Literary Portrayals of Belle Epoque Female Bonds

Irene Carrasco

ABSTRACT

This book explores fictional representations of female homosociality in a group of female - authored, middlebrow novels published in France between 1880 and 1914 in order to include women's writing of the Belle Epoque within the narratives of the literary and cultural history of friendship and further our understanding of gender identities in the long nineteenth-century. Novelistic portrayals of female homosociality are compared to the models of female bonding described in didactic or orthodox literature of the time so as to highlight the various innovations made, in relation to this theme, by the texts under consideration. Using the novel as a forum in which ideas about women's identities and their relationships could be reflected upon and negotiated, some Belle Epoque female authors engage with the limitations and possibilities of female relationships in fiction as a way to participate in contemporary debates about modern and traditional womanhood. In particular, the representation of female homosociality constitutes one of the literary devices through which the figure of the *femme moderne* comes into being on paper, and reflects the authors' engagement with a form of female modernism that problematizes the dichotomy between 'high' and 'popular' literature, giving shape to women's experience of modernity. The Introduction briefly traces the history of female friendship in France, before considering the ambiguous notion of romantic friendship and discussing predominant models of female interaction as outlined in nineteenth-century didactic literature. It explains why the Belle Epoque constitutes an interesting time from the point of view of female homosociality, establishes relevant scholarship, and details the methodological premises upon which this research is based. Chapter One considers the different roles played by physical intimacy between fictional female friends in two *romans de mœurs* by Daniel Lesueur, and situates these roles within the context of the medical and social discourses on the female body that dominate the turn of the century, and that determine the types of female identity available to women at that time. Chapter Two examines three female *Bildungsromans* by Gabrielle Réval, Colette Yver, and Marcelle Tinayre in order to identify different models of female mentorship through which the tensions between biological and spiritual motherhood, love and friendship, marriage and career, conventional and progressive femininity are played out. Chapter Three focuses on the portrayal of female communities in schoolgirl fiction by Yvette Prost and Gabrielle Réval, highlighting how the characters' experience of intellectual rivalry and intellectual friendship within the fictionalized world of the Third Republican school subverts dominant notions about presumed female nature and sociability. Chapter Four investigates female-based love triangles in three novels by Yvette Prost, Daniel Lesueur, and Colette Yver. By redefining the figure of the Other Woman and by establishing a feminine economy of generosity based on sacrifice and on the exchange of men, these texts posit women as the guarantors of the family and the moral health of the nation in the context of French degeneration, simultaneously upsetting negative stereotypes about female jealousy and sexual rivalry. The Conclusion offers an overview of the findings of this thesis, before pointing toward further avenues for research.

TABLE OF CONTENTS

INTRODUCTION

Female Friendship: 'The Troubling Silence between the Lines'?

The expression 'the troubling silence between the lines' was used by historian Alan Bray in his seminal work on the history of friendship, *The Friend* (2003), to indicate the seeming lack of evidence regarding the public and political dimension of female friendship in early modern archives.[1] In this introduction, I wish to employ Bray's expression in a different sense, calling attention to the way in which, for a long time, French women have been marginalized or erased from the cultural history of friendship. With regard to the nineteenth century, the 'troubling silence between the lines' concerns French women's exclusion from traditionally androcentric definitions of friendship, their apparent absence from ongoing discussions on the value of this relationship, the scarcity of positive representations of female friendship in canonical literature, and the small amount of research conducted on this topic in French scholarship. At first glance, some of the most well-known French novels from the nineteenth century suggest that female friendship was non-existent or, at best, dangerous when it was not simply replaced by rivalry. In *Madame Bovary* (1857) the heroine Emma is utterly lonely, in *La Cousine Bette* (1846) Bette and Valérie's alliance is evil and threatening, in *La Chartreuse de Parme* (1839) Gina and Clélia are in competition for Fabrice's affection, and in *Boule de Suif* (1880) Elisabeth is the object of other women's contempt, just to mention a few examples. However, the picture provided by such canonical literary representations and by the few studies dedicated to this topic remains incomplete, or even inaccurate, as long as we do not attend to how French women themselves imagined and represented their relationships, and to what ends. In focusing on female-authored, middlebrow fiction from the period 1880–1914, this thesis seeks to include women's writing of the Belle Epoque within the narratives of the literary and cultural history of friendship in the long nineteenth century.

In this introduction, I am going to provide a brief outline of the discourses and practices of female friendship in French history, subsequently turning my attention to the much-debated notion of female romantic friendship. I will then discuss the ideal of female friendship in nineteenth-century France, as presented in conduct books and essays from this period, and will explain why the Belle Epoque constitutes an interesting time for the

[1] See Alan Bray, *The Friend* (Chicago; London: University of Chicago Press, 2003), p. 10. Bray's claim, however, has been contested by recent scholarship that uncovers female friendship in the early modern world, such as Penelope Anderson's *Friendship's Shadows* (2012) and Amanda Herbert's *Female Alliances* (2014).

study of women's relationships in literature. After considering to what extent the topic of female homosociality has been treated in French scholarship, particularly with regard to nineteenth-century and Belle Epoque literature, I will highlight the methodological premises upon which my research is based.

Female Friendship in French History

Even though we can assume that women have been establishing relationships among themselves at least as long as men have, for many centuries these rarely gained public attention, thus leaving behind a smaller quantity of traces than have relationships between men. As Marianne Legault has recently stated, 'the expression of friendship between women is located precisely within this lack, this literary and historical emptiness, this omission or socio-historical erasure.'[2] The good deal of attention accorded to friendship in our contemporary society has encouraged a flowering of scholarship across the humanities and the social sciences investigating its nature and significance in different periods and cultures. These studies, conducted from diverse perspectives, combine a rich set of sources and methodologies, and allow us to better locate female friendship in the past. Two of the most recent contributions to the field are *Friendship: A History* (2007) edited by Barbara Caine, and *The Social Sex: A History of Female Friendship* (2015) by Marilyn Yalom and Theresa Donovan Brown.[3] The first study follows the evolutions of the concept and practices of friendship in the Western world over the past 2500 years, drawing special attention to its continuities and discontinuities, and effectively illustrating how, for a long time, the discourse surrounding friendship largely remained the preserve of men. The second one seeks more openly to re-evaluate female friendship and restore its history.

As these studies convincingly argue, female friendship received little attention in the Bible, where the few positively represented images of female bonding, such as the relationships between Ruth and Naomi or Mary and Elisabeth, tend to be more easily interpreted as family stories rather than friendship stories.[4] As for classical ideals of friendship elaborated by Greek and Latin philosophers, they were strongly androcentric and

[2]Marianne Legault, *Female Intimacies in Seventeenth-Century French Literature* (Farnham: Ashgate, 2012), p. 11.
[3]*Friendship: A History*, ed. by Barbara Caine (London: Equinox, 2007); Marilyn Yalom with Theresa Donovan Brown, *The Social Sex: A History of Female Friendship* (New York, NY: Harper Perennial, 2015).
[4]Yalom and Donovan Brown, *Social Sex*, pp. 15–26.

usually stressed the importance of the civic and moral characters of this bond. For instance, Aristotle's *Nicomachean Ethics* and Cicero's *De Amicitia*, two of the most influential texts on the subject, similarly depict friendship as a privileged relationship between equals, based on virtue, freedom, symmetry, and reciprocity. It goes without saying that all these requirements were supposed to be met primarily by men.[5] Aristotle's definition of a friend as 'another self' or as 'one soul dwelling in two bodies', as well as other images and principles pertaining to the Western philosophical tradition, continued to resonate, although not unchallenged, at least until the nineteenth century, along with the assumption of women's unsuitability for friendship. Later on, Christianity expanded this notion, bringing an emotional and spiritual element into the definition of friendship. Under the Christian impulse, a new sensibility regarding ideas of closeness, warmth, and intimacy in interpersonal relationships developed. In this context, medieval nuns and Beguines who lived in sex-segregated communities set about writing one of the first chapters in the history of female friendship.[6] Their letters, memoirs, treatises, and poetry are some of the earliest testaments to friendship between women, and interestingly highlight the close connection between female literacy and the possibility, for women, of voicing their own views of the subject of friendship.

Even though in his well-known essay *De l'Amitié (*1580), Montaigne firmly denied once again women's ability to be friends with either men or women,[7] positive representations of female mutual support and solidarity started to emerge more and more strongly during the sixteenth and seventeenth centuries. In particular, at the beginning of the early modern period, increased possibilities for self-education in restricted circles of aristocratic women, especially in Italy and France, allowed female authors to enter more effectively the ongoing discussion of friendship.[8] According to Colette Winn, Marguerite de Navarre, who in her writings associated female friendship with solidarity as well as with creativity, can be considered the first woman writer to have claimed women's natural inclination and suitability for this relationship.[9] In truth, even before then, Christine de Pizan's *Le Livre de la cité des dames* (c.a. 1405) proposed heterogeneous models of female bonding, which resisted those

[5]Yalom and Donovan Brown, *Social Sex,* pp. 27–39. For a discussion of the classical ideals of friendship, see also Dirk Baltzly and Nick Eliopoulos, 'The Classical Ideals of Friendship', in *Friendship*, ed. by Caine, pp. 1–64, and Constant J. Mews, 'Cicero on Friendship', in *Friendship*, ed. by Caine, pp. 65–72.

[6]Yalom and Donovan Brown, *Social Sex*, pp. 49–81.

[7] 'Joint qu'à dire vrai, la suffisance ordinaire des femmes, n'est pas pour répondre à cette conférence et communication, nourrice de cette sainte couture: Ni leur âme ne semble assez ferme pour soutenir l'étreinte d'un nœud si pressé, et si durable'. See Michel de Montaigne, 'De l'amitié', in *Essais de Michel de Montaigne: livre premier*, ed. by Emmanuel Naya, Delphine Reguig-Naya, Alexandre Tarrête (Paris: Gallimard, 2009 [1580]), pp. 366–82 (p. 371).

[8]Carolyn James and Bill Kent, 'Renaissance Friendship: Traditional Truths, New and Dissenting Voices', in *Friendship*, ed. by Caine, pp. 111–64 (pp. 145–52).

[9]Colette H. Winn, 'Aux origines du discours féminin sur l'amitié… Marguerite de Navarre, *La Cloche* (1541)', *Women in French Studies*, 7 (1999), 9–24.

androcentric definitions of friendship that usually excluded women.[10] Later on, the female-centred world of the French salon became particularly representative of the way in which women took upon themselves the task of reshaping friendship, in both literature and real life. Madeleine de Scudéry's works, in particular the novel *Clélie* (1654-61) and, later in her life, the *Conversations* (1686), made of her one of the major theorists of friendship of the seventeenth century.[11] The well-documented friendship between Madame de Sévigné and Madame de La Fayette, a relationship lasting over forty years, also exemplified extremely well the centrality of friendship in the lives and works of this highly educated and privileged group of women, usually referred to as the *précieuses.*[12]

Although friendship, for a long time, has been considered the prerogative of the ladies of leisure, and a clear mark of their status, it is worth noting that from the late middle ages to the eighteenth century working-class women from the rural and urban areas were also involved in forms of female sociability. The *Spinnstube* or *veillée*, a socializing gathering bringing together young women to spin during the evening, could in fact be considered as the popular equivalent of the salon.[13]

As noted by David Garrioch, in Europe the eighteenth century was marked by several shifts in the perception of female friendship.[14] Many philosophers, insisting on the rational nature of this bond, continued to doubt or even entirely deny women's aptitude for friendship. Such inability was attributed, in particular, to their lack of virtue and rationality, and to their tendency to compete for men's attention, a behaviour mainly dictated by the primacy of love in their lives.[15] Not only male philosophers, but female moralists as well, such as Madame de Lambert in her *Traité de l'Amitié* (published after her death in 1736) and Madame Thiroux D'Arconville in *De l'Amitié* (1761), were very sceptical about the existence of solid and

---

[10]Alexandra Verini, 'Medieval Models of Female Friendship in Christine de Pizan's *The Book of the City of Ladies* and Margery Kempe's *The Book of Margery Kempe*', *Feminist Studies*, 42.2 (2016), 365-91.

[11]Julie Candler Hayes, 'Friendship and the Female Moralist', *Studies in Eighteenth-Century Culture*, 39.1 (2010), 171–89 (pp. 174–75).

[12]See Yalom and Donovan Brown, *Social Sex*, pp. 101–20. Moreover, Anne Vincent-Buffault has argued that there was a link between the creation of a public literary sphere, the sociability of the salons, and the popularity of the topic of friendship: 'Il existe une accoitance entre la sociabilité des salons, des cafés, et le thème de l'amitié. Ce thème, traité dans les conversations et les publications, est l'occasion d'offrir le spectacle de la moralité de l'espace publique littéraire. Il permet une autocélébration de ces « laboratoires » animés de sociabilité, de ces lieux de rencontre et d'intimité non familiales où des sujets sont débattus entre égaux.' See Anne Vincent-Buffault, *L'Exercice de l'amitié: pour une histoire des pratiques amicales aux XVIIIe et XIXe siècles* (Paris: Editions du Seuil, 1995), pp. 107–108.

[13]Tammy Proctor, 'Home and Away: Women, Popular Culture and Leisure', in *The Routledge History of Women in Europe since 1700*, ed. by Deborah Simonton (London; New York: Routledge, 2006), pp. 299–340 (p. 310).

[14]David Garrioch, 'From Christian Friendship to Secular Sentimentality: Enlightenment Re-evaluations', in *Friendship,* ed. by Caine, pp. 165–214. The content of the next two paragraphs borrows from this chapter, unless otherwise stated in footnotes.

[15]The theme of female rivalry, a recurrent object of discussion across history in philosophy as in literature, will be treated at more length in Chapter Four on 'Female Rivalry and Love Triangles'.

sincere bonds between women. Poor education and society's expectations rather than female nature itself were at the origin of the failure of women's bonding. By contrast, friendship between the sexes, at least under certain circumstances, represented a more achievable possibility.[16] Despite these reservations, both men and women novelists became increasingly concerned with the topic of female friendship. Authors such as Madame Riccoboni, Françoise de Graffigny, Isabelle de Charrière, Mlle Poulain de Nogent, Pierre de Marivaux, and Jean-Jacques Rousseau offered several portraits of variously successful, intimate, conflictual, or subversive relationships between female characters, and explored the tensions between female friendship and marriage or love. In particular, Rousseau's portrait of the relationship between Claire and Julie in *La Nouvelle Héloïse* (1761) became one of the most significant and influential representations of female friendship in literature and even a model of behaviour for women in real life. Novels of this period usually tend to inform their readers about what friendship should be and additionally allow them to engage with the implications of complex or uncommon friendship situations that they could not have been able to experience otherwise. According to Isabelle Tremblay, in this period female friendship, especially in epistolary novels, often paves the way to the heroine's happiness, fulfilment, and personal achievement.[17] By contrast, the topic of male friendship received less attention in literature itself, since it was not perceived to involve the same complexities and potential dramatic tensions characterizing female friendship.

The new models of friendship promoted by the educated elites from the middle to the late eighteenth century progressively challenged previous, traditionally masculine models of civic, intellectual friendship, by becoming intimate and exclusive, distinctively emotional, and more closely associated with the private sphere, which is to say, at least to a certain extent, with women. True friendship now involved feelings of complete trust, openness, self-disclosure, fusion, and devotion. Its growing sentimentality corresponded to a set of rhetorical gestures such as kisses, caresses, and exchanges of miniature portraits, rings, or locks of hair. Most of all, the sentimental character of friendship was reflected in the employment of a more emphatic, tender, often eroticized language, that could be found in novels as well as in personal writings, such as letters and private diaries. All these features were in fact manifest not only in literary representations but also in actual behaviours, the two interacting in a constant, dialectical way.[18] The gradual feminization of the ideal of

---

[16]Candler Hayes, 'Friendship and the Female Moralist', pp. 175–82.

[17]Isabelle Tremblay, 'De la solitude à la solidarité: l'amitié par lettres sous la plume de Mlle Poulain de Nogent', in *Solitaires, Solidaires: Conflict and Confluence in Women's Writing in French,* ed. by Elise Hugueny-Léger and Caroline Verdier (Newcastle upon Tyne: Cambridge Scholars Publishing, 2015), pp. 27–41 (p. 28).

[18]According to Garrioch, with the increase of the literacy rate different social groups started to adopt the sentimental language employed in literature to discuss friendship. At the same time, I would argue, it is possible

friendship thus started to place women at the foreground of its history. This ideal was exploited by some of them in order to assert their moral and intellectual equality with men, and sometimes it was even considered as a viable alternative to marriage or convent life.

In addition to the aforementioned aspects, historians have found that during the eighteenth century female friendship could also assume a more public character, especially in France, where elite women founded numerous and very popular masonic lodges.[19] Moreover, in the same country, women bonded together in participating in the French Revolution and created, particularly between the 1780s and the 1790s, several short-lived female clubs and societies, thereby experiencing a peculiar kind of connection that has been labelled 'patriotic friendship'.[20] However, with the French Revolution and the subsequent strengthening of women's domestic roles, at the beginning of the nineteenth century female friendship partly lost its political aspect and became increasingly subordinated to family life.[21]

The next section of this introduction will focus on the nineteenth century and, in particular, on the notion of 'female romantic friendship', the model of friendship to which, according to historians and literary critics, middle and upper-class women usually adhered during that period. The analysis of the current debate surrounding this notion will show to what extent this category has become controversial and confusing, and will lead to a clarification of the terms and concepts adopted in this thesis.

Nineteenth-Century Female Romantic Friendship: A Source of Debate

In the nineteenth century, female friendship continued to be experienced in different ways in accordance with individual women's conditions and social status. Working-class women were usually involved in public forms of sociability within the specific context of the neighbourhood. Their living conditions prevented them from taking part in the ritual of visiting or from accessing those forms of domestic sociability that were such common features of upper-class women's lives; gatherings between them might rather be made of 'stolen minutes of conversation on the street or shouted gossip between open windows, a shared

---

to assume that fictional representations were at least in part a reflection of social practices and shaped the content of novels. See Garrioch, 'From Christian Friendship to Secular Sentimentality', in *Friendship*, ed. by Caine, p. 199.

[19]Janet M. Burke, 'Freemasonry, Friendship and Noblewomen: The Role of the Secret Society in Bringing Enlightenment Thought to Pre-Revolutionary Women Elites', *History of European Ideas*, 10.3 (1989), 283–93.

[20]Yalom and Donovan Brown, *Social Sex*, pp. 135–42.

[21]In October 1793, the aforementioned female clubs were outlawed by the Convention. In 1795, women were prohibited from gathering in the streets in groups of five or more.

cup of tea or even a drink in a pub or café'.[22] However, the relationships of mutual assistance and interdependence they could share outside the family, which were fundamental to their survival in a context marked by hardships and poverty, were not commonly perceived by them as authentic friendships, but more as necessary forms of comradeship and reciprocal solidarity. Too much closeness and intimacy were generally more feared than wished for, on account of the problems potentially brought by gossip and envy, and also because of the concerns about losing the larger support of the neighbourhood by creating particular attachments.[23]

As for bourgeois and elite women, historians have pointed out the spread, by the mid-nineteenth century, of an increasing number of female organizations involved in social, political, educational, religious, or philanthropic matters, which constituted prime socializing opportunities for them and encouraged the creation of female communities and networks of solidarity. Indeed, whether the associations they joined and the causes they championed had a strictly conservative or a more subversive character, nineteenth-century women found new venues for socialization in the public arena through their collective commitment to charitable works. Moreover, in the context of their private lives, women acted as kingpins of sociability. Elite women's social responsibilities, in fact, generally involved managing and maintaining the relations with relatives, friends, acquaintances, and their husbands' business partners. As hostesses, women dominated the social scene. They organized dinner parties, evening gatherings, and balls; they set the rules on social occasions, and 'saturated the social space with the color and volume of their clothing, their furniture arrangements, and their presence in every detail of the domestic site'.[24] As representatives of their family, they were constantly engaged in rounds of visits, whose nature, frequency, and length were determined by precise rules. For example, the Baronne d'Orval lists twelve different types of visits, describing extensively the kind of conversation to engage in and the behaviour to adopt in every circumstance.[25] On this topic, Bonnie G. Smith has remarked that 'performed with greater frequency, constant visiting was a sign of *caritas* at work in the binding of women, as representatives of the family, into a unity'.[26] From 1830 until 1914, it

---

[22] Proctor, 'Home and Away', in *The Routledge History of Women*, ed. by Simonton, p. 316. Proctor's observations refer in particular to working-class English women. However, Proctor also cites a study highlighting the significance of Parisian cafés as socializing venues for working-class French women, i.e. Haine W. Scott, *The World of the Paris Café* (1996).

[23] Marc Brodie and Barbara Caine, 'Class, Sex, Friendship: The Long Nineteenth Century', in *Friendship*, ed. by Caine, pp. 223–77 (pp. 248–55).

[24] Bonnie G. Smith, *Ladies of the Leisure Class: The Bourgeoises of Northern France in the Nineteenth Century* (Princeton; Guildford: Princeton University Press, 1981), p. 129.

[25] Baronne d'Orval, *Usages mondains: guide du savoir-vivre moderne dans toutes les circonstances de la vie*, 6th edn (Paris: Victor-Havard et Cie, 1901), pp. 93–132.

[26] Smith, *Ladies of the Leisure Class*, p. 133.

was also customary for women to have a fixed reception day for entertaining guests, usually during the afternoon or the evening.[27] Furthermore, these women frequently engaged in all sort of leisure activities, such as attending gardens, theatres, performances, and other social events.

According to critics today, however, the historical and literary model that best describes how women interacted during the nineteenth century, in Western societies, is the one commonly known under the name of 'romantic friendship'. From the 1970s onwards, the study of nineteenth-century female romantic friendship has raised issues concerning the embodiment of female friendship and its relation to homosexuality, this debate leading to a questioning of the definition of friendship itself. What romantic friendship was or what it involved remains an open question. The term usually refers to the passionate, intimate, nurturing, emotional, and physical bonds that nineteenth-century women established with one another in the United States and in western European countries.[28] The role of romantic friendship in nineteenth-century American society was first highlighted by the feminist historian Carroll Smith-Rosenberg in 'The Female World of Love and Ritual: Relations between Women in Nineteenth-Century America' (1975).[29] This influential article unearthed the existence of a segregated and exclusive female world in which relationships between women 'ranged from the supportive love of sisters, through the enthusiasm of adolescent girls, to sensual avowals of love by mature women' and provided them with emotional and physical support throughout their lives. Smith-Rosenberg insisted on the social acceptability of these relations and on their compatibility with heterosexual marriage, at least until new cultural taboos introduced in the twentieth century broke them off. She further suggested that we view 'sexual and emotional impulses as part of a continuum or spectrum of affect gradations strongly effected [sic] by cultural norms and arrangements', thus pointing out not only that friendship is a dynamic concept determined by cultural and historical specificities, but also that it could be useful to understand female relationships through the prism of a 'continuum' that blurs the lines between different forms of bonding.[30]

---

[27] *A History of Private Life IV: From the Fires of Revolution to the Great War,* ed. by Michelle Perrot (Cambridge; Mass: Belknap Press of Harvard University Press, 1990), pp. 274–77.

[28] Leila J. Rupp claims that those friendships survived well into the twentieth century. See Leila J. Rupp, 'Romantic Friendship', in *Modern American Queer History*, ed. by Allida M. Black (Philadelphia: Temple University Press, 2001), pp. 13–23. For a discussion of romantic friendship in the eighteenth century, see Susan S. Lanser, 'Befriending the Body: Female Intimacies as Class Acts', *Eighteenth-Century Studies*, 32.2 (1998), 179–98.

[29] Carroll Smith-Rosenberg, 'The Female World of Love and Ritual: Relations between Women in Nineteenth-Century America', *Signs*, 1.1 (1975), 1–29.

[30] Smith-Rosenberg, 'The Female World', pp. 2, 28–29.

The idea of the 'continuum' has been subsequently articulated in different ways by prominent critics such as Adrienne Rich and Eve Kofosky Sedgwick. Rich proposes that all women exist on a 'lesbian continuum' that embraces 'many forms of primary intensity between women, including the sharing of a rich inner life, the bonding against male tyranny, the giving and receiving of practical and political support'.[31] In her view, this broad range of woman-identified experiences is primarily defined by its resistance to 'compulsory heterosexuality' and to male domination rather than by sexuality.[32] Furthermore Sedgwick, discerning an asymmetry in the functioning of a male versus a female spectrum of relations, alludes to a certain smoothness and unbrokenness between female homosociality and homosexuality, further stating that 'an intelligible continuum of aims, emotions, and valuations links lesbianism with the other forms of women's attention to women: the bond of mother and daughter, for instance, the bond of sister and sister, women's friendship, "networking", and the active struggles of feminism'.[33] Drawing from some of Smith-Rosenberg's principal arguments, Lillian Faderman produced one of the most important and controversial works on female romantic friendship. In *Surpassing the Love of Men: Romantic Friendship and Love between Women from the Renaissance to the Present* (1985), female romantic friendship is partially equated with homosexuality and inscribed into its history: 'romantic friendships were in the quality and intensity of the emotions involved no different from lesbian love.'[34] However, although comparing romantic friendship to lesbian love, Faderman observes that these friendships 'were love relationships in every sense except perhaps the genital'.[35] In other words, romantic friends were women who loved other women, but this form of love was tolerated or even valued by society only so long as it was considered asexual, following the nineteenth-century assumption that women in general had little or no sexual desire. Like Smith-Rosenberg, Faderman concludes that in the late nineteenth and early twentieth centuries, with the medical naming of 'lesbianism', these friendships started to be increasingly perceived as suspicious or abnormal and were consequently suppressed.

---

[31] Adrienne Cecile Rich, 'Compulsory Heterosexuality and Lesbian Existence (1980)', *Journal of Women's History*, 15.3 (2003), 11–48.

[32] Blanche Wiesen Cook, too, proposes a similar, desexualized, and broad definition of lesbianism, asserting that: 'Women who love women, who choose women to nurture and support and to create a living environment in which to work creatively and independently, are lesbians.' See Blanche Wiesen Cook, '"Women Alone Stir My Imagination": Lesbianism and the Cultural Tradition', *Signs*, 4.4 (1979), 718–39 (p. 738). These views of lesbianism have been largely challenged and rejected by scholars who warned against the risk of ignoring or erasing the sexual component of lesbian women's lives.

[33] Eve Kosofsky Sedgwick, *Between Men: English Literature and Male Homosocial Desire* (New York: Columbia University Press, 1985), p. 2.

[34] Lillian Faderman, *Surpassing the Love of Men: Romantic Friendship and Love between Women from the Renaissance to the Present* (London: Women's Press, 1985), p. 19.

[35] Faderman, *Surpassing the Love of Men*, p. 16.

Such claims about the fundamentally asexual nature of female romantic friendship, which are partly motivated by a political desire to overturn the pathologizing model of lesbianism and emphasize the emotional intensity of women's bonding, have been differently received and often fiercely contested. In particular, scholars have argued against the utopian and reductive idea of a pre-sexual world, a lost age of innocence, later disrupted by the intervention of sexologists, in which relationships between women followed the mother-daughter model, were conceived of as non-sexual and consequently unproblematic, and were entirely approved of or even encouraged. Since then, the impact of the medical discourse on these friendships has been reconsidered, their acceptability in nineteenth-century society questioned and, in certain cases, their erotic and sexual nature proven.[36] The debate surrounding the notion of nineteenth-century female romantic friendship has thus started to generate growing confusion regarding the nature and the content of this relationship, the term 'romantic friendship' gradually becoming a sort of catch-all label applying to friendship as well as to sexual, romantic partnership.

More recent works on the subject of female romantic friendship such as Martha Vicinus' *Intimate Friends* (2004), Leila J. Rupp's *Sapphistries* (2009), and the aforementioned *The Social Sex* (2015) by Marylin Yalom and Theresa Donovan Brown confirm that this debate is ongoing. Vicinus claims that in the eighteenth century 'sensual romantic friendships' and 'sexual Sapphisms' represented two separate, although non-exclusive forms of female intimate friendships. In the nineteenth century, following the French Revolution and the spread of Romanticism, these two categories were progressively combined by women in order to create a new form of 'intimate friendship', which Vicinus describes as 'an emotional, erotically charged relationship between two women'.[37] Rupp, in a section of *Sapphistries* (2009) dedicated to female romantic friendship, provides a nuanced and complex picture of this relationship.[38] By rediscussing several examples previously considered by other critics, she shows that nineteenth-century female romantic

[36]For more details, see Terry Castle, *The Apparitional Lesbian: Female Homosexuality and Modern Culture* (New York; Chichester: Columbia University Press, 1993); Marylynne Diggs, 'Romantic Friends or a "Different Race of Creatures"? The Representation of Lesbian Pathology in Nineteenth-Century America', *Feminist Studies*, 21.2 (1995), 317–40; Sylvia Martin, '"These Walls of Flesh": The Problem of the Body in the Romantic Friendship/Lesbianism Debate', *Historical Reflections/Réflexions Historiques*, 20.2 (1994), 243–66; Lisa Moore, '"Something More Tender Still than Friendship": Romantic Friendship in Early-Nineteenth-Century England', *Feminist Studies*, 18.3 (1992), 499–520; Liz Stanley, 'Romantic Friendship? Some Issues in Researching Lesbian History and Biography', *Women's History Review,* 1.2 (1992), 193–216.

[37]Martha Vicinus, *Intimate Friends: Women Who Loved Women, 1778–1928* (Chicago: University of Chicago Press, 2004), p. xxiv. In a previous article, Vicinus defined romantic friendship as a form of lesbian desire, to be included in the history of lesbianism. See Martha Vicinus, '"They Wonder to Which Sex I Belong": The Historical Roots of the Modern Lesbian Identity', *Feminist Studies*, 18.3 (1992), 467–97.

[38]Leila J. Rupp, *Sapphistries: A Global History of Love between Women* (New York: New York University Press, 2009), pp. 127–41.

friendship could either coexist with heterosexual marriage or be in conflict with it, eventually evolving into the so-called 'Boston Marriage'.[39] It could involve or be a cover for sexual desire and acts, but not necessarily. Finally, it could find acceptance, arouse anxieties, or be policed.[40] In addition to this, Rupps draws attention to the prominence of the eroticization of same-sex friendship through history. More recently, Yalom and Donovan Brown have overtly adopted the continuum theory in their discussion of nineteenth-century romantic friendships. Although they give the name of 'passionate friends' to all those 'women loving other women passionately and even physically, with caresses and kisses, though not necessarily sexually' and cite historians who have warned us against interpreting those relationships as protolesbian, they consider 'lesbian romance' as the variant of romantic friendship falling to the extremity of the continuum 'where love intermingles with sex'.[41] These examples attest to the continuing ambiguity inscribed in the notion of romantic friendship, a category which indistinctly refers to female friendship and lesbian love alike.

In *Between Women* (2007), Sharon Marcus queries precisely this ambiguity, pointing to the extent to which the idea of the continuum has blinded us to the differences between homosocial, homoerotic, and homosexual ties, differences mainly determined by the peculiar 'content, structure, status, and degree of flexibility' of each social bond.[42] Marcus interestingly remarks that female relationships have been mainly conceptualized within the field of lesbian studies, and that the dominant tendency has consisted in conflating same-sex friendship and homosexual love, thus creating a persistent ambiguity between the two, as if every female bond was always at least potentially inhabited by lesbian desire and should be considered as a subset of lesbianism. According to Marcus:

> rather than valorize an invisibility or transgressiveness that all women's relationships share, or define women's relationships in terms of an intrinsic ambiguity that blurs the line between friendship and sexual partnership, we need distinctions that allow us to chart how different social bonds overlap without becoming identical.[43]

---

[39]Boston Marriages were marriage-like relationships between women. The name relates to their prevalence in the north-east of the United States. One of the most common examples of Boston Marriage is the case of the 'Ladies of Llangollen' (i.e. Sarah Ponsonby and *Lady* Eleanor Butler), who lived together for over fifty years.

[40]An example of how romantic friendship was policed is the Scottish legal case of Jane Pirie and Marianne Woods, two schoolteachers accused of indulging in 'scandalous' practices while in bed together. This accusation suggests that even in the early nineteenth century the definition of romantic friendship was ambiguous, and that attempts to separate affectionate behaviours and virtuous, normative friendship from allegedly suspicious and inappropriate female intimacy or sexuality could have been made well before the advent of early-twentieth-century sexology. The same episode is discussed by Moore, '"Something More Tender Still than Friendship", pp. 513–17.

[41]Yalom and Donovan Brown, *Social Sex*, pp. 57–58, 170.

[42] Sharon Marcus, *Between Women: Friendship, Desire, and Marriage in Victorian England* (Princeton: Princeton University Press, 2007), p. 4.

[43]Marcus, *Between Women*, p. 30.

For example, in her study of female relationships in Victorian culture and literature, she sets female friendship apart from unrequited love or obsessive infatuation between women and from female marriage or life partnership. Adopting Roland Barthes' definition of the 'erotic' as a set of dynamics located in 'practices of classifying, ritualization, and image-making and in emotional states' rather than in sexual acts, Marcus insists upon the distinction between homoerotic and homosexual.[44] A 'restrictive, literal definition of the sexual enables a corresponding latitude in defining the erotic in a way that does justice to the complexity and ingenuity of desire'.[45] Therefore homoeroticism, far from being a 'synonym' or a 'euphemism for lesbianism or sex between women', can be seen as one of the Victorian codes of female friendship and accounts for the playfulness and physicality involved in relationships between women who considered themselves friends, not lovers. According to Marcus, this form of homoeroticism is neither to be equated with lesbian love nor to be dismissed as an adolescent stage leading to heterosexuality. This understanding of female friendship has the advantage of possessing a certain latitude and flexibility while remaining separate from other kinds of relations.

Since the notion of romantic friendship is possibly the one most insistently referred to in discussions of female friendship in nineteenth-century Western societies, its significance and the scope of the debate surrounding it could not be ignored in a thesis that investigates representations of female homosociality in Belle Epoque France.[46] The term 'homosociality', which, in Sedgwick's own words, 'describes social bonds between persons of the same sex', applies in this thesis to female friendship as well as to female solidarity, mentorship, and rivalry. However, I intend to focus on female homosociality as distinct from female homosexuality, rejecting the view of female friendship in particular as a subset, a sublimation, or a form of lesbian love or desire.[47] The fact that friendship could turn into love, or that friendship could come out of love, or that two lovers could at the same time be friends, in fiction or in history, is not the concern of this thesis. As we have seen, the discourse on nineteenth-century female romantic friendship is characterized by a consistent disagreement about whether these relationships were sexual or platonic, whether they opened up the possibility, for women, to express and act on same-sex sexual desires or

[44]Roland Barthes, *Sade/Fourier/Loyola*, Richard Miller, trans. (New York: Hill & Wang, 1976 [1971]), pp. 3–6, 64 is quoted by Marcus, *Between Women*, p. 114.
[45]Marcus, *Between Women*, p. 113.
[46]Regarding the nineteenth century, the idea of 'female community' has also received particular attention by scholars, especially in the context of anglophone literature. See fn. 92 in this introduction.
[47]For the definition of 'homosociality', see Sedgwick, *Between Men*, p. 1, and Nils Hammarén and Thomas Johansson, 'Homosociality: In Between Power and Intimacy', *SAGE Open*, 4.1 (2014), 1–11.

rather represented an attempt to confine female behaviour to a respectable, pure, and socially acceptable form of interaction, and whether or not they should be considered as part of lesbian history. Following Marcus' lead, I call into question the utility or accuracy of placing all female relationships under the same heading of 'friendship', and the emphasis put on potential sexual desires or acts even when they may not have been present or when they were not constitutive elements of what people understood as female friendship, thus obscuring the specificity of this form of bonding. Therefore, in my discussion of representations of female homosociality in Belle Epoque French literature, I have decided not to adopt the term 'romantic friendship', a label that implies far too great a degree of confusion, ambiguity, and self-contradiction.[48]

The question that needs to be asked is how the details of female friendship and sociability were conceived of and negotiated in the context of nineteenth-century France by women and by society at large. This thesis, it should be noted, does not aim to fill an historic gap or further our knowledge of homosocial practices through the analysis of non-fiction primary source material, such as letters or diary entries; it does, however, address and explore 'the troubling silence between the lines' by considering the discursive treatment of female homosociality in middlebrow fiction, and by comparing these fictional representations to the prescriptive models of female interaction found in didactic or orthodox literature.[49] As the thesis progressed, the difficulty of defining friendship with pinpoint accuracy and a broader interest in female homosociality as a more complex and varied set of interpersonal interactions has led to a consideration of related themes, such as physical intimacy, mentorship, solidarity, community, camaraderie, or intellectual and sexual rivalry, which in Belle Epoque fiction are all part of the *imaginaire littéraire* of female homosociality. Friendship thus functions as a starting point, but also as a *fil rouge* connecting one chapter

---

[48]The aim of this thesis is not to draw rigid and arbitrary lines separating female homosociality from female homosexuality, nor to deny that sometimes female friendship might have represented for women the opportunity to explore same-sex sexuality, possibly evolving into a different kind of relationship. However, when considering the models of female friendship circulating in Belle Epoque French literature, especially in orthodox texts such as conduct manuals for girls, and given the visibility of lesbianism in French culture and the stigma attached to homosexual practices during the Belle Epoque, it seems relevant to question the continuity between female homosociality and homosexuality implied by the notion of romantic friendship. This is not to say that female friendship, as represented in Belle Epoque literature, is devoid of an erotic component. This question and the roles played by the body in novelistic representations of female friendship will be further explored in the chapter 'Female Friendship and the Body'. For a discussion of lesbianism in Belle Epoque France, see for example Shari Benstock, *Women of the Left Bank: Paris, 1900-1940* (Austin: University of Texas Press, 1986); Francesca Canadé Sautman, 'Invisible Women: Lesbian Working-class Culture in France, 1880–1930', in *Homosexuality in Modern France*, ed. by Jeffrey Merrick and Bryant T. Ragan (New York; Oxford: Oxford University Press, 1996), pp. 177–201; Nicole G. Albert, *Lesbian Decadence: Representations in Art and Literature of Fin-de-Si□cle France*, trans. by Nancy Erber and William A. Peniston (New York: Harrington Park Press, 2016).
[49]The term 'middlebrow' will be further discussed at p. 34 in this introduction.

to the next and ensuring the overall coherence of this thesis, even when the focus shifts from one particular aspect of female homosociality to another.

Each chapter will offer an in-depth exploration of one of the recurrent themes found in Belle Epoque novels dealing with the topic of female homosociality and the ways in which these selected novels support or challenge the general statements about friendship expressed in nineteenth-century French conduct manuals and essays. I hope, thus, to further our understanding of female homosociality as conceived in nineteenth-century French culture, and to demonstrate that one of the interests of these novels lies precisely in their engagement with and renegotiation of dominant ideals about women and their relationships. Although parallels between orthodox texts and fiction will be drawn throughout the thesis, the next section will provide a brief overview of the ideas outlined in didactic literature, so as to get a clearer sense of the prevailing conceptualizations of female friendship in nineteenth-century France, and better to gauge the various innovations made, in relation to these ideas, by the novels under consideration in this thesis.

The Ideal of Female Friendship in Nineteenth-Century France

Nineteenth-century French essays on friendship and conduct manuals for girls usually share similar concerns about the requirements and characteristics of friendship, the choice of a friend, and the behaviour a girl or a young woman should adopt in society and in the company of other women. The authors strive to provide an accurate definition of this bond and its principles, describing in detail its qualities and the duties it implies; they usually insist on the rarity of friendship and clearly instruct their readers on how to find a good friend and avoid the false ones. Fictional and actual friendships from the past, such as that between Patroclus and Achilles or Montaigne and La Boétie, are presented as models to imitate. Moreover, a comparison between friendship and love is often made, usually at the expense of the latter. Female friendship, however, does not seem to represent a recurrent object of interest in these texts and, excluding a few exceptions, most of the authors, like their predecessors, remain sceptical about the possibility of its existence. 'Peu d'amitié entre femmes. D'abord c'est une fiction poétique et rien de plus', is the curt observation of the anonymous author of *Les Usages du monde* (1880).[50] By contrast, some female authors write in defence of women's aptitude for friendship, usually in a way that reinforces conservative ideals of femininity. In *Lettre sur l'amitié entre les femmes, précédée de la traduction du "Traité sur l'amitié" de Cicéron*, Mme de Maussion endeavours to make Cicero's essay available to female readers and overtly criticizes negative assumptions on the subject of female friendship expressed by previous authors, such as Madame de Lambert, by highlighting the affinity between essential femaleness and the attributes of intimate friendship.[51] Borrowing from the classical ideal of friendship, this author presents virtue as the foundation of friendship and describes it as a primary bonding agent for women. The definition of 'vertu', traditionally understood as a masculine affair, is expanded by Maussion to include the set of wifely and maternal duties that women are expected to perform in patriarchal societies, according to their presumed nature. Female friends are consequently required to sustain each other in their quest to become *femmes honnêtes* and to play the role of 'honour keepers'; friendship is thought of both as a safeguard against improper behaviour and as a means for women to conform to mainstream femininity.[52]

The expectations thus put upon female friends betray a desire to legitimize this relationship by inscribing its ideal within the family, in response to perceived incompatibilities between marriage and friendship and to anxieties around women's self-disclosure within this bond. If marriage and family life seem to represent the biggest obstacles to female friendship in nineteenth-century France,[53] this bond, in turn, is often perceived as a threat to conventional ideas of women and their roles in society.[54] Therefore, relationships between women are strictly policed from a young age and virtually throughout a woman's life. One of the strategies underpinning this policy, as we have seen in Mme de Maussion's essay, consists in reinforcing an ideal of friendship that works to support traditional views of femininity. Girls and women are encouraged to cultivate their friendships insofar as these

---

[50] [Anon.], *Les Usages du monde, le savoir-vivre et la politesse chez soi, en visite, en soirée, au théâtre... Suite de conférences par un homme du monde. Suivi du guide pour la danse du cotillon* (Paris: T. Lefèvre, 1880), p. 19.

[51] Bonne de Maussion, *Lettre sur l'amitié entre les femmes, précédée de la traduction du "Traité de l'amitié" de Cicéron* (Paris: Goujon, [n.d.]).

[52] This essay will be further discussed in Chapter Two, pp. 119–20.

[53] See for example Maussion, *Lettre sur l'amitié*, pp. 13–14, or Louise Barbier-Jussy, who lists marriage and maternity among '[l]es épreuves les plus fréquentes et non les moins décisives de l'amitié', in *La Vie de l'amitié*, 2nd edn (Paris: Victorion et Cie, 1913), p. 168. Further details on the relation between marriage and female friendship in nineteenth-century France can be found in Chapter Four, pp. 237–39.

[54] Indeed, in some conduct books women are exhorted to be primarily devoted to their roles of mothers and wives and not to place leisure or friendship above those duties: 'La femme qui cherche son plaisir dans les fréquentations, dans les commérages du voisinage, au lieu de mettre sa maison en ordre et d'y retenir, d'y fixer son mari, manque de cœur, et de bon sens. Elle n'entend ni les intérêts de sa famille, ni ses propres intérêts.' See Comtesse de Boissieux, *Le Vrai Manuel du savoir-vivre: conseils sur la politesse et les usages du monde* (Paris: Gauguet et Cie., 1877), p. 13.

relations allow them to acquire and display distinctly feminine qualities, such as kindness and forbearance. In particular, historians argue that the families strongly supported particular, close, and solid friendships between serious girls. From the parents' point of view, these exclusive relationships based on intimacy, confidence, and affection represented an extension of the mother-daughter relation, and were privileged against the superficial and potentially dangerous acquaintances made in society. Most of all, they were praised for their formative value. They were understood as essential rites of passage before the discovery of heterosexual love, and as forms of training for future commitments, anticipating the kind of empathy, devotion, and selflessness which girls would be required to manifest later in life, as wives and mothers.[55]

Additional recommendations meant to regulate female friendship include the exhortation that girls choose their friends from among their family members (i.e. sisters and cousins),[56] the identification of suitable topics of conversation,[57] the monitoring of girls' correspondence by their mothers,[58] and the possibility, for the husbands, of controlling their wives' social lives by reading their letters and by deciding whom they should visit or befriend.[59]

Clarisse Juranville (1826–1906), a former teacher who from the 1860s onwards published more than thirty books in the form of teaching and conduct manuals, essays, and stories for children,[60] gives a definition of friendship that perpetuates the principles

---

[55]Vincent-Buffault, *Exercice de l'amitié*, pp. 158–62.

[56]Usually a sister, a brother, or a cousin provide a girl with the best friend she could hope for. Otherwise, she is encouraged to choose someone who shares her tastes, opinions, and moral code, and whose social condition is similar to her own, equality being the first requirement of friendship. See for example Fanny André, 'Les Distractions permises', in *Les Ennemis de la jeunesse: nouvelle série d'études morales et sociales, aux jeunes filles,* 2nd edn (Vals-Les-Bains: Imprimerie-Librairie E. Aberlen, 1897), pp. 172–84 (pp. 173–76).

[57]Even though friendship is based on sincerity and self-disclosure, there are restrictions on the kind of topics a girl can discuss with her friends: 'Elle ne prend pas les matières familiales pour texte de ses conversations avec ses amies les plus intimes et même les plus sûres. Les choses du foyer ne se racontent pas.' Men and sentimental encounters also appear among the topics a girl cannot confide: 'une jeune fille loyale ne va pas leur raconter ce qui s'est passé entre elle et l'homme dont elle a agréé la recherche ou qu'elle a découragé: seules, les petites sottes vaniteuses se font gloire de ces choses-là.' Baronne Staffe, □ □*les du savoir-vivre dans la société moderne: usages du monde*, 24th edn (Paris: V. Havard, 1891), pp. 339, 341, 345. Historians also point out that married women were pressured into being discreet about their married/sexual lives. See Gabrielle Houbre, *La Discipline de l'amour: l'éducation sentimentale des filles et des garçons à l'âge du romantisme* (Paris: Plon, 1997), p. 172.

[58]'En ce qui regarde vos amies, choisissez soigneusement vos correspondantes. N'entretenez jamais de commerce de lettres que votre mère n'ait sanctionné. [...] Toute correspondance doit passer sous les yeux de vos mères. Il leur appartient de lire ou de ne pas lire vos lettres, selon la connaissance plus ou moins approfondie qu'elles ont de vos amies. [...] [U]ne fille bien élevée n'écrit et ne reçoit rien que sa mère ne puisse voir et approuver'. See Maryan, M. and Béal Gabrielle, *Le Fond et la forme: le savoir-vivre pour les jeunes filles* (Paris: Librairie Bloud et Barral, 1896), pp. 255–56.

[59]'Il [le mari] doit donc, au début, passer sur beaucoup de choses, ne pas chercher à éloigner la mère ni les amis de sa femme, mais cependant il prendra de suite la direction des relations que sa femme désirerait continuer ou entretenir. Pour cela, il l'accompagne partout et reste près d'elle tout le temps dont il peut disposer en dehors de ses affaires'. See *Les Usages du monde*, p. 120.

[60][Anon.], *Notice sur Clarisse Juranville* (Paris: Imprimerie Larousse, 1907).

elaborated by Aristotle and Montaigne: 'Un ami, c'est un autre soi-même: en effet, quand je suis avec mon amie, je ne suis pas seule et nous ne sommes pas deux.'[61] According to this author, whose ideas are representative of the nineteenth-century French model of female friendship, this relationship implies intimacy, trust, goodwill, loyalty, constancy, and seriousness. In order to be appreciated by her friends, a girl should possess qualities such as goodness, kindness, and generosity, all of which are supposedly feminine characteristics. The concept of emulation, one of the most frequently recurring in any discussion of female friendship at the time, is unsurprisingly evoked by this author, who instructs her readers thus: 'Vous devez être un modèle pour vos amies; mais il faut aussi que vous ayez à gagner en leur société. L'émulation règne entre les amies et elles ne connaissent point la jalousie.'[62] If female friends are generally expected to act as role models and to encourage each other to conform to prescribed moral and social behaviours, girls are simultaneously told to avoid anyone who could exert a bad influence on them: 'Vous ne donneriez point votre affection à une jeune fille de mauvais caractère, dissipée, toujours en révolte contre la règle, s'appliquant en quelque sorte à être désagréable à tout le monde.'[63] This kind of recommendation reflects the belief that women in general are vulnerable to any kind of influence and can be easily corrupted.[64]

My analysis of conduct books and essays, although limited, suggests that the status of female friendship in nineteenth-century France was rather ambiguous. Leaving aside the enduring scepticism about women's ability to be friends or their supposedly natural tendency to act as sexual rivals, the practice of friendship is perceived as a valuable asset for the preservation and reinforcement of the status quo. Indeed, the qualities that girls are taught to display as friends (i.e. amiability, gentleness, altruism, patience, unselfishness, discretion,

---

[61]Clarisse Juranville, *Manuel d'éducation morale et d'instruction civique à l'usage des jeunes filles*, 13th edn (Paris: Librairie Larousse, 1911), p. 52.

[62]Clarisse Juranville, *Le Savoir-Faire et le savoir-vivre dans les diverses circonstances de la vie: guide pratique de la vie usuelle à l'usage des jeunes filles*, 27th edn (Paris: Librairie Larousse, 1879), p. 23.

[63]Juranville, *Le Savoir-Faire et le savoir-vivre*, p. 23.

[64]'Le cœur de la femme, en raison de son extrême délicatesse, de son exquise sensibilité, doit être entouré de la plus scrupuleuse circonspection. C'est une fleur que le moindre souffle peut si vite décharmer et flétrir! Le moindre contact immonde peut si vite ternir l'éclat de son innocence et de sa simplicité! Que la sagesse d'une amie chrétienne soit donc comme une sentinelle vigilante qui s'oppose au principe du mal!' See J.L.M.N., *La Voix de l'amitié* (Paris: Gervais, 1879), p. 118. Henri Marion similarly notes that '[l]e besoin de sympathiser, la disposition à s'apitoyer, à s'attendrir, peuvent être, en effet, pour la femme, des pièges et des causes de péril moral'. See Henri Marion, *La Psychologie de la femme: études de psychologie féminine* (Paris: A. Colin, 1900), p. 144. Mme de Maussion invites women to protect their female friends' reputation, to reprimand each other, and to provide good advice, but she also warns her readers to be careful and avoid 'contagion': 'plus une femme est honnête, moins elle croit que son amie ait pu cesser de l'être. Qu'elle la défende discrètement dans ses discours, qu'elle la soutienne par ses conseils; qu'elle essaie même ces réprimandes que Cicéron met au rang des devoirs de l'amitié; qu'elle tente tout pour conjurer le blâme prêt à atteindre son âme, et plus encore pour éloigner le poison de son cœur. Mais enfin, si le mal est sans remède, cette contagion n'est pas de celles que l'on doit braver, il faut s'en éloigner.' See Maussion, *Lettre sur l'amitié*, pp. 47–48.

moderation, and dignity) are understood as authentically feminine and friendship can be part of women's traineeship in conventional womanhood. Once they become adults, although expected to favour marriage and family life over friendship, women still have a role to play in each others' lives as self-appointed spies and morality enforcers. However, female relationships also represent a source of concern, insofar as women could become exposed to bad influences and, in the worst-case scenario, reject normative femininity or defy social conventions. In both cases, there is a clear need for these relationships to be strictly policed.

The next section will consider why the Belle Epoque represents a particularly interesting time from the point of view of female homosociality.

The Belle Epoque: A Self-contained Period in French Women's History

The term 'Belle Epoque' designates retrospectively the decades around the turn of the nineteenth century. Scholars offer different indications about its periodization. If the outbreak of World War I in 1914 has been unanimously recognized as the event that put an abrupt end to the Belle Epoque, its beginning has been variously dated up to thirty years back.[65] In this thesis I will focus on the years 1880–1914, which 'seem to correspond to a particularly colourful, dramatic and to some extent self-contained period both for French feminism and for French women's history'.[66] Beyond the posthumous idealization of an era regarded with nostalgia in the aftermath of the war, some historical factors have contributed to its good reputation. This period was in fact marked, in France, by political stability, colonial expansion, economic growth, scientific and technological progress, and cultural effervescence. This positive and prosperous image of Belle Epoque France, however, was counterbalanced by the disparities between the city and the countryside, the inequalities between classes, and

---

[65]For example, Eugen Weber, *France fin de siècle* (Cambridge, Mass.; London: Belknap Press of Harvard University Press, 1986) and Juliette M. Rogers, *Career Stories: Belle Epoque Novels of Professional Development* (University Park, PA: Pennsylvania State University Press, 2007) refer to the Belle Epoque as the period between 1900 and 1914, while *A 'Belle Epoque'? Women and Feminism in French Society and Culture, 1890–1914*, ed. by Diana Holmes and Carrie Tarr (Oxford: Berghahn, 2006), *Écrire les hommes: personnages masculins et masculinité dans l'œuvre des écrivaines de la Belle Époque*, ed. by France Grenaudier-Klijn, Elisabeth-Christine Muelsch, Jean Anderson (Saint-Denis: PUV, 2012), and *La Belle Époque des femmes?: 1889–1914: colloque tenu à Orléans les 5 et 6 Avril 2012*, ed. by François Le Guennec and Nicolas-Henri Zmelty (Paris: Harmattan, 2013) focus on the years between 1890–1914. Charles Rearick, *Pleasures of the Belle Époque: Entertainment and Festivity in turn-of-the-century France* (London: Yale University Press, 1985), and 'Belle Époque' in *Dictionnaire de l'histoire de France Larousse* <http://www.larousse.fr/archives/histoire_de_france/page/102> [accessed 31 August 2018] give a broader definition of this historical moment, referring to the decades between 1880 and 1914.

[66]Diana Holmes and Carrie Tarr, 'Introduction', in *A 'Belle Epoque'?*, ed. by Holmes and Tarr, pp. 1–8 (p. 1).

the contradictions inherent in the Republic itself. One of these contradictions, as observed by Diana Holmes and Carrie Tarr, was undoubtedly the status of women who, in a regime that claimed to be founded on the democratic ideals of liberty, equality, and fraternity, remained largely subservient to male authority and were still deprived of political, civic, and sometimes human rights.[67]

Even though the Belle Epoque was the theatre of first-wave feminism, 'the first sustained [women's] movement under contemporary republican institutions',[68] the struggles and claims of this heterogeneous and fragmented group[69] left most women unconcerned and appear to have achieved few results at the legal and institutional levels, especially if compared to the British and American campaigning groups.[70] Despite its limits, the movement had the merit of spelling out some of the central issues of twentieth-century feminism (e.g. equal educational and professional opportunities for women, parity in marriage, right to divorce, protection of the single mother, status of the natural children, denunciation of the double standard of sexual morality), and aroused the interest of the press, as well as the fears of a still deeply conservative society.[71] Anti-feminism, although very pronounced at the *fin de siècle*, was not a new phenomenon, the question of women's nature and roles in society belonging to a much older debate. Karen Offen has argued that in the context of the Third Republic, the 'Woman Question' was strongly interlaced with the 'Man Problem'. Throughout the nineteenth century, men put increasing efforts into the elaboration and reiteration of a discourse, not least medical, that reinforced gender differences in order to justify and reassert male supremacy. The need to rationalize female subordination and the virulence of the anti-feminist backlash at the turn of the century were

[67]Diana Holmes and Carrie Tarr, 'New Republic, New Women? Feminism and Modernity at the Belle Epoque', in *A 'Belle Epoque'?*, ed. by Holmes and Tarr, pp. 11–22 (pp. 11–12).

[68]Máire Cross, '1890–1914: A "Belle Epoque" for Feminism?', in *A 'Belle Epoque'?*, ed. by Holmes and Tarr, pp. 29–37 (p. 32).

[69]According to Karen Offen, '[b]y the beginning of the twentieth century, one could find many self-described or attributed feminisms: "familial feminists," "integral feminists," "Christian feminists," "socialist feminists," "bourgeois feminists," "radical feminists," and, of course, "male-feminists".' See Karen Offen, *Debating the Woman Question in the French Third Republic, 1870–1920* (Cambridge: Cambridge University Press, 2018), p. 171.

[70]In terms of the advancement of women's rights during the Belle Epoque, in 1880 the *loi Camille Sée* established state secondary education for girls and one year later the *loi Jules Ferry* established free, compulsory primary education for both sexes. In 1884 the *loi Naquet* legalized divorce. In 1886 married women were allowed to open a bank account without their husbands' consent and in 1907 working women were granted control over their own wages. In the same year they were given parental rights on illegitimate children, and in 1912 they could file paternity suits. However, suffrage would not be extended to French women until 1944 and equality in marriage would not be achieved until the 1970s.

[71]Indeed, as observed by Karen Offen, '[f]eminism may not have become a "mass movement" in France by 1900, but the woman question was unquestionably on many people's minds.' See Offen, *Debating the Woman Question*, p. 272.

linked to the perception of women's empowerment and the crisis of male identity.[72] Offen notes that despite their lack of legal or political authority, women's progressive emancipation and growing influence in society were largely acknowledged by their contemporaries, and also found a significant, often overlooked support on the part of male feminists.[73]

As France underwent a consistent process of modernization, women were evolving accordingly to the new educational, professional, and economic opportunities they were being offered. Among the most important of these opportunities were a broader access to education, with the establishment, from the 1880s, of state primary and secondary schools for girls, and the slow opening up, in many fields, of previously male-exclusive career paths. Other influential factors were the increased sense of mobility due to the diversification and greater availability of the means of transport, the acknowledgement of women as legitimate, self-indulgent consumers within a commercial culture, and the flourishing of newspapers and low-cost, mass-market fiction presenting a female perspective on women's lives and experiences.[74] All these elements exerted an influence on women's self-perception, ambitions, and attitudes. While during the Belle Epoque the figures of the feminist activist and the 'New Woman' were often confused and caricatured as subversive creatures deprived of femininity, thus essentially failing to provide French women with satisfying role models, a large number of women started to identify with the ideal of the *femme moderne*, 'a woman who could balance — with impeccable agility — tradition and innovation, femininity and feminism, work and family'.[75] This woman was animated by a sense of emancipation and equality, she was ready to pursue dreams outside the domestic sphere, to explore new identities, and to expand her roles. However, she did not intend to reject or entirely subvert traditional femininity, and tried to reconcile modern aspirations with conventional feminine norms. This complex and contradictory ideal of womanhood, caught between past and future, thus seems to reflect the strong tensions between conservative and progressive forces at work in these decades.[76]

---

[72]The fin-de-siècle crisis of masculinity and the rise of anti-feminism have been extensively discussed in French scholarship. See for example Annelise Maugue, *L'Identité masculine en crise au tournant du si□ le* (1987), and *Un si□ le d'anti-féminisme* (1999) ed. by Christine Bard. Works such as Pierre-Joseph Proudhon's *La Pornocratie, ou les femmes dans les temps modernes* (Paris: Lacroix et Cie, 1875) attest to the virulent misogyny of this period.

[73]Karen Offen, 'Is the "Woman Question" Really the "Man Problem"?', in *Confronting Modernity in Fin-de-Siecle France: Bodies, Minds and Gender,* ed. by Christopher E. Forth and Elinor Ann Accampo (Basingstoke: Palgrave Macmillan, 2009), pp. 43–62. Offen equally establishes a connection between women's growing power, the restoration of press freedom that allowed a wider circulation of feminist ideas, and the diminished gap between female and male physical strength due to mechanization.

[74]Holmes and Tarr, 'New Republic, New Women?', in *A 'Belle Epoque'?*, ed. by Holmes and Tarr, pp. 15–18.

[75]Rachel Mesch, *Having It All in the Belle Epoque: How French Women's Magazines Invented the Modern Woman* (Stanford, CA: Stanford University Press, 2013), p. 57.

[76]Mesch, *Having It All*, pp. 18–21, discusses the ideal of the *femme moderne* promoted by the women's press of the Belle Epoque as distinct from the figures of the feminist and the 'New Woman'. Although these

This thesis seeks to investigate the connection between those events that, during the Belle Epoque, had a particular relevance for women (e.g. the rise of first-wave feminism, and the shifting of women's condition and sense of identity due to the increasing number of educational and professional opportunities) and the different models of female interaction portrayed in female-authored novels, whether these interactions were articulated in terms of friendship, solidarity, or rivalry. As the next section will argue, the discussion of female homosociality in French literary scholarship, especially with reference to the so-called long nineteenth century, is rather limited, and many questions remain unexplored, particularly as regards the period of the Belle Epoque. For example, did the appeal for public recognition of women's claims and achievements or the creation of new types of female communities inflect the way in which female homosociality was imagined in Belle Epoque female-authored novels? To what extent and in which ways do the selected fictional representations endorse or challenge the model of female friendship described and prescribed in contemporary essays and conduct manuals for girls? How do novelistic representations of female homosociality interweave with questions related to gender identity and contribute to our understanding of how female experiences and subjectivities were discussed and negotiated in Belle Epoque literature?

Before discussing in more detail the methodological approach in which this research is grounded, the next section will provide an overview of the work that has already been conducted in cultural studies and in particular in French studies on the subject of female homosociality, especially with reference to nineteenth-century French literature and the cultural production of the Belle Epoque.

Female Homosociality in French Literary Studies: A Literature Review

The topic of female homosociality has received scarce attention in French literary scholarship, especially with regard to nineteenth-century literature. In the introduction to her

distinctions might appear somewhat arbitrary or unnecessary, I have decided to adopt her definition of the *femme moderne* as representative of the identity and condition of women during the Belle Epoque, not least because the heroines pictured in the novels discussed in this thesis largely correspond to this model and, in these texts, they are repeatedly referred to as *femmes modernes* rather than *nouvelles*. For more discussions of the 'New Woman' and the relation between 'New Women' and feminist activists, see also Holmes and Tarr, 'New Republic, New Women?', in *A 'Belle Epoque'?*, ed. by Holmes and Tarr; and Mary Louise Roberts, *Disruptive Acts: The New Woman in Fin-de-Siècle France* (Chicago, IL; London: University of Chicago Press, 2002). For further exploration of the often overlapping labels f*emme nouvelle*, *femme moderne*, *femme émancipée* and *Eve nouvelle*, see Offen, *Debating the Woman Question*, pp. 181–203.

book on female homoerotic desire in seventeenth-century French novels, Legault deplores the lack of research concerning literary representations of lesbianism in French studies. On the contrary, it seems to me that until now scholars have been far more interested in female homosexual relationships than in friendship or solidarity between women.[77] This is probably due, at least in part, to the fact that representations of female friendship have often been interpreted as devices dissimulating or concealing homosexual romances, the two bonds often being conflated by literary critics, especially within the field of lesbian studies.

At present, we have at our disposal very few studies on the topic of female friendship in French literature, whether as a specific focus or as part of a broader discussion of friendship. Janet Todd's *Women's Friendship in Literature* (1980), even though focused on eighteenth-century novels, remains one of the most relevant works in the field.[78] In her study, Todd explores how French and English authors (for example Denis Diderot, Jean-Jacques Rousseau, the Marquis de Sade, and Madame de Staël) have portrayed interactions between women. She identifies five different categories of female friendship: sentimental, erotic, manipulative, political, and social. In addition, she discusses a set of recurrent motifs that intermingle with these representations, retracing patterns that tend to differ along gender or national lines. For example, according to her analysis, male French eighteenth-century authors were more interested in the depiction of erotic and manipulative relationships between women and in female narcissism, while women authors in general tended to privilege the representation of sentimental, social, and political friendships. She concludes that female friendship in eighteenth-century novels enables characters to 'balance a skewed psychology, ease loneliness, teach survival and create power', allowing them to define themselves in relation to one another, outside the reference to heterosexual relationships.[79]

Susan Yates' *Maid and Mistress* (1992) is one of the rare studies specifically dealing with relationships between female characters in nineteenth-century French novels, even

---

[77]The list of previous works in French literary studies assembled by Legault, *Female Intimacies*, p. 6, includes Elaine Marks, *Homosexuality and French Literature* (1979); Terry Castle, *The Apparitional Lesbian* (1993); Lillian Faderman, *Chloe Plus Olivia* (1995); Marie-Jo Bonnet, *Les Relations amoureuses entre les femmes* (1995), and Elizabeth Susan Wahl, *Invisible Relations* (1999). We could add to her list the already cited Lillian Faderman, *Surpassing the Love of Men* (1985); Joan E. DeJean, *Fictions of Sappho, 1546–1937* (Chicago: Chicago University Press, 1989); Jennifer Waelti-Walters, *Damned Women: Lesbians in French Novels, 1796–1996* (Montreal; London: McGill-Queen's University Press, 2000); Emma Donoghue, *Inseparable* (2010); Juliette Dade, 'Ineffable Gomorrah: The Performance of Lesbianism in Colette, Proust, and Vivien', *Women in French Studies*, 20 (2012), 9–20; Gretchen Schultz, *Sapphic Fathers* (2014); Nicole G. Albert, 'La Lesbienne, nouvelle héroïne de la Belle Époque', in *La Belle Époque des femmes?,* ed. by Le Guennec and Zmelty (2013), pp. 89–99, and *Lesbian Decadence* (2016). On the subject of female friendship, Legault cites only Élaine Audet, *Le Cœur pensant: courtepointe de l'amitié entre femmes* (Québec: Loup de gouttière, 2000).
[78]Janet M. Todd, *Women's Friendship in Literature* (New York: Columbia University Press, 1980).
[79]Todd, *Women's Friendship*, pp. 413–14.

though her analysis is limited to the peculiar cross-class relation between mistress and servant.[80] These relationships are found to be constructed in terms of both rivalry and alliance, and sometimes the two figures are inscribed in the text as female doubles: 'The maid and the mistress are revealed as indispensable to one another, just as they are necessary and complementary halves of the whole that is Woman', and 'even in the texts where she is a central figure, the servant exists as much as a comment on her mistress as in her own right. Part of her function is to throw light on the personality and career of her mistress, whether through contrast or whether she repeats the same pattern at a humbler level'.[81] Yates also notes that these friendships cannot be considered subversive, but represent rather 'an instinctive means of satisfying their [women's] need for intimacy and support in a universe that has treated them harshly'.[82] She compares them to the bond between mother and daughter or between sisters, concluding that maid and mistress, as female characters, share the same destiny of loss and disappointment, and are finally reduced to their similarities regardless of their class or personality. It is interesting to observe that, according to Yates' analysis, even though these female relationships do not openly oppose or challenge the patriarchal system, they seem nonetheless to be shaped as reactions against or retreats from it.

In 1999, a section of the annual issue of *Women in French Studies* was dedicated to 'L'amitié féminine'. This section includes a collection of nine essays spanning the sixteenth to the twentieth centuries, and considers both how female authors experienced friendship in real life and how they portrayed it in their literary works.[83] Among these nine, two focus on literature of the nineteenth century. The first one, Amy Reid's compelling essay on the Goncourt brothers' *Renée Mauperin* (1863), defines female friendship as 'naturalism's blind spot'.[84] Confronted with the objective impossibility of observing the interactions occurring between women in their absence, male naturalist authors, in this example the Goncourt brothers, revert to the heterosexual romance model as a means to interpret female friendship. The adoption of such a strategy accounts for their understanding of this relationship as a form of lesbianism, leading them to attribute male characteristics to one of the female characters (this is the case for the character of Renée Mauperin), and to insert a male voyeur consciousness in their plot. However, this taboo female relationship arousing

---

[80]Susan Yates, *Maid and Mistress: Feminine Solidarity and Class Difference in Five Nineteenth-Century French Texts* (New York: Peter Lang, 1992). This study examines five novels, in particular: *Eugénie Grandet* (1833), *Germinie Lacerteux* (1865), *Une vie* (1883), *Un cœur simple* (1877), *Pot-Bouille* (1882).
[81]Yates, *Maid and Mistress*, pp. 5, 128.
[82]Yates, *Maid and Mistress*, p. 129.
[83]*Women in French Studies*, 7 (1999).
[84]Amy Reid, '*Amitié Féminine*, Naturalism's Blind Spot: The Case of the Goncourt's *Renée Mauperin*', *Women in French Studies*, 7 (1999), 88–100.

fears of gender ambiguity, its representation is finally deleted from the conclusion. According to Reid, the theme of female friendship, in this context, evidences the epistemological limitations of a genre.

Tama Lea Engelking's contribution to the same volume focuses on Natalie Clifford Barney's salon and her relationship with Lucie Delarue-Mardrus, in an effort to highlight the value of friendship within this literary circle beyond the lesbian experiences shared by its members. The emphasis is put on Barney as a literary patroness who fostered nurturing female friendships, encouraging her friends' creativity and providing them with emotional and material support. Her long-lasting friendship with Delarue-Mardrus, established after a brief love affair, is a case in point because of its influence on the content of Delarue-Mardrus' own work, which became increasingly feminist and woman-orientated. In discussing the novel *L'Ange et le Pervers* (1932), Delarue-Mardrus' *roman à clef* about her relationship with Barney, Engelking equally stresses the importance given to friendship rather than to sexuality.[85]

The 2010 special issue of *Women in French Studies* focuses on female solidarity and competition. This collection brings together ten essays exploring historical and fictional collaborations and rivalries among women in different times and contexts, for example the workplace, courts, or convents. In the introduction to the volume, Laurence M. Porter interestingly observes that 'while male bonding and "homosociality" have always been recognized and are being increasingly studied, female equivalents that have attracted critics' attention are usually limited to Lesbian examples [...] or lightly dismissed as somehow insignificant', and the study of female groups other than the erotic dyad and the family have been largely neglected until now.[86] Within this collection, only Porter's 'The Convent as a Paradoxical Site of Women's Autonomy in Post-Revolutionary Autobiography and Fiction' deals with nineteenth-century French literature. Porter discusses in particular how George Sand in her novel *Lélia* (1839) and Victor Hugo in *Les Misérables* (1862) represent the convent as an 'ultimately unsuccessful but still admirable experiment by decent, misguided women who created an island of independence within a limited, sharply separate feminosocial space sanctioned by the male-dominated Church [...] [and] began

---

[85]Tama Lea Engelking, 'The Literary Friendships of Natalie Clifford Barney: The Case of Lucie Delarue-Mardrus', *Women in French Studies,* 7 (1999), 101–16. The American expatriate Nathalie Clifford Barney (1876–1972) hosted a literary salon in Paris, Rue Jacob, for over sixty years and in 1927 founded an *Académie des Femmes.* Openly lesbian, she supported women's creativity throughout her life and was herself a novelist and poet. Lucie Delarue-Mardrus (1874–1945) was a prolific French poet, novelist, and artist linked to Barney's circle.

[86]Laurence M. Porter, 'Introduction', in *Cooperation and Competition in Communities of Women*, ed. by Julia Simms Holderness and Laurence M. Porter (= *Women in French Studies*, Special Issue 2010), pp. 10–14 (p. 10).

imaginatively to explore possibilities for depicting the dynamics of cooperation within a non-pathological cloistered community'.[87]

The essays recently collected in *Solitaires, Solidaires* (2015) provide a colourful and diversified, although limited, overview of the tensions between female solidarity and solitude in historical and literary representations offered by women writers from the seventeenth to the twenty-first centuries. Regarding literary analysis of nineteenth-century novels, the only fictional work taken into account is Liane de Pougy's *L'Insaisissable* (1898).[88] De Pougy, in transposing her love life into fiction, describes the socially marginalized position of a courtesan. Stigmatized and rejected, not least by other women, the heroine of her novel experiences exclusion and loneliness. Even the interactions with other courtesans are generally represented as conflictual, and female solidarity is usually replaced by rivalry and jealousy. De Pougy, however, in trying to cast a more positive light on the figure of the courtesan, nuancing her image of *femme fatale* and highlighting her resemblance to other women, constructs a case for her inclusion within the female community by which she feels judged. The redemption of her character, like the redemption of De Pougy herself in real life, represents an attempt to put an end to this form of female solitude and renew the character's ties with society.

A few additional articles have been published on the subject of female homosociality in nineteenth-century French literature. In 'Le Thème de l'amitié féminine chez un "tendre ami des femmes"' (2009), Maria Scott discusses the different forms that female homosociality takes in works by Stendhal, while in 'Educating Nélida and Valentia: Female Mentorship in Two Works by Marie d'Agoult', Hope Christiansen highlights the role played by strong and emancipated female mentors in the formation of the eponymous heroines.[89]

This brief survey, although presenting us with a stimulating variety of analyses, approaches, and ideas, shows that the amount of research conducted on the topic of how female homosociality is represented in Belle Epoque literature is still far from being exhaustive or even extensive. The only Belle Epoque novel considered by the aforementioned studies is Liane de Pougy's *L'Insaisissable*. Jennifer Waelti-Walters' pioneering work, *Feminist Novelists of the Belle Epoque* (1990), contains scattered references to female friendship and solidarity in female-authored Belle Epoque French

[87]Laurence M. Porter, 'The Convent as a Paradoxical Site of Women's Autonomy in Post-Revolutionary Autobiography and Fiction', in *Cooperation and Competition*, ed. by Simms Holderness and Porter, pp. 76–89 (p. 78).

[88]Philippe Martin-Horie, 'Liane de Pougy: *L'Insaisissable* ou les chemins de la rédemption', in *Solitaires, Solidaires*, ed. by Hugueny-Léger and Verdier, pp. 59–73.

[89]Maria Scott, 'Le Thème de l'amitié féminine chez un "tendre ami des femmes"', *L'Année stendhalienne*, 8 (2009), 101–15; Hope Christiansen, 'Educating Nélida and Valentia: Female Mentorship in Two Works by Marie d'Agoult', *Nineteenth-Century French Studies*, 44.3/4 (Spring–Summer 2016), 235–49.

novels, while Juliette Rogers' *Career Stories* (2007) offers a discussion of female mentorship and communities in Belle Epoque women's novels.[90] To my knowledge, no book-length study specifically focusing on female homosociality in nineteenth-century or Belle Epoque French literature has been produced.[91] This lack becomes more apparent if we consider how much attention the topic of female homosociality has received in anglophone literature and scholarship.[92] My thesis addresses the need to conduct further research into this topic, a need already highlighted by Sharon Marcus in 2009, when in the conclusion of her study on female homosociality in Victorian England she observes: 'A book focused on one country in one century also begs the question of how specific its claims are; to answer that would require a comparative synthesis of existing work and fresh research.'[93] This thesis thus aims to provide a new piece of 'fresh research', in order to further our understanding of how women's relationships and identities are constructed in literature.

---

[90]In *Feminist Novelists of the Belle Epoque: Love as a Lifestyle* (Bloomington; Indianapolis: Indiana University Press, 1990), Jennifer Waelti-Walters alludes to the importance of female relationships in Lucie Delarue-Mardrus, *Marie, fille-mère* (1906), Liane de Pougy, *Idylle saphique* (1901), Gabrielle Réval, *Un lycée de jeunes filles* (1901), and Colette Yver, *Les Cervelines* (1903). Claude Lemaître's novel *Ma soeur Zabette* (1902) is referred to as the only text characterized by the absence of any kind of female network of support. Rogers, *Career Stories* will be further discussed in Chapter Two, pp. 96–98, 113–15; Chapter Three, pp. 154, 180; and Chapter Four, p. 233. The only brief allusion to female friendship in Beth W. Gale's A *World Apart: Female Adolescence in the French Novel, 1870–1930* (Lewisburg, PA: Bucknell University Press, 2010) concerns Rachilde's novel *Son printemps* (1912).

[91]This account, except for Todd's *Women's Friendship in Literature*, was specifically limited to studies that examine the representation of female friendship in nineteenth-century French novels. Other essays in *Women in French Studies*, 7 (1999) and *Solitaires, Solidaires* (2015) consider real-life relations between nineteenth-century French women authors and female networks of solidarity established through women's press. On the subject of female friendship in poetry, see for example Medha Nirody Karmarkar and Régine Kern's article 'L'amitié féminine dans les oeuvres d'Isabelle de Charrière et de Marceline Desbordes-Valmore', *Cincinnati Romance Review*, 15 (1996), 134–43. Recently, Michelle L. Miller, *Material Friendship* (2008) has discussed friendship in Early Modern French literature. Some studies have addressed more broadly the practice or conceptualization of friendship in French history and culture, for example Anne Vincent-Buffault, *Exercice de l'amitié* (1995), and *Men and Women Making Friends in Early Modern France* (2015), ed. by Lewis C. Seifert and Rebecca M. Wilkin.

[92]For discussions of representations of female homosociality in nineteenth-century anglophone literature, see for example Nina Auerbach, *Communities of Women: An Idea in Fiction* (New York: ToExcel, 1998 [1978]); Pauline Nestor, *Female Friendships and Communities: Charlotte Brontë, George Eliot, Elizabeth Gaskell* (Oxford: Clarendon Press, 1985); Tess Cosslett, *Woman to Woman: Female Friendship in Victorian Fiction* (Atlantic Highlands, NJ: Humanities Press International, 1988); Sarah Annes Brown, *Devoted Sisters: Representations of the Sister Relationship in Nineteenth-Century British and American Literature* (Aldershot; Burlington: Ashgate, 2003); Sharon Marcus, *Between Women* (2007); and Helena Michie, *Sorophobia: Differences among Women in Literature and Culture* (Oxford: Oxford University Press, 1992). See also Barbara Caine, 'Taking up the Pen: Women and the Writing of Friendship', in *Friendship*, ed. by Caine, pp. 215–22, and Brodie and Caine, 'Class, Sex, and Friendship', in *Friendship*, ed. by Caine, pp. 223–42.

[93]Marcus, *Between Women*, p. 260.

Methodology

Different critics have argued that novels constitute a privileged field of enquiry for the study of social relationships in the nineteenth century. For example, Sharon Marcus has observed that 'nineteenth-century novels consist almost entirely of accounts of social relationships — bonds between individuals and the ways that communities respond to those bonds'. Barbara Caine has noted that 'throughout the nineteenth-century, it is to fiction rather than to philosophy that one needs to turn to find extended discussions of friendship', and Anne Vincent-Buffault has found that in nineteenth-century France the topic of friendship becomes more extensively treated in fiction, poetry, and educational literature than in philosophical treatises.[94]

As stated by Pauline Nestor:

> Literature is commonly seen as offering its own unique insight into a period. More than simply another source of opinion, literature in any age provides access to deeper levels of consciousness, liberating its own truth in fiction. [...] This inclination to privilege the insights offered by literature is particularly marked in regard to the nineteenth century when the popularity of fiction made it perhaps the most potent form of social commentary.[95]

Novels represent the main focus of my own investigation into the reality of female homosociality in the Belle Epoque because they bear, unavoidably, the marks of the social, political, and cultural circumstances in which they were produced, and, above all, they inform us about the ideals that inspired their authors and the models their readers had at their disposal. Those novels that constitute the primary corpus of this research are written by women, are about women, and are for women. The centrality of a female heroine and her social interactions, the possibility of accessing, through literature, a female perspective on women's lives and relationships, and the fact that these texts were primarily intended for and widely consumed by a female cross-class readership count among the main criteria determining the selection of the corpus, regardless of the fact that the novels belong to different genres (e.g. *roman de mœurs*, *Bildungsroman*, schoolgirl fiction, adultery novel).

---

[94]Marcus, *Between Women*, p. 8; Barbara Caine, 'Taking up the Pen', in *Friendship*, ed. by Caine, p. 215; Vincent-Buffault, *Exercice de l'amitié*, p. 76.

[95]Nestor, *Female Friendships and Communities*, pp. 2–3.

Although heterosexual love is usually at the centre of the plot, various depictions of female homosociality are inscribed in these texts, and perform different narrative and ideological functions.[96]

In privileging full-length narratives written from a female standpoint, I am not implying that female writing offers automatic access to authentic female experience, or that women authors' views on the topic of female homosociality are necessarily more meaningful, accurate, or positive than those expressed by their male colleagues, but rather wish to interrogate how women writers understand, imagine, and negotiate female homosociality in literature, as a way to discuss and spread ideas about the possibilities of modern womanhood. If we stand by Marcus' claim that 'heterosexual women's lives can only be fully understood if we attend to their friendships with women', a close examination of novelistic portrayals of female homosociality can contribute to our comprehension of female subjectivities as constructed during the Belle Epoque.[97] According to Diana Holmes, 'around the turn of the century the number of women-authored texts which deal more or less explicitly with the question of female identity and experience suggests a significant circulation and negotiation of women's issues through literature.'[98] Rachel Mesch situates these texts within the context of 'Belle Epoque literary feminism', a new discursive space that she describes 'primarily as a work of imagination: of examining, exploring and most fundamentally, fantasizing about what the fully realized modern woman could be'.[99] The novels here examined play an important role in encouraging their (female) readers to reflect on their position within the changing yet conservative world of the Belle Epoque. They communicate different views on women and their places in society, and constitute a privileged space in which female experiences can be represented, discussed, and reflected upon, and cultural norms can be supported or subverted. Fictional representations of female homosociality can be understood as part of this broader, more articulated discourse on modern womanhood carried out in Belle Epoque female-authored literature. Even more importantly, this thesis will argue that such representations constitute one of the literary devices through which the *femme moderne* comes into being on paper.

Looking at novelistic representations of female homosociality in the Belle Epoque allows us to investigate women authors' engagement with modernism at the time of its

---

[96]According to Holmes, '[u]ntil around 1910, the romance plot rarely stood alone, but rather was woven into a dense, multi-stranded narrative, which appealed to several dimensions of (particularly but not solely female) experience.' See Diana Holmes, *Romance and Readership in Twentieth-Century France* (Oxford: Oxford University Press, 2006), p. 24.

[97]Marcus, *Between Women*, p. 8.

[98]Diana Holmes, *French Women's Writing, 1848–1994* (London; Atlantic Highlands, NJ: Athlone, 1996), pp. 19–20.

[99]Mesch, *Having It All*, p. 8.

emergence. The group of novels analysed in this thesis can generally be classified as 'middlebrow fiction'. I employ this slippery term to indicate a genre that occupies the middle ground between 'high' and 'popular' literature; a form of art accessible to a wide readership, which offers a pleasurable reading experience while treating serious topics such as female education, employment, and marriage.[100] The privileging of plot, mimesis, and immersion over stylistic innovation and formal experimentation discourages the establishment of a straightforward link between these texts and the modernist (male) canon. However, scholars have been arguing for the recognition of female forms of modernism in addition to those of the male elitist avant-garde.[101] In particular, Holmes makes the case for 'un modernisme au féminin', which reflects an alternative experience of modernity and focuses more often (but not exclusively) on content rather than form.[102] Most interestingly, among the differences between the masculine and feminine genres, Holmes points to the importance of interpersonal relationships in the latter. While the male modernist hero is usually a solitary individual, in perpetual conflict with society, '[d]ans le roman féminin, le soi est bien plus un soi-en-relation, défini en grande partie par ses rapports à l'autre'.[103] Holmes further indicates that the stress put on relationships spans the extra-diegetic and intra-diegetic levels, and concerns both the reader's identification with the heroine and the relationships established among female characters in the text.[104] In this thesis, I wish to explore in more detail the ways in which, during the Belle Epoque, the redefinition of female identities in fiction is connected to the representation of homosocial relations between female characters. In particular, I will argue that these representations, while sometimes reinforcing traditional gender identities, can also exert a 'queering effect' and question the stability of binary gender oppositions by charting the development of fictional *femmes modernes* who, in their

---

[100]In a short article appeared in the *New Yorker* in 2011, Macy Halford defines the middlebrow 'as an important part of how ideas are circulated in our culture among different strata of society (specifically, among groups with varying levels of wealth, education, and access to "high" or "avant-garde" culture)'. See Macy Halford, 'On "Middlebrow"', *New Yorker*, 10 February 2011. Diana Holmes inserts most of the novels analysed in this thesis in the category of the 'middlebrow' in 'Mapping Modernity: The Feminine Middlebrow and the Belle Époque', *French Cultural Studies*, 25.3/4 (2014), 262–70. In 'Modernisme et genre à la Belle Époque: Daniel Lesueur, Marcelle Tinayre, Colette', in *F(r)ictions Modernistes du Masculin/Féminin, 1900–1940*, ed. by Andrea Oberhuber, Alexandra Arvisais, Marie-Claude Dugas (Paris: PUF, 2016), pp. 49–62 (p. 53), Holmes defines the middlebrow as 'une littérature lisible [...], ciblant un lectorat « moyen », qui offre le plaisir d'une histoire captivante tout en abordant des thèmes pertinents pour les lecteurs'.

[101]See for example Rita Felski, *The Gender of Modernity* (London: Harvard University Press, 1995), and Katherine Mullin, 'Modernisms and Feminisms', in *The Cambridge Companion to Feminist Literary Theory*, ed. by Ellen Rooney (Cambridge: Cambridge University Press, 2006), pp. 136–52.

[102]Holmes, 'Modernisme et genre', in *F(r)ictions Modernistes*, ed. by Oberhuber et al., pp. 52–58.

[103]Holmes, 'Modernisme et genre', in *F(r)ictions Modernistes*, ed. by Oberhuber et al., p. 55.

[104] Holmes, 'Modernisme et genre', in *F(r)ictions Modernistes*, ed. by Oberhuber et al., p. 56. Among the other differences identified by Holmes figure a more optimistic vision of modernity, the adoption and adaptation of realist modes of narration, and a larger readership. Moreover, although pointing to the value of female friendship, Holmes contends that 'l'importance du rapport à l'autre se manifeste encore plus dans ces textes par le rôle central joué par l'amour passionnel'.

interactions with other female characters, progressively learn how to appropriate and display both masculine and feminine attributes and break conventional codes of behaviour. It is my contention that the construction of modern, somewhat subversive female subjectivities through the literary depiction of women's relationships represents one of the distinctive features of the proposed 'modernisme au féminin'.

If in Belle Epoque literature the figure of the *femme moderne* complicates any rigid notion of femininity, the idea that gender identity is not a permanent, immutable, biologically determined category, but rather a social construction, has been formally theorized by twentieth-century feminist thinkers. In particular, Simone de Beauvoir in *Le Deu□ □e Sexe* (1949) argues that sexual difference has been historically and socially constructed in patriarchal societies through the circulation of myths and the employment of hierarchical, antithetical categories (e.g. nature, passivity, sensitivity vs culture, activity, rationality), which posit men as the dominant norm and women as the inferior Others.[105] Hélène Cixous starts her essay 'Sorties' from *La Jeune Née* (1975) by claiming that this vertical dualism organizes our society and renders women unthinkable outside such oppositions, subsequently pointing to the establishment of a feminine economy in which social codes, values, and the very understanding of gender can be revised.[106] In *Bodies that Matter* (1993), Judith Butler further highlights the possibility of deconstructing sexual difference as something inherent to the instability of the binary system and its constructions.[107] As we shall see, under the pen of some Belle Epoque female authors, the homosocial relations imagined in fiction create a peculiar interpersonal space, a 'feminine economy' of sorts, within which female characters can sometimes free other female characters from restrictive gender norms.

As noted by Marion Krauthaker, among others, the patriarchal system (i.e. the socio-political and ideological structure based on the primacy of men) and the binary logic that supports it underpin the organization of nineteenth-century French society. However, during this century the idea that the individual has some responsibility in defining his own identity starts to emerge, and some evolutions occur in the literary representation of 'masculine' and 'feminine' identities.[108] As a matter of fact, gender instability has been widely exploited in literature, from Ovid to Shakespeare, and certainly in nineteenth-century French literature

---

[105]Simone de Beauvoir, *Le Deuxi□ □e Sexe I: les faits et les mythes* (Paris: Gallimard, 1976 [1949]).
[106]Hélène Cixous, 'Sorties', in *La Jeune Née*, by Catherine B. Clément and Hélène Cixous (Paris: Union Générale d'Editions, 1975), pp. 114–246.
[107]Judith Butler, *Bodies that Matter: On the Discursive Limits of "Sex"* (Abingdon, Oxon; New York, NY: Routledge, 2011 [1993]). The works of these and other scholars such as Luce Irigaray, René Girard, and Eve Kosofsky Sedgwick provide the theoretical framework for the analysis of Belle Epoque fictional representations of female relationships and identities, and will be further discussed in the various chapters.
[108]Marion Krauthaker, *L'Identité de genre dans les œuvres de George Sand et Colette* (Paris: Harmattan, 2011), pp. 45–49, 63.

prior to the Belle Epoque, for example in authors such as Balzac, George Sand, and Stendhal.[109] As regards Belle Epoque female authors, the strongest attacks against strict gender codes and stereotypes can be found in works by Rachilde and Colette, who variously exploit the device of gender instability to create aesthetic emotions, defy (literary) conventions, and promote the plurality of female identity in literature.[110] Moreover, during the same period, the press significantly contributes to the blurring of strict gender divides. Guillaume Pinson argues that 'à partir de 1900, certains périodiques passent de l'expression de l'angoisse de la masculinisation [de la femme] à une forme de revendication qui intègre des éléments tirés de la sphère traditionnellement masculine'. For example, the magazine *La Vie heureuse* 'autorise un certain croisement entre les sphères masculine et féminine' and 'une forme de virilité, de force conquérante, est revendiquée [par la femme]'.[111] This research, it should be noted, does not look at the image of the *femme moderne* as a final product, either in fiction or in the press, but rather considers it as a literary figure in construction. It focuses on one of the devices which, in practice, allows for her presence in fiction, and contends that representations of female homosociality are often used by Belle Epoque female authors to deconstruct gender and redefine modern femininity, in a context where traditional gender norms are still far from being systematically questioned or rejected. This is all the more surprising if we consider that, in nineteenth-century France, relationships between women were usually meant to reinforce the status quo and women's place within it, as didactic literature but also much popular, orthodox literature of the Belle Epoque continue to suggest.

As regards the choice of authors and primary texts, the works of fiction analysed in this thesis have been carefully selected among an initial corpus of sixty novels published between 1880 and 1914. These texts were singled out because I considered them to be either representative of some common pattern or major trend or because, on the contrary, they helped me to illustrate a specific point. In both cases, they have been chosen because they present a particular interest from the point of view of female homosociality, and allow us to explore the intersections of this topic with issues related to the female body, work, education, marriage, heterosexual love, and the moral regeneration of the French nation. In offering a close reading of these texts, I do not aim at exhaustiveness, but rather hope to show that by 'reading in detail', i.e. by focusing on a particular aspect of these novels, as

---

[109] According to Alison Finch, gender instability became a hallmark of nineteenth-century French fiction, particularly thanks to women writers. See Alison Finch, *Women's Writing in Nineteenth-Century France* (Cambridge: Cambridge University Press, 2000), p. 229.
[110] For extensive discussion of gender deconstruction in Colette's fiction, see Krauthaker, *Identité de genre*.
[111] Guillaume Pinson, 'La Femme masculinisée dans la presse mondaine française de la Belle Époque', *Clio*, 30 (2009), 211–30 (pp. 219, 220).

opposed to treating Belle Epoque female authors as an indistinct group and their writing as a whole, it is possible to make a case for the artistic value of some non-canonical texts of the Belle Epoque.[112] Better-known and widely studied contemporary authors like the aforementioned Colette and Rachilde have not been included in this corpus by reason of the little attention they give to female homosociality or the ambiguity they create between homosociality and homosexuality.[113]

All the writers considered in this thesis, Louise-Marie Compain (1869–1940), Yvette Prost (1874–1949), Gabrielle Réval (1870–1938), Marcelle Tinayre (1877–1948), and Colette Yver (1874–1953) belong to the same generation of writers, with the exception of the slightly older Daniel Lesueur (1860–1921) and Thérèse Bentzon (1840–1907). These women were generally born in provincial France and usually came from similar middle-class backgrounds.[114] They all benefited from the new educational and career opportunities arising under the Third Republic, first as graduates of the new *lycées féminins* or even *Écoles Normales*, and later on as teachers, journalists, and professional novelists.[115] They hosted literary salons, were actively involved in some kind of female support system,[116] collaborated with the same journals, such as *La Fronde* and *Femina*, and participated in public speaking activities, giving talks about several topics, including female education, religion, and marriage. During their lives, all of them achieved, to different degrees, both popularity and official recognition. For example, Rotraud Von Kulessa identifies Daniel Lesueur, who won several prizes of the *Académie Française*, including the *prix Montyon*, the *prix Vitet*, and the *prix Archon Despérouses*, as 'la femme la plus couronnée de

---

[112]I am borrowing the expression 'reading in detail' from Naomi Schor's study *Reading in Detail: Aesthetics and the Feminine* (New York; London: Routledge, 1987), which investigates the status of the detail as an aesthetic category, and proposes a connection between the detail and the feminine. Although adapting it for my own purposes, I retain the spirit of Schor's expression insofar as I consider the representation of female homosociality as one of those seemingly marginal and neglected details whose consideration can open up the discussion about the aesthetic value of a fictional work.

[113]Although Colette's *Claudine à l'école* (Paris: A. Michel, 1958 [1900]) could have been considered in Chapter Three on 'Female Communities in Schoolgirl Fiction', I have decided to exclude this novel. This is partly due to the fact that there is a tendency to interpret the female relationships represented in this text as allusions to lesbianism. But even when the novel permits access to some facet of female homosociality (i.e. female intellectual rivalry), I have privileged other texts, whose treatment of the topic was more extensive or relevant and better served the purpose of my analysis.

[114]For example, Gabrielle Réval, pseudonym of Gabrielle Elise Victoire Logerot, native of Lorraine but born in Viterbo (Italy), was the daughter of an infantry captain. Marcelle Tinayre, born Marguerite Suzanne Marcelle Chasteau in the Limousin, was the daughter of an artist. Her mother, Louise Chasteau, was a trained teacher and school director. Colette Yver, pseudonym of Emilie Antoinette de Bergevin, was born in Normandy, the daughter of a civil servant. Daniel Lesueur, pseudonym of Alice Jeanne Victoire Loiseau and native of the department of Seine, was the daughter of a shopkeeper.

[115]For more information about the authors' educational background and their links with the Third Republican school, see Chapter Three, pp. 151–52.

[116]For example, in 1904 Lesueur, Réval, Bentzon, and Tinayre were among the members of the first, all-female jury of the *Prix Femina*, initially called *Prix Vie Heureuse*. Yver won the prize in 1907 and later on also became a member of the jury. Compain was not connected to this particular female network of artistic support, but she was engaged in other female communities, such as the *Union française pour le suffrage des femmes*.

l'époque'.[117] In 1900, Lesueur was the first female author to receive the *Légion d'honneur*, and in 1907 she was also the second woman after George Sand to be elected as a member of the committee of the *Socitété des Gens de Lettres*. In 1900, Marcelle Tinayre was awarded the *prix Montyon* for *Hellé*, one of the novels analysed in this thesis. Her novel *La Maison du péché* (1902) was re-edited 40 times, translated into nine languages and, according to France Grenaudier-Klijn, it was 'the only French novel reviewed in James Joyce's *Critical Writings*'.[118] Colette Yver won the *Prix Femina* in 1907 for her novel *Princesses de science*, considered later in this thesis, and was also awarded the *Légion d'honneur* in 1931. Yvette Prost received the *prix Sobrier-Arnould* of the *Académie Française* in 1923 for the novel *Les Belles Vies manquées*, and Gabrielle Réval was honoured with the *prix d'Académie* in 1938 for her overall body of work.

The chapter 'Female Friendship and the Body' begins this thesis by pursuing and complicating a reflection on the value of physical intimacy in women's relationships, an element which, as highlighted in this introduction, can be seen as one of the most ambiguous aspects of nineteenth-century female friendship. The chapter considers the different roles played by physicality in Belle Epoque novelistic portrayals of female friendship, and situates these roles within the context of the medical and social discourses on the female body that dominate the turn of the century. My analysis focuses on two *romans de mœurs* by Daniel Lesueur, *Justice de femme* (1893) and *Lèvres closes* (1898); occasional parallels are drawn with a male-authored novel, Henri Rabusson's *L'Amie* (1886), and with Louise-Marie Compain's *L'Un vers l'autre* (1903). After examining the connection, in fiction, between physical appearance and identity in couples of female friends, my analysis provides some explanations for the degree of physical tenderness and playfulness involved in Belle Epoque literary representations of female homosociality. In particular, by using Judith Butler's notion of 'performativity', I will show that fictional displays of affection between women can be revealing of the artificial nature of femininity, or alternatively, in the case of arguably more interesting fictions, can signify women's ability to appropriate their bodies as instruments through which they can produce their own meanings and exert agency.

Female dyads are also at the centre of the second chapter, on 'Female Mentorship and the Making of the *Femme Moderne* in the Female *Bildungsroman*', which pays particular attention to the connection existing between novelistic representations of female mentoring

[117]Rotraud Von Kulessa, *Entre la reconnaissance et l'exclusion: la position de l'autrice dans le champ littéraire en France et en Italie à l'époque 1900* (Paris: Honoré Champion, 2011), p. 126.
[118]France Grenaudier-Klijn, 'The Mother as *Femme Fatale*: God, Eros, and Thanatos in Marcelle Tinayre's *La Maison du péché*', in *Aimer et Mourir: Love, Death, and Women's Lives in Texts of French Expression*, ed. by Eilene Hoft-March and Judith Holland Sarnecki (Newcastle upon Tyne: Cambridge Scholars Publishing, 2009), pp. 128–51 (p. 136).

practices, the emphasis put on women's role as educators, and the fact that the authors themselves were often acting as mentors to their readers, possibly using the mentor figure as their literary double and as an indirect representation of the didactic value of literature itself. The focus of the thesis thus shifts from emotional intimacy as expressed by physical means to emotional intimacy in the form of intellectual support. By considering three Belle Epoque female *Bildungsromans*, Gabrielle Réval's *La Cruche cassée* (1904), Colette Yver's *Les Cervelines* (1903), and Marcelle Tinayre's *Hellé* (1899), the chapter identifies unsuccessful and successful mentorship models, through which the conflicts between biological and spiritual motherhood, love and friendship, marriage and career, decadent aristocracy and Republican bourgeoisie, past and future, conventional and progressive femininity are played out. The study of these tensions, which can be partly explained through the use of René Girard's notion of mimetic desire, will lead to the interpretation of fictional mentorship relationships in terms of 'vertical' or 'horizontal' homosociality, and will point to the establishment of a literary 'counter-discourse' on the meanings of modern womanhood.

Turning my attention from one-to-one relationships to larger group dynamics, in the third chapter on 'Female Communities in Schoolgirl Fiction' I will consider how changes in the field of female education inflected the way in which female homosociality is imagined in fiction and will show how female identities are reshaped accordingly. Yvette Prost's *Salutaire orgueil* (1907) will be read alongside the more conservative *Yette: histoire d'une jeune créole* (1880) by Thérèse Bentzon, in order to trace some of the variations occurring in Belle Epoque fictional representations of female school communities. I will then offer a close reading of Gabrielle Réval's *Les Sévriennes* (1900), additionally drawing a brief parallel to her second novel, *Lycéennes* (1902). My discussion will call attention to the fact that the public, cross-class space of the Third Republican school, as imagined in early twentieth-century schoolgirl fiction, provides women with a new socializing venue in which the notion of community is constructed both in terms of intellectual rivalry and intellectual friendship, two forms of bonding of which women, traditionally, were thought incapable. As we shall see, in this context the heroines overstep class and gender boundaries unpunished, and challenge conservative notions of female passivity by asserting themselves against each other and by collectively adhering to more complex and subversive types of femininity.

In the fourth and final chapter on 'Female Rivalry and Love Triangles', the focus shifts from intellectual to sexual antagonism, and from schoolgirl fiction to the adultery novel. By looking at the female-based erotic triangles portrayed in Yvette Prost's *Salutaire orgueil* (1907), Daniel Lesueur's *Nietzschéenne* (1908), and Colette Yver's *Princesses de science* (1907), I will show how the novels redefine the figure of the Other Woman and create a slippage between rivalry and friendship. In establishing a feminine economy of generosity based on sacrifice and on the exchange of men, the female characters of these novels cooperate to guarantee the solidity of the family and the moral health of the nation in the context of French degeneration, simultaneously upsetting common assumptions about women's innate jealousy, disloyalty, and tendency to compete over men.

Finally, the Conclusion will assess the findings of this research, reflect on its limits, and indicate paths for further inquiry, which were beyond the scope of the present study.

CHAPTER ONE

Female Friendship and the Body

Introduction

The female body has been a central issue in feminist theory at least since the publication of Simone De Beauvoir's *Le Deu□ □ e Sexe* (1949). In this seminal essay, Beauvoir argues that women, as culturally constructed 'Others', have, historically, been defined by their bodies and trapped in immanence. According to Beauvoir, 'la femme, comme l'homme, *est* son corps: mais son corps est autre chose qu'elle.'[1] As Beauvoir notes, at the biological level women's reproductive functions have subordinated the female body to the interests of the species. Alienated, insofar as they are confined to maternity and domesticity, women have been denied the possibility of actively participating in the construction of the world; their bodies do not belong to them, but rather constitute an obstacle in their path to self-affirmation.

The theoretical framework provided by Beauvoir is particularly useful when we think about the perception of the female body in the context of nineteenth-century France and the centrality of that perception to the definition of womanhood. During this century, the justification of gender difference, one of the principles underpinning the structure of French society, was a question of significant interest not only to those concerned with philosophy and religion, but also to scientists. In particular, male experts situated the origin of women's distinctive behaviour and social identity in their anatomical and physiological specificities, the female body being considered as the key to feminine nature. This idea, promulgated at the end of the eighteenth century in works such as Pierre Roussel's treatise *Syst□me physique et moral de la femme* (1775), Pierre Cabanis's *Rapports du physique et du moral de l'homme* (1802), and Julien Joseph Virey's *De la femme sous ses rapports physiologique, moral et littéraire* (1825), was still in force during the Belle Epoque.[2] For example, in 'La Psychologie des sexes et ses fondements physiologiques', a long article that appeared in the *Revue des Deux Mondes* in 1893, the French philosopher Alfred Fouillée insists on the

---

[1]Beauvoir, *Deuxi□ □e Sexe I,* p. 69. Italics in the original.

[2]For a discussion of these texts, see for example James F. McMillan, *France and Women, 1789–1914: Gender, Society and Politics* (London; New York: Routledge, 2000); Yvonne Knibiehler, 'Les Médecins et la « nature féminine » au temps du Code civil', *Annales. Économies, Sociétés, Civilisations*, 4 (1976), 824–45, and 'Le Discours sur la femme: constantes et ruptures', *Romantisme*, 13–14 (1976), 41–55.

fact that virtually any aspect of women's existence can be explained by reference to their bodies, thereby 'scientifically' proving that nature itself has destined women to family life. Fouillée goes as far as to assert that women's refusal to fulfil their natural mission of child-bearer and companion would entail the destruction of society.[3] Similarly, the philosopher and pedagogue Henri Marion devotes an entire chapter of his essay *La Psychologie de la femme* (1900) to the ways in which female physiology determines the attributes of women and their place in the world.[4]

Nineteenth-century French society was the theatre of multiple discourses on the female body, and women's biological nature was integral to the different types of identities available to them. As highlighted by Jennifer Waelti-Walters, among others, after the French Revolution:

> As the bourgeois wife and mother increasingly became an icon of idealized domesticity, images of women polarized and became less varied. On the one hand were desexualized 'angels of the house' (to quote Virginia Woolf), and on the other hand were sexually coded women divided into economically determined strata.[5]

In the context of the Belle Epoque, women continued to be defined either as mothers or sexual objects, as *femmes honnêtes* or *filles publiques*. The Third Republic, concerned by depopulation and preoccupied by the question of how best to educate productive citizens, exalted women's roles as mothers and wives while 'doctors were also promoting a medical view of "woman" primarily in terms of her child-bearing and child-rearing social role'.[6] At this time, the private, sacred, and passive maternal body, exemplified by the figure of the Virgin Mary, a mother dissociated from her sexuality and subordinated to male authority, was both medically and legally regulated.[7] Indeed, from the second half of the century, the female body and the experience of maternity became increasingly medicalized. Moreover, according to the 1804 Civil Code, which was still operative during the Belle Epoque, women's bodies were the properties of their husbands, and mothers had no legal rights over

---

[3]Alfred Fouillée, 'La Psychologie des sexes et ses fondements physiologiques', *Revue des Deux Mondes*, 119 (1893), 397–429.
[4]See Henri Marion, *La Psychologie de la femme: études de psychologie féminine* (Paris: A. Colin, 1900). In particular, 'Les Données physiologiques', pp. 49–70.
[5]Waelti-Walters, *Damned Women*, p. 3. According to Beauvoir: 'L'homme a toujours essayé de dissocier les deux aspects de la féminité: maternel et sexuel.' See Beauvoir, *Deuxi□me Sexe I,* p. 256.
[6]McMillan, *France and Women*, p. 101.
[7]The Immaculate Conception became a dogma in 1854. On the figure of the Virgin Mary as one of the ideal incarnations of womanhood, see for example Beauvoir, *Deuxi□me Sexe I,* pp. 284–85, Stéphane Michaud, *Muse et Madone: visages de la femme de la Révolution française aux apparitions de Lourdes* (Paris: Éditions du Seuil, 1985), and Julia Kristeva, 'Stabat Mater', in *The Kristeva Reader,* ed. by Toril Moi (New York: Columbia University Press, 1986), pp. 160–86.

their children. In stark contrast to the maternal body, there was the sexual, public, and dangerous body of the prostitute or the *femme fatale*, an object of fear and fascination often represented in art and literature and equally controlled by the law.[8]

Public discourses about the maternal and the sexual body need to be understood in connection with one of the dominant mindsets of *fin-de-siècle* France: degeneration. As argued by Richard Thomson:

> Degeneration was a means of structuring debate about social concerns of grave national import, be they specifically medical — such as the persistence of tuberculosis or syphilis — or more generally medico-social — like falling birth rate or rising alcoholism — and even wide socio-political problems including crime, terrorism and crowd control.[9]

While the Republic encouraged women to fight against the lowering rate of natality by producing more babies (i.e. more future soldiers and mothers), thus contributing to the regeneration of society, the prostitute's body, vessel of venereal diseases and moral corruption, needed to be held in check. The health of France itself putatively depended upon these principles.

In addition to the maternal/sexual dichotomy, the female figure continued to be invested with the traditional role of muse, her body being called upon to express conventional ideals of beauty and femininity, in a constant tension between nature and artificiality. Moreover, the nineteenth-century medical discourse on the hysterical body, with its association of female sexuality, maternity, and pathology, reinforced a negative perception of women's corporeality. As observed by Janet Beizer, hysteria, a feminine disease studied and discussed from ancient Egypt onwards, became a 'sociocultural category' in France during the last third of the century, contributing to the view of the female body as inconstant, uncontrollable, frantic, and capricious.[10]

As mothers and wives, prostitutes and *femmes fatales*, muses and hysterics, women of the Belle Epoque were constantly associated with their physicality, their bodies constituting a locus of cultural meanings largely imposed by men. As argued by Patricia Tilburg, however, the period of the Belle Epoque also represents a 'significant moment of

---

[8] According to French law, prostitutes needed to declare their activity and submit to regular medical examinations. For more detail, see for example Alain Corbin, *Les Filles de noce: misère sexuelle et prostitution, 19ème et 20ème siècles* (Paris: A. Montaigne, 1978).

[9] Richard Thomson, *The Troubled Republic: Visual Culture and Social Debate in France 1889–1900* (New Haven; London: Yale University Press, 2004), p. 23.

[10] Janet L. Beizer, *Ventriloquized Bodies: Narratives of Hysteria in Nineteenth-Century France* (Ithaca, N. Y.; London: Cornell University Press, 1994).

transition regarding French attitudes toward the body'.[11] Indeed, the *morale laïque* promoted by the Third Republic and diffused through the newly-instituted secular school posited a strong connection between body and 'soul', physicality and morality, gestures and emotions, and paid particular attention to issues of hygiene and physical health. 'Fin-de-siècle health and physical education curricula presented French girls in particular with a persistent linking of physical beauty and moral goodness', encouraging women to think of their body as the expression of the 'soul' and an instrument of moral improvement.[12] According to Tilburg, if in the secular Republic 'the physical and moral were mutually dependent and mutually sustaining', the active and positive role accorded to the body finally allowed women to consider their corporeality as a fundamental part of their whole being, a part that was deserving of attention, rather than an obstacle in the path to moral perfection, as traditionally asserted by the Church.[13]

If it is true that this secular attitude, as identified by Tilburg, contrasted with the Catholic devaluation of the body and its exaltation of woman as a spiritual being, Fouillée, whose text was associated at the beginning of this chapter with a continuation of previous thinking rather than a shift away from it, similarly notes, nevertheless, that:

> une loi psychologique bien connue veut que chaque état d'âme et ses signes extérieurs soient indissolublement associés: non seulement l'état d'âme produit son expression au dehors, mais l'expression, à son tour, tend à éveiller l'état d'âme. [...] En s'exerçant à être belle, la femme s'est exercée à être bonne.[14]

As this passage indicates, the insistence on the link between the psychological and the physical was hardly new or disruptive in itself. However, what Tilburg's research interestingly highlights is the unprecedented emphasis put on physical fitness and the celebration of the female body 'as an instrument for the dictates of one's will', suggested by the examples of popular and influential sportswomen, actresses, and music hall performers.[15] I would argue that it is this implied connection between body and mind (i.e. thoughts and intentions) suggested by Tilburg's use of the word 'will', rather than the connection between body and

---

[11] Patricia A. Tilburg, *Colette's Republic: Work, Gender, and Popular Culture in France* (Oxford: Berghahn Books, 2010), p. 159.
[12] Tilburg, *Colette's Republic*, p. 137.
[13] Tilburg, *Colette's Republic*, p. 51.
[14] Fouillée, 'La Psychologie des sexes', p. 425.
[15] Tilburg, *Colette's Republic*, p. 155.

'soul' (i.e. emotions and moral or personal qualities), that represents a significant change in women's perception of their physical selves during the Belle Epoque.[16]

In the same period, radical feminists such as Nelly Roussel and Madeleine Pelletier, who supported neo-Malthusianism and fought for the right to contraception and abortion, legitimized female desire and strongly defended the idea that women needed to take control over their own bodies as a means to emancipation. No matter how controversial and unpopular their positions were, these women were nonetheless publicly declaring that 'the woman desires as well as being desired' and that 'woman alone is mistress of her body, no matter what'.[17]

In this chapter I propose to explore how Belle Epoque fictional representations of female friendship intersect with the multiple discourses on the female body existing at this time, variously confirming, subverting, or adding something new to them. Looking at the topic of female friendship through the lens of the body is interesting for various reasons. First of all, the very fact that women are represented in their relation to one another entails a complication of the usual dichotomies (e.g. sexual versus maternal) which are a product of the male gaze, as it was constructed in the period under analysis. According to Peter Brooks, among others, 'vision is typically a male prerogative, and its object of fascination [is] the woman's body, in a cultural model so persuasive that many women novelists don't reverse its vectors'.[18] However, when two female characters interact, they appropriate the act of seeing and become subjects, and/or they become objects of *female* perception. Secondly, the body offers an interesting perspective from which to reflect on the authenticity of female homosociality. As argued in the introduction of this thesis, the question of whether it was even possible for women to establish meaningful and sincere relationships with one another was a recurrent topic of discussion in French (and European) literature and philosophy in the nineteenth century and beyond.[19] Belle Epoque novelistic representations of physical interactions between female friends often address the question of authenticity, either by positing a continuity between body and mind which reinforces the idea of women

[16]The terms 'body', 'mind', and 'soul' will be employed hereafter with the connotations indicated in this paragraph. In particular, the term 'soul' should not be understood, in this thesis, in connection with its traditional religious meaning.

[17]See 'Nelly Roussel on birth control and "The Freedom of Motherhood"', in *Feminism of the Belle Epoque: A Historical and Literary Anthology*, ed. by Jennifer Waelti-Walters and Steven C. Hause (Lincoln; London: University of Nebraska Press, 1994), pp. 241–51 (p. 248), and in the same volume 'Madeleine Pelletier on the right to abortion', pp. 252–62 (p. 254).

[18]Peter Brooks, *Body Work: Objects of Desire in Modern Narrative* (Cambridge, Mass.; London: Harvard University Press, 1993), p. 88. A major reference for the notion of men as 'gaze bearers' and women as 'images' to be looked at is Laura Mulvey, 'Visual Pleasure and Narrative Cinema', in *Film Theory and Criticism: Introductory Readings*, ed. by Leo Braudy and Marshall Cohen (New York: Oxford University Press, 1999), pp. 833-44.

[19]See pp. 6–11 in this thesis.

being able to communicate and foster strong connections with one another through their bodies, or by reducing female physical intimacy, and by extension female friendship, to a response to masculinity or a mere manifestation of traditional femininity.

These questions will be investigated through the analysis of two *romans de mœurs* written by Daniel Lesueur: *Justice de femme* (1893) and *L□vres closes* (1898), which both deal with the topic of female adultery.[20] Parallels with these two novels will be drawn with another female-authored fictional work, Marie-Louise Compain's *L'Un vers l'autre* (1903), and with Henry Rabusson's *L'Amie* (1886).[21]

The first novel, *Justice de femme*, focuses in particular on the difference between male and female infidelity and on the conflict between individual happiness and social duty, suggesting that a woman's search for fulfilment outside the institution of marriage is doomed to failure.[22] The narrative centres on Simone Mervil, a respectable young woman married for love with a successful composer, Roger, who is several years her senior. When Simone accidentally finds out about Roger's unfaithfulness, a sense of revenge, boredom, and curiosity leads her to start a liaison with her husband's friend and colleague Jean d'Espayrac, a dashing young poet. However, Simone soon regrets her decision and, in order to break things off with Jean, she leaves Paris for the south of France, where she joins her dearest friend, the beautiful and daring Gisèle. Jean's attempts at reconquering her affections are unsuccessful, and while Simone readily resumes her marriage and gives birth to a second child, Jean becomes Gisèle's lover. Later on, during an episode in which Simone protects Gisèle's honour and life at the cost of her own reputation, Jean's (unrequited) feelings for his past mistress are rekindled and he finally decides to leave Gisèle, who subsequently commits suicide. The novel takes another tragic turn when Simone realizes that her second child is in fact Jean's son. The boy dies abruptly during his stay at boarding school, where he has been sent at Simone's initiative, in an attempt to hide the truth of his paternity from Roger. Shattered by guilt and unable to overcome this loss, Simone falls ill and eventually dies. Her last words are addressed to her daughter Paulette, whom she warns against making the same mistakes.

L□vres closes, whose title draws on the lexical field of the body, was the first novel to appear in serialized form in the magazine *La Fronde*, upon its launch in 1897. As noted by

---

[20]Daniel Lesueur, *Justice de femme* (Paris: A. Lemerre, 1893), and □ *□vres closes* (Paris: A. Lemerre, 1898). These novels have been classified as *romans de mœurs* by Diana Holmes in 'Écrire les hommes: la masculinité dans les romans de Daniel Lesueur', in *Écrire les hommes*, ed. by Grenaudier-Klijn et al., pp. 93–111 (p. 97). Further references to these novels are indicated by the abbreviations *Justice* and □ *□res*.

[21] Marie-Louise Compain, *L'Un vers l'autre* (Paris: P.-V. Stock, 1903); Henry Rabusson, *L'Amie* (Paris: Calmann-Lévy, 1886). Further references to these novels are indicated by the abbreviations *UVA* and *Amie*.

[22]For further discussion of Lesueur's novelistic portrayal of marriage and adultery, see Holmes, 'Écrire les hommes', in *Écrire les hommes*, ed. by Grenaudier-Klijn et al.

its contemporary critics, the novel tackles the question of whether an adulterous wife can remain an honourable and respectable woman regardless of social prejudices.[23] In spite of its focus on heterosexual relations, the plot pays particular attention to the relationship between the heroine Marcienne de Sélys and her sister-in-law Charlotte after the latter's discovery of Marcienne's infidelity toward Charlotte's brother, Édouard. When the keeping of Marcienne's secret causes Charlotte to fall out with Édouard and fall ill, Marcienne, her claims to happiness and freedom notwithstanding, ends the affair with Philippe and, to Charlotte's delight, goes back to her husband.

In the first section of this chapter, I will discuss in which ways the portrayal of the female friends' physical appearance intermingles with Belle Epoque ideals of womanhood. The second section will consider novelistic representations of female friendship in which physical intimacy between women tends to be depicted as an artificial performance, a reaction to masculinity, or a reassertion of femininity. The last two sections will focus on representations of female friendship in which the characters, by knitting together mind, soul, and body, are able to establish more profound and truthful connections, experiencing a considerable degree of agency within their relationships by means of their body.

Female Friends, Physical Appearance, and the Ideals of Womanhood

The representation of female homosociality implies by definition the presence of at least two women in the text, and one of the interesting aspects of the novels considered in this chapter is that rather than reducing all women to a single ideal, they portray different female identities. In Belle Epoque novels, female couples, whether they are friends or rivals, are often depicted as antithetical, and called upon to embody polarized versions of womanhood, the secondary female character usually functioning as the heroine's opposite. In fact, the tendency is to associate women by complementarity or contrast rather than similarity; each female character dramatizes a distinctive, generally conventional kind of femininity. When the contrast is depicted as sharp and unequivocal, these representations seem to serve the patriarchal ideology, in the sense that women are presented with limited options and can identify either with one end of the female spectrum or with the other, in a way that sustains the maternal/sexual dichotomy.

---

[23]See the anonymous book review 'Revue Littéraire: *Les* □ *vres closes*, par Daniel Lesueur', *La Justice*, 9 April 1898, p. 2.

In fiction, this opposition between female characters is conveyed from the outset by their physical appearance and it is often indicated by hair colour, a sign of female desire that, traditionally, associates women with different value systems. In Western culture, this distinction relates to the perceived duplicity of the female body, 'a source of pleasure and nurturance, but also of destruction and evil', a perception that, as already noted, has led to the split within femininity between the maternal and the sexual, the pure and the impure, the good and the evil, the soul and the body.[24] The opposition between the fair and the dark-haired heroine, in particular, recalls the archetypal contrast between Mary and Eve, the mother and the temptress, the virgin and the whore. The coding of hair colour was a well-established trend in nineteenth-century fiction. In *Devoted Sisters* (2003), a compelling study of the representation of sisters in nineteenth-century Anglophone literature, Sarah Annes Brown reflects on the way in which authors create disparities between the sisters' physical and moral identities, and argues that colouring 'always has a signifying role, and is a key factor in determining a sister's character'.[25] A literary trope whose origins date back to Greek drama, the pairing of dark and light heroines, as Brown suggests, signals the Biblical contrast between beauty or sexual attractiveness and fertility, passion and restraint, but also, in Freudian terms, the tension between Eros and Thanatos. Brown further explains that while nineteenth-century novels usually invite both hero and reader to choose between sisters, they also create the conditions for a blurring of fixed categories and stereotypical female roles, deconstructing female characters in order to question and destabilize fictional typologies. This is notably the case for Madame de Staël's novel *Corinne* (1807), 'a potent literary influence during the whole of the nineteenth century', in which 'each sister [Corinne and Lucile] can perhaps better be interpreted as a series of negotiations around the polarities of womanhood rather than a fixed and stable site of meaning.'[26] In a book-length study focusing on the representation of hair in Victorian culture and literature, Galia Ofek similarly discusses the 'dichotomized division of women into fair and safe as opposed to dark and dangerous', for example in authors such as Charles Dickens and George Eliot. While golden hair is usually associated with 'truth, loyalty, domesticity, and purity, [...] sexual passivity, lack of ambition and unworldliness', dark hair is a 'marker of dangerous femininity'.[27] As indicated by Anne-Marie Thiesse, stereotypes concerning the heroine's hair

---

[24] Susan Rubin Suleiman, 'Editor's Introduction', in *The Female Body in Western Culture: Semiotic Perspectives*, ed. by Susan Rubin Suleiman (= *Poetics Today*, 6.1/2 (1985)), pp. 5-8 (p. 5).

[25] Sarah Annes Brown, *Devoted Sisters: Representations of the Sister Relationship in Nineteenth-Century British and American Literature* (Aldershot; Burlington: Ashgate, 2003), p. 7.

[26] See Brown, *Devoted Sisters*, pp. 14, 15.

[27] Ofek also points out that 'both models of femininity exist only so long as they can be contrasted in order to reaffirm each other', and in the chapter 'Sensational Hair', she examines how authors of sensational fiction from the 1860s onward challenge and subvert the social and literary conventions related to hair. See Galia

colour constantly reappear in Belle Epoque popular literature, where the blonde heroine is presented as the innocent victim, the red-haired heroine as the *femme fatale*, and the brunette as the one situated between the other two, the angel and the demon.[28]

In her texts, Daniel Lesueur repeatedly places a blonde heroine in contrast with a brunette, often perpetuating the opposition between docile, pure, virtuous heroine on the one hand, and subversive, sensual, wicked female figure on the other.[29] To what extent do the representations of female friends in *Justice de femme* and *Lèvres closes* reflect this tendency? In *Lèvres closes*, Marcienne, who is in her late thirties, is described by the narrator as a charming woman with brown hair, green eyes, and a supple body which has preserved the attractiveness of its youth:

> A trente-huit ans, elle était moins éclatante peut-être, mais plus séduisante qu'à vingt-huit, d'un charme plus vivant, plus tentateur, plus subtil, accru de tout ce que les sensations et la pensée, goûtées avec réflexion et ardeur, peuvent ajouter de vertigineux aux prunelles et aux lèvres d'une femme.
>
> Elle gardait beaucoup de jeunesse dans la démarche et dans la taille [...] Son front, ses tempes restaient purs de toute ride sous le retroussis audacieux des cheveux châtains. Et Mme de Sélys, quand elle daignait rire, gardait le rire de ses vingt ans, d'une sonorité de cristal dans la blancheur lumineuse des dents étincelantes. (*Lèvres*, 7–9)

Her description is punctuated by adjectives such as 'séduisante', 'tentateur', 'audacieux', which suggest a continuity with the image of the passionate and uncontrolled dark heroine. On the other hand, Charlotte, almost ten years younger than Marcienne, is presented as an appealing and delicate young woman, with a pale complexion, light-blue eyes, and blonde hair:

> Charlotte Fromentel, à vingt-neuf ans, conservait, dans sa silhouette vive et gracile, ses gestes menus, son teint de lait où seraient tombés des pétales de rose, dans l'étonnement de ses purs yeux clairs sous le désordre joli de ses frisons d'or pale, un délicieux air d'enfance, cette fraîcheur exquise d'âme et de chair qui fait dire de certains petits êtres qu'ils sont « à croquer ». (*Lèvres*, 19)

Ofek, *Representations of Hair in Victorian Literature and Culture* (Farnham: Ashgate, 2009), pp. 186, 199, 116, and 183–210. See also the discussion of the motif of fair, younger heroines versus dark, older women in fairy tales in Sandra Gilbert and Susan Gubar, *The Madwoman in the Attic: The Woman Writer and the Nineteenth-Century Literary Imagination* (New Haven; London: Yale University Press, 2000 [1979]).

[28]Anne-Marie Thiesse, *Le Roman du quotidien: lecteurs et lectures à la Belle Epoque* (Paris: Editions du Seuil, 2000 [1984]), pp. 150–51.

[29]See, for example, Gilberte and Sabine in *Haine d'amour* (Paris: A. Lemerre, 1894) or Georgette and Clary in *Comédienne*, 20th edn (Paris: A. Lemerre, 1898).

Charlotte's physical characterization is imbued with expressions evoking chastity and innocence, and throughout the text she is often compared to a fragile and endearing doll, animal, or child.

Similarly, in *Justice de femme,* Simone Mervil, at the beginning of the novel a young woman in her twenties, is described as one of those 'tendres âmes à peine vêtues de chair' who might have inspired the early painters portraying the Madonna (*Justice*, 14). Of the two friends, she is the ethereal beauty exuding purity and nobility, even though she is also a vain Parisian concerned with her looks and outfits, the use of the two labels, 'madone' and 'Parisienne', complicating her characterization from the outset (*Justice*, 14). By contrast, Gisèle Chambertier is described as a tall and slim brunette who artificially colours her hair with copper tones, this detail being repeated several times in the novel, as if to associate her character with inauthentic or improper femininity (*Justice*, 27, 172, 253). Her description indicates that she is a beautiful, sensual, and voluptuous woman full of life, with 'des yeux sombres de langueur', 'de vertige', and 'sous les ongles roses, comme dans la pourpre des lèvres, un sang vigoureux et coloré'.[30] When Simone and Gisèle's physical appearances are placed under the scrutiny of the male characters' gazes, they clearly reflect the traditional dichotomy of the woman-mother versus woman-lover. For example, at the beginning of the novel, Jean is attracted to Simone and Gisèle in very different ways, perceiving the former as 'une sœur d'âme' and the latter, one might say, as *une sœur de la chair* (*Justice*, 31). Simone, this 'fine blonde créée pour les bonheurs intimes', interestingly reminds him of 'ses premiers rêves purs, les caresses de sa mère', and closely resembles 'l'idéal de droiture, de simplicité, de chasteté féminines, qui avaient fait battre les cœurs de ses aïeux', whereas '[p]rès de Gisèle, ses sens lui parlaient un langage clair' (*Justice*, 32). Roger, Simone's husband, perceives the two female characters in the same reductive, polarized way, never suspecting his virtuous wife of infidelity and generally disapproving of her friendship with Gisèle, 'cette amie un peu compromettante' (*Justice*, 60). Like Jean, M. Chambertier considers Simone as '[une] madone' and believes that she could exert a good

---

[30]Lesueur, *Justice*, p. 27. Moreover, I would like to call attention to Gisèle's 'chair blanche' and to her 'teint du visage avec sa délicatesse de camélia'. As observed by Hermeline Pernaud, paleness of skin is one of the main features of female beauty in Belle Epoque France and it is often associated with death: 'La ressemblance avec un être mort devient un critère de beauté à part entière [...] [C]ette passion pour les corps cadavériques va surtout être mise en avant à la Belle époque, par une ode à la beauté des corps blancs.' In this case, it is possible to draw a parallel between Gisèle's paleness and her tragic destiny. Indeed, Gisèle will commit suicide by asphyxiation in a bedroom full of white lilies, these flowers recalling her fair complexion reminiscent of camellia. See Hermeline Pernaud, 'La Belle Époque au Bois Dormant', in *La Belle Époque des femmes?*, ed. by Le Guennec and Zmelty, pp. 47–62 (p. 53).

influence on the wild and capricious Gisèle (*Justice*, 39, 263).[31] When Gisèle's body becomes the object of the female gaze, the perception of this character as a sensuous creature is reinforced, as confirmed by the scene in which Simone watches Gisèle eating some fresh sea urchins in the little square of the town of Giens:

> Elle se fit ouvrir plusieurs coquilles, et elle resta debout, rieuse, d'une si fine élégance dans ce décor de vie pauvre et de sauvage nature, humant la pulpe rouge de ces bêtes qui ont un goût de fleur et de marée. Simone, malgré sa propre détresse d'âme, subit le charme de cette femme et de ce lieu. Plus tard — plus tard!... — en pensant à Gisèle, c'est ainsi que souvent elle devait la revoir: mangeant des oursins dans le pan d'ombre d'une maison simple, aux lignes sèches découpées sur le bleu violent d'un ciel méridional, avec un arôme de mer dans l'air tranquille, et, tout autour, une sensation de chaleur et d'espace. (*Justice*, 137–38)

This representation of Gisèle appeals to different senses, namely sight ('revoir'), smell ('humant', 'arôme de mer'), and taste ('goût de fleur et de marée'). Her image is associated with '[la] sauvage nature', with 'une sensation de chaleur et d'espace', and her 'charme' exerts its power on men and women alike. Of the two friends, Gisèle is undoubtedly the one embodying dangerous femininity.[32]

The contrast between the characters is further accentuated by the differences inscribed in their own perception and use of the body. Marcienne's relation with her body is undeniably more complex than Charlotte's and emerges at different levels. On the one hand, Marcienne is concerned about ageing. Even though her charm has evolved and increased with maturity, she fears the imminent loss of her physical beauty which, at the same time, will probably entail the loss of her lover. At a certain point, she asserts that: 'La vie, c'est d'être jeune, d'être beau et d'aimer' (*L□vres*, 15). In this sense, she seems to perceive her ageing body as an enemy. On the other hand, she conceives of her body as a means to experience freedom and pleasure. In particular, she delights in the practice of different sports, more or less suitable for a lady, such as horse-riding, ice-skating, and cycling; she craves

---

[31] Nineteenth-century conduct books and essays often insist on emulation as a key component of female friendship. The idea that Simone could exert a good influence on Gisèle and that, vice-versa, Gisèle could be a bad influence for Simone, a fear expressed by both Roger and Jean (*Justice*, 60, 123), reflects the belief that female friends should serve as models of good behaviour for one another and that girls or women should be kept away from dangerous influences.

[32] Gisèle's identification with the sensual woman and her unrestrained sexuality are further suggested by the fact that she does not wear a corset, a choice that arouses the disapproval of other women. See Lesueur, *Justice*, p. 28. Beauvoir notes that, historically, '[l]es coutumes, les modes se sont souvent appliquées à couper le corps féminin de sa transcendance' and the female body '[a été] paralysé par de vêtements incommodes et par les rites de la bienséance'. See *Deuxi□ □e Sexe I*, pp. 266, 267.

physical activity, movement, and fresh air, and she is compared to 'une hirondelle sauvage', a symbol of grace, independence, and *joie de vivre* (*Lèvres,* 8). More importantly, having achieved a perfect sexual *entente* with her lover, Marcienne now considers her body as a source of sensual pleasure. By contrast, Charlotte completely ignores the logic of erotic desire. Even in marriage, she has conserved a sort of chastity that makes her speak with shame and disapproval of anything relating to bodily pleasure, and she seems to value her body only in terms of motherhood. The contrast between different perceptions and uses of the body may appear less sharp in the case of Simone and Gisèle, considering that Simone herself gets briefly involved in a love affair with Jean, giving in to passion outside marriage. However, in Simone's case the experience of sensual love is represented as a moment of weakness that she goes on to regret bitterly, and her attitude seems to have little in common with the explicit desire for love and sensual fulfilment unrelentingly expressed by Gisèle.

Moreover, the relation of the four characters to motherhood is reflected by their bodies and creates a parallel between Simone and Charlotte versus Gisèle and Marcienne. In fact, both Simone and Charlotte consider motherhood as a blessing, even though for Simone the birth of her second child will ultimately turn into a punishment. Both of their bodies can be said to be primarily maternal, the experience of motherhood being central to their lives. On the contrary, Gisèle's thin body, 'presque trop maigre', observes the narrator, and her 'minces hanches', as well as Marcienne's reckless and rebellious use of the body evidenced by the practice of unwomanly sports, suggest their unsuitability for maternity, one of the core values promoted by the Third Republic (*Justice*, 27, 28). By contrast with Charlotte and Simone's maternal bodies, Marcienne and Gisèle's bodies appear free and pleasure-seeking, even though the possibility of expressing their desires and experiencing autonomy outside heterosexual marriage ultimately remains very limited. In spite of these constraints, it would appear that these bodies are not trapped in immanence or subjected to the needs of the species,[33] but rather represent the means through which Marcienne and Gisèle assert their subjectivities and exert their wills.

In both *Justice de femme* and *Lèvres closes*, the representation of the female body contributes to the definition of the characters' personalities and their roles in society by creating an opposition between them. The blonde heroine (Simone/Charlotte) and the brunette (Gisèle/Marcienne) are invested with some of the traditional values associated with their hair colour. They symbolize different relations to Belle Epoque moral propriety and, in this sense, Lesueur seems to encourage a traditional reading of the female body by

[33]See our earlier reference to Beauvoir's observations on the female body, as expressed in *Le Deuxième Sexe*, discussed at p. 41 in this thesis.

associating it with conflicting and simplistic versions of femininity (conventional/disruptive, mother/lover). However, the author also challenges the virtuous/fallen woman dichotomy by adding supplementary layers of signification to these coded types, thus making the heroine's body less legible and the character less predictable, while simultaneously nuancing the contrast between female friends. Although Simone adheres to the bourgeois model of the devout wife and self-sacrificing mother, she is far from being represented as unequivocally pure, innocent, and blameless, her image being quickly and irrevocably tarnished by her adultery. After that, no matter how hard she tries to clean the stain away and fit once again into the role of virtuous and unquestioning woman, she has to pay the price for having overstepped the boundaries of proper behaviour, her destiny exemplifying the harshness and injustice of the double moral standard.[34] The complication of female identities promoted by Lesueur in *Justice de femme* is clearly indicated in a passage where the narrator talks of a 'dédoublement':

> La Simone perverse de Meudon s'endormait, disparaissait, reculait à l'infini par une sorte de dédoublement. Et la Simone paisible et honnête se retrouvait elle-même, se reprenait si fortement qu'elle arrivait à douter de l'existence de l'autre. (*Justice*, 116)

The splitting of the subject, a key theme of modernist fiction, becomes, in this passage, a means of implicitly challenging traditional binary inscriptions of femininity.[35] Similarly to Simone, the darker-haired Marcienne could not be mistaken for or solely reduced to the caricature of the sensual woman indulging in emotional and physical excess. Although, in opposition to Charlotte, her marital unfaithfulness and indeed disrespect for the institution of marriage imply that she is acting against the bourgeois moral codes of the Belle Epoque,

---

[34]Simone's adultery and its tragic consequences are contrasted with her husband's Roger own infidelity. At the end of the novel, after a ten-year period, Roger has completely forgotten about his past affair with the talentless singer Netty Davidson, a liaison which, among other factors, was at the origin of Simone's decision to become Jean's mistress. While his adultery has been inconsequential, Simone, as previously mentioned, is devastated by the realization of her son's real paternity and his subsequent death. The conclusion to which Simone comes by the end of the novel, is that '[l]a nature et la société ont créé trop d'abîmes entre l'homme et la femme; trop divers sont leurs droits, leurs devoirs, leurs responsabilités, pour que leurs actes puissent être pesés à la même balance. Égales dans la douleur qu'elles infligent, leurs infidélités sont radicalement inégales au point de vue des conséquences'. See Lesueur, *Justice*, p. 303. According to Holmes, the novel can also be read as a reflection on the necessity of female sacrifice to the good functioning of society in Belle Epoque France, and this element contributes to the realism of the text. See Holmes, 'Écrire les hommes', in *Écrire les hommes*, ed. by Grenaudier-Klijn et al., p. 108, and 'Novels of Adultery: Paul Bourget, Daniel Lesueur and what Women read in the 1880s and 1890s', in *Currencies: Fiscal Fortunes and Cultural Capital in Nineteenth-Century France*, ed. by Sarah Capitanio, Lisa Downing, Paul Rowe, Nicholas White (Oxford: Peter Lang, 2005), pp. 15–30 (p. 26).

[35]In modernist fiction, the 'self needs to be understood in relation to a fragmented subjectivity which is composed of a kaleidoscope of sense impressions and memories; each complements the other'. See Michael H. Whitworth, 'Introduction', in *Modernism*, ed. by Michael H. Whitworth (Malden, Mass.; Oxford: Blackwell, 2007), pp. 3–60 (p. 26).

her respectability, superiority, and rare sense of compassion are highlighted more than once in the text and are meant to represent a source of admiration and respect for the reader. The non-judgemental voice of the omniscient narrator treats this character with a certain indulgence, and the complexity of Marcienne's personality prevents any attempt to classify her easily and categorically. For example, while Marcienne and Charlotte are arguing after the latter's discovery of her sister-in-law's infidelity, the narrator marvels at how Marcienne, confronted with Charlotte's severity and lack of sympathy, manages to maintain her dignity and composure:

> Quel secret de dignité était en cette hautaine créature [Marcienne]? Comment, dans un si tragique défilé, se maintenait-elle sur les sommets, d'une démarche noble et sûre, tandis qu'elle aurait dû se débattre d'horreur au fond du précipice? (*Lèvres*, 50)

Although Marcienne should be wallowing in shame and torment, the text ascribes to her '[un] secret de dignité', dignity being one of the attributes of respectable womanhood, and positively describes her 'démarche' as being 'noble' and 'sûre'. Indeed, contemporary critics of the novel remarked that Lesueur effectively leaves open the question of whether a woman could be, at the same time, an adulteress and a good wife.[36] More recently, in commenting on the ambiguity of Lesueur's heroines, including Simone and Marcienne, Diana Holmes has noted that 'celle qui incarne la vertu féminine en devient sa négation, ce qui met en doute la validité de ces catégories — femme vertueuse contre femme adultère — apparemment opposées et étanches'.[37] While Gisèle's identity remains clear-cut throughout the novel (at one point she is even defined as '[une] amante qui n'était pas mère', *Justice*, 209), Marcienne's body will be allowed to recover a maternal function through her relationship with Charlotte, an element that further problematizes the traditional maternal/sexual split. At the same time, the childish and non-threatening Charlotte will actively instrumentalize her body and manipulate Marcienne in order to reaffirm the status quo, thus completely subverting the conventional passive/active dichotomy.[38] The very ambiguity surrounding Lesueur's female characters, in both *Justice de femme* and *Lèvres closes*, the splitting of their personalities, the shifts of focalization, and the lack of explicit and unequivocal moral positions, I would argue, constitute part of the appeal of these novels for readers of the time and are gestures toward Lesueur's modernism.

---

[36]See [Anon], 'Revue Littéraire: *Les l[illegible] res closes*'.
[37]Holmes, 'Écrire les hommes', in *Écrire les hommes*, ed. by Grenaudier-Klijn et al., p. 99.
[38]On the conventional reading of the female body and the passive/active dichotomy, see pp. 47–49 in this thesis.

In her characterization of female friends, while exploiting some of the conventional meanings associated with female physical types, Lesueur eventually succeeds in attenuating the contrast between female friends by adding some complexity to her characters, in a way that challenges the traditional interpretation of the female body and the identification of women with standard, diametrically opposed ideals of womanhood, a conception supported by the male characters in the text but undermined by both the narrator and the female characters. If, traditionally, the representation of women has often encased each character in a single model of femininity, as if women could only belong to one end of the female spectrum or the other, Lesueur's novels, through the employment of different focalizers and conflicting perspectives, suggest that womanhood cannot be so easily polarized and women cannot be confined to simplistic, antithetical identities.

This section has considered the female body in terms of physical appearance and symbolic value. The following sections will explore in more detail how women's bodies actively interact in novelistic representations of female friendship.

Physical Intimacy and the Inauthenticity of Female Friendship?

The novels discussed in this chapter have in common the fact that interactions between female friends are often characterized by physical closeness and intimacy. Lesueur's *Justice de femme* constitutes a good example of the sensual playfulness and attraction occasionally involved in Belle Epoque fictional representations of female friendship. But how should we interpret the gestures of affection exchanged by Simone and Gisèle, their occasional need for privacy, the fascination they exert on each other, and the sensuality characterizing some of their interactions? As modern readers, we may be tempted to consider these elements as expressions of a latent homosexual desire or as proof of the fluidity existing between female homosociality and homosexuality in certain historical and cultural contexts.[39] Holmes, for example, has referred to Simone and Gisèle's friendship as being marked by 'an emotional intensity that at times has erotic undertones [...] suggesting an early example of Adrienne Rich's "lesbian continuum"'.[40] Although it is undeniable that Simone and Gisèle's relationship contains an erotic component, and while Holmes' hypothesis might constitute a

[39]See the debate surrounding the notion of nineteenth-century female romantic friendship, as discussed at pp. 11–19 in this thesis.

[40]Diana Holmes, 'Daniel Lesueur and the Feminist Romance', in *A 'Belle Epoque'?*, ed. by Holmes and Tarr, pp. 197–210 (p. 207).

plausible explanation, I would like to explore alternative, possibly less progressive interpretations for the degree of physical closeness characterizing their bond.[41] My analysis takes into account the multiple values and meanings that the narrator and characters attach to Simone and Gisèle's bodily interactions, and suggests that female physical intimacy can also be read as a reaction to masculinity and to heterosexual love, and therefore as a behaviour dependent on men and on the contingencies of the characters' relations with them. Moreover, the repetition of gestures of affection between female characters can be seen as a manifestation of conventional femininity, reinforcing gender roles. In this case, female friendship is largely assimilated to an inauthentic performance played out through the body. Finally, I will argue that in *Justice de femme* the female body is partly represented in a way that supports a negative view of women and their physicality.

The idea that Simone and Gisèle's entire relationship, including their physical intimacy, is mainly constructed as a response to men and heterosexual love is repeatedly suggested throughout the novel. Whenever the two friends meet, their conversation invariably revolves around the topic of romantic love. Whether they are talking about their husbands, their lover, their fears, or their dreams, their words betray a constant preoccupation with romantic passion and sensual fulfilment, their emotional intimacy being based on the sharing of hopes and concerns regarding the possibilities of love. Needless to say, these characters would fail the Bechdel test.[42] In a similar way, when Simone and Gisèle kiss or throw themselves into each other's arms, these gestures arguably constitute a response to the way in which they have been previously treated by men. This idea comes to the fore most forcefully in the episodes relating to Simone and Gisèle's stay in the south of France, which I am now going to examine in detail.

When Simone decides to break up with Jean, she joins Gisèle and her husband at Hyères and, at the beginning of her visit, the two friends feel closer than ever before. Their increased intimacy appears to be dictated by Simone's newly-acquired understanding of love, which makes her more sympathetic to Gisèle:

> La compréhension de toutes les fatalités de l'amour, que Simone venait d'acquérir à ses dépenses, lui ouvrait le cœur plus largement qu'autrefois pour cette Gisèle charmante et folle, [...] malgré tout, restée, sous ses excentriques dehors, plus pure qu'elle-même. (*Justice*, 128)

---

[41]The term 'erotic' is employed in this chapter in the sense indicated by Sharon Marcus in *Between Women*, following Roland Barthes' definition of the concept, as discussed at p. 17 in this thesis.
[42]On the 'Bechdel test', see *Bechdel Test Movie List* <https://bechdeltest.com/> [accessed 31 August 2018].

Simone later finds out that Jean has followed her to the south of France and becomes very unsettled. Gisèle, unaware of the reasons for her friend's distress but upset by her evident suffering, kisses her and holds her in her arms. Simone responds to this affection by laying her head on Gisèle's shoulder and an interesting conversation ensues:

> Gisèle maintenant l'embrassait, l'attirait contre elle, tout impressionnée par ce silence au fond duquel tremblait une douleur.
>
> — Alors, tu ne veux rien me dire? Tu n'as donc pas confiance en moi? Tu ne m'aimes donc pas?
>
> — Ah! Si, mignonne, je t'aime bien, toi, va! murmura Simone, en appuyant sa tête sur l'épaule de son amie.
>
> — Mon Dieu! que tu es jolie! s'écria Gisèle, qui l'écarta pour tâcher de lire dans les yeux clairs aux cils mouillés. Peut-on avoir des idées noires quand on a des yeux comme ça? Dis-donc... ajouta-t-elle tout bas avec un clignement de paupières, il n'est pas à plaindre, celui pour qui tu pleures.
>
> — Je ne pleure pour personne.
>
> — Allons donc! Est-ce qu'à notre âge il y a d'autres peines que les peines de cœur? Ah! si j'étais un homme, je saurais comment m'y prendre pour sécher ces beaux yeux-là. (*Justice*, 141–42)

On this occasion, although Gisèle is ignorant of the origin of Simone's misery, she suspects a man to be the cause of her unhappiness, and she consequently proclaims that were she a man, she would know how to comfort her. On the one hand, Gisèle's words can be read as an expression of homosexual desire.[43] On the other hand, the character might be suggesting that there is a limit to the degree of solace that friends can find in each other's company. Despite her efforts to provide emotional and physical support, only were she a man could Gisèle fully succeed in consoling Simone.

The omniscient narrator subsequently invites the reader to interpret the previous passage, and Gisèle's final comment in particular, as a form of *badinage*, as something playful and not serious ('Leur pensée ne dépassa point le badinage de cette câlinerie', *Justice*, 142). According to the narrator, Simone and Gisèle's need for affection and comfort, which they try to satisfy through physical contact, is determined by the lack of love and understanding that, as women, they experience in their relationships with men, and female physical intimacy is a compensation for this lack:

---

[43]Holmes quotes the final sentence of this excerpt when referring to Simone and Gisèle's relationship as an early example of Rich's 'lesbian continuum'. See Holmes, 'Daniel Lesueur and the Feminist Romance', in *A 'Belle Epoque'?*, ed. by Holmes and Tarr, p. 207.

inconsciemment, l'amour dont elles avaient parlé, dont elles frissonnaient sourdement, dont elles étaient pétries, mettait une suavité sur leurs lèvres, une trouble douceur au fond de leurs yeux. Et la secrète alliance contre l'homme — contre l'homme dont elles avaient souffert, dont elles souffriraient encore puisqu'elles aimeraient — les faisaient serrer plus étroitement l'une contre l'autre. (*Justice*, 142)

In this specific passage female physical closeness is clearly explained as a reaction, a form of allegiance or protection against men and heterosexual love.[44]

Afterwards, Simone confronts Jean and goes back to her husband, whereas Gisèle becomes Jean's new mistress. The description of Simone's ambiguous attitude toward her friend after the discovery of the latter's liaison with Jean supports the idea that the bond existing between these two female characters is largely shaped as a response to the contingencies of their romantic involvements with men. At the end of a tête-à-tête in which Simone unsuccessfully tries to warn Gisèle against the risk of the latter's husband discovering her affair with Jean and against her friend's foolishness in thinking that Jean would ever agree to marry a divorced woman, the text provides some possible explanations for Simone's contradictory reactions to Gisèle's behaviour:

> Ainsi, malgré l'écœurement dont la soulevaient les intrigues de son amie, malgré l'irritation que lui causait la seule idée de voir Gisèle devenir Mme d'Espayrac, Simone continuait à subir vers la personne et vers les amours de cette femme une sorte d'attirance perverse. Curiosité?... Involontaire préoccupation de Jean? Peut-être espérance inavouée de voir une autre trouver à son tour dans la faute les fruits d'amertume qu'elle-même y avait recueillis. Par moments même, il lui semblait que les âpres sentiments avec lesquels, depuis quelques mois, elle songeait à Gisèle, augmentaient sa tendresse pour cette créature de charme et de folie. Parfois, tout à coup, elle était prise du désir de la voir, et elle sautait en voiture, elle pressait son cocher, pour embrasser Gisèle deux minutes plus tôt, pour l'entendre lui chuchoter près de l'oreille quelque extravagante confidence. Et ensuite, elle se sentait troublée d'un vague remords, se demandant si, près de son amie, elle ne venait pas alimenter un reste d'amour pour M. d'Espayrac, ou du moins nourrir l'anxieux intérêt que lui inspiraient encore les sentiments et les actions de cet homme. (*Justice*, 243–44)

[44]In addition to this, it is interesting to note that, if Lesueur's work pluralizes women, thus challenging the singularity of *l'éternel féminin*, the above quotation singularizes men to boot ('l'homme'). This is a striking reversal of the common tendency to treat women as non-individualized, interchangeable objects and men as individual subjects.

From the beginning of the novel, the relationship between Simone and Gisèle is represented as ambiguous and dynamic, constantly shifting from emotional intensity to rivalry. In this passage, both the narrator and the character of Simone put forward different hypotheses in an attempt to rationalize the complex set of emotions, ranging from 'irritation' and 'écœurement' to a sort of 'attirance perverse' and 'tendresse', felt by Simone. The narrator refers to the possibility of Simone feeling a simple curiosity with regard to her extravagant friend and her love life. Her attitude could also betray a form of jealousy and possessiveness toward her ex-lover, Jean. A third hypothesis concerns the prospect of Simone secretly hoping that another woman will overstep the bounds of proper behaviour established by society and pay the harsh emotional price of her misconduct. As for Simone, she is under the impression that lately, in spite of her own bitterness, her affection for Gisèle and the need to see her have become more intense. Troubled by a vague sense of remorse, she wonders whether in reality their friendship only represents the means through which she tries to keep her love for Jean alive, or tries to satisfy her curiosity about him. This passage is representative of what Holmes calls the 'invitation to dialogue' implied by Lesueur's texts, namely the author's tendency to adopt an interrogative and inconclusive narrative stance, which leaves the door open to different interpretative possibilities without offering a definitive answer.[45]

What can reasonably be deduced from the various explanations offered by Simone and the narrator, however, is that Simone's 'attirance perverse' toward Gisèle is closely connected to her attraction to Jean. Her feelings of irritation and tenderness are not only determined by Gisèle herself and her personal qualities, but also, and perhaps primarily, by Gisèle as Jean's mistress. Arguably, Simone's desire to see Gisèle, to hug her, to hold her close, listening to her whispered secrets, could be more revealing of Simone's obsession with Gisèle and Jean as a couple than it is of female erotic agency. The various hypotheses formulated in this excerpt, reinforced by Simone's final, resting inference, largely deny the possibility of Simone being independently and genuinely concerned with or attracted to Gisèle and posit their relationship within a heterosexual framework in which their intimacy, either emotional or physical, can be understood as a reaction to men, as an attempt to retreat from them and, ultimately, to maintain a connection with them. This kind of intimacy risks having a depoliticizing and disempowering effect on female friendship to the extent that, to use an expression proposed by Pat O'Connor, it represents a sort of 'palliative coping', a

---

[45]It should be noted that Holmes refers more generally to 'unresolved contradictions at various levels', noting in particular the contradiction between the novels' conservative closures and the sympathetic treatment of the heroines promoted by the use of internal focalization and free indirect speech, the *dénouement* remaining open to different interpretations. See Holmes, 'Novels of Adultery', in *Currencies,* ed. by Capitanio et al., p. 26.

temporary and limited form of consolation which distracts women and prevents them from actively engaging in the struggle to improve their situation.[46]

Moreover, it is possible to argue that Simone's interest in Gisèle as Jean's mistress reflects a dynamic of fascination with and revulsion at the kind of femininity embodied by her friend and the distinctive way she positions herself within the Belle Epoque moral economy. In *Justice de femme* Lesueur puts two different female characters in a nearly identical situation and shows the effects of their choices. The difference between Simone and Gisèle's attitude is indicated early in the novel by Gisèle herself, in a long passage that is worth quoting at length:

> Moi, je cultive mon MOI (pour employer une expression dont les hommes n'auront pas seuls le privilège). Toi, tu cultives un tas de vieux préjugés; tu cultives des ombres; l'opinion d'autrui, la morale de la portière, le code conjugal tel que ces messieurs l'ont fait à notre usage et à leur plus grand profit. Tu acceptes des devoirs que tu ne discutes même pas. Penser t'effarouche, vivre te fait peur. Tu n'oses t'interroger; tu te défies de ce que ton cœur, de ce que ta raison, de ce que tes sens te répondent. Ton innocente petite personne te fait l'effet d'un monstre qu'il faut sans cesse tenir en bride... Moi, que je sois bonne ou méchante, peu m'importe! Ce qui m'occupe, c'est de satisfaire ma méchanceté ou ma bonté. Je m'étudie pour savoir au juste ce que je veux, et, quand je le sais, je le fais. Qu'est-ce que les autres peuvent m'apprendre là-dessus? (*Justice*, 29–30)

According to Holmes, Gisèle belongs to that group of secondary female characters that, in Lesueur's novels, claim 'the right to uncompromising self-fulfilment, scorning the attempts to reconcile duty and desire, the wish to combine concern for the other with concern for the self, that characterise romance heroines', and 'represent the danger of excess, of a lack of emotional control, of an incautious flouting of social proprieties'.[47] Although both Simone and Gisèle commit adultery and are ultimately punished by death (Gisèle takes her own life while Simone does not survive the loss of her son), Gisèle's unapologetic pursuit of her desires and her relentless, reckless defiance of the Belle Epoque system of values sets her apart from Simone. If in a way Gisèle's experience of adultery mirrors Simone's, her attitude toward infidelity and her conduct with Jean are different. Gisèle's self-confidence and her ability to defy social prejudices, which she manifests in her relationship with Jean, are at the origin of Simone's puzzlement and attraction to her friend when, at the end of the

[46]Pat O'Connor, *Friendships between Women: A Critical Review* (New York: The Guilford Press, 1992) p. 30, cited by Karen Hollinger, *In the Company of Women: Contemporary Female Friendship Films* (Minneapolis; London: University of Minnesota Press, 1998), p. 24.
[47]Holmes, 'Lesueur and the Feminist Romance', in *A 'Belle Epoque'?*, ed. by Holmes and Tarr, pp. 206–207.

aforementioned tête-à-tête, the narrator and she explore the reasons for her ambiguous reactions to Gisèle. In other words, Simone's feelings of attraction/repulsion with regard to Gisèle, as Jean's mistress, dramatize her feelings of attraction/repulsion with regard to a different kind of womanhood and the possibilities it entails, especially in the sphere of romantic love, and not only a fascination with her friend's body or personal qualities. This explanation reinforces, at least to some extent, the complicity between female friendship, physical intimacy, and heterosexual love established by the text.

However, the notion of triangular desire, as conceptualized first by René Girard and later on by Eve Kosofsky Sedgwick, allows us to consider a different possibility. According to both Sedgwick and Girard, in structures of triangular desire the bond established between desiring subjects is stronger and more significant than the bond that each subject might create with the desired object, the latter functioning as a conduit for their desire for each other.[48] If this were understood to be the case for Simone, Jean, and Gisèle, then it would be possible to talk of a different connection between these fictional female characters and to interpret their physical intimacy as a manifestation of homosexual desire. What should be noted is that the text does not erase all ambiguity around Simone and Gisèle's relationship and their physical interactions. On the contrary, it encourages the reader to consider different interpretations. Those discussed in this section (i.e. physical intimacy between female friends as a reaction to men and heterosexual love, and fascination with another woman as the embodiment of a different type of womanhood), although perhaps less progressive than interpretations that privilege the theme of female homosexuality, are suggested repeatedly throughout the text and should at least be added to the list of interpretive possibilities.

As a response to masculinity, female physical intimacy in the work of Lesueur appears to be largely subordinated to the heterosexual plot and, in this sense, it is difficult to read it as a possible sign of strong and spontaneous female *entente*. A further way of interpreting the physicality involved in these examples is to consider to what extent this aspect of women's interactions can be revealing of the constructedness of Belle Epoque femininity. Belle Epoque novels often suggest that physical manifestations of affection between women, when they do not break the rules of good behaviour, are considered standard practice and can be understood as expressions of essential femininity. In this regard, it might be useful to evoke Judith Butler's notion of 'gender performativity':

---

[48] See René Girard, *Mensonge romantique et vérité romanesque* (Paris: Grasset, 1961), and Sedgwick, *Between Men*. The notion of triangular desire will be further discussed in Chapter Two, pp. 128–29, and Chapter Four, pp. 200–201.

> [G]ender is in no way a stable identity of locus of agency from which various acts proceed; rather, it is an identity tenuously constituted in time — an identity instituted through a *stylized repetition of acts*. Further, gender is instituted through the stylization of the body and, hence, must be understood as the mundane way in which bodily gestures, movements, and enactments of various kind constitute the illusion of an abiding gendered self.[49]

According to Butler, gender is a socially constructed identity created through the reiteration of bodily acts.[50] I propose to consider the repetition of affectionate gestures among fictional female friends, in *Justice de femme* and in some other novels of this period, as part of those enactments reinforcing traditional gender roles and promoting conventional ideas about women.

Nineteenth-century French society largely endorsed affectionate modes of interaction between women.[51] These behaviours were partly explained as the result of female education and could be understood as expressions of mainstream femininity. Indeed, whether a young girl was educated at home, in a convent, or in a public school, her socialization occurred in an almost exclusively female context where, by means of the interactions with other girls and women, she was taught to conform to a traditional model of femininity, learning to perform the various tasks that nature and society had assigned her. Women were perceived as sensitive and emotional, and were encouraged to be caring, tender, affectionate, and loving. At the same time, they were often thought to be frivolous, flirtatious, and coquettish.

In some Belle Epoque novels, female friendship allows the female characters to display all these supposedly feminine qualities through their bodies. On the one hand, the models of female friendship described in these novels recreate the kind of physical tenderness that apparently existed between mothers and daughters in this period.[52] Following this model, the female body interacts with other women in a way that contributes

---

[49]Judith Butler, 'Performative Acts and Gender Constitution: An Essay in Phenomenology and Feminist Theory', in *Writing on the Body: Female Embodiment and Feminist Theory*, ed. by Katie Conboy, Nadia Medina, Sarah Stanbury (New York: Columbia University Press, 1997), pp. 401–17 (p. 402). Italics in the original.

[50]In *Bodies that Matter*, p. xxviii, Butler defines 'performativity' as the 'power of discourse to produce effects through reiteration' and proposes that we see sex as the materialization of discourses through the body.

[51]According to Vincent-Buffault, in nineteenth-century France '[l]a liberté de ton dans l'épanchement, dans l'expression des émotions et de la sensualité, dans les gestes de l'effusion était totalement admise entre jeunes femmes'. See Vincent-Buffault, *Exercice de l'amitié*, p. 222.

[52]According to historians, in the nineteenth century the mother-daughter relationship, at least in the case of bourgeois women, had attained unprecedented levels of intimacy. See Yvonne Knibiehler, 'Bodies and Hearts', in *A History of Women in the West, 4, Emerging feminism from Revolution to World War*, ed. by Georges Duby and Michelle Perrot (Cambridge, Mass: The Belknap Press of Harvard University Press, 1993), pp. 325–68 (p. 355).

to defining the character as unmistakeably feminine, which is to say maternal, warm, and demonstrative. On the other hand, fictional female friends are often represented as mimicking heterosexual love, as if women were incapable of establishing genuine and authentic connections through their bodies. In support of this interpretation, the authors of nineteenth-century conduct manuals for girls sometimes denounce physical displays of affection between friends as affectations revealing the coquettish nature of women rather than as expressions of sincere friendship. For example, in an early nineteenth-century treatise on female friendship, Mme de Maussion writes:

> Anacharsis raconte que l'Amitié voyant un jour deux femmes qui s'embrassaient étroitement auprès de son autel, leur dit, que le goût des plaisirs les unissait en apparence, mais que leurs cœurs déchirés par la jalousie, le seraient bientôt par la haine. N'ayant pas, comme la déesse, le don de pénétrer au fond des cœurs, je me garderai de rien dire d'aussi sévère aux jeunes personnes, qui se prodiguent devant le monde les témoignages d'une trop vive affection; je me contenterai de leur représenter que ces caresses, ces élans affectés, ressemblent quelquefois aux amorces qu'emploie la coquetterie; telle n'est pas l'expression de cette pure union des cœurs, de cette belle et sage amitié.[53]

In this passage, physical intimacy between female friends is not read as an expression of true affection or desire but rather as a sign of coquetry that works against the understanding of female friendship as a strong, meaningful relationship.[54]

Belle Epoque representations of female friendship often support this earlier view and reduce women's friendship to a bodily performance devoid of meaning. For instance, in Henry Rabusson's novel *L'Amie* (1886) Gisèle and Germaine, who consider themselves to be best friends, repeatedly manifest passionate tenderness for each other in the presence of Maxime, Gisèle's husband. At the beginning of the novel, for example, when they meet under the eyes of Maxime after a few years separation: 'Les deux amies s'étaient mises à causer avec cette volubilité, cette puissance d'expansion et cette furie caressante qui caractérisent les intimités de femmes' (*Amie*, 5). During another encounter, still in the presence of Gisèle's husband:

[53]Maussion, *Lettre sur l'amitié*, pp. 71–72.

[54]A century later, Abel Bonnard, the author of another essay on friendship, also describes gestures of affection between women as excessive and meaningless, defining female friendship as the 'impuissante imitation de l'amour'. See Abel Bonnard, *L'Amitié* (Paris: Hachette, 1928), pp. 133–34.

[Germaine] disait à son amie, lui prenant la taille, lui baisant les cheveux et lui prodiguant les noms d'animaux utilisés entre jeunes filles qui s'aiment:

— Que je suis heureuse de te voir, de rester près de toi, mon chat, mon rat, mon lapin chéri! (*Amie*, 65)

According to the narrator, physical intimacy is a distinctive feature of female friendship and one of the constitutive elements of mainstream femininity. Gestures such as 'se prendre par la taille' or 'baiser les cheveux' are so trivial that they can be unambiguously performed in front of a husband. While Germaine is represented as a coquette whose playfulness is part of her perverse personality, the serious and irreproachable Gisèle adopts similar forms of behaviour when sharing confidences with Germaine or turning to her for consolation:

Gisèle se pencha sur son amie et la tint longuement embrassée, murmurant à son oreille, avec de douces paroles et les noms tendres, quelque peu provinciaux, qu'elles avaient accoutumé de se donner entre elles, la confidence des angoisses et des tourments où elle se débattait. (*Amie*, 198)

What is interesting is that such passionate and effusive behaviour occurs between two women whose friendship is ultimately revealed to be very superficial and fragile. From the beginning of the novel their relationship is in fact marked by a tension between friendship and rivalry, and is doomed to failure. Despite the repetitive and ostentatious display of physical affection between the two women, *L'Amie* is yet another story of betrayal and deception, and the erotic component of women's relationships, as represented in this novel, contributes to the portrayal of female friendship as a bodily parade lacking authenticity.[55]

If hugs, kisses, and caresses are commonplace among female friends and relatives in Belle Epoque fiction, in the case of Lesueur's *Justice de femme* some allusions to the inappropriateness of its heroines' behaviour are made, but only when the two are in the company of servants and acquaintances. In fact, although women were allowed to express their emotions in appropriate contexts, nineteenth-century French conduct manuals discourage female friends from unrestrained displays of affection in public and codify the way in which they should greet each other at formal gatherings such as receptions and

[55]Another element worthy of attention in Rabusson's novel is the idea that 'toute liaison de femmes un peu durable suppose deux natures opposées, quelque chose comme une nature mâle à côté d'une nature femelle'. This idea supports the view of female friendship not as a relationship in its own right but rather as an imitation of heterosexual relationships. See Rabusson, *Amie*, p. 35.

parties.[56] At the beginning of the novel, when Simone first pays a visit to Gisèle, the two friends spontaneously kiss each other in the presence of the three other women attending Gisèle's afternoon tea, a gesture endorsed by nineteenth-century French codes of polite behaviour (*Justice*, 27). Even when meeting in front of their husbands in the public space of the theatre, the two women exchange a kiss (*Justice*, 220). By contrast, the way in which Simone and Gisèle part at the end of their first encounter, after Jean's arrival at Gisèle's afternoon tea, appears more problematic: 'En disant adieu à son amie, elle [Simone] ne put se tenir, malgré la présence des étrangères, de la serrer en une longue étreinte, de l'embrasser à plusieurs reprises' (*Justice*, 38). In this instance, the presence of strangers makes Simone's exuberance seem out of place. Simone's unchecked impulse is subsequently explained by the narrator: 'Un élan de cœur, le regret d'un mouvement de jalousie à l'égard de Gisèle, un besoin de câline sympathie, provoquèrent cette explosion de tendresse' (*Justice*, 38). The narrator suggests that Simone has acted out of a need for affection but also, simultaneously, out of a sense of guilt, thus alluding to the sentiment of jealousy and antagonism coming into play between these two characters. More importantly, what should be noted here is that Lesueur's text seems in line with the recommendations addressed to women in conduct books. These manuals offer evidence that women were expected to show a certain composure when interacting with others, especially since it was considered impolite to play favourites during receptions.[57] This kind of consideration may account for the fact that, according to the narrator, Simone and Gisèle should show some restraint ('se tenir') and not give in to the excessive behaviour adopted on this occasion.

Simone and Gisèle's reunion after an eight-month separation is once again marked by affectionate, almost exaggerated tenderness. At this point, Simone has long left her lover and has had a baby while Gisèle, who does not suspect Simone and Jean's past affair, has become Jean's new mistress. Simone is aware of the rumours concerning Gisèle's liaison with Jean and, although she is unsure of how she feels about her friend/sexual rival, when the two women finally meet they greet each other in a warm, passionate way:

> Ce fut une telle effusion de câlineries, de baisers, d'épithètes mignardes, que chacune des jeunes femmes, dans la griserie de l'entraînement de cette minute, ne distingua pas si elle cédait à sa propre tendresse ou à la contagieuse tendresse de l'autre. (*Justice*, 201)

---

[56] 'Elle ne prodigue pas à ses amies des démonstrations hyperboliques d'affection, ne leur saute pas au cou à tout propos, ne les accable pas d'appellations mignardes.' See Baronne Staffe, □ □*les du savoir-vivre*, pp. 273–74.

[57] See for example *Les Usages du monde*, p. 27, and Maryan and Béal, *Le Fond et la forme*, p. 209.

The arrival of a servant abruptly cuts off their intimacy and forces them to separate. However, a few moments later 'Gisèle embrassait à nouveau son amie, car, à pas discrets, le domestique avait quitté la chambre', this episode signalling once again the impropriety of Gisèle and Simone's display of affection and their need for discretion (*Justice*, 202). As in the previous example, it is fair to assume that Gisèle and Simone are required to check themselves and to show more self-possession only in the presence of people who do not belong to their most intimate circle. Indeed, considering the characters' social status (they are both presented as affluent and well-bred ladies), their occasional reserve primarily appears to be dictated by a rigorous etiquette which encourages them to conform to rigid standards of dignity and self-control.

If physical effusions between fictional female friends, although reinforcing certain gender stereotypes about women being maternal or coquettish, are occasionally portrayed as being too self-indulgent and unladylike, when women overstep the boundaries of proper social behaviour their conduct is also negatively associated with hysteria, another alleged attribute of femininity, purportedly determined by women's biological nature. In both *Justice de femme* and *L'Amie* there is a certain tendency to represent women as incapable of controlling their bodies and as overwhelmed by their sensual instincts. In the case of Simone and Gisèle, not only do they impulsively ignore social codes of behaviour and repeatedly kiss in front of strangers, but the narrator describes the physical euphoria of one of their encounters using the term 'griserie' (*Justice*, 201). *Le Trésor de la Langue Française* defines this word as an 'excitation physique qui étourdit, état comparable à l'ivresse', an 'exaltation produisant souvent une certaine altération du jugement, de la pensée'.[58] Moreover, we read that Simone 'se sentait fondre [...] d'une tendresse dissolvante' for Gisèle (*Justice*, 203). Rabusson similarly portrays female physical intimacy as being characterized by a 'furie caressante' (*Amie*, 5. My italics). The employment of these expressions ('griserie', 'tendresse dissolvante', 'furie caressante'), in conjunction with the fact that some female characters are explicitly labelled as 'folles' (e.g. 'cette Gisèle charmante et folle', *Justice*, 128) suggest that women are unable to rationally govern their own bodies and remain the victims of sensations. Female friendship seems to 'dissolve' the boundaries of the female body. Undisciplined, excited, excessive, even 'furious', the friend's body is partly assimilated to the hysterical body which, by definition, is unstable, convulsive, and capricious. These representations thus seem to reinforce a negative view of women and their corporeality,

[58]*Le Trésor de la langue française informatisé: dictionnaire de la langue du XIXe et du XXe si□ le (1789–1960).*

leaving the reader to wonder how the characters could possibly establish truthful, profound relations through bodies that they cannot control.

In many ways, then, it is possible to think of the bodily interaction between Simone and Gisèle in *Justice de femme* as something different from the expression of authentic female intimacy or the manifestation of genuine desire between women. Whether their physical closeness is the result of circumstances related to men or a performance in which the female body is used to reassert traditional femininity and conventional ideas about gender, their friendship often remains confined to the realm of the inauthentic.[59]

Female Friendship and the Body as a Producer of Meanings

In the next two sections, I would like to shift my focus, by considering representations of female friendship in which physical and emotional intimacy between women tend to be portrayed as meaningful and sincere rather than feeble and artificial. Moreover, I will explore ways in which the female friend's body, far from being a mere object of the (male) gaze, becomes a powerful instrument of expression, self-affirmation, and communication, through which the nature of the relation itself is collaboratively defined and, in certain cases, the conventional presentation of the female body is subverted, allowing female characters to experience a certain degree of agency within their relationships.

With regard to nineteenth-century French women, Vincent-Buffault has observed that 'le corps tient une place importante dans l'exploration des affects qui les lient'.[60] Belle Epoque novelistic representations of female friendship occasionally confirm the existence of a link between emotional and physical intimacy for women, portraying characters who rely

---

[59]Sharon Marcus has observed that fictional representations of female friendship in Victorian England are similarly characterized by intense physicality. In the Victorian age, female friendship represented a component of conventional femininity which reinforced gender roles. However, Marcus' analysis convincingly shows that this relationship also 'provided women with a sanctioned realm of erotic choice, agency, and indulgence', allowing them to 'display affection and experience pleasurable physical contact outside marriage'. See Marcus, *Between Women*, pp. 57, 62. So far, the interpretation I have offered of Simone and Gisèle's friendship in *Justice de femme* is different, in the sense that their physical closeness often appears to be constructed as an artificial performance which rarely translates into the expression of authentic affection or desire. This is not to say that their relationship is entirely devoid of authenticity in itself, nor that the text categorically excludes other hypotheses, but rather that this particular way of representing physical intimacy between women (i.e. as a response to masculinity or as an assertion of femininity) is not necessarily a manifestation of emotional intimacy or an expression of female agency. Simone and Gisèle's difficulty in establishing a profound and meaningful connection through their bodies, signalled for example by their failure in interpreting each other's bodily signals, will be further discussed later on in this chapter, p. 78. By contrast, Simone's perception of Gisèle as an object of beauty and desire more positively attests to women's ability to take pleasure in the appreciation of other women's physical charms. This question will be further discussed in this chapter, p. 70.
[60]Vincent-Buffault, *Exercice de l'amitié*, p. 223.

on touching as a means for bonding and sharing, using their bodies to establish stronger, more truthful connections. These representations show the centrality of the body to female friendship, and present the erotic dimension of this relationship in a generally positive light. In the examples that I am going to discuss, female characters express and communicate emotional intimacy, mutual understanding, and support through physical contact. Their interactions can be corporeal, intellectual, and emotional all at once, in a way that reconciles the body with the mind, showing that women, far from being the hapless victims of nature, can exert control over their bodies. Their relationships imply the presence of complex feelings of attraction, a tendency to appreciate other women's physical charms, and the ability to interpret each other's gestures and expressions. Although the body is central to the enactment of female friendship, physicality is represented in a way that goes beyond the maternal/sexual, platonic/erotic, passive/active dichotomies. Physical proximity, for example, does not simply translate into maternal or coquettish behaviour, and the characters usually appear to be in control of their bodies, purposefully using them to manifest friendship and solidarity, their gestures being occasionally invested with a political value.

One of the most striking aspects of the novels considered in this chapter is the fact that the female characters are constantly intent on scrutinizing, decoding, and admiring each other's bodies. These characters pay close attention to other women's looks, they enjoy female physical beauty, and are fascinated by each other, simultaneously attracted by the aesthetic and personal qualities of their friends. For example, in *L'Un vers l'autre*, a novel that will be further discussed later on in this section,[61] when observing her mother-in-law:

> Laure la trouvait belle à souhait ce soir-là dans sa simple toilette de soie noire garnie de jais, qui faisait valoir son teint mat, ses traits fins éclairés par des grands yeux bruns pensifs et affectueux. Tout de suite la jeune fille s'était sentie attirée par le charme qui émanait de cette femme douce, réservée, un peu timide. Elle avait reconnu la présence d'une âme sérieuse comme était la sienne. (Compain, *UVA*, p. 8)

The mother-in-law's prettiness and the simplicity of her clothes seem to correspond to the moral qualities that Laure has immediately and instinctively appreciated in this woman (i.e. 'douceur', 'réserve', 'timidité') and perfectly mirror her 'âme sérieuse'. The connection between physical attributes and personality is also stressed in the description of the eyes, characterized as 'pensifs' and 'affectueux'. When Laure first meets her new boss, the school director Germaine, she looks at her attentively and thinks:

---

[61] For a summary of the novel, see p. 76 in this thesis.

> Elle est bien jolie avec ses cheveux blonds qui ondulent autour de son visage ovale, illuminé de grands yeux verts, doux et volontaires à la fois. Mais elle est un peu trop pâle et ses paupières sont cernées de noir. Elle est trop mince aussi en sa robe brune, et j'aimerais qu'elle eût les doigts moins blancs. Je crois que je l'aimerai. (*UVA*, 172)

Germaine's pleasant looks match the purity of her soul and Laure appears to be both physically and emotionally attracted to her (she finds her 'jolie' and she believes that she is going to love her). Her eyes are defined as 'doux' and 'volontaires'. The other details of her aspect (i.e. 'paleur', 'cernes noires', 'minceur') are the corporeal signs of her emotional state and anticipate the description of her daily struggles in her role of school director. Laure instantaneously wishes that Germaine had 'les doigts moins blancs' and it is worth asking whether this kind of remark does not betray an awareness of the connection between mental and physical well-being rather than a preoccupation with aesthetic standards.

A similar link between the moral and the physical is suggested by the fact that, in Lesueur's novel *Lèvres closes,* Charlotte's first impression of Marcienne is conveyed by a suggested correspondence ('harmonie') between the latter's soul ('âme') and her body ('paysages extérieurs des gestes, des regards'), in a passage that presents itself as symbolist in orientation:

> Une magie d'attirance lui capta le cœur. Elle [...] sentit chez sa future belle-sœur la nature profonde, aux adroites avenues sans détour, les lointaines harmonies de l'âme avec les paysages extérieurs des gestes, des regards, avec les frissons de la voix. (*Lèvres*, 25–26)

This correspondence between the emotional and the physical resonates with Tilburg's observations about the perception of the body as a vessel of moral beauty and the expression of one's personality as promoted by French Republican ideology.[62] To the extent that women's physical appearance, in these novels, is understood as a manifestation of their personal qualities (e.g. sweetness, determination), rather than as symbolic of certain universal characteristics (e.g. passivity, hysteria), these representations arguably

[62]Tilburg has been discussed at pp. 43–45 in this thesis. As I am going to argue further below, to my mind, novelistic representations of bodily interactions between female friends stress not only the traditional link between 'body' and 'soul' (i.e. body and emotions or personal attributes), but also the link between 'body' and 'mind' (i.e. body and thoughts or intentions), the gestures performed by fictional female friends conveying the characters' feelings but also other meanings. The link between 'body' and 'mind' rather than 'soul' is also implicitly suggested by Tilburg's research.

encourage female readers to think of their own bodies as articulate and expressive rather than as idle or hysterical. Moreover, the female characters' active engagement with the act of looking, in particular the way in which their 'scopophilia' (i.e. the erotic pleasure of looking) parallels their 'epistemophilia' (i.e. the desire to know the other), posits women as the knowing subjects and allow them to infer or elaborate their own meanings when watching other women's bodies.[63]

A further, somewhat different example of women's ability to appreciate female attractiveness is provided in *Justice de femme*, where Simone is fascinated by Gisèle Chambertier because she is beautiful and socially in demand, to the extent that M. Chambertier's unwanted attentions flatter Simone because he is the husband of one of the most sought after women in Paris (*Justice*, 40).[64] During one of their encounters, Simone remains under Gisèle's spell, the latter's charm being so powerful that '[Simone] se sentait fondre pour elle d'une tendresse dissolvante et douce' (*Justice*, 203). She remarks that her friend looks extremely beautiful and, gazing at the details of her physical appearance, is unable to decide what exactly constitutes Gisèle's renewed appeal (*Justice*, 203–204). The episode in Giens, previously quoted in this chapter,[65] also confirms Simone's inclination to perceive Gisèle's body as an object of desire. Simone's enjoyment of female beauty suggests that (heterosexual) women, as well as men, can take an erotic interest in femininity, an idea that broadens the definition of female friendship.[66] Whether these novels stress the link between women's appearance and their personal qualities, or objectify the female friend's body in a way that highlights the erotic dimension of female homosociality, the female gaze is invested with considerable power.

A close reading of Lesueur's novel *Lèvres closes* allows us to further highlight the roles played by the body in Belle Epoque representations of female friendship. This analysis also contributes to a better understanding of the nature and dynamics of Marcienne and

---

[63]Brooks employs the terms 'scopophilia' and 'epistemophilia' in his essay *Body Work*. My use of the term 'scopophilia', in this thesis, does not necessarily imply a connection with sexual desire.

[64]The triangle between Simone, M. Chambertier, and Gisèle offers a good example of René Girard's model of mimetic desire.

[65]See p. 51 in this thesis.

[66]I am indebted to Sharon Marcus' insights regarding Victorian women's objectification of the female body, an attitude deemed compatible with heterosexuality and mainstream femininity. 'Women took note of other women's attractions not only as models to emulate but as pleasurable objects to consume. Women who felt physically attracted to other women were not seen as less feminine because of the attention they lavished on other women's bodies, but more so. Luxuriating in women's charms and viewing women as physical objects are activities some now think of as the prerogative of men. Lesbian enjoyment of women's bodies is considered an appropriation of masculine desire, while heterosexual women are often imagined as inspecting one another in a spirit of hostile rivalry, unable to enjoy feminine beauty unless narcissistically admiring their own. Victorians, however, saw both men and women as inclined to appreciate women's looks.' See Marcus, *Between Women*, p. 61.

Charlotte's relationship. The way Marcienne and Charlotte negotiate the meanings of non-verbal communication shows that they have developed a good knowledge and understanding of each other's feelings and reactions. During their encounters, a variety of messages are conveyed through the signals consciously or unconsciously sent by the body, these signals reinforcing, completing, or contradicting what is said by words or revealing what words cannot express. The lack of gestures itself can be remarkably telling. For example, when the two women meet after Charlotte's discovery of Marcienne's unfaithfulness toward her husband Édouard, Charlotte's disappointment and vexation are revealed at once by the seriousness of her facial expression and even more strongly by the lack of common gestures of affection between female friends or relatives, such as hugs and kisses. In this situation, Charlotte immediately takes her brother's side by ignoring Marcienne and displaying a great deal of affection toward him. While Édouard is oblivious to his sister's peculiar attitude, Marcienne quickly realizes that something is wrong and tries to interpret Charlotte's behaviour:

> Elle [Charlotte] s'avança, dans un sérieux inaccoutumé de son minois de candeur. Le pétillement des traits, des yeux, s'éteignait sous une ombre de gravité. Marchant droit à M. de Sélys, elle lui mit les bras au cou, l'étreignit d'un grand baiser silencieux, sans répondre au: « Bonjour Lolotte », gaiement lancé par Marcienne. [...] Marcienne, surprise que Charlotte ne lui eût pas encore rendu sa bienvenue gentille, et la voyant s'attarder d'une câlinerie si grave au cou de l'avocat, se rappela certaines bouderies de la petite quand elle-même s'était raidie en orgueil ou en volonté contre Édouard. (*Lèvres*, 19–20, 27–28)

As long as the three characters remain together Charlotte avoids directly speaking to Marcienne, she looks coldly at her, is nervous and laughs 'd'un rire faux'. Marcienne pays close attention to her expression, noting the 'nervosité de la bouche, navrement des prunelles, tout le joli visage contracté, douloureux' (*Lèvres*, 29). When Charlotte is finally forced into conversation by Marcienne and addresses a few words to her, the reason for her unusual attitude becomes suddenly apparent not only because of what she says (Charlotte refers to the skirt Marcienne wears for cycling and in whose pockets she has inadvertently left proof of her affair), but mostly because of the tone of her voice. After this realization, Marcienne turns pale and feels 'les yeux de Charlotte boire sa pâleur' (*Lèvres*, 30). In other words, three messages have been rapidly and almost silently exchanged between the two friends: Charlotte suspects Marcienne's betrayal; Marcienne discovers that Charlotte's suspicions have been aroused; Charlotte realizes that Marcienne is now aware of her suspicions and is probably confirming them. While these shocking revelations take place,

Édouard is utterly unaware of what is going on. He takes no notice of Charlotte's hostility toward Marcienne nor of the strange uneasiness between the two friends; he is not part of the real conversation that is unfolding under his eyes and distractedly decides to leave the room (*Lèvres*, 33).

During this first encounter, some of the aspects of non-verbal communication so central to the interaction between female friends have already emerged, in particular in terms of looks, facial expressions, tone of voice, and facial paling. When Marcienne and Charlotte interact en-tête-à-tête in the following chapters, a variety of elements pertaining to the non-verbal dimension of communication insistently come into play, performing various functions. Once of these functions is the expression of emotions, following the Belle Epoque belief that 'tout ce que l'âme éprouve retentit sur l'organisme, et, par exemple, se reflète sur la figure; la figure est comme le miroir des sentiments'.[67] At different moments both Marcienne and Charlotte blush, turn pale, smile, cry, and find themselves unable to control the contractions of their facial muscles or the sudden raising of their chests, thus manifesting, often unintentionally, a wide range of feelings including shame, surprise, distress, sadness, frustration, and suffering. For example, when after the departure of Édouard Charlotte and Marcienne are left alone and an explanation is in order, Marcienne's eyes light up with 'l'ardeur et le droit de vivre' (*Lèvres*, 36). Marcienne often manages to display a sense of confidence and respectability through her gaze. Similarly, when Charlotte looks at Marcienne, the former's eyes betray or explicitly convey indignation, disapproval, or incomprehension. Charlotte also manifests her repugnance through particular gestures. For example, her movement in handing Philippe's letter, the proof of Marcienne's adultery, to her sister-in-law is described as a 'geste de dégoût [...] sur ce papier qu'elle écartait comme une chose immonde' (*Lèvres*, 37–38). Later on, she tries to manifest her contempt with a smile: 'Un sourire avisé, furtif, d'un dédain qui s'appliquait, vint soulever la lèvre, puis se fondit dans le gercement d'un frisson' (*Lèvres*, 49). Moreover, both Marcienne and Charlotte give physical responses in reaction to a provocation or a particularly hurtful remark. For example, when Charlotte suddenly switches from informal *tutoiement* to *vouvoiement*, 'Marcienne fléchit sous le désastre que représentait cette syllabe [vous]. Elle s'assit à son tour. Instinctivement elle prit refuge près de son petit bureau' (*Lèvres*, 39).

In addition to the display of emotions, bodily signals can reveal the character's inner thoughts and real intentions or can be aimed at provoking a specific reaction from the interlocutor. As regards the revelation of one's true thoughts and feelings, for example, when

[67]Henri Marion, *Leçons de psychologie appliquée à l'éducation* (Paris: A. Colin et Cie, 1882), p. 28.

Charlotte accuses Marcienne of shamelessly sacrificing her respectable marriage in the name of sensual pleasure, Marcienne refuses either to admit or deny this observation. However, 'sur le beau visage de Mme de Sélys, depuis le cou jusqu'aux racines des cheveux relevés, la marée rose du sang surgit d'un flot brusque, s'étendit, resta' (*Lèvres*, 52). This blushing, not followed by explicit words, is interpreted as a confession and defined by the narrator as a 'rougeur d'aveu' (*Lèvres*, 54). When, in the midst of the quarrel, Charlotte starts to cry, she feels inwardly lost 'à sentir qu'en face de sa belle-sœur coupable, elle ne parvenait pas à la haïr, qu'elle subissait toujours son charme tendre, sa domination d'altière douceur, et qu'une tentation lui venait d'aller pleurer sur son épaule' (*Lèvres*, 46). In her confusion, Charlotte instinctively feels the need to cry on Marcienne's shoulder, thus sensing her own contradictory desire to be consoled by and reconciled with the very person who is causing her distress. However, she does not act on this desire and the temptation does not translate into an act. Although Marcienne is profoundly moved by Charlotte's tears, it is only when she, Marcienne, cries that the two women share a passing moment of physical and emotional rapprochement (*Lèvres*, 61–62, 118). It has already been noted that the tone of voice can convey a message beyond its verbal content. The same is true for looks. For instance, when Marcienne fears that Charlotte could inadvertently reveal her secret, she looks at her with 'des yeux d'inquiètude et de supplication', not formulating her request aloud but still trying to send her a message (*Lèvres*, 125).

Among the functions performed by the female body in *Lèvres closes* and in other novels of this period, the expression of emotions might appear as the most conventional. As observed by Holmes, popular fiction in the Third Republic, for example, firmly stresses the connection between feelings and gestures and treats the body as the mirror of the soul. In particular, Holmes refers to 'a sort of pathetic fallacy [which] operates whereby emotional states translate directly into physical symptoms' and considers this device as one of those distinctive elements of mass fiction, whose aim is to produce 'a relaxing and reassuring ease of interpretation' for readers with limited education and leisure.[68] More recently, however, Holmes has argued that, for Lesueur, 'objectivation' (i.e. the 'rendering of psychology and emotion through external event', a device that she adopts in her *romans populaires*) constitutes a more effective technique to show the 'interplay between inner and outer realities' than the strategies conventionally used in the *roman psychologique* or in the *roman à thèse*.[69] What is even more interesting from the point of view of female homosociality is the portrayal of the female body as a means to establish and reinforce female bonding and

[68]Holmes, *Romance and Readership,* pp. 26, 31.
[69]Holmes, 'Mapping Modernity', p. 265.

as expressive not only of emotions but also of intentions and thoughts. Marcienne and Charlotte accord a considerable degree of attention to body language, constantly gazing at one another, trying to interpret the other's expressions and movements, and often aware of the parallel and secret conversations taking place beyond words. This treatment of the female body not only contributes to a more positive representation of female friendship (women are able to interact through their bodies in a way that is both autonomous and significant), but it also challenges the view of the female body as passive or uncontrollably hysterical, as the key to a feminine nature that reduces women to mothers or mistresses, as a passive object of beauty for men to admire, use, and reproduce. These novelistic representations closely intersect with those discourses that, during the Belle Epoque, were reinforcing the union between body and mind and were promoting an understanding of the female body as an instrument of self-determination and agency that women needed to control in order to achieve their emancipation.[70]

It is important to note that the non-verbal elements discussed above are not peculiar to female friendship but are part of human communication and, even in this novel, they are similarly present when the female characters interact with their husbands or lovers. However, Édouard often proves unable to decode his wife's gestures and physical reactions or to guess her state of mind. He is indifferent to Marcienne's feelings and, most of the time, his desiring gaze arguably perceives her body as a mere erotic object. For example, at the beginning of the novel, Marcienne is annoyed by the fact that he cannot pick up on her discomfort, and when he lightly professes himself certain of Marcienne's love for him, Édouard fails in interpreting his wife's subsequent pallor and the changing expression of her eyes as expressions of her inner life:

> « ... puisque vous m'aimez, Marcienne. »
>
> A ces mots, à cet accent, Mme de Sélys devint très pale. Toute droite devant son mari, elle le contemplait. Quelque chose d'insondable approfondissait les magnifiques prunelles. Mais lui les trouva seulement plus attirantes, plus expressives; et il allait, cet époux vieilli, prononcer une parole d'amant, lorsqu'un coup de timbre, vibrant dans la cour, dispersa les émotions différentes de leurs deux âmes. (*Lèvres*, 18)

Édouard does not take notice of the trouble written in Marcienne's eyes; on the contrary, he finds her stare more charming and is going to react inappropriately, possibly by pronouncing some tender words, until the ring of a bell defuses their 'émotions *différentes*', the latter

---

[70]These discourses have been analysed at pp. 44–45 in this thesis.

adjective signalling that the two characters are not on the same wavelength and cannot communicate effectively through their bodies. In referring to Charles Bovary's inability to read Emma's body, Peter Brooks observes that the 'eyes are traditionally the mirror of the soul, that part of the body which gives access from the physical to the spiritual [...] His [Charles'] gaze seems to have no grasp on the other's reality'.[71] If Édouard, like Charles, fails in 'reading' his wife's mind, if he fails in deploying those mentalizing abilities that, according to psychologists, allow us 'to treat other agents as the bearers of unobservable psychological states and processes, and to anticipate and explain the agents' behavior in terms of such states and processes', it is worth asking whether such failure depends on the fact that these male characters do not attribute a mind to the female characters.[72]

However, Édouard, who was oblivious to Marcienne and Charlotte's silent conversation at the beginning of the novel, pays closer attention to their body language during their encounter with Philippe at the theatre, when Charlotte inadvertently arouses his suspicions by preventing the two men from shaking hands (*Lèvres*, 147–49). Generally speaking, he seems more prone to detect the meaning of his sister's body signals rather than his wife's (*Lèvres*, 157–67). Moreover, Marcienne and Philippe, '[qui] s'aiment avant tout de tous leurs sens' and whose bodies speak the language of passion, are usually successful in deciphering each other's thoughts and emotions through their gestures and expressions (*Lèvres*, 78).[73] Philippe even uses Marcienne's body as a sort of canvas where he can impress the marks of their tormented love, of his lust and jealousy, and Marcienne enjoys the idea of bearing the signs of his ardent desire for her on her skin (*Lèvres*, 86–97). What is interesting to note is that in this novel the male gaze is often blinkered or inadequate, which means that cross-sex non-verbal communication sometimes fails, whereas Marcienne and Charlotte possess a remarkable and consistent ability to interact through their bodies by linking body signals to mental states. This ability is compared to and often proves to be even more effective than that of two lovers (Marcienne and Philippe) or brother and sister (Édouard and Charlotte).

Similar observations concerning the relevance of the female body and the power of the female gaze in representations of female friendship apply to other Belle Epoque novels, such as for example *L'Un vers l'autre*. Published in 1903, *L'Un vers l'autre* was considered the major literary accomplishment of the journalist and feminist activist Louise-Marie

---

[71]Brooks, *Body Work*, p. 91.
[72]See 'Theory of Mind' in the *Internet Encyclopedia of Philosophy* <https://www.iep.utm.edu/theomind/#SH1c> [accessed 31 August 2018].
[73]The narrator also remarks: 'Ah! Comme ils auront été amants par les yeux!'. See Lesueur, *L□ res*, p. 190.

Compain.[74] Divided into three sections, it tells the story of Laure Prevel, an intelligent and strong-minded young woman who, soon after her marriage to the honest but old-fashioned and uncompromising Henri Deborda, rebels against her husband's tyranny and subsequently leaves him in order to become a teacher in a provincial school. Both characters evolve painfully during their time apart, Laure finding comfort in the presence of her sympathetic school director Germaine, until they finally find their way back to each other by entering into a more progressive ideal of marriage, one founded on respect and equality. The female characters represented in this novel often refuse to experience their interactions as one-dimensional and frivolous corporeal performances. For example, at the end of an episode in which the heroine Laure opens her heart to her cousin Madeleine, a moment to single out for its emotional intensity and the mutual understanding achieved by the two characters, the narrator observes: 'Elles s'embrassèrent calmement. La profondeur de leur émotion supprimait les gestes et les paroles banales', as if in certain circumstances the usual display of physical contact would be unnatural and meaningless, the expression of a deeply felt emotion only requiring a quiet hug (*UVA*, 148).

As in *Lèvres closes*, female characters in this novel show a peculiar ability to read each other's body. For example, Laure is the only character in a room full of people to notice 'une expression de tristesse inaccoutumée sur la physionomie de sa cousine Avilard' and is instinctively affected by her distress (*UVA*, 10). Later on, confiding to Madeleine her decision to leave her husband, the narrator observes that 'tandis qu'elle parlait, elle observait Madeleine et, dans les regards de sa cousine, puisait la force de continuer son récit douloureux', since in the latter's eyes she found 'une surprise émue, une sympathie profonde, une approbation douloureuse et enthousiaste', signals of the understanding and support she was looking for (*UVA*, 145). Listening to her story, Madeleine's feelings come to the surface through her body and seem to transform her physical appearance:

> Le visage chiffonné et banal de la femme de l'inspecteur paraissait transfiguré, si fortes étaient les émotions qui bouleversaient son cœur. Ses yeux bleu pâle brillaient d'un éclat inaccoutumé et de grosses larmes venaient parfois humecter les paupières déjà ridées, sillonner les joues qu'une couche légère de fard seule faisait roses encore. (*UVA*, 145–46)

---

[74]See Rachel Mesch, 'Marie-Louise Compain', in *Le Dictionnaire universel des créatrices*, ed. by Béatrice Didier, Antoinette Foque, Mireille Calle-Gruber (Paris: Éditions des femmes, 2013), pp. 1023–24.

In the following excerpt, the tenderness and mutual sympathy existing between Laure and Germaine are manifested by explicit words in conjunction with looks, smiles, and the touching of hands, an affectionate gesture often occurring between female characters:

> Avec un sourire, elle [Laure] ajouta, captivante:
>
> —Voulez-vous me permettre de vous dire que je vous aime bien?
>
> —Mais, moi aussi, répondit Germaine presque gaiement, en lui serrant la main.
>
> Un instant elles se regardèrent avec une émotion secrète, et dans les yeux de l'autre chacune lut une douce confiance. (*UVA*, 214)

In *L'Un vers l'autre*, as in *Lèvres closes*, when the female body expresses emotions, as it often does in traditional literature, female friends show a peculiar, almost exclusive ability to perceive and decode bodily signals. This ability, along with the purposeful use they make of their bodies, puts them in a privileged position and allows them to perform active roles.

The image of touching hands, a recurring gesture in *L'Un vers l'autre*, is one of the most significant examples of the female characters' aptitude to knit together body, soul, and mind in order to produce meanings and communicate. For instance, Laure, regretting the shame she has briefly felt in being seen walking down the street with Marie Collard, decides to defy social conventions and publicly shake hands with her, as if to assert her sympathy vis-à-vis this woman.[75] When Madeleine wants to show Laure support and encouragement after her decision to leave her husband and become an independent woman, the first thing she does is to clasp her hands energetically (*UVA*, 146). During Laure and Germaine's first encounter, the latter, fearing that she has offended Laure, lays her hand on her trembling fingers while expressing by words all her respect and compassion for her (*UVA*, 174). The two repeatedly clasp each other's hands throughout the novel when they need reassurance and consolation, for example after a disagreeable conversation with the school inspector or when exchanging intimate confidences (*UVA*, 212, 214, 235, 245).[76]

[75]Marie Collard is a marginal character in the story. The daughter of a waiter, she lives with Maniot, one of Henri's colleagues, with whom she has had two children. Since the couple are not married, Marie is the victim of social prejudices. According to Belle Epoque social conventions, Laure and Marie cannot be officially introduced or talk to each other, let alone act in a friendly manner. Laure's attitude toward Marie on this occasion is in fact one of the causes of Laure and Henri's first fight and I read their handshake as an example of gestures having a political potential. See Compain, *UVA*, p. 64.

[76]Perhaps it is in this sense that physical contact has been defined by Yalom and Donovan Brown as one of the 'ingredients that seem basic to women's friendship' across history. See Yalom and Donovan Brown, *Social Sex*, p. 344.

Interestingly, even in *Justice de femme* when Simone, unwilling to share the secret of her adultery, refuses Gisèle's support, the narrator employs a metaphor comparing the possibility of female emotional intimacy to a caressing hand:

> [E]lle avait peur — dans son trouble — de se laisser amollir par cette amicale tendresse, par cette complicité câline de femme qui pressent et absout l'amour; [...] elle se raidissait contre l'instinctif besoin de faire toucher les plaies de son cœur à une main légère, caressante... (*Justice*, 141)

In this excerpt, the reference to some of the principal aspects of nineteenth-century female friendship, namely self-disclosure, understanding, and comfort, is constructed using terms drawn from the lexical field of the body and relating to touching and sensations, such as 'amollir', 'câline', 'se raidir', 'toucher', 'plaies', 'main', and 'caressante', suggesting the existence of a link between the emotional and the physical. Moreover, this passage further supports the idea that Simone and Gisèle usually fail in establishing a profound and honest relationship and in supporting each other. In addition to this, while Simone and Gisèle display their emotions and try to communicate through their bodies, they are often oblivious to each other's physical reactions or unable to interpret them. Gisèle, in particular, rarely takes notice of Simone's turning pale and being upset, nor does she attach a particular meaning to her gestures and expressions. For example, when Simone finds out that after their break-up Jean has followed her to the south of France, she desperately wishes to leave on a scheduled day-trip with Gisèle and her husband in order to avoid him, and begs her friend not to change their plans. However:

> Gisèle se mit à rire devant l'ardeur de cette supplication. Si fine qu'elle fût, elle ne pouvait soupçonner quel désir affolant de fuite mettait une prière anxieuse dans les yeux et sur les lèvres de son amie. Elle crut à l'enfantin plaisir espéré de cette excursion. (*Justice*, 132)

Similarly, when some time later Simone, fearing that Gisèle is about to confess her affair with Jean, turns pale, shrinks from her and 'avec la main étendue, comme un enfant qui veut se préserver d'un coup' tries to prevent her from telling this secret, Gisèle is once again unconcerned by her friend's gesture (*Justice*, 204–205). These examples show that Simone and Gisèle are usually unable to read each other's bodies and successfully interact through them as other fictional female friends do, further confirming their failure in achieving that profounder union between the emotional and the physical that often contributes to characterize female friendship as authentic in Belle Epoque novels.

Before carrying the analysis of these novels any further, I would like to highlight some interesting parallels between novelistic and visual representations of female sociability and the body in Belle Epoque France. As argued by Linda Nochlin in her influential essay *Women, Art and Power* (1988):

> representations of women in art are founded upon and serve to reproduce indisputably accepted assumptions held by society in general, and by artists in particular, [...] about woman's weakness and passivity; her sexual availability for men's needs; her defining domestic and nurturing function; her identity with the realm of nature; her existence as object rather than creator of art; the patent ridiculousness of her attempts to insert herself actively into the realm of history by means of work or engagement in political struggle.[77]

In a later work, Nochlin recapitulates how the female body has been treated in (nineteenth-century) art using the following words:

> women's bodies have always served as allegorized objects of desire, of hatred, of elevation, of abasement — of everything, in short. That is the point: woman's body has never 'counted' in itself, only with what the male artist could fill it with, and that has always, it seems, been himself and his desires.[78]

Bran Dijkstra, among others, discusses at great length how *fin-de-siècle* European artists variously associate the female figure with nature or mythology, representing it in timeless contexts and depriving it of any individuality, or else link it with ideas of vice and degeneration, portraying either women's bestiality and uncontrollable sexuality or their essential weakness and passivity.[79] Nineteenth-century artistic representations of the female body, it should be noted, largely echo those popular and scientific discourses which, during the Belle Epoque, present women's bodies as receptacles of meanings imposed by men rather than as instruments through which women themselves can produce their own meanings. Nochlin stresses this very point when, discussing the female nude in the nineteenth century, she asserts: 'Muse or model, mistress or mother, asleep or awake, the nude female can inspire, perhaps reproduce, but cannot *produce* or *create*.'[80] In this

---

[77]Linda Nochlin, 'Women, Art and Power', in *Women, Art and Power and Other Essays* (London: Thames and Hudson, 1991 [1988]), pp. 1–36 (p. 1).
[78]Linda Nochlin, *Representing Women* (London: Thames and Hudson, 1999), p. 131.
[79]Dijkstra offers many examples drawn from French visual culture, including paintings of women together. See Bran Dijkstra, *Idols of Perversity: Fantasies of Feminine Evil in Fin-de-Si□ le Culture* (New York; Oxford: Oxford University Press, 1986).
[80]Nochlin, *Representing Women*, p. 136. My italics.

sentence, Nochlin lists the traditional types of identities (i.e. 'muse', 'mistress', 'mother') which, as discussed at the beginning of this chapter, were typically available to Belle Epoque women and which were anchored in a particular understanding of women's nature, further indicating the difficulty for them of creating their own meanings through the body.[81]

More recently, Tamar Garb has pointed out a striking difference between male and female portraiture in the nineteenth century and before. While portraits of men are traditionally required to inform the viewer about the subject's personality, his social status, and his profession, and the act of looking consequently implies an intellectual encounter with the image, portraits of women constitute rather a projection of male desires and an exercise in technical skills, the woman remaining 'ultimately unknowable because she was purely physical', 'a decorative surface, and empty shell which needed to be cloaked and adorned in the style of the moment'.[82] The traditional iconography of bourgeois femininity, in particular, presents women as mere objects of beauty to be juxtaposed with other objects, mindless creatures devoid of character, leading an existence of fashionable idleness in the domestic space. Alfred Stevens' *Le Salon du peintre* (1880) offers a good example of this particular way of portraying the female body, and could be compared to the images usually found in women's magazines (Annex a and b). Indeed, as observed by Anne Higonnet, in fashion plates 'what matters is not one person or one image but the infinitely reproducible spectacle of femininity. [...] No individual presence emanates from the fashion print because no individual is posited as prior to its image'.[83] When women are portrayed together, their bodies remain anonymous, unidentified. Not only are they virtually indistinguishable from one another and treated as interchangeable, but they do not even seem capable of establishing relations among themselves, their bodies simply mirroring each other.[84]

However, critics have noted a shift occurring in the conceptualization of the female portrait at the end of the nineteenth century, which can be equated with the positive representations of the female body found in novels of the same period. Female artists of the Belle Epoque, in particular, challenge conservative iconic models of femininity through their

---

[81] See pp. 42–43 in this thesis.

[82] Tamar Garb, *The Body in Time: Figures of Femininity in Late Nineteenth-Century France* (Seattle: University of Washington Press, 2008), pp. 46, 51. Debora L. Silverman raises the same point in *Art Nouveau in Fin-de-si□ le France: Politics, Psychology, and Style* (Berkeley: University of California Press, 1989), where she discusses Camille Mauclair's article 'La Femme devant les peintres modernes' (1899), also used by Garb. Marie-Jo Bonnet similarly observes that in nineteenth-century France 'l'idéal du beau prôné par le système des Beaux-Arts exige des femmes sans caractère, sans visage propre'. See Marie-Jo Bonnet, *Les Deux Amies: essai sur le couple de femmes dans l'art* (Paris: Éditions Blanche, 2000), p. 131.

[83] Anne Higonnet, *Berthe Morisot's Images of Women* (Cambridge: Harvard University Press, 1992), p. 95.

[84] 'She existed in and for what she mirrored, and unless she mirrored the world of man, she mirrored brute nature, the world of woman, herself. Thus, paradoxically, as long as woman lived among women, she lived alone, completely self-contained. She mirrored other women and other women mirrored her'. See Dijkstra, *Idols of Perversity*, p. 132.

depiction of the New Woman.[85] In paintings such as Louise Breslau's *Portrait des amies* (1881) or *Les Amies, Effet de contre-jour* (1888) women are represented as highly individuated, thinking subjects, that assert their individuality (Annex c and d). Soberly dressed, dignified, and unidealized, their expressions reveal their character and inner life. Their common engagement in intellectual or creative activities attests to a seriousness of purpose and characterizes them as modern women.[86] These paintings can be associated with the photographs of professional women circulating in Belle Epoque magazines, which, by contrast with fashion plates, display the female figure in time, in its association with work, power, and intellect. Insofar as these images present the female body as productive of meanings and as revealing of a woman's identity, thoughts, and purpose, they seem to go hand in hand with certain Belle Epoque novels.[87]

Female Friendship and the Body as a Vehicle of Agency

The privileged role played by the female body in *Lèvres closes* and in other novels of the same period suggests that women could appropriate both the act of looking and their own bodies, actively using the latter to express emotions, convey meanings, and communicate. In this section, I am going to discuss additional ways in which the body could be used by women to foster complex relationships with each other, define the structure and quality of these relationships in their own terms, and experience agency.

The nature of Marcienne and Charlotte's friendship, in particular, is revealed in the following excerpt by the silent way in which their bodies interact before the two women start talking. At this moment, the two friends are finally left alone and Charlotte is determined to confront Marcienne on the subject of her presumed infidelity. While it might be expected that the former would be, at least temporarily, in a position of power and superiority, on the contrary:

---

[85] According to Garb, these changes were also promoted by the aesthetic requirements of Realism and Naturalism starting from the 1860s. See Garb, *The Body in Time*, pp. 56–61. Silverman also observes this phenomenon in *fin-de-siècle* art. See Silverman, *Art Nouveau*, pp. 69–70.

[86] On Breslau's paintings, see Garb, *The Body in Time*, p. 61. Breslau's work has been discussed in somewhat different terms by Marie-Jo Bonnet in her study of visual representations of lesbianism. See Bonnet, *Les Deux Amies*, pp. 164–68.

[87] Regarding the link between Belle Epoque novelistic and visual representations of female homosociality, it is worth noting that feminist propaganda of this period appropriates the image of touching hands, a gesture often recurring in novels of this period, as already mentioned, in order to symbolize female agency and solidarity, collaboration and mutual support, as Hélène Dufan's poster for the first issue of the magazine *La Fronde* illustrates (Annex e).

> Droite, la tête légèrement renversée en arrière, de toute sa fierté raidie elle [Marcienne] écrasait la timidité de Charlotte. Celle-ci, blanche et comme mourante, les lèvres tirées par un frémissement, les jambes amollies, dût s'asseoir. Elle défaillait. (*Lèvres*, 36)[88]

Marcienne and Charlotte's bodies clearly manifest that their relationship is not one between equals. The power relation is unbalanced and Marcienne usually stands in a position of superiority. In another passage, the narrator explicitly observes that Charlotte is 'étreinte par cette superiorité', the verb employed belonging, interestingly, to the lexical sphere of physicality (*Lèvres*, 51). When their altercation seems to have come to an impasse, Marcienne and Charlotte stand up face to face. At this moment, 'la douceur intime et ancienne de leur amitié resurgit. Un long flot de tendresse monta, dans une horreur étonnée de la lutte' (*Lèvres*, 60–61). Charlotte apologizes, Marcienne starts to cry, and finally:

> Elles s'étaient rapprochées. Elles s'étreignaient à présent, frémissantes de sympathie, d'angoisse. La tête blonde s'appuyait sur l'épaule plus haute. L'aînée entourait la cadette de ses bras, avec un bercement imperceptible, comme pour une petite fille que l'on console. (*Lèvres*, 62)

Later on, the reasons for their conflict taking over again, the distance between Charlotte and Marcienne becomes physical as much as mental and emotional. This is indicated in a passage that can be singled out for its unusual absence of verbs: 'Un retour d'hostilité sur cette parole. Un recul. [...] Les fronts et les cœurs de nouveau redressés. Les yeux durcis. Une désolation d'espace entre les âmes' (*Lèvres*, 63–64). The effect of immediacy thus obtained in this scene puts the accent on the visual dimension of the narration, on the characters' gestures, expressions, and movements, almost as if these were stage directions. A further example of the asymmetry and the general functioning of the characters' relationship is given when a few days later Charlotte, who claims to be sick, welcomes Marcienne in her *cabinet de toilette* where she lies on a chaise longue. While begging Marcienne to give up her affair, '[elle] se coula en bas de la chaise longue, glissa à terre, posa ses mains jointes sur les genoux de sa belle-sœur' in an attitude of submission, prayer, and supplication (*Lèvres*, 116–17). Marcienne, upset by this gesture and feeling more vulnerable, takes Charlotte in her arms, forces her to lie down again, then sits down on the carpet and lays her head near Charlotte's head, starting to cry. At this point they both start

---

[88]Moreover, during this discussion the narrator observes that Charlotte 'manquait totalement du prestige que réclamait son rôle'. See Lesueur, *Lèvres*, p. 45.

to call each other by tender names, such as 'ma pauvre chérie' and 'ma mignonne' (*Lèvres*, 118). Even though this may appear as a reversal of the situation, Marcienne now being in a position of submission, she is the one still dictating the terms of their interaction. All Charlotte can do in this circumstance is try to withdraw, and even when she does Marcienne tells her: 'Ne t'écarte pas de moi, chère petite' (*Lèvres*, 119). At the end of their conversation, softened by Charlotte's good nature and naivety, Marcienne kisses her to dissimulate a smile in a gesture of maternal tenderness (*Lèvres*, 121). From all these examples, we can deduce that Charlotte and Marcienne's hierarchical relationship is constructed in the following way: understanding and emotional affinity entail physical proximity and allow the performance of maternal gestures, such as the tender rocking of the childish Charlotte, whereas disagreement rapidly translates into physical distance and gestures of hostility. This is a further confirmation of the strong connection existing between physical and emotional intimacy in women's relationships.

What is even more striking, as I am going to demonstrate, is that Charlotte and Marcienne's bodily interactions and the power dynamic they enact contribute to the redefinition of the characters' roles as women and question the stereotypes generally associated with female physical types, thus challenging the traditional reading of the female body. Even though in one of the passages describing Marcienne and Charlotte's rapprochement the narrator employs the terms 'aînée' and 'cadette', these appellations being normally used in relation to sisters, and despite the fact that Marcienne and Charlotte often call each other 'sœur' and 'petite sœur', I propose to read their friendship in terms of the mother-daughter model rather than the more egalitarian sororal model. The mother-daughter model is suggested not only by the lack of equality in their relationship and by the maternal gestures occasionally characterizing their bodily interactions, as highlighted above, but also by Charlotte herself who thinks of Marcienne as a 'sœur aînée, *maternelle* à sa jeunesse', and by Marcienne who often calls Charlotte 'ma pauvre *enfant*' and thinks of her as 'une âme dont elle avait un peu la charge', 'innocente comme ton [de Charlotte] dernier-né' (*Lèvres*, 50, 54, 62, 106, 119. My italics). While Charlotte admires Marcienne, regards her as a role model, and is in awe of her, Marcienne constantly shows great affection toward Charlotte and, like a mother, is animated by a strong sense of responsibility and protection toward her. Marcienne and Charlotte's unequal friendship encompasses a wide range of emotions and attitudes, from warmth, affection, and admiration to disagreement and hostility, and it implies a power dynamic of control and submission, all of these being reflected in the way that their physical interactions unfold.

In a previous section on 'Physical Intimacy and the Inauthenticity of Female Friendship?', I suggested that when the physical intimacy between friends assumes a maternal character, their interaction can be read as a way to confine women to traditional gender roles, reducing female friendship to a display of conventional femininity with the risk of depriving it of its authenticity. However, in this case Lesueur's decision to apply the mother-daughter model to Charlotte and Marcienne's relationship has a different effect. Through her friendship with Charlotte, Marcienne, whose sterile body asserts with energy its 'puissance passionnelle' in the relationship with Philippe, is enabled to recover a maternal function (*Lèvres*, 55). In this way, instead of restricting Marcienne's body and identity to a single role, Lesueur seems to allow her character to go beyond the split between the maternal and the sexual body. The text gives Marcienne the possibility of identifying with both identities (i.e. mistress and mother), thus blurring the lines between these traditional dichotomies. In this sense, Marcienne's character evokes the image of *la mère qui jouit* proposed by Julia Kristeva in *Des chinoises* (1974), a figure reconciling the two roles usually available to women in patriarchal societies, that of the idealized, desexualized mother disconnected from her body, and that of the erotic woman who, on the contrary, is all body.[89] Lesueur's text suggests not only that the active female body can simultaneously perform different functions and roles, but that, through the interactions with other women, a woman can acquire and combine multiple identities in different ways.

In addition to these elements, I would like to discuss another instrumental, active function played out through the body in novelistic representations of female friendship. This function comes into play when one of the heroines exerts, through her body, an influence on her friend's life, feelings, and behaviour, eventually affecting other characters and the plot itself. The example of Charlotte Fromentel in *Lèvres closes* is a case in point. Charlotte is in fact physically affected by her choice not to reveal Marcienne's secret, the first symptom not surprisingly being to keep her mouth shut as the title of the novel announces. At the same time, she actively instrumentalizes her body to prevail against Marcienne's resolutions and change the course of events. A few days after their first confrontation, Charlotte 'se disait souffrante, s'enfermait', and as her husband Jacques remarks: 'Lolotte n'est pas plus malade que moi. C'est un caprice' (*Lèvres*, 102). Hearing these words, Marcienne immediately feels responsible for Charlotte's condition and her emotions are altered by this awareness:

[89]Julia Kristeva, *Des chinoises* (Paris: Editions des Femmes, 1974).

> Celle-ci se troublait à constater la mâle sollicitude des deux hommes pour l'aimable et fragile créature si profondément atteinte par sa faute [...] Non seulement elle [Charlotte] gardait les lèvres closes, mais elle ne laissait échapper aucun symptôme involontaire de ce qui devait la tourmenter si cruellement. Marcienne en ressentit une émotion où la gratitude et la pitié se mêlaient d'impatience. (*Lèvres*, 104–105)[90]

From now on, Charlotte undergoes physical changes. When Marcienne, following Jacques' advice, goes to see her, 'l'air d'enfance dont s'imprégnaient ses joues fines et rondes, ses traits menus, devenaient plus sensibles par la claire gravité des yeux' (*Lèvres*, 102). When they subsequently spend an evening at the theatre, Marcienne:

> examinait Lolotte et la trouvait changée, même de visage. Quelque chose d'arrêté, de durci dans les traits. Ce n'était plus le flou enfantin, la fleur de chair toujours pétrie de sourires et creusée de fossettes. L'azur des yeux ne pétillait plus comme une source au soleil, mais s'immobilisait, s'assombrissait en surface d'abîme. (*Lèvres*, 127)

After her quarrel with Édouard, Charlotte is definitively taken ill. The reader finds out about Charlotte's malady in a passage focalized on Philippe and presented using free indirect style:

> Oui... c'est vrai... il le sait bien, cette ennuyeuse petite Mme Fromentel est très malade. Et Marcienne assure que c'est à cause d'eux [Marcienne et Philippe]. Une fièvre cérébrale survenue à la suite d'une scène avec M. de Sélys, où la jeune belle-sœur, qui avait surpris leur secret, se serait laissée malmener, accuser d'on ne sait quoi, plutôt que de les trahir. (*Lèvres*, 174)

Charlotte starts to spoil Marcienne and Philippe's intimacy by progressively becoming a 'présence, invisible mais si gênante, glissée dans leur tête-à-tête' (*Lèvres*, 175). If initially Marcienne 'n'accusait pas leur amour du crime involontaire', after a while she tells Philippe: 'Ce sont nos baisers qui la tuent' (*Lèvres*, 178, 180). Charlotte, through her illness, manipulates Marcienne, making her feel guilty. From the moment Marcienne starts to blame herself (and Philippe) for Charlotte's condition, her relationship with both Philippe and Édouard is affected: because of Charlotte's malady, Marcienne spends more time with

---

[90]It is also interesting to observe that Jacques, who considers Marcienne as Charlotte's 'modèle' and 'bon ange', says to her: 'Un mot de vous la guérira', thus introducing the idea that a woman's words and actions can have an impact on her female friend's body. As we will see, this idea is further reinforced in the text by Charlotte's illness, apparently caused by Marcienne's behaviour, paralleled by the fact that the instrumentalization of Charlotte's sick body affects Marcienne's decisions. See Lesueur, □ □*vres*, p. 105.

Édouard and is distracted from Philippe. Charlotte's sick body thus works as a sort of weapon. Its active power is clearly highlighted in the following excerpt, focalized once again on Philippe and featuring free indirect style:

> Ah! la malencontreuse personne que cette petite Mme Fromentel! Quel besoin avait-elle eu de découvrir leurs secrets, de se mêler de leurs affaires, de tomber dans une espèce de crise de nerfs [...] finalement de tout bouleverser avec sa fièvre cérébrale — une maladie faite exprès, qu'on ne pouvait pas mettre au compte de quelque microbe. (*Lèvres*, 200)

According to the text, Charlotte's 'maladie faite exprès', an expression suggesting Charlotte's intentionality, has changed everything ('tout bouleverser'). In the pages following this passage, Philippe also considers that if Charlotte dies, her death would bring Marcienne closer to Édouard and away from him. Finally, Charlotte effectively breaks the couple apart when she expresses her last wish on her death bed, once again asking Marcienne to leave Philippe (*Lèvres*, 209–10). Marcienne keeps her promise and the reader soon discovers that Charlotte did not die after all:

> Charlotte Fromentel ne mourut pas. Elle fut sauvée par ce qu'on est convenu d'appeler un miracle, et ce qui n'est que l'enchaînement d'effets très apparents à des causes très secrètes [...] Charlotte assura Marcienne que c'était son serment qui l'avait retenue au bord du tombeau. (*Lèvres*, 222–23)

Of course, Charlotte's recovery is a slow one, and Marcienne has to go with her to the south of France:

> Sa victoire définitive était à ce prix. Elle serait retombée malade d'inquiétude si elle avait dû rester seule, au loin, durant de longues semaines, laissant Marcienne exposée au dangereux vertige, et la sécurité de son frère au péril d'une défaillance. (*Lèvres*, 224)

Charlotte's malady and her recovery thus ensure her victory ('victoire') over Marcienne's will and desires, and guarantee the preservation of the status quo for Édouard's benefit.

Charlotte's body ultimately is the means through which the whole plot develops. On the one hand, Marcienne's adultery, her very unclosed lips, affects Charlotte's body, insofar as she is visibly consumed by the secret she keeps or, in other words, by the fact of keeping her own mouth shut. On the other hand, Charlotte's sick body influences Marcienne's feelings and actions because Marcienne feels responsible for her illness. Moreover, Charlotte's body exerts a broader impact on the story, since she more or less deliberately instrumentalizes it to provoke Marcienne and Philippe's break-up. This instrumentalization allows Charlotte to protect her brother and his marriage, thus ultimately reinforcing the existing order. What is interesting is that in *Lèvres closes* the sick female body instead of being weak, passive, and fragile, puts Charlotte in the position of the tormentor rather than the victim and allows her to play an active role in the story, even though initially one would not expect such a behaviour from a candid, innocuous, and submissive woman like her (the blonde heroine). The unusual status acquired by Charlotte entails a temporary reversal of the power relation between the two female characters and further questions the conventional reading of the female body. It is important to note that this reversal is possible only insofar as Marcienne, as Charlotte's friend, agrees to pay attention to, and to attribute a particular meaning to, her physical display of distress. In other words, the form of agency experienced by Charlotte through her body is possible only insofar as the novel sustains the idea that female friendship implies a connection between body and mind, that a friend's actions and words can affect another woman's body and that, in return, the female body can affect another's woman behaviour, even though in this case the result of this mechanism has nothing to do with women's emancipation.

In *Justice de femme* Simone also instrumentalizes her body, although in a very different way. Thanks to an anonymous letter, Gisèle's husband discovers the time and place of Gisèle and Jean's meeting. Simone, alerted by Gisèle's mother-in-law and concerned by the lovers' safety, rushes to the place of their encounter in order to warn them before the arrival of the suspicious husband. Once introduced into the house, the same where she used to meet Jean when they were having an affair, Simone desperately tries to persuade Gisèle to leave the place at once. However, when she discovers that Gisèle is the author of the anonymous letter and that she has planned everything in order to be caught by her husband, get a divorce, and become Jean's legitimate wife, Simone understands that all her efforts are in vain and decides to abandon Gisèle to her fate. At this moment Gisèle's husband arrives at the gate and Gisèle finally realizes the danger of the situation. Not only could her husband kill her or Jean, but according to French law if he comes with a police officer and proceeds to the 'constatation d'adultère' he will be able to file for divorce against his wife, depriving her of any title, money, and dignity, and preventing her from marrying her accomplice, a punishment that Gisèle considers worse than death itself. Therefore, Gisèle begs Simone to save her and:

> Comme un éclair, la même pensée les frappa. Simone pouvait se substituer à Gisèle!... Mme Chambertier, d'un geste à la fois de violence et de supplication, poussa son amie vers la chambre où se trouvait Jean. Déjà même, elle lui enlevait son chapeau, elle cherchait à lui dénouer les cheveux. (*Justice*, 259)

Simone, after a brief hesitation, voluntarily takes Gisèle's place:

> Quand Simone entendit rouvrir la porte de la chambre, elle se cacha le visage dans ses mains, pensant que ses cheveux et sa taille suffirait à justifier Gisèle sans qu'elle eût besoin de se laisser reconnaître. (*Justice*, 262)

This episode has an impact on all the characters involved, on their relationships, and on the course of events. First of all, Simone has literally protected Gisèle with her own body. Thanks to this substitution, the two women have deceived Gisèle's husband thus preventing him from ruining Gisèle's life. Gisèle's husband, who actually recognizes Simone, now considers her a loose woman and unsuccessfully tries to become her lover. For his part, when he sees Simone, Jean realizes that he is still in love with her:

> Quand il l'avait vue [...] prendre sur elle, si simplement, la honte de l'autre, et défaire ses cheveux blonds pour mieux avoir l'air de la pécheresse [...] il avait compris tout ce que, dans son cœur à lui, elle avait laissé de passion nostalgique et d'inexprimés regrets. (*Justice*, 263–64)

As for Gisèle, Simone has sacrificed her honour to her friend and now she cannot forgive her for putting her in this difficult position. Their friendship will never recover from the accident. Later on Simone will find out that Gisèle, left by Jean, has committed suicide. At the end of the novel, after many years, following her son's death Simone falls ill and asks to be brought to the south of France, where she had spent the summer with Gisèle and where she finally dies.

At this point, it is important to stress the fact that, in *Justice de femme,* women are repeatedly instrumentalized, treated as 'commodities', and considered interchangeable by men, as usually happens in patriarchal societies.[91] In fact, in the course of the novel Jean substitutes Simone with Gisèle, as his mistress, and Gisèle's husband similarly tries to substitute Gisèle with Simone by asking her to become his lover. In this particular episode,

---

[91]On the notion of 'women as commodities', see Luce Irigaray, *Ce sexe qui n'en est pas un* (Paris: Editions de Minuit, 1977).

however, the female body is instrumentalized and purposefully substituted by the women themselves in order to serve their own purposes (i.e. to protect Gisèle from her husband). Women's body is thus presented, once again, as a powerful vehicle of agency.

Conclusion

Given the centrality of the body to the definition of women's identities and experiences in the Belle Epoque, the purpose of this chapter was to show in what ways novelistic representations of female friendship intersect with contemporaneous scientific and popular discourses on the female body. If during the Belle Epoque women continued to be largely defined by their bodies, it was often men, and not women themselves, who produced the cultural meanings attached to them. As mothers, prostitutes, muses, or hysterics, women were often reduced to their physical selves and presented as the victims of biology or as passive objects of beauty to be displayed for the pleasure of a desiring male subject. The novelistic representations of female friendship discussed in this chapter both support and problematize these views.

In particular, in these novels, the traditional contrast between female characters, signalled by their physical appearance, can be nuanced and complicated in a way that subverts the conventional reading of the female body, thus suggesting that women cannot be confined to polarized and unequivocal versions of femininity. A blurring of the rigid dichotomies characteristically imposed by the male gaze is made possible by the very fact of representing two women interacting with one another and appropriating the act of seeing. As knowing subjects, women scrutinize and interpret each other's bodies, the latter becoming, for a change, the objects of *female* perception and appreciation. Moreover, in the case of Lesueur's novels, the modernist motif of fragmentation, which emerges through the splitting of the female characters' sense of identity, the deployment of multiple focalizers, and the absence of clear-cut moral positions, contribute to a dismantling of the conventional coding of female body types by creating ambiguity around the female characters. The representation of multilayered, ambiguous, somewhat contradictory female personalities does not entirely erase traditional inscriptions of femininity from Lesueur's texts, but the characteristics associated with these categories are shuffled around and some common expectations are contradicted, in a way that gives space to what Hélène Cixous will refer to, well after Daniel Lesueur's era, as 'l'infinie richesse de leurs [les femmes] constitutions singulières'.[92]

While physical intimacy between fictional female friends is sometimes represented as an inconsequential reaction to masculinity or an inauthentic bodily performance that strengthens the association of women with their traditional roles, other representations attest to Belle Epoque women's changing perceptions of their physical selves and to their efforts to reconcile the physical, the emotional, and the intellectual in order to express their desire to establish stronger connections, occasionally performing gestures which are invested with political meanings. Certain representations, particularly in *Justice de femme*, remain open to different interpretations, but it can be argued that they partially reinforce a negative view of female physical intimacy, and by extension of female friendship, insofar as they subordinate it to the heterosexual plot and present it either as a response to men or as a way to perform and reaffirm mainstream femininity. The female body also acquires a negative connotation whenever the friends' behaviour oversteps the boundaries of Belle Epoque politeness and is subsequently condemned as unladylike or even hysterical. By contrast, other representations, such as those found in *Lèvres closes* or *L'Un vers l'autre*, portray the female body as an active instrument of self-expression and an effective vehicle of female agency. In spite of the social norms that operate to codify and constrain it, in its interactions with other women the body manifests emotions, thoughts, and intentions, and it is used to communicate, to negotiate the terms of the relationship, to acquire and combine multiple identities (e.g. those of mistress and surrogate mother in the case of Marcienne), or to exert an impact on other characters and on the course of events.

My reading of fictional inscriptions of female bodies has offered a number of different perspectives on a long-standing debate over the authenticity of women's relationships. I have shown that the different ways in which female bodily interactions are represented allow the authors to characterize women's relations as genuine and meaningful, especially when a continuity between body and mind is promoted, or, on the contrary, as lacking depth and sincerity. In all of these ways, fictional representations of female friendship effectively operate to challenge, even while sometimes also confirming, Belle Epoque ideas about the female body and, more generally, about women's identities and their relationships. These novels thus lead us to re-evaluate our own ideas about Belle Epoque conceptions of female corporeality, and our views on these female authors as the active participants in contemporary debates about women, friendship, and the body.

---

[92]Hélène Cixous, 'Le Rire de la Méduse', *L'Arc*, 61 (1975), 39–54 (p. 39).

CHAPTER TWO

Female Mentorship and the Making of the *Femme Moderne* in the Female *Bildungsroman*

Introduction

Chapter One focused on the portrayal of physical intimacy between fictional female friends and the values attached to the female characters' appearance and bodily interactions, calling attention to the intersections between the embodiment of female friendship, the authenticity of female bonding, and the problematization or reinforcement of Belle Epoque assumptions about women's nature and identities. While this chapter still concerns itself with female dyads, the focus will move from emotional intimacy as expressed through the body to emotional intimacy in the form of intellectual support, and from friendship to mentorship. This introductory section will offer a preliminary discussion of the didactic value of women's writing in nineteenth-century France, the genre of the *Bildungsroman*, and the definition of mentorship.

Traditionally, women's writing has often served didactic purposes. In the nineteenth century, female authors of children's or didactic literature, such as for example the Comtesse de Ségur, found greater acceptance in society insofar as they were using literature to fulfil their 'natural' task of moral educators. In *La Petite Sœur de Balzac* (1989), an essay on nineteenth-century French women writers, Christine Planté has commented on women's difficulty in practising *l'écriture pour l'écriture* and on their need to justify their literary ambitions by evoking external reasons. In particular, Planté defines *écriture didactique* as a form of literary instrumentalization and moral propaganda confining women to a genre deemed both useful and appropriate.[1]

Under the early Third Republic, women continued to write a great deal of non-fictional, prescriptive texts such as etiquette manuals, textbooks, but also journal articles on fashion and housekeeping. Different as they may appear, their content is often similar and, what is more important, all these texts share a common purpose: to inform, counsel, and instruct the reader about codes of good practice and behaviour in conformity with the values and expectations of Belle Epoque French society. The tradition and practice of these popular

---

[1]Christine Planté, *La Petite Sœur de Balzac: essai sur la femme auteur* (Lyon: Presses Universitaires de Lyon, 2015 [1989]), pp. 151–60.

forms of writing continued to be linked to the educational role attributed to women in society. During the Belle Epoque, this educational role, which was conventionally associated with the figure of the mother, was also connected to the figures of the teacher (at primary and secondary levels) and the feminist activist. Teachers were in fact considered as the mentors par excellence, while feminists, regardless of the different orientations of the various groups, aimed at educating other women, not least by disseminating ideas through essays and conferences.[2] It is not a coincidence that the majority of the conduct books for girls analysed in this thesis were written by female authors. Even more importantly, most of the writers whose novels I take into account were teachers; they were contributing articles to women's magazines and, in some cases, even wrote conduct manuals and gave public lectures.[3] In all these ways, the authors were arguably positioning themselves as the wiser, more experienced *mentors* who shared their advice with the younger generations or, more simply, with other women.[4]

The didactic, sometimes moralizing aspect of women's writing emerged not only in articles, conduct books, essays, and children's stories, but also in the novels that women writers were specifically addressing to an adult female audience. For example, in discussing the *roman catholique*, a genre that was particularly popular between the 1870s and the First World War, Ellen Constans has observed that:

> selon les milieux catholiques, c'est dans la famille et par les femmes, les mères, que passe la transmission de la « saine morale » et des « bonnes idées ». Et qui mieux qu'une femme pouvait écrire pour les femmes, parler aux femmes? L'auteur-femme reste dans le domaine imparti à son sexe, elle prolonge par l'écriture fictionnelle son rôle d'éducatrice.[5]

---

[2]Real-life examples of teachers and feminists who used writing as a means to educate a female readership were Clarisse Juranville and Hubertine Auclert. The former was not only a teacher but also the author of a considerable quantity of didactic and moral texts addressed to young girls. The latter, one of the most well-known feminist activists of her period, was also a journalist and public speaker.

[3]Daniel Lesueur, Gabrielle Réval, and Yvette Prost all worked as teachers at some point in their lives. For more information, see Chapter Three, pp. 151–52. Both Lesueur and Réval wrote conduct books and, in one of those, Réval even defines herself as a 'guide'. See Daniel Lesueur, *Pour bien tenir sa maison* (Paris: Pierre Lafitte et Cie., 1911); Gabrielle Réval, *Pour bien connaître ses droits* (Paris: Pierre Lafitte et Cie., 1913), and *L'Avenir de nos filles* (Paris: Hatier, 1904), p. 15. In addition to this, over the years, Daniel Lesueur, Gabrielle Réval, Marcelle Tinayre, Colette Yver, and Marie-Louise Compain delivered conferences and public lectures on topics as diverse as literature, religion, foreign countries, feminism, and women's issues. All contributed articles to various magazines, such as *Femina* and *La Fronde*.

[4]It should be noted that female mentorship also played an important role in the careers of these authors. Indeed, during the Belle Epoque women often acted as *patronnes* in the literary and artistic contexts through the creation of salons, professional associations, or prizes, thus supporting and facilitating other women's access to the creative fields. For example, when starting her literary career, Gabrielle Réval received the support of well-known women writers, such as the journalist Séverine and the playwright Jeanne Marni. Réval hosted a literary salon which was attended, among others, by Marcelle Tinayre, Lucie Delarue-Mardrus, and Caroline de Broutelles, the founder of the *Prix Femina*. Réval herself became a member of the jury and additionally celebrated the talent of some of her colleagues in *La Chaîne des dames*, 5th edn (Paris: G. Crès, 1924).

[5]Ellen Constans, *Ouvri□ □ de lettres* (Limoges: Presses Universitaires de Limoges, 2007), p. 105.

According to Constans, these novels consist in '[r]écits d'éducation (de dressage?), qui se doivent de préparer l'adolescente à sa destinée d'épouse et de mère'.[6] More recently, Marie Kawthar Daouda has highlighted the role of a particular genre, the *roman édifiant*, in shaping the writing of those authors who made their appearance in the French literary panorama from the 1870s onwards. Mainly addressed to a female readership, these novels can be defined as 'recueils de modèles à imiter' responding to a specific conception of women's writing and reading. As explained by Daouda, women were commonly thought to be influenced and transformed by what they read, and female authors were consequently expected to provide their readers with good examples to follow, as mothers would do with their children, in a way that reinforces the link between maternal, educational, and authorial functions: 'La parole féminine est légitime dès lors qu'elle double la fonction biologique de transmission de la vie par une fonction morale de perpétuation de l'ordre social.'[7] Rotraud Von Kulessa points to the educational value of female-authored literature and to the perceived compatibility between women's writing and the maternal role of women as the main arguments still put forward by female authors during the Belle Epoque to legitimize their literary activity.[8]

If, in the case of the *romans catholiques* and *édifiants*, literature was put at the service of a conservative agenda, the female authors studied in this thesis championed a variety of ideas, arguably feminist, in fictions that often combined the genre of the *Bildungsroman* with the novel of ideas and the popular romance.[9] In this sense, Belle Epoque female novelists can be thought of as mentoring their readers through the medium of their fiction, at least to the extent that they tend to prove the validity of a thesis and dramatize the consequences of women's choices, in narratives which are often organized around the conflict between personal freedom and society's expectations. Margaret Cohen discusses how early nineteenth-century authors of sentimental novels (e.g. Mme Cottin) play with the logic of the

---

[6]Constans, *Ouvri□ □ □de lettres*, p. 127.
[7]Moreover, in comparing the *Bildungsroman* with the *roman édifiant*, Daouda argues that in the latter the heroine's access to society and adulthood is made possible by the presence of female figures acting as role models and embodying the ideal of the 'bienveillance féminine', that she defines as '[un] engendrement de l'esprit [qui] dépasse de beaucoup les cadres fixés par le roman édifiant d'inspiration catholique'. See Marie Kawthar Daouda, 'L'Anti-Salomé: représentations de la féminité bienveillante au temps de la Décadence (1850–1920)' (unpublished doctoral thesis, Université Européenne de Bretagne, 2015), pp. 19, 25, 33, 39.
[8]For more details, see Von Kulessa, *Entre la reconnaissance et l'exclusion*, pp. 184–95.
[9]Holmes employs the term 'feminist romance' with reference to 'a novel of ideas, with an explicit thesis, but [...] also a love story'. See Holmes, *Romance and Readership,* p. 34. The novels studied in this chapter present some of the main characteristics of the *Bildungsroman*: the heroine leaves her house and, in some cases, moves from the provinces to Paris; she is presented with a series of obstacles to overcome; by the end of the novel, she claims her rightful place within the social system, although this is not always a conventional one. Further clarification of my use of the term *Bildungsroman* is provided below.

classic or Realist novel as analysed by Barthes, by creating texts in which hermeneutic and proairetic codes work in parallel and function to demonstrate a truth established at the outset, building 'an increasingly crushing sense that the conflict between collective welfare and individual freedom is inevitable'. As argued by Cohen, in these novels 'there is no structural moment when the narrative comes to a close. The anguishes of the double bind can be prolonged as long as characters are willing and able'.[10] The novels considered in this chapter depart from this pattern by attempting a reconciliation between individual happiness and societal duty, by allowing the heroine either to enter into a marriage based on respect and equality, or to pursue a career in which her skills are put at the service of society.

With regard to Belle Epoque female authors, Waelti-Walters has noted that:

> Some lecture, some analyze, some prefer subversive description, and a few of them seem to have created critical structures unawares. Whatever their strategy, they have something important to say about human experience from a female perspective.[11]

Although I do not mean to imply that a didactic purpose always lies behind Belle Epoque women's fiction or is necessarily at the centre of the authors' concerns, it is possible to generally think of these works as a means to circulate, discuss, and negotiate ideas about women's lives and identities. Sometimes these ideas come to the fore regardless of the fact that the authors may have made certain choices purely in order to create dramatic tension and build effective narrative structures rather than to inform or instruct their readers. Nevertheless, this chapter will argue that in the case of our selected Belle Epoque novels of female development, the representation of female mentoring, the form of homosociality which concerns us in this chapter, can be read as a sign of the authors' vocation to guide their readers and, possibly, as an oblique representation of the didactic value of literature itself, insofar as these fictional bonds seem to extend beyond the world of the text itself, mirroring the author-reader relationship. I will further argue that the novelistic portrayals of female mentorship offered by these authors represent a continuation of the strong didactic tradition existing within the European literary canon in general, and within French female-authored educational literature in particular, but also, because of the progressive ideas supported in these texts, a subversion of its often conservative character.

Much scholarship has been dedicated to the genre of the *Bildungsroman*, 'one of the most successful and one of the most vexed contributions that German letters have made to

---

[10]Margaret Cohen, *The Sentimental Education of the Novel* (Princeton, NJ: Princeton University Press, 2002 [1999]) pp. 61–62.
[11]Waelti-Walters, *Feminist Novelists*, p. 180.

the international vocabulary of literary studies'.[12] First coined by philologist Karl Morgenstern in 1819 and then popularized by Wilhelm Dilthey in 1870 in his critical discussion of Johann von Goëthe's novel *Wilhelm Meisters Lehrjahre* (1795–96), for the past two hundred years the term has been used in different, more or less inclusive ways, and critical debates around the genre's historical, aesthetic, and ideological boundaries continue today. Although I am aware of the theoretical distinctions between the *Bildungsroman* and its subgenres (i.e. *Erziehungroman*, *Entwicklungroman*, *Berufsroman*), each covering various ideas of education, growth, maturation, self-discovery, development, apprenticeship, coming-of-age, and artistic formation, in this thesis I employ the label 'female *Bildungsroman*' as a broad category to designate Belle Epoque novels depicting the formation of the heroine as an individual through her social interactions.

The choice of focusing on the female *Bildungsroman* entails some considerations about the exclusion of female protagonists from traditional definitions of the genre and about the differences between male and female narratives of development. In a recent overview of feminist criticism of the genre, Anna Bogen points out two different approaches: the first one treats the female *Bildungsroman* as a genre *à part* and, by highlighting the latter's distinctive qualities, it aims at developing a female canon; the second one argues for the impossibility of the female *Bildungsroman*'s existence, before the late twentieth century, due to women's historical realities in patriarchal societies.[13] I shall not go into the details of the debate, but limit myself to presenting some general remarks which are relevant to my own discussion of Belle Epoque novels of female development. Although, in consideration of the disagreements highlighted above, talking of a female *Bildungsroman* can be problematic in itself, it should be noted that the protagonist's gender undoubtedly affects the structure and themes of this narrative. Male and female fictional trajectories differ insofar as, at least in the nineteenth century, women's autonomy and agency are limited by social conventions and female growth does not imply the individual's integration into the public sphere, but rather leads to a private, domestic destiny of wifehood and motherhood. If Franco Moretti identifies marriage as one of the characteristic elements of the *Bildungsroman*, particularly

---

[12]Tobias Boes, 'Modernist Studies and the *Bildungsroman*: A Historical Survey of Critical Trends', *Literature Compass*, 3.2 (2006), 230–42 (p. 230).

[13]Anna Bogen, *Women's University Fiction, 1880–1945* (London: Pickering & Chatto, 2014), pp. 11–13. For further discussion on the female *Bildungsroman* see Lorna Ellis, *Appearing to Dimish* (1999); Susan Fraiman, *Unbecoming Women* (1983); Rita Felski, 'The Novel of Self-Discovery', *Southern Review* (1986); *The Voyage In* (1983), ed by Abel Hirsch and Langland Abel; Esther Kleinbord Labovitz, *The Myth of the Heroine* (1986); Annis Pratt, *Archetypal Patterns in Women's Fiction* (1981); and Patricia Ann Meyer Spacks, *The Adolescent Idea* (1981). A more recent contribution is Giovanna Summerfield and Lisa Downward, *New Perspectives on the European Bildungsroman* (2010).

in the British literary tradition,[14] Juliette Rogers argues that for the male hero marriage is only 'a form of reward', whereas for the female heroine it 'is not a by-product but rather the main goal of the protagonist's quest'.[15] According to Rogers, the presence of a romance plot and the absence of strong mentorship relations are among the factors setting the Belle Epoque novel of female professional and educational development apart from the classic male *Bildungsroman*.[16] By contrast, for Jenny Odintz, one of the main interests of the *Bildungsroman* lies in 'its engagement with the formation of the gendered individual through education and other social processes, whereby girls, in coming of age and becoming women, were encouraged to emulate ideal patterns of feminine behavior and development'.[17] In her study, Odintz points out three elements that are specific to the female *Bildungsroman*: female maturity implies the 'awareness of social position as women, or [the] recognition and critique of society's demands on female individuals'; female friendships are represented in these texts as 'more than mere models for initiation into patriarchal society'; novels of female development gesture toward the constitution of female communities formed by readers, writers, and texts.[18] All the elements indicated by Rogers and Odintz as distinctive of the female *Bildungsroman*, i.e. the role played by female relationships, the interrogations around female identity and women's position in society, the inscription of the romance plot within the narrative, and the creation of reading communities, will be relevant to my discussion of female mentorship in the Belle Epoque female *Bildungsroman*.

As regards the specific form of female homosociality studied in this chapter, a mentorship relation can be broadly defined as a bond established between a wiser person who provides guidance, the mentor, and another who receives it, the protégé. In a thesis exploring the topic of female mentoring in French novels between 1650 and 1750, Ashley S. Headrick notes how the concept of mentoring is characterized by a 'universal vagueness about its origins and what it means', this relation being viewed either as a personal,

[14]In referring to the *Bildungsroman* as 'the "symbolic" form of modernity', Moretti distinguishes between novels belonging to the classification order (the English novel of marriage) and novels belonging to the transformation order (the French novel of adultery). For Moretti, the two categories translate different attitudes toward modernity and youth, and rely on opposing principles (identity vs change, fulfilled teleology vs open ending, stability vs instability, freedom vs happiness). See Franco Moretti, *The Way of the World: The Bildungsroman in European Culture*, trans. By Albert Sbragia (London: Verso, 2000 [1987]), pp. 3–13.
[15]Rogers further argues that at the beginning of the twentieth century, in spite of the presence of a romance plot, marriage is no longer represented as the heroine's main goal in novels of female professional and educational development. See Rogers, *Career Stories*, pp. 76–77. I will discuss in this chapter how the novels considered in my analysis subvert the ideal of romantic love.
[16]Rogers, *Career Stories*, pp. 50, 52.
[17]Jenny Odintz, 'Creating Female Community: Repetition and Renewal in the Novels of Nicole Brossard, Michelle Cliff, Maryse Condé and Gisèle Pineau' (unpublished doctoral dissertation, University of Oregon, 2014), p. 16. Rogers' remark, in contradiction with Odintz's statement, about the absence of strong female mentor figures in Belle Epoque novels of female development will be further discussed below.
[18]Odintz, 'Creating Female Community', pp. 138–39.

emotional, and nurturing bond or, to the extent that it is inserted in larger power structures, as a political tie.[19] In discussing the myths and models of mentoring in literature, Headrick refers to the Homeric *Hymn of Demeter* as a source for mentoring relationships between women and defines the female mentor as a threshold figure intervening at moments of transition to offer the heroine wisdom, support, and shelter, her presence in literature suggesting that female mentors were 'an essential part of a young woman's coming of age in France in the seventeenth and eighteenth centuries'.[20] Although the *Petit Larousse illustré* (1906), in defining the word *mentor* as 'Guide, gouverneur d'un jeune homme', seems to limit the scope of this relation to interactions between men, the female characters studied in this chapter are no strangers to the roles of mentor and *protégée*, and, as we shall see, the relationships that they foster with each other are not only nurturing and emotional but, above all, political.[21]

In this chapter, I am going to focus on three Belle Epoque novels of female development: Gabrielle Réval's *La Cruche cassée* (1904), Colette Yver's *Les Cervelines* (1903), and Marcelle Tinayre's *Hellé* (1889).[22] These texts have been selected for the importance that they accord to the representation of female mentorship during the heroine's passage from adolescence to adulthood but also at other times of need. In particular, they illustrate the crucial roles played in the heroine's life by a more experienced female character, who exerts an impact on the development of her subjectivity and tries to influence her choice of a path to follow.

My analysis of female mentoring in these texts builds upon Juliette Rogers' aforementioned remarks on the mentor figure in Belle Epoque women's novels of educational and professional development. Rogers defines the search for a positive role model or mentor as one of the 'mainstays of the traditional Bildungsroman plot'.[23] However, according to her observations:

> [M]ore often than not, Belle Epoque women's novels lack a powerful mentor figure. The reasons for this lack are varied: in certain fields, such as the sciences, there were few women in positions of authority who could mentor the younger female colleagues. The men in power

[19] Ashley S. Headrick, 'Women Mentoring Women in French Literature 1650–1750' (unpublished doctoral dissertation, University of North Carolina, 2006), pp. 43–48.
[20] Headrick, 'Women Mentoring Women', pp. 50–55, 154–55.
[21] *Petit Larousse illustré: nouveau dictionnaire encyclopédique*, 3, ed. by Claude Augé (Paris: Librairie Larousse, 1906).
[22] Gabrielle Réval, *La Cruche cassée* (Paris: Calmann-Lévy, 1904); Marcelle Tinayre, *Hellé* (Paris: Nelson and Calmann-Lévy, n.d. [1904]); Colette Yver, *Les Cervelines* (Memphis, Tenn.: General Books, 2012 [1903]). The novels will hereafter be referred to as *Cruche, Hellé*, and *Cervelines*. All in-text page references are to these editions.
[23] Rogers, *Career Stories*, p. 114.

often abuse their position and don't take their female students seriously. In other domains, such as education, where the staff was entirely female, the mentor figures are distant and cold or their behavior provides inappropriate examples for their students.[24]

Rogers refers in particular to Marguerite in Réval's novel *Sévriennes* (1900) and Claudine in Colette's *Claudine à l'école* (1900), suggesting that '[b]ecause both Marguerite and Claudine have difficulties finding women in positions of authority whom they could emulate, they must develop their own definitions of the femme nouvelle'. Later on, she offers the counterexample of Laure in Compain's *L'Un vers l'autre* (1903) who, on the contrary, is able to achieve the strong kind of mentor-disciple relationship usually found in the male *Bildungsroman* and is never disappointed with her female role models.[25] Rogers' observation about the absence of 'a powerful mentor figure' in Belle Epoque women's novels, while no doubt applicable to many of the novels of educational and professional development she studied, is nuanced by the examples offered by the novels considered in this chapter.

One of the features that the three novels share is the presence in the text of a *femme moderne*, a strong, educated, and economically independent female character who has achieved or has the potential to achieve a greater degree of agency and freedom without necessarily rejecting every aspect of conventional femininity (i.e Mme Villebau in *La Cruche cassée*, Jeanne Bœrk in *Les Cervelines*, and Hellé herself in *Hellé*). As noted by Beth Gale:

> The idea of the New Woman contains an altruistic element. The New Woman does not merely claim educational rights for herself; she then passes her knowledge on to the next generation. Having attained a certain level of confidence and autonomy, she then works to prepare girls to participate in society and effect positive change.[26]

A mentoring function thus seems to be inscribed in the figure of the *femme nouvelle* and also, I would argue, in that of the *femme moderne*.[27] The female mentor, however, could

---

[24]Rogers, *Career Stories*, p. 50.
[25]Rogers, *Career Stories*, pp. 99, 103. Compain's *L'Un vers l'autre* has already been discussed in Chapter One, pp. 68–69 and 75–77. Réval's *Sévriennes* will be further discussed in Chapter Three, pp. 178–92.
[26]Gale, *A World Apart*, p. 93.
[27]On the distinction between *femme moderne* and *femme nouvelle*, see p. 25 in this thesis. In both *La Cruche cassée* and *Hellé* the expression 'femme moderne' is privileged over that of 'femme nouvelle'. See *Cruche*, p. 186 and *Hellé*, p. 46. The example of Hellé, who is the *femme moderne* in the text, differs from those found in the other two novels and corresponds more closely to those heroines evoked by Rogers, who lacking a satisfying female role model are encouraged to become themselves the *femmes modernes*. As for Jeanne Bœrk, although smoking cigarettes and refusing the traditional roles of wife and mother, this character has a very feminine appearance and little in common with the stereotypically mannish 'New Woman' that, in Belle Epoque France, was still largely perceived as a foreign import and ridiculed.

also be a character defined in opposition to the *femme moderne*, as is the case with Mme Marboy in *Hellé*.

In offering a close reading of these novels, I seek to better understand what kind of influence fictional women exert on each other within a mentorship relation and to highlight the fact that what lies at the heart of these texts is always the definition of womanhood itself. Fictional female mentors, in fact, can actively contribute to or try to prevent the shaping of the heroine as a *femme moderne*, guiding her through a period of changes and negotiating with her the meanings and possibilities of womanhood. In this sense, the portrayals of female mentorship considered below can be said to constitute different examples of 'vertical' or 'horizontal' homosociality, whose narrative function is to subvert or maintain the gender status quo within the fictional world of the novel. For the purpose of this research, the term 'vertical' homosociality will be used to talk about relationships that allow women to challenge traditional institutions and exert forms of power, while 'horizontal' or normative homosociality will be used with regard to 'relations that are based on emotional closeness, intimacy, and a non-profitable form of friendship' in harmony with the existing social order.[28] The latter more closely resembles the models of female homosociality described in nineteenth-century and Belle Epoque conduct books and essays on friendship, which required women to sustain each other in conforming to mainstream femininity and in performing traditional duties.[29] Insofar as these novels tend to disrupt, or at least problematize, the 'dominant discourse' about women's relationships and, more generally, about femininity carried out in normative literature, they contribute to establishing an ideological 'counter-discourse' on the values and identities of Belle Epoque women.[30] At the same time, in more strictly literary terms, the three novels variously deconstruct the model of romantic love, redefine the notion of the heroine, and describe a new kind of quest for her, thus contributing to the modernization of the novel at the turn of the century.

---

[28]The distinction between 'vertical' and 'horizontal' homosociality is proposed by Nils Hammarén and Thomas Johansson, 'Homosociality: In Between Power and Intimacy', *SAGE Open*, 4.1 (2014), 1–11 (p. 5).

[29]For a discussion of these models, see pp. 19–23 in this thesis.

[30]For Richard Terdiman, the 'dominant discourse' organizes social existence and reproduction, presenting itself as transparent, self-evident, universal, internalized and ubiquitous. 'Counter-discourses' develop different modes of opposition against the 'dominant discourse' and these modes can be either thematic or formal. Although Terdiman dedicates a whole chapter to the *Bildungsroman*, he argues that 'the genre's tactic was not to *subvert* the dominant but rather to seek to *recontain* it' (p.87). For Terdiman, by providing an initiation into the post-revolutionary cultural system, this genre exposes the existence of the dominant discourse and its contradictions but posits itself on a continuum between complicity and denunciation. See Richard Terdiman, *Discourse/Counter-discourse: The Theory and Practice of Symbolic Resistance in Nineteenth-century France* (Ithaca; London: Cornell University Press, 1985), in particular the chapter 'Discourses of Initiation', pp. 85–116. As we shall see, the novels analysed in this chapter seem to be more explicit than those considered by Terdiman in their questioning of dominant values.

The following sections will offer separate discussions of the three novels and the ideas emerging from each text, starting with Réval's *La Cruche cassée* (1904).

La Cruche cassée **and the Conflict between Biological and Spiritual Mothers**

Gabrielle Réval's *La Cruche cassée* (1904) is a feminist novel of ideas about the redefinition of the concept of 'female honour'. Its major contentions concern the need for a new moral code for the modern woman, the right to free love, and the defence of the unwed mother.[31] The title refers to Jean-Baptiste Greuze's painting *La Cruche cassée* (1773), the image of a young girl allegorizing the awakening to sensual love and the loss of virginity. The novel's heroine, the twenty-one-year-old Aline, is repeatedly compared to and associated with this image (*Cruche*, 126, 143, 159).

At the beginning of the novel, Aline is expected by her mother, a vain woman of aristocratic origins with a very conservative view of women's role and destiny in society, to marry the older and rich town doctor in order to rescue her family from its debts. Unwilling to consent and determined to work so as to earn a living for herself and her family, Aline takes refuge at her godmother's house, where she gets a feminist education and simultaneously falls in love with Mme Villebau's nephew, Maurice. Although reciprocating her love, Maurice, who is legally unable to get a divorce from his mad wife, a woman he has never loved but to whom he is bound by duty and honour, cannot marry Aline. However, the two, with Mme Villebau's consent, become secretly engaged. When Aline's mother discovers that her daughter has a lover, she kills Maurice and, therefore, goes to prison. A grief-stricken Aline subsequently moves to Paris where, with the unwavering support of her father, brother, and godmother, she finds a job and gets increasingly involved with a feminist charity sheltering pregnant women. Eventually, she falls in love with another man who accepts her past and she is reconciled with her repentant mother, thus being rewarded for her honesty and courage.

In discussing novels published in the period 1890–1910, Gale has pointed out that 'the theme of weak family bonds returns repeatedly, and helps to explain the characters' need to seek emotional fulfilment outside the home' and, I would argue, the need to seek

[31]For Marcel Ballot, a contemporary reviewer, the novel tackles two main issues: that of the 'fille-mère' and that of the possibility, for a man, of divorcing his mad wife. See Marcel Ballot, 'La Vie Littéraire. Le Roman féministe: *La Cruche cassée*; *Le Ruban de Vénus* par Mme Gabrielle Réval', *Le Figaro*, 8 October 1906.

guidance and more effective role models elsewhere, especially when the figure of the biological mother appears inadequate or disappointing.[32] In this case, although respecting and loving her mother, Aline rejects her as a role model and increasingly questions the ideal of womanhood to which she urges her to conform, to the point that even her loving but weak father notes: 'mon enfant, tu te montres chaque jour différente de l'idée que ta mère s'est faite de toi!' (*Cruche*, 30). The way in which Aline challenges her mother's authority and, even more importantly, the fact that the novel's ending endorses the daughter's choices (in the final scene, it is the mother who, like a chastened prodigal son, comes back home to be forgiven by her daughter, *Cruche*, 344), mark a break away from the pattern set by earlier novels. As argued by Alison Finch, early nineteenth-century women's fiction usually promotes filial duty and devotion. In these novels, the daughter's rebellion is only temporary and the parent's position is usually reinforced.[33] Another significant difference between Réval's novel and previous fiction can be found in the representation of the biological mother. In pre-1830 fiction and well into the nineteenth century, according to Finch, mothers tend to be idealized as being unconditionally loving and self-sacrificing, or they are 'conveniently dead'. In any case, they are rarely represented in a negative way.[34] By contrast, I would argue, the selfish, manipulative, and controlling Mme Robert, Aline's mother, more closely resembles the 'deranged, destructive' mother-figure, 'the hyperbolically haughty or oppressive matriarch', who opposes the young girl's self-determination, often by promoting an arranged marriage.[35]

Mme Robert's mission in the text is to ensure the preservation of the status quo through the education of her daughter. In a passage that highlights the characteristics she values in a woman, Mme Robert tells Aline:

> [I]l importe que pour les autres, tu [Aline] sois toujours la jeune fille chrétienne, sage, soumise, prudente, et au-dessus de tous les soupçons; tu as un bien plus précieux que toi-même, c'est ta réputation. (*Cruche*, 59)

---

[32]Gale, *A World Apart*, p. 67. Sarah Vandegrift Eldridge has observed a similar tendency in German fiction: 'authors depict intergenerational misunderstandings and disagreements about likeness or obedience as most acute in biological relationships, whereas foster parents or surrogate parental figures often appear more attuned to more modern notions of individuality and development.' See Sarah Vandegrift Eldridge, *Novel Affinities: Composing the Family in the German Novel, 1795–1830* (Rochester, NY: Camden House, 2016), p. 57.

[33]Finch, *Women's Writing*, p. 42.

[34]Finch, *Women's Writing*, pp. 44–45.

[35]Finch, *Women's Writing*, pp. 45–46. On the contrary, in Réval's novel as in earlier fiction, the father is a more positive, less oppressive figure. See Finch, *Women's Writing*, pp. 47–48.

Although acknowledging the existence of a double standard ('le monde est sévère pour les femmes, il est tout indulgence pour l'homme. Il admet deux honneurs'), Mme Robert reproaches her daughter for 'son esprit de discussion' and declares: 'Toujours il en a été ainsi, et nous n'avons qu'à obéir aux lois qu'ont respectées nos mères' (*Cruche*, 60, 61). Mme Robert's language and her views seem to be modelled after those characterizing conduct books of this period and her sentences often sound didactic. For example, she occasionally employs peremptory maxims, as in the following excerpt: 'Je me rappelle d'une phrase qui dès ma jeunesse m'a servi de règle: « Rien n'est plus habile qu'une honnête conduite »' (*Cruche*, 60). Because Aline repeatedly expresses reservations about her mother's principles, the tone of the dialogue between these two characters is often polemical. Aline and her mother disagree on many topics, including the question of female education and employment. While Aline regrets not having had the chance to push her studies any further, Mme Robert finds her education sufficient to become a good wife, her daughter not being in need of a degree or a job like any ordinary, poor girl: 'Aline avait souhaité poursuivre ses études au delà du brevet élémentaire: rudement on lui fit entendre qu'une petite fille bien née n'avait pas besoin d'être instruite comme une pauvresse' (*Cruche,* 27). These words remind us to what extent the ideal of womanhood promoted by Mme Robert is linked to the question of class (this model of femininity only concerns the 'bien nées', i.e. bourgeois and upper-class women), and also point to the subversive power of education, the means through which a modern woman can attain her independence and possibly elude the social expectation that she marry and make babies. When Aline begs her mother to let her work and achieve economic independence instead of getting married to the doctor ('laisse-moi travailler librement, je gagnerai ma vie, j'ai du courage, ne me condamnez pas à manger un pain qui me répugne', *Cruche*, 110), Mme Robert strongly opposes her wishes and replies:

> Ah! tu es bien de ton temps... de ce temps qui abolit le passé, les traditions du foyer et vous tourne la tête, en vous promettant salaire, bonheur, liberté, liberté surtout! Comme si la femme pouvait s'affranchir de tout ce qui fait sa vie, et risquer, pour une utopie, de jeter le désordre dans la famille [...] [J]e veux maintenir ce qu'avant nous d'autres ont respecté, et si les miens sont incapables de comprendre leur devoir, c'est moi qui le leur apprendrai... (*Cruche*, 111)

Mme Robert's aim is to teach ('apprendre') her daughter what her 'devoir' is, convincing or forcing her to adhere to a conservative kind of femininity. In this passage, the word 'liberté' (which is repeated twice) is negatively associated with the terms 'utopie' and 'désordre'. In the context of *fin-de-si□cle* degeneration, women's freedom is perceived, by Mme Robert, as a threat to the stability of the family and, by extension, society. Mme Robert's discourse is set in opposition to those pronounced by the most progressive and emancipated female characters found in Réval's novels, who frequently employ the very same word, 'liberté', in a positive sense, any time they discuss the condition of women and their possibilities.[36] Despite Mme Robert's insistence, Aline does not submit to her mother's will and looks for support and understanding outside her family, by turning to a woman who embodies a different type of femininity and whose actions are guided by other principles.

Interestingly, Mme Villebau is first mentioned in the text in the passage describing Aline's education:

> Aline pianota, broda, dessina, sous les yeux de sa mère; mais, pendant les longues heures que celle-ci consacrait aux visites, l'enfant se jetait éperdument sur les livres de la bibliothèque ou sur les ouvrages que sa marraine, madame Villebau, lui envoyait de Paris. Madame Villebau, veuve d'un camarade du capitaine Robert, était un écrivain des plus connus et des plus aimés: elle s'intéressait à la vie de sa filleule, cherchant, par des lectures et une correspondance assez régulière, à orienter la pensée indécise, la rêverie de cette grande enfant. (*Cruche*, 27–28)

The mentoring role Mme Villebau plays in Aline's life is highlighted from the outset, her primary function being to 'orienter' Aline and allow her to improve her education. Mme Villebau first performs this task through the medium of literature and writing. She regularly corresponds with her god-daughter ('une correspondance assez régulière') and also sends her books ('les ouvrages') from Paris.[37] Moreover, Mme Villebau is a successful writer. The professional identity of this mentor figure and her attempts to guide Aline 'par des lectures' seem to stress the link previously discussed between female mentoring, the educational role of women, and literature.

With regard to the genre of the *roman édifiant*, Daouda observes that at the end of the nineteenth century the character of the teacher is replaced, in this kind of novel, by 'la femme-auteur mise en abîme', which functions as a 'double littéraire chargé d'expliciter la

---

[36]In Réval's novel *Sévriennes* (1900), the word 'libre' is repeated twenty-four times, the word 'librement' five times, and the word 'liberté' nine times.

[37]In this respect, the representation of female mentorship in Réval's novel follows the pattern set by earlier fiction. As noted by Hope Christiansen in an article focused on Marie d'Agoult's *Nélida* (1846) and *Valentia* (1847), in these texts both heroines are introduced to reading material by their female mentors. The 'autodaxie' allows them to gain a better understanding of their condition as women and prepares them to receive the lessons later provided by their mentors. For Christiansen, 'the combination of independent study and guidance from their mentors constitutes the very kind of education that d'Agoult desired for all women, one governed by reason.' Similar elements can be found in Réval's novel, as discussed in this section. See Christiansen, 'Educating Nélida and Valentia', p. 242.

volonté morale de l'auteur'. According to Daouda, this shift is linked to the growing presence of women in the literary field, to the fact that female writing starts to promote discourses that go beyond the 'discours édifiant', and to the possibility of representing female benevolence as existing outside the familial sphere.[38] Daouda thus remarks that '[l]a projection de la femme auteur de romans édifiants dans un personnage relayant sa pensée, faisant à la fois office de double autobiographique et d'éducateur, est un procédé récurrent'.[39] In *La Cruche cassée*, which, as already noted, can be considered as a feminist novel of ideas interweaving the *Bildungsroman* and the romance plots, Réval adopts this very strategy, insofar as the character of Mme Villebau is invested with an educative function and serves as the author's fictional double. Indeed, Mme Villebau shares with Réval a number of views on the position of women in society, for example in terms of women's education, career, and social awareness. In the aforementioned manual *L'Avenir de nos filles*, which also appeared in 1904, Réval comments on the societal changes occurring at the turn of the century and on the fact that marriage does not represent the main aspiration or the only option available to women any more. For Réval, freedom and responsibility should be the two principles at the core of girls' education. Moreover, mothers have a new duty toward their daughters, which consists in attending to their future by orienting them toward a suitable career. Independence is here presented as the key to happiness. However, like Mme Villebau, Réval is far from hostile to the ideals of marriage and motherhood. On the contrary, she believes that girls should choose a profession that allows them to reconcile their natural (i.e. maternal) and social functions, because '[i]llusion ou réalité, la tendre image de la femme s'appuyant à l'homme, « comme la vigne s'appuie à l'ormeau », rattache dans une commune palpitation les cérébrales qui s'émancipent, aux autres femmes, heureuses de vivre obscures au foyer conjugal'.[40]

The idea that a female mentor-author can educate her *protégée*-reader through books, as Mme Villebau and, possibly, Réval herself are attempting to do, and the idea that women in general can use literature as an instrument to enlighten and support other women, are further reinforced later on in the text, when Aline reads Jeanne Marni's novel *Celles qu'on ignore* (1899) and Georges de Peyrebrune's *Les Fr□res Colombe* (1880) to the

---

[38]Daouda, 'L'Anti-Salomé', p. 38.
[39]Daouda, 'L'Anti-Salomé', p. 38.
[40]Réval, *L'Avenir de nos filles*, p. 303. The ideas discussed in this paragraph can be found in 'L'Appel aux mères: conclusion', pp. 293–303. In a 1911 interview meant to prove that Réval's opinions and the kind of feminism she promotes are unthreatening to men, Réval makes the case for women's evolution through intellectual development but not for their emancipation. She insists that marriage and motherhood remain women's preferred choices, that education makes those who can marry better companions for men, and not their rivals, while allowing those who cannot marry to be independent. See Joseph Bois, 'La Femme de demain', *Le Temps*, 26 August 1911.

women of the 'Refuge des femmes enceintes', where she starts to build up a library. Aline is in fact convinced that these texts have the potential to provide comfort and guidance to the women she is assisting (*Cruche*, 293, 301, 303). Even though in *La Cruche cassée* the reader is never explicitly addressed, the reference to these texts seems to create an intertextual space in which the reading community built within the novel appeals to and mirrors the real-life community composed by Réval's, Marni's, and Peyrebrune's readers. It is in this sense that the possibility of establishing female mentoring bonds mediated by literature is invested with a considerable power and seems to extend beyond the boundaries of the text, Aline's *Bildung* through books paralleling the readers' *Bildung*.

Aline is initiated into the principles of feminist thought by Mme Villebau, who is defined by the narrator as 'l'incarnation de l'âme moderne' (*Cruche*, 126). After having openly confessed to her godmother: 'j'ai des forces à utiliser, cette vie rétrécie me pèse, je souffre de mon ignorance, marraine!' (*Cruche*, 129) she receives a training on women's rights and claims:

> Aline regardait avec étonnement sa marraine: c'était la première fois qu'elle entendait défendre les idées féministes, si ridiculisées dans sa petite ville. Elle écoutait attentive, de plus en plus surprise, madame Villebau lui expliquant les revendications de la mère, de l'épouse à son foyer, les lois du travail, de la concurrence, la propriété du salaire. (*Cruche*, 130)

Mme Villebau makes up for Aline's self-acknowledged ignorance by instructing her in the areas of knowledge deemed important for women, which indeed broadly correspond to the topics discussed by Réval herself in the aforementioned essay *Pour bien connaître ses droits* (1913).[41] Although these feminist ideas might not have been entirely new to Aline, until then they had only been treated with scorn by her conservative entourage. However, now that they are spoken of by Mme Villebau, the figure whose authority and worthiness Aline recognizes, they acquire value and credibility. Unlike those of Mme Robert, Mme Villebau's words function, as language philosopher J. L. Austin would have put it, as 'perlocutionary acts'. Perlocutionary acts indicate 'what we bring about or achieve *by* saying something, such as convincing, persuading, deterring, and even, say, surprising or misleading'.[42] While Mme Robert's words go unheard, Mme Villebau's are effective because uttered in the right conditions; in particular, they offer new, valid answers in the changing world of the Belle

[41] See Réval, *Pour bien connaître ses droits.*
[42] John Langshaw Austin, 'Lecture IX', in *How to Do Things with Words: The William James Lectures delivered at Harvard University in 1955* (London: Oxford University Press, 1962), pp. 108–19 (p. 108).

Epoque, and they are pronounced by someone whose authority is recognized by the other person participating in the act.[43] Mme Villebau then goes on to contradict and ridicule the scientist Paul Broca's misogynistic assumptions about women's intellectual inferiority and talks of a 'renaissance féministe', her opinion thus being held up against that of male experts (*Cruche*, 130–31).

When discussing with her nephew Maurice the question of female honour and the rights of the unwed mother, Mme Villebau addresses Aline and invites her to become more informed and aware:

> Ma chérie, je n'ai pas le dessein de blesser tes oreilles, mais tu n'es plus une gamine: dans la vie, il y a de telles iniquités qu'il faut de bonne heure s'habituer à considérer les êtres et les faits sous un angle exact. (*Cruche*, 144)

In telling Aline that she is not a 'gamine' any more, Mme Villebau is suggesting that her access to adulthood entails the understanding of women's inferior position in society. This kind of conversation marks Aline's spirit and the stay at her godmother's house clearly represents a transformational experience for her:

> Aline, un peu rouge, suivait madame Villebau; son esprit tendu cherchait à comprendre ces idées, si différentes des idées qu'on lui avait apprises, et son cœur s'associait à la généreuse révolte de sa marraine. Sur la route, le soleil, très haut, jetait derrière eux l'ombre trapue et déformée du groupe. Ainsi la vie, allant par les chemins, déformait les idées! Et plus la lumière se haussait dans l'esprit, plus petites et plus laides devenaient les ombres vivantes que projette sur terre l'harmonieuse et puissante réalité. (*Cruche*, 149)

In this excerpt, the word 'révolte' acquires a positive connotation and Aline's (liberating) process of education is described through the use of an analogy which recalls Plato's allegory of the cave. Moreover, the use of free indirect speech indicates transformation, not just by its content but also by the fact that it suggests an in-between position, due to the slips and ambiguities that it creates between character and third-person narrator. Aline's evolution is also confirmed in the following sentence, in which the narrator observes how the effects of Mme Villebau's influence start to counteract those provoked by the actions of Aline's mother: 'Peu à peu, elle [Aline] livrait son esprit et son cœur; tout ce que l'autorité

---

[43]On the necessary conditions to be satisfied for the utterance to be performative and on the cases in which the performative utterances misfire, see Austin, 'Lecture II' and 'Lecture III', in *How To Do Things With Words*, pp. 12–24 and 25–38. Similar observations about felicitous versus infelicitous utterances apply to the other couples of successful and unsuccessful mentors discussed later on in this chapter.

étroite et vétilleuse de la mère avait soigneusement comprimé, s'épanouissait dans la joie' (*Cruche*, 153). Even though Mme Villebau never encourages Aline openly to rebel against her mother, but rather to affirm her own will while still respecting her family, the type of initiation provided by the two older women tends toward two conflicting ideals of womanhood: the *femme traditionnelle* and the *femme moderne*. In following her godmother's lead, Aline is starting to remove herself from her biological mother's example and from the kind of femininity she represents, progressively growing into a *femme moderne*.[44]

Since Mme Villebau believes that '[l]es actes feront plus que des paroles' (*Cruche*, 146), Aline is encouraged to act upon the new principles she is learning and actively engages with the feminist movement by taking part in charity activities. On the subject of female charity work, historians remind us that women's engagement with social problems could represent a conservative force. For example, Bonnie Smith has argued that nineteenth-century rich bourgeois women of northern France 'attempted to convert their domestic vision to social policy' and 'approached thorny public problems from a familial and theological perspective'.[45] Discussing the topic of female charity, Smith has observed that:

> women's concern with women and children had important consequences. Not only did the domestic perspective of women determine their choice, it set the conditions for the reception of charity. Women monitored the behavior of their beneficiaries and revealed in the organization of their societies a firm intention to mold members of their sex into their own image, and thereby to extend, multiply, and strengthen their own domestic standards until they became a social norm.[46]

In other words, these charitable ladies were less prone to help women who did not conform to their standards (e.g. unwed mothers and fallen women) and, through their charitable institutions, they sought to perpetrate a series of conservative and anachronistic beliefs on women and society, 'molding' other women according to restrictive definitions of womanhood.[47] Although in *La Cruche cassée* Réval suggests that women should always be

---

[44]Subsequently, Aline will continue to improve her education in Paris, by attending feminist conventions in her new role of stenographer. See *Cruche*, p. 308.

[45]Bonnie G. Smith, *Ladies of the Leisure Class: The Bourgeoises of Northern France in the Nineteenth Century* (Princeton; Guildford: Princeton University Press, 1981), pp. 134, 135.

[46]Smith, *Ladies of the Leisure Class*, p. 138.

[47]According to Anne Martin-Fugier: 'La philanthropie n'a évidemment rien de révolutionnaire [...] Elle maintient en place la structure, la renforce. Cette tâche conservatrice est dévolue aux femmes des classes aisées.' See Anne Martin-Fugier, *La Bourgeoise: femme au temps de Paul Bourget* (Paris: Grasset, 1983), p. 212. For Smith, however, these conservative positions increasingly came under attack toward the end of the century under the anti-Catholic impetus of the Third Republic. For more details, see Smith 'Society: Charity versus Capitalism', in *Ladies of the Leisure Class*, pp. 123–61.

concerned with the dignity and well-being of other women, and although this involves being sympathetic toward unwed mothers and their children (indeed, Mme Villebau strongly defends the 'idée de la maternité toujours et partout légitime', *Cruche*, 147), some of the novel's plot details indicate that only those women who decide to assume their parental role and keep their children are worthy of the kind of attention and help that female networks of support, along with the institutions, can provide. For example, during the stay at her godmother's, Aline pays a visit to Louise, an unmarried young mother generously rescued by Mme Villebau. Aline is indignant at the thought of Louise abandoning her new-born baby and, with Maurice's complicity, persuades her to keep him in exchange for a job (*Cruche*, 158–63). However, in the novel this moralizing attitude is not directly linked to a form of Catholic feminism and the ideas promoted are overall progressive.

Once in Paris, Aline starts to visit the 'Refuge des femmes enceintes' on behalf of her godmother and gets increasingly involved with this open-minded charity. The refuge as well as the woman who first welcomes Aline, 'une vieille infirmière en coiffe, l'air souriant et maternel, comme il convient à l'entrée d'une *nursery*', are described in positive terms. Moreover, it is specified that in the institution '[l]e culte est libre' and women are not expected to be religious or to take part in any sort of religious practice (*Cruche*, 294). Mademoiselle Guémadeuc, the director of the charity, interestingly points out that women of all classes and conditions arrive at the institution: 'des filles de gens riches qui ont été jetées dehors après leur faute, des travailleuses, ouvrières, institutrices, artistes, des servants, des rôdeuses, des femmes sortant de prison' (*Cruche*, 296). An illegitimate or unwanted pregnancy is presented as a social problem that brings women together regardless of their social background and that needs to be faced collectively, requiring women to join forces against male tyranny and social prejudice in order to reaffirm their (maternal) rights. When Aline first meets these 'fallen women', she introduces herself by saying: 'Je suis venue à vous, mes amies, comme une sœur', thus evoking the concept of female solidarity and sorority, a concept restated in the sentence: 'fraternellement elle cherchait à consoler, à relever les misérables' (*Cruche*, 300, 302). In addition to being motivated by feminist principles, Aline feels close to these women because she identifies with them. In fact, she considers that, had she not been lucky, she could have found herself in their situation (*Cruche*, 298). From that day on, she takes an active interest in the fate of these rejected mothers; she solicits the support of other women ('Aline recueillait des secours, intéressait à ces malheureuses quelques jeunes employées de la librairie') and starts to put together 'le premier fond d'une bibliothèque' (*Cruche*, 303). The novel thus shows how, having turned into a *femme moderne* with the support of her godmother, Aline becomes more and more concerned with the education, rights, and general welfare of other women. It is not a coincidence that one of Aline's first actions consists in reading books to these women and starting a library; books were in fact the first instrument through which Mme Villebau, at a distance, tried to guide and support her *protégée*. In this sense, both Mme Villebau and Aline confirm Gale's assertion about the 'altruistic element' involved in the idea of the New Woman, whose purpose in fiction was to instruct and awaken other women.[48]

In addition to providing a moral and political education, Mme Villebau allows her *protégée* to access the professional field and become economically independent. When Aline realizes how deeply her family has sunk into debt, she asks for her godmother's financial support (a support readily given), but she also resolves to pay the debt off with her own work. However, Aline lacks any kind of professional training and she needs to be rather secretive about her plans because her family, especially her mother, strongly opposes her will. Therefore, she seeks her godmother's advice, first by letter and then in person (*Cruche*, 50–51, 131). Mme Villebau preaches a kind of moderate feminism according to which women should primarily aim at finding their happiness and independence within a marriage founded on equality. In fact, more than once she invites Aline to consider marriage as a desirable option, warning her about the difficulties that a solitary life involves (*Cruche*, 123–25, 201).[49] However, she also believes in women's right to work and is more than willing to help her god-daughter to find a job. Therefore, she buys her a typewriter, she asks her nephew to train her, and she temporarily hires her as her personal assistant. She also introduces her into a broader professional network, so that Aline will be able to continue working once she gets back to her parents' house (*Cruche*, 131). After Maurice's death, with Mme Villebau's support, Aline moves to Paris and obtains a job in a publishing house, where she works first as a typist and then as a stenographer (*Cruche*, 282). In providing Aline with a moral and political education and in promoting her access into a profession, Mme Villebau helps her *protégée* to achieve her emancipation not only in the sense of a passage from childhood to adulthood, but also in that of an evolution from *jeune fille* to *femme moderne*.

Mme Villebau also performs more traditional mentoring tasks throughout the novel. For example, she constantly offers Aline both emotional and moral support. Any time she

---

[48]On Gale's discussion of the New Woman, see p. 98 in this thesis. In discussing Marie d'Agoult's *Nélida*, Christiansen talks of 'a striking effect of *dédoublement*, with Nélida, like Élisabeth, setting in motion a psychological metamorphosis in someone with the potential to do and be so much more in life', when she mentors another student. Moreover, Nélida takes upon herself the task of accomplishing her mentor Élisabeth's dream of actively promoting working-class women's collective welfare. See Christiansen, 'Female Mentorship', pp. 244–45.

[49]As previously discussed, this attitude is in line with the ideas expressed by Réval herself in *L'Avenir de nos fille* and elsewhere. A similar message is conveyed in other novels of this times, for example in Compain's *L'Un vers l'autre*.

faces a problem or a moral dilemma, or requires some help, Aline turns to her godmother or her godmother spontaneously intervenes. This happens in particular when Aline is in need of moral guidance and her own mother's advice is unsatisfactory. For example, when Aline initially refuses to marry the doctor, she replies to her mother's observations by saying: 'Jamais marraine ne me conseillera d'oublier, par intérêt, le respect de moi-même', and when she realizes that her father is unable to support her, '[t]oute sa pensée se tourne vers sa marraine' (*Cruche*, 110, 112). Subsequently, she writes to her:

> Aidez-moi, secourez-moi… Vous savez que mon cœur ne s'est donné qu'à vous, qu'il vous aime pour tout ce qu'il y a en vous de généreuse audace, de franchise et de bonté. Aidez-moi, aidez-moi; je vous apporte mes bras, mon cerveau, mon courage, mais sauvez mon rêve de n'être qu'à celui que j'aimerai et qui quelque part m'attend! (*Cruche*, 113)[50]

If Aline has already given her godmother her heart ('cœur'), it is now her brain ('cerveau'), her ability to work ('bras'), and her bravery ('courage') that she wishes to develop with the assistance of her mentor. In evoking a need to cultivate at the same time the heart, the brain, the body, and the spirit Aline seems to claim the right to adhere to a more progressive model of femininity, which values intelligence, strength, and boldness along with the more traditional quality of sensibility. In response to Aline's cry for help, Mme Villebau temporarily provides her with a shelter, another of the classical functions of the mentor.[51] While Aline considers this as an opportunity to 's'entendre secrètement pour un travail rémunérateur' and escape the prospect of marriage (*Cruche*, 84), her mother wrongly believes that:

> Ce petit voyage aura son utilité; Aline, auprès de madame Villebau, l'exquise Parisienne, oubliera un peu sa sauvagerie, elle prendra auprès d'elle le goût du monde, connaîtra les douceurs de la fortune. On ne vit pas de pain sec, de solitude et d'eau fraîche, madame Villebau le lui dira. (*Cruche*, 107)

Ironically, while both Aline and her mother perceive the utility of Mme Villebau's offer of shelter, they understand this usefulness in very distinctive ways. In fact, in recognizing Mme Villebau's mentoring role, Mme Robert clearly hopes that under the influence of this woman Aline will be encouraged to attach more importance to money ('fortune') and social status

[50]In this passage, as in the rest of the novel, Aline employs *vouvoiement*, a form that indicates the hierarchical nature of her relationship with Mme Villebau.

[51]Moreover, after Maurice's death, Mme Villebau and her faithful servant Sophie come to take care of Aline and her family, and the offer of shelter and protection is renewed through an invitation to Paris, where Aline moves into a new apartment with her brother and father and then starts to work. See *Cruche*, pp. 260–63.

('goût du monde'), and will be persuaded to marry for convenience, thus following the traditional path that her parents have in mind for her. For her part, Mme Villebau's stated aim is to reinforce the bond with her god-daughter and obtain her trust: 'je veux que ton séjour ici t'attache un peu plus a moi. Ta mère ne souhaite que ton respect et ton obéissance; moi, je réclame ta confiance et ta tendresse' (*Cruche*, 172). Aline repeatedly declares that she finds herself content in the company of her godmother, and at one point she also admits that she regrets not having a mother like her (*Cruche*, 122). At this point, Mme Villebeau readily takes on a maternal role:

> — Mais, ta mère, je le suis un peu puisque je suis ta marraine! Je n'ai pas encore pu m'occuper de toi, parce que la vie m'avait séparée des tiens; [...] maintenant que tout s'éclaire, j'ai le loisir d'être maman. Va, abuses-en, j'ai une telle soif d'être aimée, de connaître enfin ce que j'ai désiré toute ma vie, les baisers d'un enfant, les doux mots qui câlinent et qui consolent!
>
> — C'est ainsi, marraine, que je vous ai aimée! (*Cruche*, 122)

While modelled on the mother-daughter model and involving physical tenderness and gestures of affection (e.g. 'un long baiser sur le cou', 'en caressant tendrement la main de la jeune fille', *Cruche*, 122, 142), as we have seen, this relationship is to be understood primarily in the sense of a spiritual mothering, the kind of nurturing involved being intellectual as well as emotional.[52]

Mme Villebau also plays an important role in the context of Aline's sentimental life and, as her mentor, she acts in accordance with the traditional female role of the *chaperonne* as well as that of the *entremetteuse*.[53] At the beginning of the novel, Aline seeks her godmother's advice following the reception of a 'bouquet d'amour' from an unknown admirer (*Cruche*, 44). To Aline's disappointment, it will be later discovered that the secret admirer is the old doctor Vimart. Torn between marrying a man she does not love for economic reasons and disobeying her own mother, Aline, as usual, looks for Mme Villebau's opinion and support. Although the latter generally insists upon the importance of marriage in a woman's life, she also believes that her *protégée* should follow her heart and be allowed to choose

[52]On this topic, see also Susan Hennessy's discussion of the representation of 'maternité stérile' in Naturalism, and Marie Kawthar Daouda's discussion of the figure of the teacher as a 'mère spirituelle'. Susan S. Hennessy, 'La Maternité stérile: une analyse des mères spirituelles dans *Au bonheur des dames*, *La joie de vivre*, *Le rêve* et *L'argent*', *Excavatio: Emile Zola and Naturalism*, 2 (1993), 103–109, and Daouda, 'L'Anti-Salomé', pp. 31–38.

[53]The 'entremetteuse' is defined by the *TLFI* as the 'Personne — généralement une femme — qui sert d'intermédiaire dans une intrigue galante'. The relation between female homosociality and heterosexual love will be further discussed in Chapter Four on 'Female Rivalry and Love Triangles'.

her own husband (*Cruche*, 113, 123–25), an attitude that resonates with Réval's own belief that a girl's education should be based on the principles of freedom and responsibility.[54] During Aline's visit, Mme Villebau brings her god-daughter and her nephew close together. Before introducing the two young characters, she tells Aline Maurice's sad story and asks for her help: 'Je compte sur ta gaîté, sur ton entrain pour le distraire; il faut tâcher de le sauver; à nous deux nous y arriverons, une autre fera le reste' (*Cruche*, 141). Mme Villebau encourages their physical proximity, for example by persuading Aline to stitch a flower to Maurice's jacket, a gesture after which Maurice takes the heroine's hand and kisses it (*Cruche*, 150). Aline is not only intrigued by Maurice, but she also considers that: 'par reconnaissance pour sa marraine, autant que par pitié pour Maurice, il était de son devoir de réconforter celui qui cachait sa souffrance', and asks him to accompany her to visit Louise, the unwed mother rescued by Mme Villebau (*Cruche*, 158–64). Afterwards, Aline and Maurice start to work together on research for Mme Villebau and their intimacy rapidly grows. If, at first, Mme Villebau feels 'soucieuse', she then understands that the two have genuinely fallen in love and considers that destiny 'a amené cette enfant près d'elle, pour en faire sans doute l'épouse de Maurice' (*Cruche*, 164–67, 173). During a day out in Nancy, Mme Villebau, who chaperones the two lovers in a rather casual and relaxed way, confirms to one of her friends her hope to give Aline away to her nephew, and that day the two get secretly engaged (*Cruche*, 187–89).[55] It is only when she realizes that Maurice cannot legally divorce his wife and marry Aline that Mme Villebau regrets having encouraged their feelings and tries to convince her god-daughter to give up this relation. However, at the same time, the godmother exhorts Aline always to be true to herself and makes clear that she trusts her to make her own choices (*Cruche*, 202–205). The two lovers finally decide to remain secretly engaged and to wait for each other. At that point, Mme Villebau, who on the whole approves of the engagement, acts as their intermediary during their time apart, while also inviting Aline to be honest with her parents and explain the situation to them, a resolution that Aline never manages to keep (*Cruche*, 216–17, 226–27). After Maurice's death and Aline's recovery, the godmother continues to be as supportive and understanding as ever toward her *protégée* who, at the end of the novel, decides to get on with her life and gets engaged to another man (*Cruche*, 240–41).

---

[54]On Réval's professed opinions about female education, see p. 104 in this thesis.

[55]The importance for young women to be chaperoned on all occasions is often highlighted in conduct manuals of this period. Although the following example refers to young brides, the same recommendation applied to unmarried girls, possibly even more forcefully: 'Dès les premiers temps de son mariage, une jeune femme ne doit pas sortir seule; elle vivra encore presque comme une jeune fille et prendra toujours son mari pour mentor; elle se fera accompagner, dans ses promenades, par sa mère ou une de ses sœurs, ou, si elle n'a ni l'une ni l'autre, elle choisira pour sortir avec elle une amie plus âgée de respectabilité incontestée.' See Baronne d'Orval, *Usages Mondains*, p. 75.

Throughout the text, Mme Villebau remains at Aline's side and actively guides her through her transition from *jeune fille* to *femme moderne* by providing an education which is at the same time feminist, professional, and sentimental, and also by constantly offering shelter, emotional support, and advice, thus playing a major role in Aline's life. This relationship can arguably be defined as a 'vertical' one, to the extent that it enables Aline to challenge both parental authority and social prejudices, distancing herself from the rigid and suffocating example set by her biological mother and breaking off from tradition. Although, by the end of the novel, Aline does not claim for herself an unconventional place in society, she becomes more aware of women's rights and condition, while also turning into an active, economically independent individual, who acts upon her principles and is free to choose her own partner.

Les Cervelines and Female Friends as Mediators of Desires

If female mentoring in *La Cruche cassée* follows the traditional pattern of the older woman mentoring a younger girl and fits the mould of the hierarchical mother-daughter model, *Les Cervelines*, on the contrary, portrays a mentorship relation between friends who are on an equal footing. According to Juliette Rogers, Colette Yver's *Les Cervelines* (1903) belongs to a new category of Belle Epoque novels of professional development where the typical *Bildungsroman* quest plot interweaves with the romance plot. In this kind of novel the two narratives are in conflict; they are modified and rewritten in alternative ways, but the general purpose of displaying the heroine's process of maturation is maintained.[56] The title *Les Cervelines* designates a new type of female character, the 'brainy woman' who pursues a professional career, often in a male-dominated field, and lives her life independently, eventually rejecting the two most common options available to women of that time, marriage and motherhood. As noted by Rogers, Belle Epoque women and heroines were taught that 'they should not seek such attributes as power, domination, and authority'.[57] By contrast, the 'brainy woman', she observes, is usually a smart and confident overachiever driven by a strong desire for knowledge, recognition, and self-affirmation, who poses a threat to male domination. Rogers distinguishes between two types of 'Cervelines': the 'pure brainy women', who 'dismiss conventional femininity and embrace the sanctioned male role

[56]Rogers, *Career Stories*, pp. 115, 117–18.
[57]Rogers, *Career Stories*, p. 116.

entirely', and the 'seduced brainy women', who are tempted 'by the idea of fulfilling traditional feminine roles at the same time as the masculine ones'.[58] In discussing Belle Epoque women's intellectual emancipation, Andrea Oberhuber similarly refers to the centrality of the conflict between intellectual and marital aspirations. For Oberhuber, the figure of the 'jeune femme savante' raises two kinds of issues. At the social level, there is the necessity, for young women, of reconciling newly acquired intellectual skills and professional goals with a society that still expects them to consider marriage as their primary vocation. At the literary level, the appearance, in fiction, of a new model of femininity constitutes a new source of narrative and dramatic tension, due to the incompatibility between the heroines' aspirations and social expectations about marriage and family life.[59]

Yver's novel recounts in parallel the stories of two 'brainy women' living in a provincial town: the twenty-six-year-old Marceline Rhonans, a high-school history professor who also gives public lectures and conducts pioneering research on ancient history, and the twenty-two-year-old Jeanne Bœrk, a brilliant and very determined medical intern completely absorbed by her professional ambitions in a male-dominated field. Two local doctors, Paul Tisserel and Jean Cécile, fall in love respectively with Jeanne and Marceline and propose to them. While Jeanne dismisses without the slightest hesitation Paul's offer of marriage, Marceline, who reciprocates Jean's feelings, briefly contemplates the prospect of renouncing her career in order to marry him, as he requires her to do, but finally decides to break up with him and subsequently leaves on a research trip to Beirut.

Rogers rightly describes Jeanne and Marceline as 'isolated loners, pioneers in male-dominated fields' who lack the support of female colleagues or older female mentors but who, as friends, can rely on each other by developing 'a strong and equal association that helps them to survive difficult experiences in their work'.[60] In addition to this, I would argue that Jeanne and Marceline's friendship is presented as a mentorship relation, if not in the professional domain, certainly in the broader context of their personal lives, and that a form of female mentoring is established between the younger but 'pure' cerebral woman, Jeanne, and the temporarily 'seduced' one, Marceline.[61] If we try to situate this text within the wider context of the French literary canon, it is possible to trace its lineage back to such works as Molière's plays *Les Précieuses ridicules* (1659) and *Les Femmes savantes* (1672), whose plots also centre upon two young heroines and their possible marriages to their suitors.

[58]Rogers, *Career Stories*, pp. 120–21.
[59]See Andrea Oberhuber, 'Cervelines ou Princesses de science? Les entraves du savoir des jeunes héroïnes dans les romans de la Belle Époque', *Romantisme*, 165.3 (2014), 55–64.
[60]Rogers, *Career Stories*, pp. 126, 133.
[61]According to Rogers, Marceline is originally a 'pure brainy' woman who, for a moment, is tempted by love, but eventually returns to her original identity. For more details, see Rogers, *Career Stories*, pp. 121–28.

However, as we shall see, the portrayal of Marceline and Jeanne's relationship and the way in which this portrayal affects the narrative operate to challenge this literary tradition. Indeed, as already noted by a contemporary critic, '[ces] types absolument remarquables de femmes distinguées par leur intelligence [...] n'ont rien de commun avec les précieuses que Molière a ridiculisées.'[62]

As noted by Rogers, Jeanne and Marceline are atypical heroines within both the quest and the romance plot lines. On the one hand, they lack the naïveté and vulnerability of the classical romance heroines, and on the other hand, unlike the usual *Bildungsroman* protagonists, they both appear to know what they want and to have a straightforward path ahead of them. However, even though Marceline seems effectively to reconcile her intellectual and personal life, a conflict exists between the two aspects of her complex personality, her intellectual and 'masculine' side and her more sentimental and 'feminine' side.[63] In her case, love and the temptation to start a family become a serious obstacle, which she must overcome by choosing between marriage and career, between the private and the public and, ultimately, between the traditional and the modern female role. Jeanne and Marceline are confronted with the same dilemma, since they both receive a marriage proposal, but they react in different ways. Even though Marceline tries to interfere with Jeanne's decisions and to advise her, Jeanne already knows her own mind and refuses to be counselled. On the contrary, Marceline has many doubts and is in need of guidance. Thus, at a critical moment of her life, a time of transition, the relationship with Jeanne becomes the main factor influencing her decisions, her understanding of her own desires, and the way in which she defines herself.[64] In *Les Cervelines*, the temporary practice of mentoring appears to be a fundamental, if overlooked aspect of Marceline and Jeanne's friendship at a particular stage of their lives, and contributes to the resolution of the conflict that lies at the heart of the novel.

Although at the beginning of the text both heroines are described as active, intellectually powerful, and self-reliant women with a fulfilling life, the contrast between Jeanne and Marceline is repeatedly highlighted and becomes ever more marked as the

---

[62]E. Marion, 'Les Romans de Colette Yver', *Foi et vie*, 1 April 1924, pp. 360–66 (p. 361). Whether this is intentional on the part of the author or not, I would argue that Molière's *Les Femmes savantes* serves as an intertext for Yver's novel and allows her to inscribe her work into a well-established literary tradition, even while challenging said canon. The parallel suggested at first glance by a similarity in titles and subject matter (both *Femmes Savantes* and *Cervelines* deal with the stories of intellectual women) is supported by more specific elements that will be further highlighted in fn. 73 and 77 in this chapter.

[63]Rogers, *Career Stories*, pp. 119, 125, 127, 128. In describing Marceline, the narrator talks of an 'âme féminine', 'âme de savante et âme de jeune fille en même temps'. See *Cervelines*, p. 16.

[64]This is possible insofar as mentoring, as noted by Headrick, can be a 'dynamic found in friendship' and 'the specific practice of mentoring is a temporary one' within a more complex relationship. See Headrick, 'Women Mentoring Women', pp. 36, 55.

story progresses. First of all, this opposition is unsurprisingly established in terms of their physical appearance and, when the characters are first introduced, it is signalled by their colouring in association with a few telling details:

> L'une [Jeanne], de haute taille, blonde, enveloppée d'une cape blonde comme ses cheveux; l'autre [Marceline], frêle, vêtue de noir, portant en arrière de ses bandeaux bruns un canotier uni, comme les saints leur nimbe. (*Cervelines*, 1)

In opposition to the frail Marceline, Jeanne is often described as a lively and well-built woman. When they physically interact, this contrast becomes even more accentuated:

> Jeanne Bœrk serrait dans ses grandes paumes campagnardes la fragilité de sa main [de Marceline] maigriotte. Sa main était une petite chose d'ivoire blanc attachée à un poignet de fillette, le tout d'une finesse d'aristocratie très accentuée. (*Cervelines*, 15)

These elements hint at the heroines' characters and at their different positions within the plot, already suggesting that, between the two, Jeanne is the sturdier one, the one uncompromisingly attached to her principles and positively convinced of her life choices. Moreover, the text seems to value Jeanne above Marceline by symbolically associating her with a positive image of France. Indeed, the name Jeanne Bœrk suggests an interesting connection with the figure of Jeanne D'Arc, an emblem of French nationalism but also of female independence and leadership. As noted by Caroline Igra, after the events of the Franco-Prussian war and the Commune and until the end of the century, the myth of the maiden Sainte Jeanne 'reemerged to represent hope and regeneration'. This figure was the 'perfect symbol of glory and strength' for a nation that wanted to reassert its standing in Europe and rebuild its identity.[65] The surname Bœrk, to the extent that it is typical of the provincial area of Alsace-Lorraine, also promotes the idea of a healthy attachment to 'la terre', Jeanne being a vigorous and hearty countrywoman. By contrast, Marceline's aristocratic appearance and origins (her real name is in fact 'de Rhonans', but she has rejected her patronymic along with her disapproving family) situate her within the lineage of a decadent aristocracy whose obsolete values must be dismissed by a modern woman in construction.

---

[65]Caroline Igra, 'Measuring the Temper of her Time: Joan of Arc in the 1870s and 1880s', *Konsthistorisk tidskrift/ Journal of Art History*, 68.2 (1999), 117–25 (p. 117).

Initially, Jean tends to confuse the two friends:

> A l'amie de Jeanne Bœrk il avait prêté, depuis qu'il entendait prononcer partout son nom, les virilités froides de cette belle fille, jusqu'à sa force corporelle, jusqu'à l'impassibilité de son âme, sa sécheresse cachée. (*Cervelines*, 22)

However, when he is in the presence of the two women, he realizes that the difference inscribed in their appearance ('Jeanne Bœrk bruyante, dont s'épanouissait le visage charnu et rose, Marceline plus aristocratique, plus finement charmante', *Cervelines*, 31) also corresponds to a difference in personality ('[Jean Cécile] comprit entre les deux amies une effroyable distance d'âme; elles étaient, l'une et l'autre, à des plans totalement inégaux de pensée', *Cervelines*, 33).[66] Marceline herself often reflects on the similarities and disparities between Jeanne and her, this process of identification and rejection paralleling her doubts throughout her experience of self-discovery. At the beginning of the novel, Marceline thinks: 'Je suis une créature de travail. [...] Jeanne Bœrk et moi sommes pareilles en cela; mais elle est moins tentée que moi par mille choses' (*Cervelines*, 31). In discussing the topic of romantic love with Jean, she also declares: 'Vous allez nous juger mal, Jeanne et moi qui partageons là-dessus la même opinion' (*Cervelines*, 47). However, when Jean contemptuously tells Marceline that Jeanne is nothing but a 'brainy woman', Marceline, who is succumbing to her love for him, states: 'Je ne suis pas une Cerveline', a declaration that makes him understand the true nature of her feelings for him (*Cervelines*, 57). During a decisive conversation between Jeanne and Marceline, when Jeanne herself proudly confirms that she is ' [une] Cerveline' ('j'en suis une et je m'en fais gloire; quand on n'est pas une Cerveline, on a bien des chances pour être une écervelée'), Marceline tries to distinguish between 'Cerveline' and 'cérébrale', the latter being animated by 'une intelligence forte et créatrice' but also able to experience 'tous les autres courants de la vie':

> La différence qu'elle venait d'énoncer entre la cérébrale et la Cerveline était celle-là même qu'elle croyait exister entre son amie et elle. Elle cherchait désespérément à accorder la cérébralité puissante qu'elle se sentait et la tendresse qu'elle portait au fond du cœur. (*Cervelines*, 71)

[66] The male characters express a positive assessment of Marceline and hold her up against Jeanne, as discussed in this chapter, p. 123.

Eventually, Marceline will acknowledge her similarity with Jeanne and will choose to revert to her original status of 'Cerveline' in a more conscious and decisive way, a decision heavily influenced by her friend.

Before considering the impact that Jeanne's words exert on Marceline, it is important to understand what kind of relationship they have developed over time. Jeanne and Marceline first met as doctor and patient, when Marceline was affected by a bad fever and Jeanne took good care of her. Since then, their relation has turned into a friendship characterized by familiarity, mutual understanding, trust, and reciprocal support. When Jeanne pays a visit to Marceline in her apartment, we read that:

> Elle entra délibérément, s'enfonça dans le couloir étroit et obscur à demi, et monta l'escalier seule, sachant qu'elle était chez elle dans ce petit logis discret et confortable de son amie. (*Cervelines*, 15)

When they are in each other's company, the two friends are relaxed and adopt unceremonious manners, smoking cigarettes, traditionally a male bonding activity, in companionable silence:

> Elles fumèrent d'abord sans rien se dire, ayant si rarement, dans leur vie laborieuse, le loisir de ces moments de bien-être, de ces minutes oisives, où elles pouvaient ne pas penser. (*Cervelines*, 16)[67]

The nature of their bond is highlighted in the following excerpt:

> [Marceline] était entourée de très près d'amitiés, et celle de Jeanne Bœrk, froide et forte, édifiait à sa vie morale un invisible soutien. Jeanne était capable d'être une amie serviable et loyale. Toutes deux s'aimaient un peu comme deux bons camarades heureux de se trouver ensemble et tacitement prêts à se dévouer l'un a l'autre. [...] Sans qu'il y eût entre elles la moindre tendresse, elles étaient sûres l'une de l'autre comme deux choses accotées ensemble, et qui tiennent de leur point de contact leur équilibre. (*Cervelines*, 19)

The friendship between Jeanne and Marceline is defined as 'froide et forte', devoid of the 'tendresse' that was often thought to characterize women's relationships in the nineteenth

---

[67]For Alison Finch, 'inhibitions [about smoking and drinking], although still active in a majority of late-nineteenth-century women writers, were showing signs of being cast aside by some. [...] In Rachilde, women smoke both tobacco and hashish, specifically identifying these as masculine activities now being "appropriated".' See Finch, *Women's Writing*, p. 177.

century. Moreover, the two women are referred to as 'deux bons camarades heureux', the switching of grammatical gender contributing to a challenge to sex conventions by creating an instability around gender.

The language employed in the above excerpt, along with the evocation of the intellectual and 'masculine' dimensions of Jeanne and Marceline's relationship, produce a shift from the conventional model of female friendship promoted by prescriptive literature toward a new ideal of women's relations that blurs gender boundaries. The discourse on female friendship found in nineteenth-century conduct manuals for girls, in fact, usually supports a traditional ideal of womanhood, at least in the sense that the qualities women are taught to display as friends (amiability, gentleness, altruism, patience, unselfishness, discretion, moderation, and dignity) are understood as authentically feminine. For example, when in her essay entitled *Lettre sur l'amitié entre les femmes*, Mme de Maussion declares that 'aussi bien que les hommes, *les femmes savent être amies*', she grounds women's propensity to friendship in a gendered discourse on female nature, insisting on the compatibility of womanly qualities such as selflessness, tenderness, and nurturing with the requirements of friendship:

> Les femmes, si visiblement destinées à aimer, à soigner, à consoler, les femmes, dont toute l'existence est dans le sentiment, pour qui l'oubli d'elles-mêmes doit être un principe, et le soin de tout ce qui les entoure un devoir continuel, les femmes pourraient-elles bien ne pas connaître l'amitié?[68]

Mme de Maussion gives full credit to the belief that women's friendship belongs to the realm of sentimentality and that, in women, emotions take priority over reason, when she asks: '[Q]ui doit plus que les femmes être soumis à cet empire des sympathies, s'il est vrai que le pouvoir de la raison le cède trop souvent chez elles à celui du sentiment?'.[69] Additionally, she explains:

> [L]a science des femmes c'est la connaissance de leurs devoirs. Les vertus des femmes c'est l'accomplissement de ces mêmes devoirs. Ce sont ces devoirs qu'elles doivent mettre en *leur commerce*, dans ces devoirs qu'elles doivent s'entr'aider, s'encourager, se servir mutuellement d'exemple ou de conseil, dans ces devoirs encore qu'elles doivent complaire et se réjouir entre elles. [...] [C]ombien ne devons-nous pas trouver un plus grand motif d'union dans les honorables fonctions que la nature et la société nous confient; quel attrait

[68]Maussion, *Lettre sur l'amitié*, pp. 6, 122. Italics in the original text.
[69]Maussion, *Lettre sur l'amitié*, pp. 12–13.

plus puissant que cette communauté de sentiments et d'intérêts; quel lien plus naturel que ces rapports de devoirs et de jouissances, pour toutes celles qui en font la première affaire, l'honneur et la joie de leur vie?[70]

By stating that women's 'science', 'vertu', and 'commerce' all relate to those specific duties that both nature and society have assigned to women, Mme Maussion is suggesting that male and female friendship are based on different values. If it is true that, as Greek and Latin philosophers used to say, true friendship is based on virtue, male and female virtue, for Mme de Maussion, are two different things. In particular, women's virtue concerns the performance of traditional wifely and maternal tasks. Mme Maussion supports the idea that male friendship is primarily intellectual, whereas women are expected to bond over matters concerning the domestic sphere. As we have seen, Jeanne and Marceline's friendship contradicts this model. As friends, these two women occasionally act in unfeminine ways and cultivate a series of traits deemed at the time to be masculine. Unburdened by marriage or maternity and thriving on their intellect, what they pursue together is not the ideal of the traditional woman, but rather that of the modern woman. The subversion of male and female models of friendship is further reinforced in the text when, in commenting on Jean and Paul's relationship at a moment when the two friends have not seen much of each other, the narrator observes that: 'Les amitiés masculines ont de ces intermittences, elles s'impressionnent de la moindre influence, elles pâlissent et deviennent fades sous la moindre de leur passion' (*Cervelines*, 23). This remark is very surprising if we consider that traditionally it is women, and not men, who are accused of being shallow and impressionable, and of entertaining fleeting and superficial relationships.[71] Furthermore, this passage proposes an interesting female personification of male friendship, a rhetorical device which itself tacitly and comically subverts gender binaries.

In the aforementioned excerpt,[72] the perception of Jeanne as an 'invisible soutien morale' and the belief that 'leur point de contact' is the source of their 'équilibre' attest to the potential of this relationship to involve an aspect of mentoring. It is interesting to note that a later passage focalized on a male character suggests that Jeanne and Marceline might mutually influence each other and, as a result, Jeanne may become more feminine. After one of Marceline's public lectures, Tisserel, thinking about Jeanne and her behaviour, observes in fact that:

[70]Maussion, *Lettre sur l'amitié*, p. 69–70. Italics in the original text.
[71]See 'The History of Female Friendship in France', pp. 7–11 in this thesis.
[72]See p. 118 in this thesis.

> Comme jamais, ce jour-là, elle avait été bonne et charmante. Toute enfiévrée encore du triomphe de Marceline, elle ne parlait que de cela, elle s'oubliait pour son amie, elle jouissait à sa place, elle donnait l'illusion d'une femme affectueuse, d'un cœur. C'était cet aspect nouveau qui achevait de la perfectionner aux yeux de Tisserel: elle se féminisait tout à fait, elle était presque touchante. (*Cervelines*, 23)

In this case, the male gaze reasserts the same stereotypes about female relationships that we can find in nineteenth-century conduct manuals and essays, according to which women could and should support and encourage each other in the path to becoming 'des femmes honnêtes', a process that it is here indicated by the verb 'se féminiser'. However, as will be discussed below, this idea is corrected later on in the text by Jeanne and Marceline's narrative perspectives.

No matter how strong the tie between them is, Jeanne and Marceline's friendship is not without occasional clashes, arguments, and misunderstandings, and a feeling of estrangement can occur between them. Divergences of views and attitudes arise from their characters. In particular, Marceline has a weaker, 'feminine' side that she tries to conceal from Jeanne, sometimes unsuccessfully, and which is at the origin of their tensions or lack of mutual understanding, as well as of Jeanne's refusal to be guided or influenced by Marceline. Even though, as previously discussed, Marceline's house feels like home to Jeanne, the former denies her friend access to her bedroom, the physical space which reflects her half-acknowledged femininity, and therefore hints at a small sense of dissatisfaction with her life, or at least with the solitude that her current life involves:

> Tout ce qui était encore en elle intimité, mystère, et femme, se remisait comme accessoires encombrant dans sa chambre. Mais encore était-ce un lieu fort peu connu; toutes ses amies, et Jeanne Bœrk, la plus aimée de toutes, n'en avaient jamais ouvert la porte. C'était la chapelle secrète; et ce fort esprit sentait s'offenser en soi une pudeur imprécise à laisser voir à d'autres femmes le portrait de sa mère autour duquel elle mettait des fleurs, et l'oreiller de son lit où elle s'enfonçait quelquefois le soir pour cacher ses larmes d'isolée. (*Cervelines*, 16)

The distinctive feminine qualities possessed by Marceline and referred to as 'intimité', 'mystère', and 'femme' represent '[des] accessoires encombrant[s]' and Marceline feels 'une impudeur imprécise' at the idea of making them visible to Jeanne, who more than once expresses her contempt for these attributes. The noun 'accessoires' seems to suggest that femininity is socially constructed and artificial, and the term 'encombrant' additionally implies that it is an unnecessary burden to get rid of. In truth, this expression holds the resolution to the novel's dilemma, which consists in Marceline's rejection of the traditional female destiny (i.e. marriage, motherhood, and domesticity), a rejection that signals a desire to become more like Jeanne.

When further on Jeanne and Marceline talk about religion, love, or marriage the discrepancies between their personalities become more apparent. For example, the narrator observes that Marceline's 'esprit contenait dix fois celui de son amie' and that '[e]lles étaient faites toutes les deux de telle façon que la plupart du temps, quand Marceline parlait, Jeanne Bœrk n'entendait qu'une fraction de sa pensée' (*Cervelines*, 17). Even when Marceline enthusiastically discusses her dreams and ambitions, in particular her intention to earn enough money to quit her teaching job, travel, and write a comprehensive history of Antiquity, 'Jeanne Bœrk ne comprenait, ne pouvait comprendre qu'à demi les émotions, les vibrations, la poésie de cette femme' (*Cervelines*, 18). When Marceline stops talking:

> Il y avait dans son enthousiasme quelque chose de sacré que profanait l'indifférence de l'étudiante, et sa vision s'acheva secrètement [...] Elle ne parlait plus. Jeanne Bœrk, somnolente, froissait dans ses doigts une dernière cigarette, sans penser à rien. (*Cervelines*, 18-19)

Even though Marceline is discussing her professional goals, at this stage her language and attitude still seem to confine her, at least to a certain extent, into a conventional female identity ('émotions', 'poésie', 'femme', 'sacré'), something that Jeanne, who is neither 'sensible' nor 'nerveuse' and who practises her profession certainly with a fierce passion, but also with a sort of cold and rational professionalism, is always inclined to scorn or, as in this case, ignore (*Cervelines*, 17). In a similar way, when Jeanne visits Marceline, bringing her future love interest Jean along:

> [Jean et Marceline] se mirent à parler de choses banales, ce qui causait à Jeanne Bœrk une sorte d'agacement. Elle s'ennuyait. [...] [N]on seulement son amie et le médecin échangeaient des lieux communs, mais encore ne s'occupaient nullement d'elle; et c'était un détail qui la gênait toujours. (*Cervelines*, 32)

This passage is revealing of the sort of annoyance felt by Jeanne any time Marceline overlooks her and behaves in a way that she, Jeanne, deems unfit or unworthy of her friend. Jeanne consistently refuses that part of Marceline's personality which makes her less 'Cerveline' and more 'femme', and, in this situation, she displays a strikingly unfeminine feature, insofar as her egotism is in contradiction with the social expectation for women to be selfless and patient.

At the end of this meeting, Jean himself, comparing Marceline and Jeanne, will remark: 'Celle-là [Marceline] est très femme [...] Elle est à mille lieues de l'autre' (*Cervelines*, 33). Jean's position is set in opposition to that of Jeanne and is aligned with that of Paul, who also praises Marceline's femininity and, in a speech reported by Jean, clearly states that 'Mademoiselle Rhonans est meilleure qu'elle [Jeanne]' (*Cervelines*, 57). From these male perspectives, Marceline is rated higher than Jeanne, insofar as she remains 'très femme' regardless of her intellectual qualities. Such qualities are in fact viewed by the male characters as threatening. When describing the encounter between Marceline, Jeanne, and Jean, the focalization on the male character conveys this exact idea: 'Entre elles deux, il [Jean] avait pris un siège petit où s'amoindrissait encore son être frêle. Il s'intimida parmi ces mentalités vigoureuses de femmes qui le dominaient' (*Cervelines*, 31). Even more interestingly, in this example gender stereotypes are dramatically overturned by the attribution of 'male' qualities to the female characters (e.g. 'vigoureux'), and vice versa by that of 'female' traits to the male characters (e.g. 'frêle'), something that happens repeatedly in the text.

Although the relationship between Marceline and Jeanne is solid and sincere, the gulf between the two friends widens when Marceline, solicited by Jean, pleads Tisserel's cause and tries to convince Jeanne not to stubbornly refuse his repeated and sincere offers of love. When first discussing the matter with Jean, Marceline actually takes the side of her friend, recognizing that she is an 'exceptional' woman with her own path to follow: 'Jeanne Bœrk n'est pas une femme semblable à une autre femme, monsieur; les conditions de sa vie en font un être d'exception' (*Cervelines*, 43). However, Marceline, who even earlier in the novel 's'attendrissait de la [Jeanne] penser aimée' (*Cervelines*, 17), now agrees to speak in Tisserel's favour. She immediately regrets her choice, considering that: 'cette bonne Jeanne est faite pour devenir un grand savant, un *homme cé□ □re*. Il n'est pas possible de briser une pareille carrière. Comment me suis-je embarquée en cela!', but still keeps her promise and goes to see her (*Cervelines*, 44).[73] On this occasion, Jeanne and Marceline first try to defuse the situation, but when Marceline openly accuses Jeanne of being too proud and goes on to emphasize how good it would be to accept Tisserel's proposal, her friend is both surprised and concerned ('— Marceline, êtes-vous folle? [...] vous dites des choses ridicules auxquelles vous ne m'aviez pas habituée', *Cervelines*, 45). Marceline also tries to reason

[73]The employment of the expression 'homme célèbre', in italics in the original text, is another example of the deconstruction of gender stereotypes and the blurring of boundaries promoted in this text.

with Jeanne by evoking utilitarian arguments (e.g. having a husband would be a guarantee of good reputation for Jeanne and would protect her from inappropriate behaviour on the part of her male colleagues). However, Jeanne's views on marriage are very clear from the outset and she never wavers on this topic. From the first time Marceline mentions to Jeanne the possibility of marrying Tisserel, the narrator wonders: 'Qu'aurait fait en somme d'un mari cette créature souverainement occupée, de qui la vie était orientée déjà sans retour dans le chemin du travail scientifique, et qui prenait là toutes ses joies, son intérêt, sa raison d'être' (*Cervelines*, 17). On the same occasion, Jeanne herself declares to her friend:

> J'en ai trop vu dans ma salle, de pauvres malheureuses exténuées, vieillies, tuées par cette noble vie de famille que l'on prône tant, la maternité, les soucis et le reste. Et je me demande pourquoi, oui vraiment je me demande pourquoi j'irais troquer mon sort agréable avec cette existence. (*Cervelines*, 17–18)

It is through her work that Jeanne, as lucid and discerning as ever, has had the opportunity to cast a look over the reality of women's private lives and has developed a negative view of marriage and maternity. This view, as formulated in the above passage, constitutes an open critique of the status quo.[74]

At the end of one of their conversations, Jeanne explicitly asks Marceline what she would do were she in her shoes and Marceline, after a brief hesitation, admits that she would be tempted by the possibility of domestic happiness. In this case, not only does Marceline's attempt at mentoring Jeanne fail miserably, but a simple interjection from Jeanne is sufficient to make a significant impression on her, serving as a clear signal of Jeanne's greater potential as a mentor:

> — Moi, si quelqu'un m'aimait de la manière dont monsieur Tisserel vous aime, ma belle Jeanne, je crois positivement que je me laisserais tenter par ce bonheur.
>
> — Oh! Marceline! Allons donc! s'écria la Cerveline indignée.
>
> Cette interjection de Jeanne la poursuivit longtemps et lui fut un thème à des méditations qui dépassèrent de beaucoup en portée le romanesque incident actuel.
>
> — Jeanne est plus forte que moi, pensait-elle [...] Elle a raison [...]

---

[74]This excerpt can fruitfully be read in parallel with the words pronounced by Armande at the very beginning of *Les Femmes savantes*, when after defining marriage as a 'vulgaire dessin' she deplores the condition of married women. Like Jeanne, Armande laments the lot of married women, referring to their duties as 'des pauvretés horribles'. See Molière, *Les Femmes savantes*, ed. by Georges Couton (Paris: Gallimard, 1999 [1672]), p. 27.

Le problème la tourmentait partout, dans la rue, à son cours de lycée. [...] Fallait-il être forte comme Jeanne? (*Cervelines*, 45, 46)

The situation gets even more complicated when Marceline, entering Jeanne's room, interrupts an awkward moment between her and Tisserel, who has just proposed and has been refused with great resolution. Marceline's inappropriate attempts to defend Tisserel increase Jeanne's irritation. The latter mercilessly blames Marceline for her weakness, accusing her of forgetting the principles they used to share, and goes as far as to tell her 'je vous ai trouvée stupide' (*Cervelines*, 50). Later on, Marceline 'avait toujours à l'esprit le cas de conscience de Jeanne' and is jealous because of the love that her friend has been able to inspire in a man (*Cervelines*, 51). This episode leads to Jeanne and Marceline's temporary estrangement: 'La bonne entente que jusqu'ici n'avait pas cessé entre elle et Jeanne Bœrk était troublée par un sentiment étrange que ne définissait ni l'une ni l'autre' (*Cervelines*, 53), and Marceline eventually gets closer to Jean, loses interest in her job, and seriously contemplates the prospect of marriage.

Before giving a definitive answer to Jean, however, Marceline decides to take a week to consider his offer thoroughly. At this point, Jeanne providentially reappears in her life and, in her mentoring role, influences the novel's outcome. Initially:

> En la reconnaissant, Marceline fut prise d'un froid glacial [...] [E]lle ne pouvait l'admirer ; son amitié pour elle était même diminuée. [...] D'un autre côté, elle avait peur des théories de Jeanne, qui allaient peut-être ravager le secret très cher dormant en elle [l'amour de Marceline pour Jean]. Elle la condamnait, mais Jeanne la condamnerait aussi. Il y avait désormais un abîme entre elles. (*Cervelines*, 69–70)

Marceline seems to be concerned about the possible effects of Jeanne's opinions on her growing feelings for Jean, another sign of Jeanne's influence over her. However, shortly after, when Jeanne presses her hand with affection, a gesture whose relevance has been highlighted in the previous chapter, Marceline is reminded of 'la force d'amitié franche et saine, presque exclusive' of Jeanne and regrets her hard feelings (*Cervelines*, 70). Jeanne then starts to talk about her involvement with some children that she is tending and healing in her role as apprentice doctor, and this represents the pretext for a broader discussion on the social role of women.[75] By appealing to Marceline's understanding of social reality as an

---

[75] Jeanne's attitude toward these children can be considered as revealing of the 'impérissable instinct de femme demeuré au fond d'elle-même' despite the fact that, according to the text, she is a 'fière fille, exempte de sensibilité et de faiblesse, que rien n'émouvait à faux, qui ne connaissait pas d'impressionnabilité nerveuse'.

'engrenage' in which everyone has a role to play, Jeanne denounces women's confinement to their reproductive function, defends women's freedom, and claims a different place for herself in society:

> Je me défends d'être un rouage, je fais d'abord ce qui me plaît, et je me moque de ma fonction sociale. La femme doit être mère, n'est-ce pas? Je la connais, celle-là. Mais suis-je libre, oui ou non, de choisir la vie qui me convient? Je suis comme vous, je ne comprends pas les inutiles, et au fond, je suis un peu de votre système. Mais pouvez-vous dire que je sois inutile? Est-ce que je n'ai pas ma fonction sociale? [...] Moi, ma chère, sans mari et sans enfants, je me trouve une femme absolument complète, et si vous le voulez, quoique je m'en inquiète fort peu, dans l'engrenage social, j'estime que je fonctionne admirablement. (*Cervelines*, 71)

Jeanne forcefully asserts that a woman who rejects marriage and motherhood is not to be considered as useless or worthless within the system. Her words clearly contradict the traditional discourse about women's mission in society, a discourse that, at the time, was promoted not only by men, but also by those feminists who claimed women's social rights on the basis of their reproductive and maternal functions. This speech strongly affects Marceline, who finds herself 'séduite, conquise et émérveillée'. When she attempts to reconcile her confused desires by indicating the difference between 'Cerveline' and 'cérébrale', Jeanne contradicts her and explains that only one aspect can prevail, either the intellectual or the sentimental one: 'Il faut toujours que dans un être quelque chose prédomine [...] quand c'est le tour de l'amour ce n'est plus celui de la pensée; il me semble que je ne dois rien vous apprendre' (*Cervelines*, 71). In this case, the verb 'apprendre' is arguably a key word.[76] Even though Jeanne presents her views as self-evident, she is clearly, although maybe unintentionally, instructing and advising Marceline on the choice to make.

Jeanne then insists on the fact that women can pursue different destinies and reiterates her and Marceline's own uniqueness and similarity:

> Je crois bien, grand Dieu! qu'il faut se marier, que tout le monde se marie! Mais — attendez — sauf ceux dont la fonction est ailleurs. N'ayons pas de fausse modestie; des femmes

---

See *Cervelines*, p. 70. While certain features of traditional femininity (e.g. emotionality, weakness, impressionability) do not apply to Jeanne's character, her attention to children proves that she has not rejected this ideal of womanhood entirely. This element supports my argument for Jeanne being a *femme moderne* more than a New Woman. See fn. 27 in this chapter.

[76]On this occasion, Jeanne also observes that in her case it is certainly 'le cerveau' that prevails, while in Tisserel's case, it is rather 'le cœur', thus offering yet another example of the subversion of gender stereotypes. See *Cervelines*, p. 71.

comme vous et moi ont autre chose à faire que de fonder un ménage; nous devons être assez lumineuses pour rendre, en ce sens, service à nos semblables et payer notre dette à la communauté humaine. Est-ce bien dit? De sorte que, pour nous, l'amour serait sans excuse, puisqu'au lieu de se présenter sous la forme d'un devoir, il ne ferait que nous arracher à notre mission naturelle qui est purement intellectuelle. (*Cervelines*, 71)

As noted by Rogers, Jeanne's words present a strong feminist element and echo those pronounced by a well-known feminist activist of the Belle Epoque, Nelly Roussel, who similarly questions women's confinement to traditional roles and claims their right to choose their own path in life.[77] Indeed, in this passage Jeanne subverts once again Belle Epoque assumptions about female roles and identities by using the word 'naturel' in association with women's intellectual mission and, even though she is unaware of her friend's private struggles, she points Marceline toward the right path to follow.[78]

The effect of Jeanne's discourse on Marceline is immediate, as the following excerpt attests:

Les velléités qu'avait eues à plusieurs reprises Marceline de se confier à cette unique amie, de lui conter les chagrins indéfinis, les mélancolies, les inquiétudes, les troubles qui la possédaient depuis qu'en secret elle aimait, tout ce besoin d'expansion qui est une des bases de l'amitié fut irrévocablement refoulé sous les paroles de Jeanne. Elle eut honte d'avoir aimé [Jean] Cécile. [...] Jeanne Bœrk et sa froide sapience ressuscitaient devant elle la Marceline d'autrefois qui pensait et parlait ainsi avant cette aventure de faiblesse, et qui n'était plus. (*Cervelines*, 71, 72)

Two elements in particular are worthy of note: first of all, when Jeanne temporarily assumes the role of the mentor, this dynamic seems to overrule their friendship. In fact, the 'besoin d'expansion', which is to say the openness and intimacy which are common traits of female

[77]See Juliette M. Rogers, 'Feminist Discourse in Women's Novels of Professional Development', in *A 'Belle Époque'?*, ed. by Holmes and Tarr, pp. 183–95 (pp. 188, 190, 191).
[78]Jeanne's assertions recall Armande's invitation for her sister to pursue higher goals and focus on her intellectual development instead of marriage. Surprisingly enough, however, Jeanne's argument also echoes one of those put forward by Henriette, who similarly proclaims that women should be free to take on different roles and responsibilities in society. While Armande tells her sister: 'À de plus hauts objets élevez vos désirs [...] Loin d'être aux lois d'un homme en esclave asservie / Mariez-vous, ma sœur, à la philosophie', Henriette responds: 'Le Ciel, dont nous voyons que l'ordre est tout-puissant, / Pour différents emplois nous fabrique en naissant [...] Habitez, par l'essor d'un grand et beau génie, / Les hautes régions de la philosophie, / Tandis que mon esprit, se tenant ici-bas, / Goûtera de l'hymen les terrestres appas.' However, while in *Les Femmes Savantes*, as in *Les Précieuses Ridicules*, women's intellectual ambitions are ridiculed and the possibility of occupying a different place in society is ultimately denied, the message conveyed by Yver's text is radically different, since by the end of the novel both Jeanne and Marceline decide to pursue their professional careers, ultimately choosing their friendship and their jobs over romantic love and marriage. See Molière, *Femmes Savantes*, pp. 27–29.

friendship in the Belle Epoque, is suppressed. Moreover, Jeanne forcefully puts Marceline in front of her old self and helps her to overcome her difficulties by indirectly encouraging her to appropriate once again the status of 'Cerveline'. In the following days, '[l]a vision souriante de Jeanne Bœrk planait sur ses pensées en *idéal*. Elle ne la condamnait plus maintenant, mais l'admirait. Comme elle la trouvait libre, belle et forte!' (*Cervelines*, 77. My italics). As this passage makes clear, Jeanne has become Marceline's role model, the 'idéal' after which she is going to shape her own behaviour. Bearing the example of her friend in mind, Marceline confesses to Jean: 'j'étais éclairée subitement sur ma véritable fonction ici-bas' and refuses his marriage proposal, finally asserting: 'Je suis une Cerveline!' (*Cervelines*, 78, 80). With these words, Marceline achieves her journey of self-discovery, claiming for herself the possibility of defining who she is, as her friend Jeanne unapologetically does.

The power of Yver's novel lies in the tension between career and marriage, which ultimately becomes a tension between two opposing and seemingly irreconcilable ideals of womanhood, the *femme moderne* and the traditional woman. In the novel, the ambassadors of these conflicting models are primarily Jeanne and Jean, who share the same root name in the feminine and masculine form, and work against each other, functioning almost as split figures, as the two sides of the same coin. In fact, Jeanne rejects Marceline's sentimental, feminine side, which is exactly the aspect most appreciated by Jean and, vice versa, Jean tries to suppress Marceline's masculine, intellectual side, which is the aspect most valued by Jeanne. In having Marceline choose between Jean and Jeanne, Yver obliges her heroine not only to choose between love and friendship, but also between two different models of female and human existence. Eventually, Marceline embraces the more progressive model of femininity proposed by another female character and discards the conventional one offered by a patriarchal figure as potential husband and household leader. Not only do the novel's ending and Marceline's final decision seem to endorse the ideal of womanhood championed by Jeanne, but even when we consider the internal dynamic of Marceline and Jeanne's relationship, the text always privileges Jeanne's position, by showing Marceline's attempts at influencing Jeanne as unsuccessful and Jeanne's mentoring practice as successful.

One useful way to understand the functioning of Jeanne and Marceline's mentorship relation is to apply René Girard's notion of mimetic desire to their friendship. In *Mensonge romantique et vérité romanesque* (1961), Girard explains that desires are not autonomous or spontaneous and that they have little to do with the object toward which they are directed. Instead, they are generated and mutually reinforced through the bond established between the desiring subject and the mediator, the latter constituting both a role model to imitate and an obstacle to overcome. According to Girard, '[l]e désir selon l'*Autre* est toujours le désir d'etre un *Autre*', this dynamic revealing the nineteenth-century fascination with the Other.[79] In *Cervelines*, insofar as Jeanne tells/teaches Marceline what she should want and pursue, she arguably acts as a mediator for her friend's desire to become a *femme moderne*. Girard further argues that in internal mediation (i.e. the situation in which the distance between desiring subject and mediator is minimal, as is the case for two characters inhabiting the same diegetic world) two reversed but identical triangles are superimposed.[80] In other words, the desiring subject also serves as a mediator fuelling the desire of the other person. Indeed, Jeanne and Marceline mutually strengthen their wish to focus on their careers and reject traditional femininity. The opposition between the two characters, which Marceline temporarily claims by saying that she is not a 'Cerveline' (*Cervelines*, 57), becomes emptier the closer they get. In opposition to Girard's model, in which proximity usually brings about hatred and competition, Jeanne and Marceline's renewed closeness deepens their reciprocal love and respect. Moreover, the place occupied by Jeanne within this triangular structure of desire is rather unconventional as she is not the mediator of a desire for heterosexual romance; she is not a sexual rival exciting the heroine's desire for a man, a role often conferred upon female characters in literature, or the mediator of a traditional female role.[81]

Indeed, one of the most innovative aspects of this novel is the fact that female friendship/mentorship ultimately delegitimizes the romance plot, Marceline's adherence to Jeanne's lifestyle and views leading her to reject marriage, remain free, and achieve her professional goals in the public domain. In this sense, the relationship between Jeanne and Marceline can be understood as a 'vertical' one, its representation challenging the tradition of female characters privileging love and marriage over female friendship or career. In this way, Yver contributes to the creation of a positive new narrative for the modern heroine, as other authors of this period, such as Colette in *La Vagabonde* (1910), were also doing.[82] Moreover, the two sub-plots of *Les Cervelines* reinforce the feminist undertone of the text. The successful playwright Eugénie Lebrun, Jean's first romantic interest, like Jeanne and

[79]Girard, *Mensonge romantique*, p. 89. Italics in the original text.
[80]Girard, *Mensonge romantique*, p. 104. On the difference between external and internal mediation, see Girard, *Mensonge romantique*, p. 18.
[81]The topic of female sexual rivalry will be further discussed in Chapter Four on 'Female Rivalry and Love Triangles'. Sharon Marcus talks of fictional female friends 'mediating a suitor's courtship, giving a husband to the friend or the friend to a husband, or helping to remove an obstacle to the friend's marriage', thus introducing the heroine to her traditional role of wife and mother. See Marcus, *Between Women*, p. 82.
[82]Colette, *La Vagabonde* (Paris: Fayard, 1953 [1910]). By contrast, other contemporary authors, for example Marcel Prévost in *Les Vierges fortes* (1900), depict female characters who similarly reject traditional female roles but fail in pursuing their intellectual ambitions and in attaining their autonomy.

Marceline remorselessly chooses freedom over marriage. By contrast, the pure and undemanding Henriette Tisserel, an emblem of traditional femininity, tragically dies, thus depriving Jean of the possibility to experience love as he intends it.[83]

However, placing *Les Cervelines* within the broader context of Yver's literary production and reading it in parallel with her views on women's emancipation raise a series of questions. Different critics, including Simone de Beauvoir, Jennifer Waelti-Walters, and Diana Holmes have commented on Yver's feminism or lack of it.[84] As for contemporary reviewers of the novel, they generally perceived Yver's text as a misogynistic critique of intellectual women who refused to marry. For example, Jean Lionnet notes:

> durant tout le cours du volume, on sent percer comme une rancune sourde contre ces émancipées « qui ont gardé de la femme, et de la meilleure, tout, sauf le cœur, *et le cœur, souvent même, sauf l'amour* »; et l'on est fort étonné que Mme Colette Yver ne soit pas un homme; car, enfin, ce sont là des griefs qu'il appartiendrait au seul sexe masculin d'invoquer.[85]

An anonymous critic rightly observes that the conflict between heart and mind, as represented in Yver's novels, implies that women are unable to reconcile intellectual and domestic tasks, the same problem being pointed out by Jane Misme, who refers to this topic as 'une des plus plaisantes inventions de l'anti-féminisme'.[86] Yver herself, in her anti-feminist essay *Dans le jardin du féminisme* (1920) 'targets in particular the *cervelines* whose brains have atrophied their hearts'.[87] In a context marked by fears of depopulation, anxieties about the stability of the family, and the presence of a strong pro-natalist discourse, criticism of emancipated women who reject marriage and maternity to pursue their careers abounded, and although 'Mme Colette Yver est elle-même une « Cerveline » et une « Princesse de Lettres », ce qui rend invraisemblable sa condamnation', even her later novels, *Princesses*

---

[83]Eugénie Lebrun appears at the beginning of the novel and is the first 'Cerveline' in whom Jean is disappointed. Henriette, Tisserel's younger sister, is desperately in love with Jean, who is too focused on Marceline to give her any thought until it is too late; Henriette dies of an unattended tuberculosis. As noted by Oberhuber, 'avec elle, disparaîtront l'amour sacrificiel et l'image du féminin faible qui demeure autrement sans écho dans *Les Cervelines*'. See Oberhuber, 'Cervelines ou Princesses de science?', p. 59.

[84]For example, Beauvoir considers Yver's fiction anti-feminist whereas Waelti-Walters proposes to see this author as a 'closet feminist'. For an overview of these critics' arguments, see Hope Christiansen, 'Grappling with Feminism in the Belle Époque: Colette Yver's *Princesses de science* and *Les Dames du palais*', *MLN*, 130.4 (2015), 946–62.

[85]Jean Lionnet, *L'Évolution des idées chez quelques-uns de nos contemporains* (Paris: Perrin et Cie, 1905), p. 133. Italics in the original text.

[86][Anon.], 'Une nouvelle romancière: Colette Yver', *La Liberté d'opinion*, April-May 1907, pp. 93–95, and Jane Misme, 'Cœur ou Cerveau', *La Française*, 21 January 1912, p. 1. In her article, Misme discusses Yver's *Princesses de science* and Prost's *Salutaire orgueil*. Her quotation refers particularly to the latter text, but it can apply to *Les Cervelines* as well.

[87]Christiansen, 'Grappling with Feminism', p. 960.

de science (1907) and *Les Dames du palais* (1909), suggest that women should give up their professions for the sake of their husbands and children, and celebrate female abnegation.[88]

Yver expresses her opinion on female professionalization in an article that appears in the magazine *Femina* in 1907. According to her, when women do not have the opportunity to marry, they can still live a life 'pleine, féconde, intéressante et noble, — surtout assurée et libre' through their careers. However, '[s]i le mariage se présente alors l'anomalie cesse, la combattante dépose ses armes et rentre dans les conditions naturelles, s'offre à l'amour, à la maternité, à la royauté secrète du foyer, et son mari aura en elle une amie intellectuelle, vaillante et supérieure.'[89] Yver's position is not very different from that of other female authors of this period, who similarly endorsed the idea that marriage and career were fundamentally incompatible, for women, and that while women should have the opportunity to earn their living, if given the chance, they should privilege marriage.[90] However, as noted by Hope Christiansen, '[t]here is marked difference between what Yver claims she did and what her characters and stories tell us', or, one might say, between the beliefs she expressed in articles and essays and the underlying message of *Les Cervelines*.[91] In spite of the nuances and inconsistencies of Yver's discourse, what clearly emerges from *Les Cervelines* is that, as already pointed out by Oberhuber, at least 'du point de vue des protagonistes, le roman se termine sur une vision positive des modes de vie autonomes qu'adoptent Jeanne et Marceline'.[92]

---

[88]Alice Berthet, 'Droits de la femme: quelques clichés sur le féminisme', 10 October 1911. According to Jules Bois, '[d]ans *Princesses de science*, Mme Colette Yver avait pris nettement parti contre les savantes, pour les « servantes de l'ignorance ».' For Marion, it is through 'le renoncement, le sacrifice de leur moi pour le salut du foyer' that Yver's heroines 'deviennent belles, admirables, vraiment supérieures'. See Jules Bois, 'Revue des livres: *Les Dames du Palais*, par Mme Colette Yver', *Les Annales*, 20 March 1910, pp. 277–80 (p. 277), and Marion, 'Les Romans de Colette Yver', p. 362.

[89]Colette Yver, 'Le Choix d'une carrière: enquête Femina', *Femina*, 1907.

[90]On Réval, see p. 104 in this thesis. The ending of Compain's novel *L'Un vers l'autre* also suggests that women should not privilege career over love, but rather enter into a more progressive form of marriage.

[91]Christiansen, 'Grappling with Feminism', p. 961.

[92]Oberhuber, 'Cervelines ou Princesses de science?', p. 60. For Holmes, 'the attraction of the feminist position she [Yver] opposes is by no means underestimated'. See Holmes, *French Women's Writing,* p. 50.

Hellé and the Rejection of Female Mentorship

After having discussed two different examples of 'vertical' homosociality, one consisting in a hierarchical, mother-daughter-like mentorship relation (*La Cruche cassée*), and the other in a temporary mentoring practice inscribed within an equal friendship (*Les Cervelines*), in this section I will consider one representation of 'horizontal' homosociality, in which the heroine rejects her mentor's guidance and refuses to conform to the traditional model of womanhood that she presents her with.

In 1900, Marcelle Tinayre's novel *Hellé* (1899) won the *Prix Montyon* of the *Académie Française*, a prize traditionally awarded 'aux auteurs français d'ouvrages les plus utiles aux mœurs, et recommandables par un caractère d'élévation et d'utilité morales'.[93] This novel has been defined by Waelti-Walters as a 'feminist and socialist utopia' about female education and marriage, in which the heroine embodies 'the pure example of Tinayre's dream: an active, autonomous woman who finds her equal and joins her life to his so that they can work together for a better future'.[94] Unlike the other novels considered in this chapter, *Hellé* is written in the first person, the authority of the narrator being ascribed to a young girl whose inherently limited perspective dominates the narrative. Moreover, unlike our other novels, *Hélle* still fits, thematically, in that post-1870 atmosphere characterized by the decline of the aristocracy and the need to find new models after the defeat of Sédan. If, particularly in *Les Cervelines*, the female characters are already evolving into *femmes modernes* and are taking on new identities, in *Hellé* change represents more of a confused, gradual aspiration.

The eponymous heroine Hellé, an orphan brought up by her uncle, has been raised to become an independent thinker with a strong sense of morality and an ability to make her own decisions in life. At the age of nineteen, her uncle brings her to Paris so that she can experience new situations and choose a companion. There she meets two men, the handsome and shallow poet Maurice Clairmont and the serious and honourable philanthropist Antoine Genesvrier. After her uncle's death Hellé, blinded by Maurice's good looks and good manners, agrees to marry him, but eventually realizes her error of judgement and breaks up with him. She then recognizes that Antoine is the better match for her and together they set about achieving their domestic happiness and contributing to social progress by means of charitable work. As observed by Gale, the novel deals on the one side

[93] See the definition of the 'Prix Montyon' in *Académie Française* <http://www.academie-francaise.fr/prix-montyon> [accessed 31 August 2018].
[94] Waelti-Walters, *Feminist Novelists*, pp. 37, 38.

with the liberal and subversive education Hellé is offered at home by her uncle, an education that sets her apart from the girls of her age and, on the other side, with the 'social education' the heroine acquires in society, within the urban landscape. The latter is mainly provided by Antoine, who encourages Hellé to put her exceptional skills at the service of others, and by Parisian ladies who, on the contrary, try to turn her into a good wife, explaining that she ought to sacrifice her skills in the interest of her husband.[95] By the end of the novel, Hellé has become a true *femme moderne*, mainly on account of the influence exerted by the male mentoring figures present in her life, first her uncle Sylvain de Riveyrac and then Antoine. One of the female characters in the text, Mme Marboy, also tries to mentor Hellé, although unsuccessfully. Her actions and words show that, potentially, fictional female mentors could function as the last bastion of the status quo. Mme Marboy consequently offers an interesting counterexample to Mme Villebau and Jeanne Bœrk.

On her arrival in Paris, Hellé considers herself to be different from and even superior to the other girls of her age, 'des êtres inachevés, demi-conscients', '[des] enfants ignorantes, vêtues de rose et d'azur' (*Hellé*, 46). At the same time, she feels utterly unprepared to face this new, more challenging social context because she has lived 'hors de [son] siècle'. A classical education and a life spent in the countryside have left her unable to fit into society (*Hellé*, 45, 46) This combination of wisdom and worldly ignorance signals that Hellé's education is incomplete and the heroine is struggling to access adulthood in a changing world. After a few weeks, everyone is treating Hellé with a 'bienveillance indifférente' and she experiences a certain loneliness (*Hellé*, 47). Later on, she will remark: 'Les jeunes filles ne m'aiment guère, parce que je leur ressemble peu et que nous n'avons aucun goût commun'; the heroine is clearly estranged at the beginning of her epic quest (*Hellé*, 72). We learn, however, that in this period: 'Une douceur nouvelle entra dans [sa] vie avec l'amitié d'une femme' (*Hellé*, 47). The relationship between Hellé and Mme Marboy is depicted as both hierarchical and affectionate, and a correspondence with the mother-daughter model is suggested from the outset. In fact, the orphaned Hellé first approaches the old woman on the pretext of her resemblance with her deceased aunt and the childless Mme Marboy promptly expresses her desire to have a daughter like Hellé (*Hellé*, 48). Throughout the novel, Mme Marboy acts as a surrogate mother, providing Hellé with emotional support and physical tenderness, to the point that Hellé will also remark: 'ma présence lui donnait l'illusion de la maternité', Mme Marboy's attitude often evidencing 'une fierté maternelle [à l'égard d'Hellé]' (*Hellé*, 65, 207). Since their first encounter, the two

[95]Gale, *A World Apart*, pp. 97–99.

women are bound together by 'sympathie', a word repeated twice in the space of a few lines; when she first addresses Hellé, Mme Marboy uses 'un ton affectueux' and even expresses a desire to kiss her (*Hellé*, 48, 49). Gestures of affection usually characterize their interactions (e. g. 'Madame Marboy posa sa main sur mes cheveux', *Hellé*, 56) and after her uncle's death, Hellé refers to Mme Marboy as one of the few persons belonging to her social circle, defining her as 'une véritable amie' (*Hellé*, 187).

Not only does Mme Marboy immediately start to fill the emotional void in Hellé's life, but when the heroine tells her uncle about this unexpected encounter, M. de Riveyrac instantly points toward Mme Marboy's potential as a mentor: 'Cette aimable vieille t'enseignera les us et coutumes du monde et ne gâtera ni ton esprit ni ton coeur', thus indicating that the older woman can help Hellé to navigate the complicated social context of Parisian salons (*Hellé*, 49). When he first escorts Hellé to Mme Marboy, M. de Riveyrac explicitly entrusts the young girl to her new mentor:

> Je ne l'ai jamais confiée à qui que ce fût, mais elle ne saurait trouver une tutelle plus charmante et plus bienveillante que la vôtre. [...] Vous trouverez Hellé fort ignorante de beaucoup de choses. [...] Elle a le cerveau d'un homme et le cœur d'une vierge. Vous l'aimerez. Et l'œuvre de toute ma vie sera achevée par vous. (*Hellé*, 50)

In this excerpt, the employment of the word 'œuvre' suggests a reference to the myth of Pygmalion. Indeed, Hellé is the 'statue qu'il [M. de Riveyrac] taillait lentement, pareille à son idéal', the perfect woman made by a man, kept away from the traditional patterns of female socialization (i.e. her aunt's influence), and still awaiting a soul (*Hellé*, 21).[96] The uncle now wishes Mme Marboy to complete Hellé's education by helping her to decipher new social codes, but also by protecting her and possibly by assisting her in her choice of husband. At this point, the appointed mentor playfully reminds him that she does not share his views on women and asks him: 'Ne craignez-vous pas que je la défigure?', her words constituting yet another allusion to the Pygmalion myth (*Hellé*, 50). Mme Marboy describes herself as 'une femme qui a eu toutes les superstitions, toutes les faiblesses de son sexe, une créature nerveuse et tendre, sensible aux idées moins qu'aux sentiments', thus ascribing to herself some of the qualities of traditional femininity (e.g. sentimentality, irrationality, excitability, *Hellé*, 51). However, M. de Riveyrac is confident that Hellé, who has always been sheltered

[96]At the beginning of the novel, Hellé observes: 'Jamais je n'avais ouvert un roman, lu un journal, écouté des confidences de jeune fille. Au seuil de la jeunesse, j'étais une statue enveloppée de voiles blancs, vivant seulement par le front qui pense.' See *Hellé*, p. 28. Additional references to the Pygmalion myth are indicated in fn. 99 in this chapter.

from negative ‘influences féminines’, will not be persuaded to give in to ‘mysticisme’ or ‘sentimentalité’ by Mme Marboy’s example or advice (*Hellé*, 51). Hellé is not a dreamer or an impressionable girl, her uncle has given her the instruments to think and there is no risk of her turning into an Emma Bovary. The conversation that ensues between the two mentors is, unsurprisingly, about female identity and the role of women in society. While they both reject the model of the New Woman embodied by the *sportswomen*, ‘êtres bizarres qui chevauchaient des véhicules d’acier’, Mme Marboy clearly defends the ideal of the ‘maman’, the ‘épouse à la vieille mode’, while M. de Riveyrac promotes the ideal of a *femme moderne* who will be the equal of her husband and will guarantee the future of French society. The political aspect of this novel thus comes to the foreground. In differentiating the *femme moderne*, who ‘n’ammolira pas l’énergie de son mari’ and ‘élèvera une race vraiment virile’, both from the mannish New Woman, who was seen as partly responsible for the weakening of French society, and from the ‘épouse à la vieille mode’, ‘tremblante ingénue [...] proie éternelle des Don Juans’, M. de Riveyrac makes a case for the education of the *femme moderne* and for the promotion of a new ideal of womanhood in the context of a widespread fear of French *dégénérescence* (*Hellé*, 52, 53).[97] By contrast, the aristocratic Mme Marboy still champions an outdated model of femininity that does not fit within the modern world and needs to be replaced.

After having received her uncle’s blessing, Hellé quickly becomes very attached to the old woman; she spends a lot of time in her company and acts as ‘la fille de la maison’. At this stage, Mme Marboy’s house provides her with a much-needed shelter where she can forget that she is ‘une étrangère’ in Paris (*Hellé*, 65). However, despite this sincere and profound affection, Hellé is perspicacious enough to spot the old lady’s flaws, which she attributes to her aristocratic origins and inadequate education, initially regarding them with a kind of benevolent compassion (*Hellé*, 54, 55). When the two start to talk about romantic love Mme Marboy is surprised to discover Hellé’s extremely lucid and disenchanted opinion about men and relationships and asks her: ‘Qui vous a si bien instruite, bon Dieu! Vous ne lisez pas de romans?’ This passage possibly constitutes an allusion to Emma Bovary and certainly refers to the romanticized, unrealistic ideas that sentimental novels were accused of circulating (*Hellé*, 56).[98] Hellé confirms that she has never read a single novel in her life and opposes her observational skills and good judgement to the biased notions other girls of her age might develop by reading sentimental novels. To prove her point, she applies her

---

[97]This passage further supports the distinction proposed by Mesch in her analysis of Belle Epoque women’s press between the New Woman and the *femme moderne*. See p. 25 in this thesis.
[98]This view of literature can be placed in opposition to that presented in *La Cruche cassée*, where novels, as we have seen, are considered as instrumental to women’s liberation. See pp. 103–105 in this thesis.

critical skills to real-life situations, this attitude reflecting her education based on 'réflexion', 'raisonnement', and 'expérience' rather than books, and she discusses the example of three couples who got married during the winter, considering them with a sort of clear-headed, ironical contempt (*Hellé*, 19, 56, 57). Mme Marboy finds her 'féroce' but Hellé shows an unusual awareness of her own character and desires. She declares that her education will prevent her from falling for a mediocre person and that she will never risk her freedom and independence for anything less than true love. Mme Marboy, who believes that 'l'amour, c'est surtout la grande illusion' and that 'le bonheur [...] habite une sphère moyenne et tempérée' (*Hellé*, 58, 59), thereby adopting a typically bourgeois position, subsequently remarks:

> je suis presque effrayée quand je considère votre avenir. Vous êtes si différente de la femme telle que je la conçois! Votre beauté, votre intelligence, l'extrême hardiesse de votre esprit seront-elles des éléments de félicité ou de désastre? La femme, à mon avis, est un être de tendresse et de sacrifice, supérieure à l'homme par le sentiment, inférieure dans l'ordre intellectuel. Je la veux appuyée au bras de l'époux, penchée sur le berceau de l'enfant, agenouillée devant Dieu... (*Hellé*, 59)

Mme Marboy's words signal the newness of the kind of femininity embodied by Hellé. In this text, the *femme moderne* is still under construction and questions are raised about the appropriateness of this model, which can potentially entail either 'félicité' or 'désastre'. In spite of this warning, Hellé immediately resists Mme Marboy's attempts to talk her into adhering to a traditional model of womanhood, according to which women must remain ignorant, or even irrational ('inférieure dans l'ordre intellectuel'), and must submit to their husbands ('appuyée au bras de l'époux'), to their maternal duties ('penchée sur le berceau'), and to religion ('agenouillée devant Dieu'). Hellé scornfully associates this model with the 'inhuman' Virgin Mary 'dont la maternité ne fut glorieuse que par la réprobation de l'amour', in a sentence that challenges the indisputability of the Marian cult, which played such an important role in girls' education at the time (*Hellé*, 59).[99] The heroine expresses doubts about the value of such an ideal ('Mon devoir est-il de me mutiler, de m'humilier, de chercher le sacrifice comme but, d'aimer la douleur?') and at the end of the conversation she strongly asserts: 'Mon devoir est de réaliser la femme que je puis être, et d'être heureuse en aidant

[99]On the link between the Marian cult and girls' education, see for example Gale, *A World Apart*, pp. 43–44. The rejection of chastity as a positive value expressed in the three novels breaks the pattern of 'expiatory femininity' that is represented in novels such as Victorine Monniot's *Le Journal de Marguerite*, 30th edn (Paris: Librairie de Périsse Frères, 1886 [1857]). On 'expiatory femininity', see Daouda, 'L'anti-Salomé'.

au bonheur d'autrui', a purpose that she will be able to accomplish only with the support/mentoring of Antoine, who will effectively complete the uncle's work by turning Hellé into a modern woman (*Hellé*, 60).[100]

Mme Marboy's unfitness to perform the role of mentor and Hellé's dismissal of her lessons are highlighted several times in the text, sometimes even by way of a male perspective. When Antoine persuades Hellé to bring help and comfort to a young unmarried mother, Marie Lamirault, he remarks that:

> toute bonne qu'elle est, madame Marboy n'a pu se défaire de certaines superstitions... Elle ne refuserait pas d'aider une fille-mère, mais elle refuserait de vous mettre en rapport direct avec elle, vous, une jeune fille, une jeune fille honnête, pure, bien élevée et qui devez ignorer le mal. (*Hellé*, 121)[101]

Later on, Hellé realizes that there are certain realities that Mme Marboy, and even her own uncle, would not let her know about (*Hellé*, 135). Mme Marboy also strongly objects to the fact that, after M. de Riveyrac's death, Hellé, 'insoucieuse du préjugé', chooses to live on her own and refuses to be chaperoned (*Hellé*, 173). Things get even worse when, during the period of Hellé's engagement to Maurice, Mme Marboy and Mme de Nébriant, one of Maurice's aristocratic cousins, constantly act as *chaperonnes* and 's'efforçaient de [la] reconquérir à leurs idées, elles essayaient de combattre le fâcheux et choquant effet d'une éducation anormale' (*Hellé*, 212-13).

Mme Marboy's intrusion into Hellé's sentimental life is one of the main aspects of their relationship. Like Mme Villebau, Mme Marboy is at the origin of her *protégée*'s encounter with her future partner. At a dinner, she places Hellé between her godson Maurice, to whom she has already introduced the young heroine on a previous occasion, and her nephew Antoine. Unlike Hellé's uncle, Mme Marboy always shows a certain predilection for Maurice, a predilection initially shared by Hellé, who is rather charmed by his manners. At this early stage, other women in the text also try to play the role of 'marieuses' and advisors to Hellé, in particular Mme Gérard, the dim-witted wife of one of M. de Riveyrac's friends. After recommending marriage as the best prospect for a young woman, Mme Gérard tries

---

[100]Further developing the Pygmalion reference, when Antoine declares his love for Hellé, he talks of '[l]a statue [qui] devenait femme' under his influence. Later on, in a silent conversation with her departed uncle, Hellé observes: 'c'est pour lui [Antoine] que vous m'avez taillé, dans un marbre incorruptible, la statue idéale qu'il devait animer en me touchant.' See *Hellé*, pp. 171, 273.

[101] Antoine confirms the hypocritical and conservative character of nineteenth-century French women's charitable work, when he asserts that '[les] femmes du monde [...] sont élégiaques et charitables pour les pauvres d'opéra-comique, les bons pauvres bien propres et bien polis, pour les filles qui se conduisent bien et les ouvriers point ivrognes'. See *Hellé*, p. 134.

to set Hellé up with an uninteresting but ambitious man in search of a wife to support his political career. When Hellé refuses his offer of marriage, Mme Gérard reacts by insinuating that Antoine is in love with her and warmly invites Hellé to distrust a man who has renounced his title and fortune, who lives as a virtual recluse, nurtures subversive ideas, and sides with 'la crapule'. However, Hellé objects decisively to Mme Gérard's calumnies and firmly refuses to be counselled by her, reducing her to tears before making up with her (*Hellé*, 102–106). After this episode, Hellé turns to her mentor and confidante for help and advice. Despite defending her nephew and acknowledging the nobility of his choices — he has in fact renounced his title and wealth to dedicate his life to the more unfortunate — Mme Marboy takes this opportunity to inform Hellé that Antoine could not make a suitable husband:

> La compagne qu'il rêve — s'il rêve — n'existe nulle part. Vous-même, Hellé, dont il admire la haute intelligence, vous-même n'auriez pas le goût, ni le courage d'associer votre vie à la vie de Genesvrier. J'avoue que si j'étais une fille de vingt ans, Antoine, tout admirable qu'il est, ne me séduirait guère. Je n'en ferais pas mon fiancé, mais je serais fière et heureuse qu'il voulût bien être mon ami. (*Hellé*, 109)

In this way, Mme Marboy discourages Hellé from considering Antoine as a possible romantic choice and subsequently stresses his difference from Maurice, whom she considers both 'aimable' and 'raffiné' (*Hellé*, 111). Just when Hellé is telling Antoine that she needs some time to carefully consider his marriage proposal, Mme Marboy pays her a visit in the company of Maurice, who has just come back from a long journey (*Hellé*, 177). It is no mystery that Mme Marboy favours their union:

> [Mme Marboy] se plut à nous réunir, Maurice et moi. Sensible à la gaieté de son filleul, à sa courtoisie, aux attentions dont il l'entourait, elle favorisait tous ses desseins. Elle s'appliquait à incliner mon âme vers Maurice. N'était-il pas tout pareil, peut-être, à son idéal de jeune fille, à l'homme qu'à mon âge elle eût aimé? (*Hellé*, 193)

In promoting this match, Mme Marboy is encouraging Hellé to choose the kind of man she would have chosen for herself in the past ('à mon âge'), at a time still removed from the new claims and aspirations of Belle Epoque women. Moreover, Mme Marboy is pressing Hellé to become the kind of woman that, according to her, she ought to be. For Mme Marboy, there is an 'homme idéal' fit for the 'femme idéale', and both can contribute to the preservation of society as it is.

When she slowly starts to realize that Maurice, to whom she is now engaged, might not be the person she thought he was, Hellé tries to confide her doubts and fears to her mentor. Marie Lamirault, the unwed mother succoured by Hellé, is at the origin of a fight between Hellé and her fiancé, and Mme Marboy readily takes Maurice's side, reminding Hellé how a *femme honnête* is supposed to behave:

> Vous méprisez l'opinion; vous raillez les convenances mondaines; et vous oubliez que vous n'êtes plus libre! Vous avez mené, jusqu'à présent, une existence anormale et tout exceptionnelle. N'espérez pas continuer cette existence en y associant votre fiancé. S'il vous faut sacrifier des habitudes, des préférences, des affections même que Maurice ne saurait approuver, n'hésitez pas ma petite amie: sacrifiez le passé à l'avenir. [...] [A]u nom de votre bonheur futur, défaites-vous de ces idées qui, amusantes, excusables chez la jeune fille, seraient intolérables chez la jeune femme. On vous a élevée comme un garçon très intelligent, dans une liberté qui convient au caractère viril et ne s'allie pas avec la réserve et la soumission féminine. (*Hellé*, 228, 229)

Mme Marboy points out the inappropriateness of Hellé's education and urges her to abandon her principles and suppress those aspects of her personality, such as her intelligence and independence, which are deemed 'masculine' and do not match the requirements of mainstream femininity, thus reinstating traditional gender stereotypes ('garçon', 'intelligent', 'liberté', and 'viril' are opposed to the 'réserve' and 'soumission féminine'). In addition to this, she points to the conflict between personal happiness and collective good, demanding that Hellé renounce 'le passé' (i.e. her dreams and ambitions) in the name of the 'avenir', by which she means Hellé's marriage and the greater good of the nation.[102] Mme Marboy then asserts that Antoine has exerted a bad influence on Hellé and that the latter is ill-prepared to be a wife, but that hopefully marriage will constitute an opportunity for redemption. When, in response to these observations, Hellé pronounces a subversive and passionate speech about women's freedom and about equality in marriage, Mme Marboy severely admonishes her: 'vous êtes bien la femme des temps nouveaux [...] vous êtes une révoltée, ma pauvre fille. La vie vous pliera et vous brisera' (*Hellé*, 230, 231). When Hellé finally cancels the wedding, Mme Marboy tries to interfere, asserting that Maurice and she are made for each other and that love will fix everything, but Hellé is too wise and resourceful to be persuaded by such weak arguments. When she opens once again her heart to Mme Marboy and explains her point of view, the incompatibility between

[102]The conflict between personal happiness and collective good and the topic of female sacrifice will be further explored in Chapter Four on 'Female Rivalry and Love Triangles'.

Hellé, 'la femme des temps nouveaux', et Mme Marboy, a defender of tradition who 'subissait l'antique influence de l'éducation qui fait la femme respectueuse de l'homme parce qu'il est homme, acceptant de la même main la caresse et joug', becomes irreconcilable and Mme Marboy ultimately rejects Hellé: 'Je n'étais plus la fille de son cœur' (*Hellé*, 257, 258).

Tinayre's novel offer an example of 'horizontal' homosociality in which the mentorship relation established between the younger heroine and the older woman temporarily provides the *protégée* with shelter, assistance, and emotional support in a time of need and transition, and exists in perfect harmony with the social order. This relationship, however, is destined to fail because Hellé, influenced by two male mentors (i.e. her uncle and Antoine) who have encouraged her to become a *femme moderne*, is determined to defy traditional conventions and stubbornly refuses her female mentor's attempts to turn her into a traditional woman. Female mentors like Mme Marboy are compliant with the status quo and the relationships that they try to foster with other women resemble the models of female interaction promoted by conduct manuals of the time, in which women were told to encourage each other in performing the tasks that society imposed on them. In this example, Mme Marboy functions as the main agent within a network of women who insistently try to educate Hellé according to conservative notions about women's place in society.[103] The novel suggests that a conservative form of female mentoring has become unsuitable and does not respond to young girls' needs and expectations any more. In fact, Tinayre portrays the relationship between Hellé and Mme Marboy as unsuccessful and represents it as an obstacle that the heroine must overcome in order to affirm herself and find her happiness, which comes in the form of a marriage of equals; Mme Marboy's influence is thus mostly ineffective and her figure is ultimately disempowered within the text to the advantage of a male figure, Hellé's true mentor and future husband Antoine, with whom the heroine will endeavour to create a better society. In this sense, the novel represents a reversal of *Les Cervelines*, in which, in order to become a *femme moderne*, Marceline needs to reject the male figure (Jean) and side with her female mentor/friend Jeanne. What both novels consistently shows is that the mentoring practices attempted by the most conventional characters, usually the descendants of a dying aristocracy, are frustrated up to the end and that the heroine chooses to follow the lead of those figures, male or female, who promote more progressive views on women's roles in a changing society.

---

[103]This network also includes Mme Gérard and Mme de Nébriant. On the other side, not only M. de Riveyrac and Antoine, but also Marie Lemirault and Mlle Frémant, 'une femme de lettres, très laide, très intelligente, pétrie de fiel et de vinaigre, réchérchée et rédoutée de tous', provide alternative role models. See *Hellé*, p. 234.

Conclusion

Belle Epoque women writers create strong female mentoring figures who not only perform some of the traditional tasks of the mentor, but more subversively contribute to the shaping of a new generation of *femmes modernes* and to the heroine's empowerment and emancipation in a changing world. These female relationships are invested with narrative power, insofar as they variously delegitimize parental and patriarchal authority, moral prejudices, and romantic love, thus hinting at the potentially crucial roles that women can play in each other's lives. The authors themselves often appear to take on this task, by means of fictional doubles and through the extension of the theme of female mentoring from the narrative content to the author-reader relationship itself, using literature as an instrument to discuss and negotiate ideas about women's experiences and identities. In this sense, the novels themselves can be thought of as 'perlocutory acts', through which the authors guide their readers.[104]

Each novel depicts a conflict between opposing ideals of womanhood. Traditional femininity is unsuccessfully promoted by female figures who are attached to a decadent aristocracy (Mme Robert, Mme Marboy, and even, to some extent, Marceline, in her failed attempts at mentoring Jeanne) or by patriarchal male figures (Jean Cécile and Maurice Clairmont). It is only by adhering to the model of the *femme moderne*, as symbolically represented by female characters who have already embraced this ideal, like Mme Villebau and Jeanne, or as supported by male characters who are more attuned to the requirements of modernity, like M. de Riveyrac and Antoine, that the heroine manages to access adulthood.

The three novels are worthy of attention for the ways in which they portray 'horizontal' and 'vertical' female homosociality and for their contribution to the social and political debate over the attributes of femininity and the roles of women. The distinction between 'horizontal' and 'vertical' female homosociality, in particular, is a reflection on the saving or potentially destructive effects that women can exert on each other's lives. In *La Cruche cassée* and *Hellé*, the blame for women's oppression and for the stability of the patriarchal system is put on matriarchal figures like Mme Robert and Mme Marboy who, for example, still see arranged or traditional marriage as the natural path for women to follow. Female mentors, however, can also exert a more positive impact on the heroine's journey, by supporting her in her process of self-determination. In this way, some Belle Epoque novels carve out a new space for women and women's relationships in fiction.

---

[104]On Austin's definition of 'perlocutory acts', see pp. 105–106 in this thesis.

It is important to note that, in addition to establishing a sort of ideological 'counter-discourse' about women and their relations, these novels also present some innovative aspects at the literary level. In particular, each text deconstructs the model of romantic love, although in different ways. The ending of *Les Cervelines* challenges the well-established literary tradition of female characters choosing love over friendship or career, as both Jeanne and Marceline refuse the possibility of becoming wives and mothers in order to preserve their relationship and to satisfy their intellectual needs. In *La Cruche cassée*, Aline cannot overcome the obstacles thrown in her way during her search for romantic fulfilment. Even though she is able to dismiss the thought of Maurice's Bertha-like, mad first wife, her lover is killed by her oppressive mother directly after she has offered him her virginity. However, Aline later falls for another man who, in order to be with her, decides to look past social prejudices and who accepts that she does not need to be chaste in order to be loved or respected. Hellé recovers in time from her crush on Maurice, the charming and superficial George Wickham of the situation, to pursue an ideal of love based on friendship and on the accomplishment of collective good. In spite of the difficulties and hesitations experienced by these female characters, none of them could be mistaken for the traditional victim-like heroine who ends up trapped in an unhappy marriage or dead, like Emma Bovary or Jeanne Le Perthuis Des Vauds.

In a period characterized by the crisis of the hero and the search for new role models, these heroines are represented as smart, rational, resilient, and capable women who can choose either to support themselves psychologically and financially, or to enter into a more equal form of marriage. By the end of the novel, they have all turned into self-assured adults who can love, work, and contribute to the welfare of society, rightfully claiming their place in the world. And this is due, in no small part, to the support of other women.

CHAPTER THREE

Female Communities in Schoolgirl Fiction

Introduction

Our discussion in the first two chapters of this thesis centred on the novelistic representation of friendship and mentoring among pairs of female characters, paying particular attention to the ways in which, more often than not, such fictional relationships serve to deconstruct gender stereotypes and promote complex, somewhat progressive ideals of femininity in fiction. This chapter will broaden the scope of our investigation by focusing on larger groups of female characters, and particularly on the homosocial dynamics occurring in female communities at school, as represented in Belle Epoque schoolgirl fiction. This introductory section will provide some information regarding the emergence of female communities and networks of support during the Belle Epoque, the progress made in terms of female education under the early Third Republic, the genre of schoolgirl fiction, and the literary idea of female community.

According to Juliette Rogers:

> The events of the Third Republic that would have the most significant impact on women's lives, both immediately and on a long-term basis, were the creation of girls' public secondary schools and women's teacher training schools (*les écoles normales*), along with the decision to require primary education for all girls.[1]

Among the main outcomes of the advancements registered in the fields of female education and professionalization under the early Third Republic, one in particular is of interest for the purposes of this thesis: the emergence of different kinds of female communities. These included communities of students and teachers within the scholastic system at all levels, communities of working women in various professional fields, some of which were sometimes still considered as male territory, but also new reading and writing communities, and a number of female networks of support, ranging from the societies boasting an explicitly feminist vocation to those institutions more generally created to foster women's presence in the cultural and public spheres. In this sense, the advent of secular, state-regulated primary

---

[1]Rogers, *Career Stories*, p. 15.

and secondary education for girls exerted a 'significant impact on women's lives', to use Rogers' expression, in terms of female homosociality.

Educational, professional, literary, and other women-oriented communities had at least one thing in common: they widened or created new spaces of exclusively female sociability. In nineteenth-century France, including during the early Third Republic, female homosociality, at least in the case of bourgeois and upper-class women, was often a private, domestic matter. A tendency to reduce women's relationships to the private sphere is evinced not only by the association of female relations with such elements as emotional intimacy, physical tenderness, or the sharing of secrets, but also by the very nature and relative narrowness of the physical space in which female interactions could occur. Nineteenth-century men could gather in a myriad of public, often entirely male socializing venues, such as for example clubs, cabarets, *bistrots*, offices, or the army, therefore creating different types of bonds among themselves, which spanned professional partnerships and comradeships or close friendships. By contrast, whether well-heeled Belle Epoque women were meeting at home during their *five o' clock* or in a *salon de thé*, in their parlours and boudoirs or in public gardens, this had little effect over the type of relationship they could foster.[2] Anne Vincent-Buffault comments on the extent to which female confinement to the private sphere reduced women's opportunities to diversify their relationships:

> Pour les hommes du XIXe siècle, les vies professionnelle, sexuelle, affective, sociale se scindent en lieux d'expériences aux frontières relativement étanches où peuvent se nouer des relations autonomes les unes par rapport aux autres : amitiés de négoce, fraternité professionnelle, sociabilité masculine, camaraderie de jeunesse [...] A l'inverse, le cantonnement, certes relatif, des femmes dans la sphère privée ne conduit pas à la différenciation des engagements affectifs.[3]

---

[2]Studies of women's leisure time in the nineteenth century inform us that during this period the association between leisure and domesticity was strengthened, even though it should be noted that women's involvement with charitable work and philanthropic activities facilitated a shift from domesticity toward the public domain. See Proctor, 'Home and Away', in *Women in Europe*, ed. by Simonton, pp. 315, 320. My discussion in this paragraph is limited to middle and upper-class women and to activities exclusively linked to female sociability. Proctor also lists a series of public leisure activities in which elite and/or middle-class women engaged, such as attending assemblies, opera performances, public trials, balls, parties, card games, races, military displays, fireworks shows, balloons ascensions and exhibitions. These were, however, activities enjoyed in the company of men, as well as of other women. As for working-class women, their life conditions often prevented them from engaging in those domestic forms of sociability that characterized upper-class women's daily schedules (i.e. rounds of visiting, the *five o' clock*), and gathered in public venues, such as the Parisian cafés, the music-hall, and public parks. Their modes of sociability followed different patterns. Therefore, the association between female homosociality and the private sphere is less or not relevant in their case. See Proctor, 'Home and Away', in *Women in Europe*, ed. by Simonton, pp. 316, 321, 322.

[3]Vincent-Buffault, *Exercice de l'amitié*, p. 244.

In discussing the symbolic division between male/public versus female/private spaces of sociability, André Rauch asks: 'qu'advient-il lorsque les femmes se mettent à fréquenter l'école puis le lycée, le café-concert et les rivages marins ?'.[4] One might narrow this question down to what happens more specifically to female homosociality when these new, public socializing venues (i.e. the *écoles de filles*, *lycées*, and *écoles normales*) are open to and attended by significantly increasing numbers of women. As we shall see, Belle Epoque literature can offer us some interesting insights into this topic.

However, it should be noted that discussion of female homosociality in the educational context is not peculiar to the Belle Epoque, as French writers of conduct books, school manuals, and essays (but also novelists) comment on the significance of friendship during adolescence throughout the whole nineteenth century.[5] Indeed, even before the introduction of mandatory secular education, friendship had a role to play in girls' life at the convent or at boarding school, when, cut off from their families, the students could feel a stronger need to foster deep and close relationships with chosen companions.[6] The value of friendship during this life stage is often highlighted in nineteenth-century essays and conduct books. For example, Mme de Maussion declares that: 'Les amitiés formées dès la jeunesse sont toujours les plus précieuses et les plus sûres, surtout pour les femmes, qui pour la plupart n'ont qu'à cette époque de leur vie la liberté d'en jeter les fondements.'[7] Auguste Wiseman, in his essay entitled *L'Amitié* (1872), confirms that adolescence, for both sexes, could be the scenario of real friendship, especially in the context of the boarding school.[8] Clarisse Juranville, in her *Manuel d'éducation morale et d'instruction civique à*

---

[4]André Rauch, *Le Premier Sexe: mutations et crise de l'identité masculine, 1789–1914* (Paris: Hachette, 2000), p. 11.

[5]According to historians, in the nineteenth century adolescence emerged as a life stage during which friendship was thought to play a crucial role in terms of the individual's development. Agnès Thiercé, for example, argues that: 'La seconde moitié du XIXe siècle donne à l'adolescence sa signification moderne et forge la classe d'âge adolescente.' Thiercé observes that female adolescence, as an age class, was recognized later than its male equivalent, and its boundaries were overall less well defined. By the end of the nineteenth century, however, this life stage usually encompassed the period between the age of 12–13 and 18–20. Adolescence was then considered a phase of 'naissance sociale', during which the importance of friendship could not be overlooked. See Agnès Thiercé, *Histoire de l'adolescence* (Paris: Belin, 1999), pp. 5–26 and 117–34. On the topic of friendship and adolescence in nineteenth-century France, see also Vincent-Buffault, 'L'Adolescence inventée', in *Exercice de l'amitié*, pp. 135–84.

[6]According to Rebecca Rogers, for example, boarding schools, especially during the first decades of the nineteenth century, represented for girls alternative families where solid and nurturing bonds between students or between students and teachers could be created, and where female friendship acquired a privileged status. See Rebecca Rogers, *From the Salon to the Schoolroom: Educating Bourgeois Girls in Nineteenth-Century France* (University Park: Penn State University Press, 2005), pp. 71–73. On girls' education and sociability in nineteenth-century France, and particularly before the 1880s, see also Gabrielle Houbre, *La Discipline de l'amour* (1997), and Anne Vincent-Buffault, *Exercice de l'amitié* (1995).

[7]Maussion, *Lettre sur l'amitié*, p. 81.

[8]Auguste Wiseman, *L'Amitié* (Paris: Bray et Retaux, 1872), pp. 153–56.

l'usage des jeunes filles (1911) also highlights the relevance, for girls, of the bonds they could foster during the school years:

> L'école, la pension, c'est en effet, en petit, une société: on vit en commun, on reçoit les mêmes leçons, on travaille de concert et on s'amuse ensemble, les relations s'établissent et l'amitié naît. Ces affections de l'aurore de la vie se conservent toujours.[9]

I have purposefully chosen, above, three examples of texts that span the so-called long nineteenth century and that testify to the consistent importance attributed to friendship during the critical and formative years of adolescence throughout this period.

By the end of the century, these years corresponded to a time when girls were often engaged in full-time education in the public, cross-class space of the Third Republican school. Thiercé underlines the impact of the educational reforms of the 1880s on female homosociality when she asserts that: 'En sortant du foyer, du cadre familial, en intégrant des structures propres à son âge, l'adolescence féminine accède à une existence collective et à une nouvelle sociabilité.'[10] If convents and boarding schools arguably were, and still are in the Belle Epoque, privileged spaces of female sociability, this is also true, and perhaps more importantly so, for Third Republican schools, in which increasing numbers of girls coming from different backgrounds are allowed to experience education as a communal reality characterized by interactions with their peers as well as with older women.

Patricia Tilburg refers to the Republican school as 'an institutional setting that, given the peculiar prominence of girls' education in political debates in the Third Republic, conveyed a wealth of cultural meaning to readers' and notes that 'the schoolgirl had become, by 1900, one of the eligible types of modern French society'. For Tilburg, it is the combined fascination with female adolescence and education that promoted the appearance of a new genre of 'girls' school novels' at the turn of the century.[11] This chapter will investigate which aspects of female homosociality are more prominent within this new literary genre and in which ways the fictional relations occurring within the world of the Third Republican school, as it is imagined and portrayed by authors who are themselves the products of this educational system, influence the characters' sense of self and their development. Before discussing these elements, I would like to provide a brief overview of female education in Belle Epoque France and explore in more detail how the progress registered in this field

---

[9]Juranville, *Manuel d'éducation morale*, p. 74. For more information about Juranville's works and life, see *Notice sur Clarisse Juranville.*

[10]Thiercé, *Histoire de l'adolescence*, p. 142.

[11]Tilburg, *Colette's Republic*, p. 77.

promoted the appearance or reinforced the presence of certain female communities. I shall subsequently highlight the ways in which both topics (i.e. female education and female communities) are relevant to the authors and novels considered in this thesis.

Given women's domestic destiny and the fact that their intellectual abilities were generally thought to be inferior to those of men, educational opportunities for nineteenth-century French girls were rather limited. Before the educational reforms of the 1880s, rich bourgeois and aristocratic ladies were sent either to convents or to private, secular boarding schools directed by non-religious women. Sometimes they attended private courses delivered by male professors and, in many cases, they were educated at home by their mothers or by private governesses. These different forms of education (i.e. religious, secular, maternal, and domestic) co-existed and were variously supported or challenged by pedagogues and politicians throughout the century. In certain cases, they continued to be preferred education choices even after the creation of primary and secondary public schools for girls under the Third Republic. The female curriculum outlined during the first half of the century and hardly modified with the advent of the public school, focused on religion, literature, history, geography, foreign languages, and the so-called *arts d'agrément.* These included dance, music, drawing, painting, and needlework, the latter being considered as the ultimate feminine art. Scientific subjects, philosophy, and the Classics (Greek and Latin) were generally excluded.[12]

The second half of the century registered a series of advancements in the field of female education, culminating in the educational reforms of the 1880s. In 1850, the *loi Falloux* envisaged the institution of primary schools for girls in towns of 800 or more inhabitants, an action rarely carried out subsequently for lack of funding, and in 1867 the minister of education Victor Duruy made an attempt to provide secondary education for girls at the national level. By 1880, the question of female education was at the heart of the political and philosophical debates between Catholics and Republicans, the latter wishing to remove women from the influence of the Church in order to educate the wives and mothers of the Third Republic in accordance with the principles of the *morale laïque.*[13] In 1881–82, with the *lois Jules Ferry*, primary education for all children from the age of six to thirteen became secular, free, and mandatory. The *Ecole Normale Supérieure de Fontenay-aux-Roses* and the *Ecole Normale Supérieure de Sèvres*, whose mission was to train the new female teaching staff, opened in 1880 and 1881 respectively. In 1880, the *loi Camille Sée*

[12]For a detailed account of female education in nineteenth-century France, see Françoise Mayeur, *L'Éducation des filles en France au XIXe siècle* (Paris: Perrin, 2008 [1979]).
[13]For a discussion of the *morale laïque* see Tilburg, *Colette's Republic.*

led to the creation of a national system of *coll□ges* (three-year program) and *lycées* (additional two years). By 1914, the number of female secondary students had increased from a few hundred to up to 38,000.[14] The secondary-school program involved the study of literature, modern languages, history, geography, and the *morale laïque,* along with an introduction to scientific subjects (arithmetic, geometry, chemistry, physics, and natural history). The curriculum also included gymnastics, hygiene, domestic economy, needlework, drawing, and music.[15]

Despite the widening educational opportunities available to women during the Belle Epoque, historians have pointed out that the educational reforms did not follow feminist principles and were not intended to encourage female emancipation. This is not surprising, given that those who promoted these reforms were hardly supportive of feminist goals. In fact, anticlerical politicians often shared with their Catholic adversaries a conservative vision of womanhood, and the education provided by the State was aimed at consolidating women's place within the family in the traditional roles of partners and educators. In the beginning, secondary education was not supposed to open the way to women's professionalization and the qualification girls could aspire to, the *diplôme d'études secondaires*, had no practical value. As stated by Rebecca Rogers:

> Republicans wanted thinking and rational wives and mothers, but they were far from advocating a rethinking of gender roles that would have led women to assume more active lives in public.[16]

However, the emphasis the school put on the value of work, the decision to train female *professeurs* to be employed in the new *coll□ges* and *lycées*, and the parents' desire to ensure their daughters' economic independence through education, brought about unintended effects that were in contradiction with the domestic ideals openly promoted by the Third Republic. Patricia Tilburg, among others, has observed that:

> Villages across France built secular public schools for their daughters as a means of forming sensible and obedient helpmeets, but officials also insisted that such schools provide girls with a practical professional training that threatened to upset traditional notions of women's social roles.[17]

---

[14]Mayeur, *Éducation des filles*, pp. 256–57.

[15]For a complete list of subjects, see Mayeur, *Éducation des filles,* Annexe IV, pp. 323–24.

[16]Rogers, *From the Salon to the Schoolroom*, p. 208.

[17]Tilburg, *Colette's Republic*, p. 24. For discussions about the effects produced by the educational reforms, often in contradiction with the intentions of the reformers, see for example: Patricia A. Tilburg, 'Work, Class,

In terms of professional degrees, female students could pass the *brevet élémentaire* in order to become primary-school teachers, while the *certificat* and *agrégation*, prepared in the *écoles normales*, allowed them to teach, respectively, in the female *collèges* and *lycées.* Little by little, female students also started to obtain the *baccalauréat* and to access higher education in increasing numbers. Their number in the universities rose from 624 in 1900 to 2547 in 1914, when they represented 10% of the student population.[18] Those girls who had gone so far as to access higher education also started to make their appearance in male-dominated professional fields such as law and medicine. Despite the small number of women actually practising these professions, the diversification of the possibilities that became available to them outside the domestic sphere, the shifts produced in terms of their sense of identity, and the potential tensions arising from the contrast between traditional and new feminine roles, became of great interest to Belle Epoque female authors, who often explored these topics in their novels.[19]

The laws passed in the 1880s promoted the emergence of female communities of students and teachers at all levels and reinforced the presence of women within prestigious male fields and within new sectors accessible to the lower class.[20] In addition to these elements, one of the main effects of the educational reforms was the rise in the literacy rate among French women of all classes, the percentage of female illiteracy dropping from 31% in 1875 to 2.7% in 1914.[21] The emergence of a new, expanded female readership created new demands in the publishing market and its existence contributed to the flourishing of women's magazines as well as to the growing success of popular fiction at the turn of the century. These factors, combined in particular with the 1881 law on press freedom and with the technological improvements registered in the field of printing, also encouraged (educated) women to pursue literary careers.[22] In this sense, the efforts made by the French

---

and Secular Girls' Education', in *Colette's Republic*, pp. 23–45; Rebecca Rogers, 'Political Battles for Women's Minds in the Second Half of the Nineteenth Century', in *From the Salon to the Schoolroom*, pp. 201–26; Juliette M. Rogers, 'Innovation and Education: Historical Contexts from the Belle Epoque', in *Career Stories*, pp. 15–42; and Beth W. Gale, 'Education, Literature and the Battle over Female Identity in Third Republic France', in *Culture Wars and Literature in the French Third Republic*, ed. by Gilbert D. Chaitin (Newcastle upon Tyne: Cambridge Scholar Publishing, 2008), pp. 103–27.

[18]See Mayeur, *Éducation des filles*, pp. 228, 237–40, 259.

[19]See Rogers, 'Innovation and Education', in *Career Stories*, pp. 15–42.

[20]While teaching positions were generally the most sought after, Juliette Rogers' study also underlines that the educational reforms allowed working-class girls to become more educated and that new employment opportunities opened up for them, for example in retailing and in the tertiary sector.

[21]Data quoted in Dominique Dinet, 'L'Éducation des filles de la fin du 18e siècle jusqu'en 1918', *Revue des sciences religieuses*, 85.4 (2011), 457–90 (p. 488).

[22]The question of female writing during the Belle Epoque, the factors that promoted or hindered women's access to literary careers, and the expansion of the female reading public have been considered by various scholars. See for example Mélanie E. Collado, *Colette, Lucie Delarue-Mardrus, Marcelle Tinayre: émancipation et résignation* (Paris: Hachette, 2003); Ellen Constans, *Ouvrières des lettres*; Diana Holmes

Republic to provide primary and secondary education for girls can be said to have produced a significant impact on women as both producers and consumers of culture during the Belle Epoque, by promoting the creation and growth of female reading and writing communities.

On the subject of female literary communities during the Belle Epoque, Melanie Collado has interestingly argued that:

> Contrairement à l'idée répandue que les femmes entretenaient toujours des rapports de rivalité entre elles, la correspondance échangée entre plusieurs femmes de lettres montre qu'elles formaient une communauté et qu'elles s'encourageaient réciproquement.[23]

In a similar way, Jennifer Milligan has observed that early twentieth-century women writers needed to create their own professional networks in order to consolidate their presence within the literary field.[24] These networks of female solidarity and sociability often took the traditional form of the literary salon. Among the numerous salons existing at the time, the one hosted in Paris from 1909 by the American writer and patroness Natalie Clifford Barney offers a good example of the way in which these venues supported female creativity and helped to foster solid bonds between women engaged in similar careers. Barney's salon functioned for over fifty years and, along with the *Académie des Femmes* that she founded at a later stage, in 1927, it played an important role in the promotion of women's writing. Her contribution has been described by Tama Lea Engelking in the following way:

> Inspired by Sappho's example, and a 300-year-long tradition of women-hosted salons, Barney created a supportive environment in her salon and *Académie des Femmes* to foster female friendship, create artistic contacts, promote an exchange of literary ideas between women, and encourage, inspire and celebrate the literary creations of her friends.[25]

'Passion, Piety, and the New Woman', in *Romance and readership*, pp. 21–45; Rogers, 'Innovation and Education', in *Career Stories*, pp. 15–42; and Von Kulessa, *Entre la reconnaissance et l'exclusion*. For contemporary discussions of the presence and status of female authors in the Belle Epoque literary panorama, see Von Kulessa, *Entre la reconnaissance et l'exclusion*, pp. 157–99.

[23]Collado, *Colette, Lucie Delarue-Mardrus, Marcelle Tinayre,* p. 33.

[24]Jennifer E. Milligan, *The Forgotten Generation: French Women Writers of the Inter-War Period* (Oxford; New York: Berg, 1996), pp. 37–39. Milligan refers both to the creation of literary salons and to the *Prix Fémina*, which I discuss below, by combining information driven from additional sources. For a discussion of solidarity among women writers in nineteenth-century France, see also Finch, *Women's Writing*, pp. 17–18.

[25]Engelking, 'The Literary Friendships of Natalie Clifford Barney', p. 104. On Barney's salon, see also Melanie Hawthorn, 'Clans and Chronologies: The Salon of Natalie Barney', in *'A Belle Epoque'?*, ed. by Holmes and Tarr, pp. 65–79. Von Kulessa provides a list and discussion of women-hosted literary salons around 1900 in *Entre la reconnaissance et l'exclusion*, pp. 147–55.

Another initiative consolidating women's presence in the Belle Epoque literary world was the creation of the *Prix Fémina* in 1904. Initially known under the name of *Prix Vie Heureuse* after the magazine whose director, Mme Caroline de Broutelles, took the initiative of establishing the literary award, this prize represented women's response to the exclusion of female authors from the *Prix Goncourt.* Granted by an all-female jury and regardless of the author's sex, in the years between 1904 and 1914 the *Prix Fémina* was awarded to four female authors (Myriam Harry, Colette Yver, Marguerite Audoux, and Camille Marbo). One of the declared aims of the prize was to create 'bonds of confraternity' between women of letters and, in the early twentieth century, the *Prix Fémina* functioned as a sort of *Académie Féminine*, working to secure women's access to cultural power and participation in literary debates, and providing them with a much needed space of literary sociability and support.[26] A sense of sociability among intellectual women was also promoted by the institution of the *Vendredis Fémina*, a series of weekly gatherings held at the *Théâtre Fémina* and mainly addressed to a female audience.[27] In the fields of journalism and theatre, the renowned feminist newspaper *La Fronde*, founded by Marguerite Durand and entirely managed by women between 1887 and 1905, constitutes an additional example of Belle Epoque female professional communities, along with the 'Halte', the *Association des Auteurs Dramatiques Féminins*, or the *Théâtre Féministe* founded by Marya Chéliga.[28]

The elements discussed above are relevant to this thesis in many ways. Most of the authors I refer to in this chapter belonged to the generation of women born in the 1870s who benefited from the educational reforms promoted by the Third Republic or were involved at some level with the educational system. For example, Gabrielle Réval graduated from the *Ecole Normale Supérieure de Sèvres* in 1890 and taught in a female high school in Niort

---

[26]On the Prix Fémina see Sylvie Ducas, 'Le Prix Fémina: la consécration littéraire au féminin', *Recherches féministes*, 16.1 (2003), 43–95; Margot Irvine, 'Une académie de femmes?', *Les Résaux de femmes de lettres au XIXᵉ siècle, @nalyses*, 3.2 (2008), 14–24; '"Des liens de confraternité?": Friendships and Factions of the Jury of the Prix Fémina (1904–1965)', in *Solitaires, Solidaires*, ed. by Hugueny-Léger and Verdier, pp. 137–50; and Von Kulessa, *Entre la reconnaissance et l'exclusion*, pp. 127–34.

[27]During the same period, the magazine *Vie Heureuse* created the *Lycéum*, a female club aiming at promoting women's intellectual exchanges. On the *Lycéum* and the *Vendredis Fémina* see Von Kulessa, *Entre la reconnaissance et l'exclusion*, pp. 140–41.

[28]On the association 'Halte', see Kimberly van Noort, 'Spectacles of Themselves: Women Writing for the Stage in Belle Epoque France', in *A 'Belle Epoque'?*, ed. by Holmes and Tarr, pp. 139–52. On the *Théâtre Fémina* and the *Théâtre Féministe*, see Von Kulessa, *Entre la reconnaissance et l'exclusion*, pp. 41–45. On *La Fronde* see, for example, Roberts, *Disruptive Acts*, and Maggie Allison, 'Marguerite Durand and La Fronde: Voicing Women of the Belle Epoque', in *A 'Belle Epoque'?*, ed. by Holmes and Tarr, pp. 37–50. Furthermore, Rachel Mesch has called attention to the particular community formed by the readers and writers of women's magazines and novels during the Belle Epoque. See Mesch, *Having it All,* p. 6. For further discussion of the networks of female solidarity and sociability created by the writers and readers of women's newspapers, particularly during the first half of the nineteenth century, see Siobhán McIlvanney, 'Scribbling Sorority: Writer-Reader Relations in the Early French Women's Press and *Le Journal des Dames*', and Lucie Roussel-Richard, 'La Naissance de la presse féminine comme réponse aux solitudes des écrivaines en France au XIXᵉ siècle', in *Solidaires, Solitaires*, ed. by Hugueney-Léger and Verdier, pp. 95–114 and 115–36.

until 1899, when she was sent away because of a liaison with a widowed man.[29] Yvette Prost graduated from the *Ecole Normale Supérieure de Moulins* in 1893 and, after having taught for a few years, became the director of a girls' school in Lapalisse.[30] Marcelle Tinayre, whose mother Louise Chasteau was an educational writer and the director of the *Ecole Normale Supérieure de Fontenay-aux-Roses*, obtained the *baccalauréat.*[31] Information about Colette Yver's educational background is scarce, but she probably attended a Catholic school in Rouen and prepared for the *brevet supérieur.*[32] Daniel Lesueur, although belonging to an earlier generation not directly affected by the reforms, resumed her studies at a later stage. In 1883 she obtained the *brevet supérieur* in Versailles and subsequently worked as a teacher.[33] The aristocratic Thérèse Bentzon, born in 1840, was home-schooled by her mother and by an English governess.[34] These writers often showed a particular interest in questions relating to women's education, professionalization, and economic status. All of them variously dealt with these topics in their fiction, placed some of their novels in the school setting and chose female teachers and students as the heroines of their stories. In addition to engaging with these subjects in their fictional works, they also produced essays and articles about them. For instance, in 1900 Lesueur wrote an essay entitled *L'Evolution féminine, ses résultats économiques (1900).*[35] As journalists, these women often

---

[29]See Gretchen van Slyke, 'Monsters, New Women and Lady Professors: A Centenary Look Back at Gabrielle Reval', *Nineteenth-Century French Studies*, 30.3/4 (Spring–Summer 2002), 347–62 (p. 356). Van Slyke garners this information from Jo Burr Margadant, *Madame le Professeur: Women Educators in the Third Republic* (Princeton: Princeton University Press, 1990), p. 169.

[30] Stéphane Hug, 'Yvette Prost: une institutrice lapalissoise en littérature', *Palacia*, 2 August 2016, <http://palicia.blogspot.co.uk/2015/10/yvette-prost-une-institutrice.html> [accessed 31 August 2018].

[31] See Waelti-Walters and Hause, *Feminism of the Belle Epoque*, p. 67, and Von Kulessa, *Entre la reconnaissance et l'exclusion*, p. 57.

[32]See Jacques Benoist, 'Mise au propre développée de mon enquête sur Colette Yver afin de rédiger un court article la concernant pour l'encyclopédie Catholicisme' <http://jacquesbenoist.free.fr/pdf/yver.pdf> [accessed 31 August 2018]; Michel Manson, 'Colette Yver: une jeune auteure pour la jeunesse de 1892 à 1900', in *Juvenilia: Écritures précoces*, ed. by Guillemette Tison (= *Cahiers Robinsons*, 15 (2004)), pp. 61–77 (p. 66); and Margaret Ann Victoria Goldswain, 'Overlooked and Overshadowed: French Women's Writing 1900–1938' (unpublished doctoral thesis, University of Western Australia, 2014), p. 104.

[33]Lesly Bessière, 'L'Ascension de Daniel Lesueur à la Belle Époque: une femme à la conquête des honneurs et des institutions littéraires' (unpublished master's thesis, Université Paris Diderot – Paris 7, 2008), pp. 11–12.

[34]See Linda L. Clark, 'Marie-Thérèse de Solms-Blanc', in *An Encyclopedia of Continental Women Writers*, 1, ed. by Katharina M. Wilson (New York; London: Garland, 1991), pp. 134–35. Her novel, *Yette: histoire d'une jeune créole* (1880), which I discuss in this chapter, is set in a Parisian boarding school and I use it in order to trace patterns that continue into or disappear from later fiction.

[35]Daniel Lesueur, *L'Évolution féminine, ses résultats économiques (1900): rapport établi à la demande du con□ □ □du commerce et de l'industrie, lors de l'Exposition de 1900* (Paris: Impr. Polyglotte Hugonis, 1900). In 1904, Réval wrote the aforementioned *L'Avenir de nos filles*. At a later period, Colette Yver wrote *Femmes d'aujourd'hui: enquête sur les nouvelles carri□ □ □féminines*, 16th edn (Paris: Calmann-Lévy, 1929). A few articles by Yver appeared in different magazines, see for example the aforementioned 'Le Choix d'une carrière'; 'La Dame employée', *La Revue Hebdomadaire*, 4 May 1918, pp. 21–45; 'Le Mariage et le travail des femmes', *Le* Correspondant, 25 April 1920, pp. 237–64; 'Causeries et digressions sur l'avenir scolaire', Les *Cahiers de la République des lettres, des sciences et des* arts, 1 June 1926, pp. 89–94. Louise-Marie Compain wrote *La Femme dans les organisations ouvri□ □ □*(Paris: V. Giard et E. Brière, 1910) and the article 'Les Conséquences du travail de la femme', *Grande Revue*, 25 May 1913.

collaborated with the same newspapers and contributed articles, for example, to *La Fronde* and *Fémina.* Moreover, they were involved in different ways with networks of female professional support. In particular, in 1904 Lesueur, Réval, Bentzon, and Tinayre were among the twenty-two members of the first jury of the *Prix Fémina*. Yver won the prize in 1907 and later on also became a member of the jury.

Considering the extent to which these authors were affected by and involved in the educational and professional evolutions characterizing French women's history during the Belle Epoque, and given their active engagement with questions relating to female education and careers as well as their participation in different networks of female support, it is interesting to explore how they approached the topic of female homosociality, and the idea of female community in particular, in novels specifically dealing with the representation of women's educational experiences. We have already seen how, for Tilburg, the advent of the Republican school and a new interest in girlhood account for the emergence of early-twentieth-century schoolgirl fiction. Similarly, for Juliette Rogers, '[t]he new education system undoubtedly influenced the type of heroines they [Belle Epoque female authors] portrayed and the way that they tackled difficult feminist issues.'[36] The question addressed in this chapter is whether this element also influenced the way in which female communities are imagined and evaluated in their novels.

Previous scholarship on the idea of female community or sisterhood in nineteenth-century fiction mostly concerns anglophone literature, and Nina Auerbach's *Communities of Women* (1978) remains one of the most important references on this topic.[37] Auerbach describes the 'literary idea' of women's community as a form of resistance existing in opposition to and outside of patriarchal reality:

> As a recurrent literary image, a community of women is a rebuke to the conventional ideal of a solitary woman living for and through men, attaining citizenship in the community of adulthood through masculine approval alone. The communities of women which have haunted our literary imagination from the beginning are emblems of female self-sufficiency which create their own corporate reality, evoking both wishes and fears. As a literary idea, a community of women feeds dreams of a world beyond the normal.[38]

---

[36]Rogers, 'Feminist Discourse', in '*A Belle Epoque'?*, ed. by Holmes and Tarr, p. 185.
[37]Additional references include Pauline Nestor, *Female Friendships and Communities* (1985); Helena Michie, *Sorophobia* (1992); Sharon Marcus, *Between Women* (2007); *Cooperation and Competition* (2010), ed. by Simms Holderness and Porter.
[38]Auerbach, *Communities of Women*, p. 5.

Auerbach further explains that: 'Since a community of women is a furtive, unofficial, often underground entity, it can be defined by the complex, shifting, often contradictory attitudes it evokes.'[39] In *Career Stories*, Rogers draws from Auerbach's discussion of this subject to comment on the depiction of official (as opposed to the 'furtive', 'unofficial', and 'underground') women's communities in Belle Epoque novels of educational development, and considers this element as one of the innovations brought into the genre of the *Bildungsroman* in France at the time. Rogers notes that these female 'learning and living environments specifically aimed at educating women' occasionally take the form of a positive intellectual utopia, a reality semi-detached from the rest of society where the heroine can freely evolve and mature, as is the case in Compain's *L'Un vers l'autre.* However, she remarks, they also 'constitute only temporary passages for the protagonists'.[40] By focusing on the representation of fictional communities of female students and teachers in a group of understudied schoolgirl novels published during the Belle Epoque, I wish to further our understanding of the way in which the idea of women's community is exploited in fiction and its implications for the way in which female identities are negotiated and reshaped through literature.

In this chapter, I will offer a close reading of Thérèse Bentzon's *Yette* (1880) and Yvette Prost's *Salutaire orgueil* (1907), subsequently turning my attention to Gabrielle Réval's *Les Sévriennes* (1900) and, to a lesser extent, *Lycéennes* (1902).[41] While the dynamics regulating the interactions between a group of girls and their teachers at the *école normale* of Sèvres and at the Lycée Maintenon can be said to represent the main focus of Réval's novels, the author of *Salutaire orgueil* insists rather on the heroine's isolation and denounces the lack of a real sense of community in the classroom. The latter text will be read alongside Bentzon's *Yette* in order to trace some of the continuities and evolutions registered in literary portrayals of female homosociality during the Belle Epoque. Prost and Réval's novels, in particular, allow us to consider alternative models of female homosociality, which are in stark contrast with the ideal of female friendship described in conduct books and essays of the Belle Epoque, but also in most contemporary fiction of the time. In their novels, in fact, the school system encourages the female characters to appropriate and

---

[39]Auerbach, *Communities of Women*, p. 11.

[40]For more details, see Rogers, 'Dreams and Disappointments: Women's Education Novels', in *Career Stories*, pp. 79–112. In this chapter, Rogers discusses various novels, including Colette's *Claudine à l'école*, Compain's *L'Un vers l'autre*, and Réval's *Sévriennes*.

[41]Thérèse Bentzon, *Yette: histoire d'une jeune créole* (Paris: Bibliothèque d'éducation et de recréation, 1880); Yvette Prost, *Salutaire orgueil* (Paris: Bibliothèque des Annales Politiques et Littéraires, 1907); Gabrielle Réval, *Les Sévriennes*, 23rd edn (Paris: Albin Michel, 1900), and *Lycéennes* (Paris: Société d'éditions littéraires et artistiques, 1902). These novels will hereafter be referred to as *Yette*, *Orgueil*, *Lycéennes*, and *Sévriennes*. All in-text page references are to these editions.

display a series of qualities, such as intellectual pride and ambition, along with a spirit of independence, which were usually deemed as unfeminine and, therefore, inappropriate for girls. The heroines become intellectual rivals, and feelings of antagonism or a desire to succeed often lead them to push the boundaries of respectable female behaviour, along with class boundaries. When not competing, their modes of interaction still subvert conventional ideas about female relationships by acquiring an intellectual character usually thought to be peculiar to male friendship.[42]

Pushing Class and Gender Boundaries in *Salutaire orgueil*

The first instalment of Yvette Prost's *roman feuilleton*, *Salutaire orgueil*, appeared in *Les Annales Politiques et Littéraires* in December 1906, and the novel was awarded that publication's prize. By 1920, it had reached its 18th edition and had been translated into English and Italian. The story is narrated in the first person by its main character, Marie Höel, a poor and orphaned girl with a crippled leg. Born in the 1870s, Marie is raised in Burgundy by her loving but ignorant grandmother. An unhappy child, she is constantly bullied by her classmates and ignored by the adults, until one of her teachers senses her intelligence and, just before her grandmother's death, encourages her to take a very competitive exam and get a scholarship in order to pursue her studies. Marie spends ten years at the *lycée*, first as a student, and then as a *surveillante*. In this context, she finds a friend and mentor in the figure of her English and music professor, the strict and dignified Mlle Esther, from whom she learns the value of hard work and the importance of taking pride in her intellectual achievements, increasingly cultivating her *esprit* and building a stoic attitude toward life. At the age of 22, Marie leaves the *lycée* and starts to work as a private piano teacher in another town, where she grows closer to Mme Elder, a wealthy old lady, who is also the director of a local women's association. An assiduous visitor at Mme Elder's, Marie slowly falls in love with the latter's volatile and tormented son, the writer Luc Elder. When Luc finally asks her hand in marriage, Marie discovers that years before he had been Mlle Esther's lover. What is worse, the two have a child together, whose very existence is still unknown to him. Animated by a sense of justice, Marie decides to give up her own happiness and breaks up

[42] As discussed in Chapter Two, Jeanne and Marceline from *Les Cervelines* also share an intellectual friendship. This novel, however, has not been included in the present chapter because it does not involve the representation of a female community, but focuses on a one-to-one relationship between two characters who are neither colleagues nor fellow students.

with Luc, so that he can marry Mlle Esther and take care of their child. Determined to forget her past and to start a new life, at the end of the novel Marie embarks for Canada.

In this chapter, I am going to focus exclusively on the first part of the novel, where Marie recounts her childhood and adolescent memories before her departure from the *lycée*.[43] Even before the school setting is introduced, Marie's interactions with the children of her neighbourhood set the tone for her experience of the Republican school system and anticipate the relations that she will entertain with her classmates. Marie grows up in a context characterized by sharp social tensions, which will only be accentuated once she enters the classroom. At the beginning of the novel, she explains:

> Les fillettes m'estimaient peu, à cause des petites robes de forme archaïque que grand' mère me taillait dans ses vieux jupons [...] D'une sensibilité très vive, je souffrais de ces milles cruautés d'enfants : regards ironiques, lèvres pincées des petites filles — déjà femmes. (*Orgueil*, 3)

The 'fillettes' Marie refers to are the daughters of the local grocer and innkeeper. Therefore, they belong to the lower middle class, while Marie, whose grandmother is a poor 'ravaudeuse', belongs to the working class. This social gap is clearly signalled by Marie's puny appearance and the ugliness of her clothes. This visual reminder of her poverty will be pointed out again and again throughout the novel. One of the first memories retold by Marie concerns the painful loss of her worthless but beloved doll, Blondine, that a group of little girls decide to throw in the river after she refuses to play according to their rules. The appearances of the dolls reflect the girls' social status and economic condition. While most of the girls have '[des] poupées modernes', Marie's doll, like Marie herself, is deformed and poorly dressed, and looks like 'une poupée-servante' (*Orgueil*, 6). When Marie refuses to let her doll play the part of 'leur bonne', asserting that she is 'une princesse', one of the girls spitefully kicks Blondine, and at that point Marie completely loses her temper:

> Je bondis sur l'insolente, je saisis ses cheveux à pleines mains, je lui griffe le visage, je lui donne des coups de pieds. Elle pousse des cris de volaille qu'on plume vivante, dans le but d'attirer les auteurs de ses jours. Sa mère survient, en effet, m'octroie une volée de gifles et me chasse de la tuilerie. J'entre chez grand mère, les joues en feu, mais l'œil sec et la tête haute. (*Orgueil*, 7–8)

[43]This novel will be further discussed in Chapter Four on 'Female Rivalry and Love Triangles', pp. 202–17.

The wild and tomboyish Marie is a far cry from the docile and virtuous child often depicted in texts addressed to a young female readership, such as the protagonist of the nineteenth-century bestseller *Le Journal de Marguerite*, a successful novel written by Victorine Monniot and published in 158 different editions between 1858 and 1914.[44] Marguerite is in fact a very wise and good-hearted young girl engaged in a constant struggle to further improve herself, who by the end of the novel attains a saint-like status. The character of Marie, on the other hand, can be aligned with the figure of the lively and somewhat bad-tempered, rough, and unfeminine young girl that can be traced back to novels such as George Sand's *La Petite Fadette* (1849), the comtesse de Ségur's *Les Malheurs de Sophie* (1859), or Stendhal's *Lamiel* (1889).[45]

The second chapter of the novel is entirely devoted to Marie's experience of the secular primary school, and offers a good example of how this text works to dismantle both social and gender prejudices. Neglected by her teacher and mistreated by virtually everyone, Marie speaks of 'débuts moroses' (*Orgueil*, 13). In particular, she fears the 'monitrices', the older girls who serve as teaching assistants and repeatedly hit her with a stick ('ma petite tête aux cheveux de filasse attirait cette baguette comme un aimant'), inflict physical violence on her ('elles serraient mon bras grêle, ou m'aplatissaient le nez au mur en me poussant un peu brusquement'), and call her names ('les monitrices me coiffaient de tous les noms de basse-cour réputés peu intelligents', *Orgueil*, 14–15). When she turns eleven, Marie is allowed to attend the same class as other children of her age, but her 'timidité maladive' prevents her from proving her worth (*Orgueil*, 16). The narrator then describes the school festival during which prizes are distributed to the best students.[46] When the teacher realizes that Marie can recite the verses of Hugo's poem better than the daughters of the town councillors, she gives her the honour of reciting them at the ceremony, regardless of her inferior social status. As explained by Marie: 'Quand une fillette était désignée pour réciter un morceau, c'était, pour elle et ses parents, une gloire sans pareille' (*Orgueil*, 17).

---

[44]See Victorine Monniot, *Le Journal de Marguerite* (1857). Data quoted from Valérie Mesgouez, 'Victorine Monniot: Le Journal de Marguerite' <http://blog.univ-reunion.fr/blogpapang/2015/06/22/victorine-monniot-le-journal-de-marguerite/> [accessed 31 August 2018].

[45]Published posthumously, *Lamiel* was written from 1839 to 1842. Alison Finch discusses the characters of Sophie and Fadette, among others, in these terms. She also observes that '[w]omen in the last third of the century were even more determined than their mid-century predecessors to focus on girls' robustness and need for physical freedom. In this, they received some support from the culture'. Finch refers in particular to Henry Gréville's heroines, as well as to Thèrese Bentzon's *Yette* and Marcelle Tinayre's *Hellé*. See Finch, *Women's Writing*, pp. 111–17, 118–21, 174, 176. On the appearance of the modern and outspoken young heroine overstepping gender boundaries, see also Gale's discussion of the Goncourts' Rénée Mauperin in Gale, *A World Apart*, pp. 25–33.

[46]With regard to school festivals and prize-giving ceremonies, Tilburg observes that these kinds of initiatives 'lauded female educational accomplishment in a new political environment, with girls from the working and middle classes at the center of attention'. Tilburg comments on the representation of these events in *Claudine à l'école* and *Salutaire orgueil*. See Tilburg, *Colette's Republic*, pp. 83–87.

Moreover, in choosing Marie over the other girls, the mistress remarks: 'il n'y a que toi, pauvre petite, qui comprennes quelque chose parmi toute cette volaille' (*Orgueil*, 18). The teacher uses the same metaphor employed first by Marie, when she talks of the 'cris de volaille' of the girl she has attacked, and then by the *monitrices*, who call Marie 'tous les noms de basse-cour'.[47] The word 'volaille' arguably has a gendered, even misogynistic connotation, insofar as it suggests that female stupidity or meekness are natural. In this case, the character in the highest power position, the mistress, validates Marie's use of the term. Oblivious to class distinctions, she raises Marie above the other children because of her intellectual superiority, allowing her to take pride in herself. In that moment, Marie observes: 'La « volaille » fixait sur moi des yeux ahuris et jaloux qui furent doux à mon orgueil naissant' (*Orgueil*, 18). The novel thus appears to argue against this gendered prejudice in the figure of Marie, even while confirming it for the general group.[48] Marie's pride, intelligence, and desire to succeed, which she manifests in her interactions with both schoolmates and teachers, are the positive forces propelling her to push the boundaries of class, along with those of conventional femininity. Because she is chosen over the more affluent girls of her class group to recite the poem, Marie defies class restrictions; because she is smart and unapologetically takes pride in her intellectual superiority, she challenges assumptions about female stupidity ('la volaille'), modesty, and submissiveness. This scene thus interestingly knits together the two themes recurring throughout Prost's novelistic portrayal of female homosociality at school: class and gender. I shall first consider in more detail the question of class, subsequently turning my attention to Prost's redefinition of girlhood.

Throughout the nineteenth century, the double device of class and sex segregation contributed to carefully isolating bourgeois and upper-class girls within an all-female context where, through their relations with other girls and women, they developed their identities and learned their social roles. Before the advent of the public school, girls usually found themselves in the company of classmates who came from a broadly similar social background. As highlighted by van Slyke, in nineteenth-century France 'schooling was supposed to reinforce the class-system and firmly anchor each individual to his or her place in it', while '[s]ocial mobility by means of education was generally condemned as "déclassement"'.[49] The subsequent democratization of primary education and the institution

---

[47]These passages are quoted at pp. 156, 157 in this thesis.
[48]In *Lycéennes*, Réval employs the image of the 'volaille' in a radically different way. The protagonist Françoise comments on the lack of collaboration and fierce rivalry characterizing interactions among students by explaining: 'ici, nous sommes en cage, comme des coqs à qui l'on fournit la pâtée avant le combat, tant pis pour celles qui ne savent point manger! on les plumera plus vite.' Her metaphor evokes ideas of female aggressiveness and intellectual competition rather than submissiveness or dullness. See *Lycéennes*, p. 84.
[49]Van Slyke, 'Monsters, New Women and Lady Professors', p. 352. According to Mayeur: 'Au XIXe siècle, les filles des milieux aisés ne sont pas en général élèves des établissements destinés aux classes populaires. Si,

of the *coll□ges* and *lycées féminins* brought about some concerns about social mixing, to the extent that those families who could afford it continued to send their daughters to convents and private boarding schools, fearing that their daughters would debase themselves in the company of girls of the lower classes.[50]

Social intermingling is rarely endorsed in manuals for girls, which for the most part consider social and moral equality as the tenets of legitimate and authentic friendship.[51] In Juranville's view, for example, similarity in social condition clearly represents one of the prerequisites of friendship: 'il est bon de chercher ses amis dans un rang ni trop au-dessus, ni trop au-dessous de soi, l'amitié ayant pour condition essentielle une égalité sociale qui ne laisse place à aucun calcul d'intérêt.'[52] By opening up the educational system to girls from all social classes, however, the Third Republic seems to challenge, at least to some extent, the principle of class segregation, taking a step toward the creation of cross-class communities of female students. The Republican school comes under attack for exposing privileged girls to the dangers of moral corruption and, at the same time, for instilling inappropriate aspirations and desires in lower-class girls, thus creating a new generation of 'déclassées', whose very existence threatens the stability of the entire nation.[53]

In one of the essays featuring in *Les Ennemis de la jeunesse: nouvelle série d'études morales et sociales, aux jeunes filles* (1897), a collection of texts offering interesting insights regarding the way in which the new school system was perceived by its contemporaries, one of the contributors, Mlle L. B. B., evokes some of the objections often raised by parents against the dangers of social mixing at school:

à côté des pensionnaires « riches », un couvent accueille des externes « pauvres », il veille à ne pas mêler sur les mêmes bancs les deux catégories. Cette ségrégation en introduit une autre: à l'époque, le sentiment est encore très fort qu'il faut dispenser à l'enfant une instruction et une éducation qui soient en harmonie avec la position sociale qu'il occupera probablement, d'après son origine. Personne n'a l'idée, et surtout pour les filles, que l'éducation, précisément, pourrait donner à l'enfant une position supérieure à celle de ses parents.' See Mayeur, *Éducation des filles*, p. 9.

[50]On this subject, Karen Offen comments: 'The conviction that daughters must be dowried and supervised either by their mothers in the home, or by nuns in convent schools, was so deeply rooted that the mere prospect of their daughters mixing with girls who might be not only "godless," but also dowryless could be interpreted as evidence of an impending slip down the social ladder.' See Karen Offen, 'The Second Sex and the Baccalauréat in Republican France, 1880–1924', *French Historical Studies*, 13.2 (1983), 252–86 (p. 265).

[51]One of the main exceptions to this rule is represented by the invitation addressed to bourgeois and upper-class women to get involved with charity work. Indeed, charity work promotes a cross-class encounter, although one that remains very hierarchical.

[52]Juranville, *Manuel d'éducation morale*, p. 53. Fanny André similarly notes: 'La première condition, me semble-t-il, ce serait qu'il existât quelque égalité entre les amies, qu'elles appartinssent à des milieux semblables', subsequently specifying that similarity in moral disposition matters more than similarity in economic status. See André, 'Les Distractions permises', in *Les Ennemis de la jeunesse,* p. 174.

[53]For L. Randon, '[s]i nos errements pédagogiques devaient continuer longtemps, leurs fâcheux résultats, accumulés par l'hérédité, finiraient par tuer notre nation.' Such comments can be easily situated within the context of *fin-de-si□ le* fears of degeneration. See L. Randon, 'Les Victimes de l'instruction', in *Ennemis de la jeunesse*, pp. 241–63 (p. 244).

Ici les craintes s'éveillent et les mères s'effarouchent: « Des jeunes filles, y pensez-vous! Et le mélange des classes ! et la contagion morale possible! » Il y a dans ces frayeurs une part, avouons-le, qui n'est digne ni des démocrates, ni surtout des chrétiens, mais elles ont quelque chose de respectable aussi.[54]

This author, however, strongly defends the Republican school's potential to develop a spirit of equality and solidarity among girls coming from different social backgrounds:

Elle [l'éducation commune] crée l'esprit de solidarité. La bonne camaraderie de l'École, le travail et les jeux en commun, les mêmes intérêts, les mêmes émotions à l'éveil des hautes idées purificatrices, élèvent l'esprit bien au-dessus des petits préjugés et des différences sociales mesquines.[55]

Mlle L. B. B. further contends that, by leading a communal life, girls are encouraged to take an interest in the activities and experiences of their fellow students, and she also alludes to a series of initiatives aimed at cultivating a spirit of fraternity across social classes.[56]

One of the most violent attacks against the Republican school comes from L. Randon, who in an essay dedicated to 'Les Victimes de l'instruction' from a section of *Les Ennemis de la jeunesse* entitled 'Grandes Hécatombes', holds the new educational system accountable for turning the students into '[des] [p]auvres âmes détachées du milieu social où la naissance les avait placées'. For Randon, the limited number of degrees and actual jobs available in teaching creates a situation in which 'elles [les filles instruites] n'ont plus aucun lien spirituel avec les personnes qui les entourent, et une barrière matérielle infranchissable les sépare des groupes humains avec qui elles communieraient', with the risk for them of resorting to prostitution or even suicide.[57]

These fears, however, were largely unwarranted. Françoise Mayeur, among others, reminds us that in spite of the school's self-proclaimed egalitarian ethos, 'la notion selon laquelle l'instruction doit être soigneusement adaptée au milieu social et au genre de vie dans lequel l'enfant, devenu adulte, est appelé à évoluer, n'a [pas] été oubliée.'[58] On this subject, Tilburg interestingly observes that while 'the architects of the Third Republic

[54]Mlle L. B. B., 'Les Lycées de jeunes filles', in *Ennemis de la jeunesse*, pp. 135–43 (p. 140).
[55]Mlle L. B. B., 'Les Lycées de jeunes filles', in *Ennemis de la jeunesse*, p. 139.
[56]Mlle L. B. B., 'Les Lycées de jeunes filles', in *Ennemis de la jeunesse*, p. 141.
[57]Randon, 'Les Victimes de l'instruction', in *Ennemis de la jeunesse*, pp. 252–53. In his essay, Randon argues that the problem of 'déclassement' concerns male and female students alike. As regards women, however, for Randon the issue of 'déclassement' becomes more urgent and generalized in the sense that, by distracting women from their natural vocations (i.e. marriage and maternity), the education offered by the Republican school dispossesses society of its mothers and wives. See pp. 256–57.
[58]Mayeur, *Éducation des filles*, p. 222.

venerated the cross-class public school' and considered education as 'a social panacea' that could reduce class difference, 'the vision of the republican schoolroom as a space for class *rapprochement* was plainly more of an aspiration in 1880 than a social reality.'[59] In fact, as already mentioned, at the turn of the century, upper-class girls often continued to be sent to private, Catholic schools or to private elementary classes attached to public secondary schools, when they did not receive their education at home.[60] Moreover, in spite of the democratization of schooling, primary and secondary schools bore little resemblance to one another in terms of class dynamics; while primary education had become free and compulsory for all, the *coll□ges* and *lycées féminins* mainly served a bourgeois, middle-class clientele.[61] In addition to this, the school curricula and textbooks propagandized republican ideals of social harmony and contentment, by inculcating social immobility, modesty, and resignation.[62]

At this point, it is important to remember that one of the main arguments put forward by the advocates of the *coll□ges* and *lycées féminins* was to further the education of the future mothers and wives of the Republic in order to narrow the intellectual gap between men and women and provide Frenchmen with more interesting, sophisticated, and rational companions. For example, in his famous public speech *De l'égalité de l'éducation*, given on April 10th 1870, Jules Ferry declared:

---

[59]Tilburg, *Colette's Republic*, pp. 24, 32.

[60]According to Porter, 'before the disestablishment of the Church in 1905, as many as 72% of primary school students were taught by nuns or priests'. Mayeur observes that 'dans les cas des lycées et collèges, les parents, par leur participation, assuraient les enfants contre la « promiscuité », redoutée beaucoup plus pour les filles que pour les garçons'. Clark highlights that '[b]y attending special elementary classes attached to *lycées* and *coll□ges* middle-class children avoided mingling with children attending regular primary schools'. See Porter, 'The Convent as a Paradoxical Site', in *Cooperation and Competition*, ed. by Simms Holderness and Porter, p. 77; Mayeur, *Éducation des filles*, p. 234; Linda L. Clark, 'The Socialization of Girls in the Primary Schools of the Third Republic', *Journal of Social History*, 15.4 (1982), 685–97 (p. 685).

[61]Mayeur refers to the 'caractère socialement sélectif de l'enseignement secondaire', noting that 'lycées et collèges de jeunes filles recrutent au-dessus des classes populaires, en-dessous des classes dirigeantes. Ils ont été créés pour la bourgeoisie aisée, ils ont surtout attiré, dans leurs débuts, la petite et la moyenne bourgeoisie'. See Mayeur, *Éducation des filles*, p. 237. Girls from the lower classes, after having completed primary education, often received a professional training at the *écoles primaires supérieures* or *cours complémentaires*, their number increasing from 9767 in 1890–1891 to 40,052 in 1912–1913. See Jean-Pierre Briand, Chapoulie Jean-Michel, *Les Coll□ □es du peuple: l'enseignement primaire supérieur et le développement de la scolarisation prolongée sous la Troisi□ □e République*. Paris, INRP/CNRS/Ecole Supérieure de Fontenay Saint-Claude, 1992, pp. 166–67, 273, as quoted by Thiercé, *Histoire de l'adolescence*, p. 142. As for the teacher training schools (*écoles normales*), they often recruited girls of 'humbler origins', who needed to make a living for themselves and for their families. See Rogers, *From the Salon to the Schoolroom*, p. 194. Like Mayeur, Rogers also remarks that: 'Because it concerned middle-class education, the flavor and tone of the new schools [of the secondary school system] bore little relation to those of the primary system.' See Rogers, *From the Salon to the Schoolroom*, p. 205.

[62]See Linda L. Clark, 'The Primary Education of French Girls: Pedagogical Prescriptions and Social Realities, 1880–1940', *History of Education Quaterly*, 21.4 (1981), 411–28 (p. 416).

Mon Dieu, mesdames, si je réclame cette égalité, c'est bien moins pour vous que pour nous, hommes. Je sais que plus d'une femme me répond, à part elle: Mais à quoi bon toutes ces connaissances, tout ce savoir, toutes ces études? à quoi bon? Je pourrais répondre: à élever vos enfants, et ce serait une bonne réponse, mais comme elle est banale, j'aime mieux dire: à élever vos maris. (*Applaudissements et rires.*)

L'égalité d'éducation, c'est l'unité reconstituée dans la famille.

Il y a aujourd'hui une barrière entre la femme et l'homme, entre l'épouse et le mari, ce qui fait que beaucoup de mariages, harmonieux en apparence, recouvrent les plus profondes différences d'opinion, de goûts, de sentiments; mais alors ce n'est plus un vrai mariage, car le vrai mariage, messieurs, c'est le mariage des âmes.[63]

If secondary education appears to have largely failed in promoting social equality, it is arguably because its ultimate goal was not to encourage social mobility or bring girls from different classes together, but rather to bring men and women of the same class closer, in order to ensure the solidity of the family. This issue can be linked to Beauvoir's observations that, in nineteenth-century France, 'les femmes ne sont pas solidaires en tant que sexe: elles sont d'abord liées à leur classe.'[64] According to Beauvoir:

Les femmes de la bourgeoisie étaient trop intégrées à la famille pour connaître entre elles une solidarité concrète; elles ne constituaient pas une caste séparée susceptible d'imposer des revendications: économiquement, leur existence était parasitaire.[65]

In other words, bourgeois women's first allegiance was usually to their husbands and families rather than to other women, especially women from the inferior classes.

Prost's novel participates in the debates surrounding the emergence of the new school system through its depiction of a heroine issued from the working class, who benefits from the new educational opportunities opening up to all girls from the 1880s onwards. The aforementioned scene in which the little Marie, purely on account of her intelligence, is assigned the much-coveted task of reciting a poem at the school festival points to the school's potential to reduce social disparities and to boost the republican value of é*galité* by way of education. The sense of egalitarianism promoted in the classroom at that specific

---

[63]Jules Ferry, *De l'égalité d'éducation: conférence populaire faite à la Salle Moli□re le 10 avril 1870 par M. Jules Ferry* (Paris: Société pour l'instruction élémentaire, 1870), pp. 27–28. Gale refers to this question in 'Education, Literature and the Battle over Female Identity', p. 105. Ferry's arguments are not entirely original. For example, in *De l'amour* (Paris: M. Levy, 1857 [1822]), Stendhal had already put forward similar ideas.
[64]Beauvoir, *Deuxi□ □e Sexe I*, p. 211.
[65]Beauvoir, *Deuxi□ □e Sexe I*, p. 190.

moment, however, is short-lived since on the day of the festival Marie, who is inappropriately dressed for the occasion, is ultimately denied the opportunity to declaim the poem. Not only do her classmates, who in the circumstance closely resemble their dolls, silently communicate their disapproval ('Mes compagnes, toutes de blanc vêtues, toutes excessivement frisées et enrubannées, me regardent en silence, avec des yeux exorbités'), but all the teaching staff, including the headmistress, agree on the fact that Marie cannot appear in front of the major and the other dignitaries (*Orgueil*, 24). When Marie is awarded the school's *prix d'honneur*, she finally gets to get up on the stage, despite her poor dress. Since 'on mène a M. le maire et aux personnages importants les plus jolies robes et les plus gentilles frimousses', the teaching assistant surreptitiously tries to lead Marie toward a fireman in the background, thus avoiding having to introduce her to the other authorities. At that point one politician, recognizing the girl who has won the prize, decides to hand Marie the book and put the paper crown on her head himself, thus reasserting the meritocracy of the Third Republican school system and levelling the social differences.[66] Overall, the representation of the social dynamics occurring in the classroom, as provided in these episodes, testifies to the contradictions of the Third Republican school and gives the lie to contemporary narratives about how state education fosters social egalitarianism. Indeed, Prost extends Marie's tense relations with the girls of her neighbourhood to the schoolroom, and her experience as a student is consistently fraught with social tensions. Even at the *lycée,* the heroine continues to lead '[une] vie déserte' and is despised by her classmates because she is 'pauvre et mal vêtue' (*Orgueil*, 56). While some of the authority figures in the text (i.e. Marie's teacher and the politician) dismiss her social inferiority by rewarding her intellectual superiority, thereby suggesting the possibility that Marie might raise herself above her social status through education and hard work, Marie's schoolmates have not learned the lesson of fraternity and solidarity that the creation of cross-class communities at school was meant to teach them.[67]

---

[66]In referring to the same scene, Tilburg observes that '[t]he egalitarian ethos of the school is preserved by this upright politician who is oblivious to class distinctions'. Reading *Salutaire orgueil* as a fictional retelling of Prost's own experience of the Republican school, Tilburg claims that 'Yvette Prost remembered the "School of the People" as an arena in which such scholastic success came only by way of painful class confrontations'. See Tilburg, *Colette's Republic*, pp. 86–87.

[67]Other novels from this period similarly represent the school as a context in which social distinctions are far from being erased. The very popular *Claudine à l'école* (1900), for example, stages a heroine who remains almost completely detached from her classmates because of her intellectual and social superiority. Beth Gale, among others, remarks that Claudine 'spends her time criticizing the environment of the school and the mental and physical weaknesses of her schoolmates', and refers to Joan Hinde Stewart, who 'also notes Claudine's basic loneliness, her lack of "authentic bonds" with parents or friends'. In this case, it is Claudine's superior social and intellectual status that creates a gap between her and the other students. For Tilburg, *Claudine à l'école* speaks of Colette's own 'middle-class remembrances' of the Third Republican School and demonstrates that she, as an adolescent, was aware of class divisions and of her privileged social position. See Gale, *A Wold Apart*, pp. 99–100, and Tilburg, *Colette's Republic*, pp. 87–88. Another example, more similar to *Salutaire*

In pushing class boundaries to assert her own worth and make a better future for herself, Marie simultaneously pushes the boundaries of respectable girlhood. Although the Third Republican school was designed to teach girls how to become truly 'feminine', which is to say kind to one another, gracious and forgiving, submissive and self-effacing, compassionate and supportive toward the poor, the mechanisms enacted within this fictional setting, as represented in Prost's novel, encourage the heroine to be competitive, dauntless, even aggressive. In other words, she becomes the opposite of what she is expected to be in Third Republican ideology. I shall now consider in more detail how the novel deconstructs the notion of respectable girlhood in the figure of Marie.

When Marie ends up first at the 'concours' and, thanks to a scholarship, is admitted as an intern at the *lycée*, she still experiences a great loneliness and all the unladylike qualities she showed as a child (i.e. pride, sense of competition, need for recognition) become more prominent. During the arrival scene, Marcelle and Madeleine, the 'jolies fillettes de mon âge' with 'le sourire aux lèvres' who are designated as Marie's helpers, contemptuously appraise the poor contents of her suitcase and start to mock her (*Orgueil*, 45). When Madeleine remarks: 's'il me fallait porter ces affreuses choses, moi qui ai la peau si fine, il me viendrait des ampoules!', Marie does not show any sign of patience or tolerance and readily stands up for herself, showing a persistent lack of traditionally feminine qualities:

> J'ai fermé la malle d'un coup sec et j'ai crié, d'une voix qui frémit:
>
> — Vous deux, allez-vous-en ! Je vous ai assez entendues!
>
> Le ton a été si péremptoire que les jeunes pécores ont pris lestement la porte, sentant bien que la petite fille qui porte de si rudes toiles sans se couvrir d'ampoules serait capable de se défendre à coups de poings.
>
> Je les poursuis jusque sur le palier, et, penchée sur la rampe, je crie à la jeune Madeleine, qui détale:
>
> — Il est bien regrettable, vous, que vous n'ayez de fin que la peau! (*Orgueil*, 46)

The 'ton péremptoire' used by Marie, her inclination 'à se défendre à coups de poings', and the way she appeals to her own intelligence contribute to the portrayal of a heroine who is very different from the ideal of the gentle and composed young lady of her time, as represented in conduct manuals.

Marie's entire social experience at the *lycée* is rather painful from the moment she sets foot in her new classroom:

---

orgueil, is Lucie Rondeau-Lezeau's 'Le Livre d'une étudiante', *Le Temps*, June–July 1914, in which the heroine Marthe, issued from a family of farmers, also experiences the hostility of her classmates.

> Autour de moi, je sens tous ces yeux d'enfants, tous ces yeux cruels, qui font l'inventaire de ma chétive personne, depuis mes cheveux blondasses, trop serrés, en une natte qui ressemble à une corde, jusqu'à mes gros souliers de veau consolidés par des clous à la tête ronde. J'entends des ricanements étouffés et des réflexions moqueuses. Je suis mal à l'aise. (*Orgueil*, 47)

This is a typical scene in the school fiction genre. This passage in particular can be associated with Charles Bovary's arrival at the *lycée* of Rouen, at the beginning of *Madame Bovary* (1856). The fact that *Madame Bovary* serves as an intertext for Prost's novel is suggested, for example, by the detail concerning Marie's shoes — Charles Bovary 'était chaussé de souliers forts, mal cirés, garnis de clous'.[68] However, although Charles and Marie experience the same hostility on the part of their classmates and initially feel embarrassed and self-conscious, their attitudes differ considerably. The heroine immediately displays that lucid self-awareness lacked by Charles and never allows herself to be victimized. After a few months, Marie sums up her social life in a short paragraph:

> Depuis mon arrivée au lycée, je n'ai pu prendre contact avec les autres élèves. Après les railleries des premiers jours, quelques romanesques, attirées par mon deuil, par ma pâleur et mon infirmité, avaient jugé intéressant de me témoigner une pitié peu discrète. J'ai accueilli cette pitié plus mal encore que je n'avais reçu les moqueries, et les lycéennes ont laissé à l'écart cette « boursière » farouche qui ne supporte ni d'être ridiculiste [sic] ni d'être plainte, et montre facilement ses griffes… (*Orgueil*, 52)

The other girls only try to approach her to the extent that she looks helpless and fragile, but Marie refuses to be pitied and readily reasserts her strength and boldness. In contrast with the earlier references to female dullness or even passivity ('la volaille'), the novel repeatedly puts forward an ideal of female determination and combativeness ('montrer les griffes').

At this point, Mlle Esther approaches Marie and invites her to take part in 'la lutte dure et farouche' (*Orgueil*, 59). According to the teacher, people can be divided into two categories, the strong ones who walk on the front lines by themselves, and the weak ones, who walk as a group in the background. Mlle Esther tells Marie that 'Il faut être parmi les premiers'; she encourages her to find her own happiness 'dans l'étude' and to become 'un esprit', 'une force', thus raising herself above other people's pity or mockery (*Orgueil*, 59–

[68]Gustave Flaubert, *Madame Bovary: mœurs de province* (Paris: Gallimard, 2001 [1856]), p. 47.

60).[69] Marie accepts Mlle Esther's invitation to consider pride as 'la base de toute ma vie morale' rather than a sin, as preached by the local priest (*Orgueil*, 61).[70] She completely adheres to these traditionally masculine principles and goes as far as to assert that 'une femme a plus d'ardeur, plus de force, plus d'endurance qu'un homme', a statement that operates to upset hierarchical gender divisions. The heroine firmly believes that by cultivating her intelligence, she can compensate for her 'infériorité matérielle', one of the main sources of the contrast with the other girls, and she wishes to '[c]onnaître un jour la joie unique de la supériorité et de la domination!' (*Orgueil*, 62). Following this conversation with Mlle Esther, Marie decides to fight to become the first of her class, thus finding her place within the social group and winning her classmates' respect, if not their friendship:

> Les autres élèves de mon âge me semblaient très lointaines et j'avais, avec elles, peu de points de contact. Depuis longtemps, elles ne songeaient plus à rire de moi. Elles disaient, en parlant de moi, dans le langage emprunté à leurs frères:
>
> — Marie Höel? Une espèce de sauvage, mais rudement calée… (*Orgueil*, 80)

This passage is a good example of the way in which Prost's text challenges stereotypes of femininity through the representation of female homosociality. In borrowing their brothers' speech and in referring to Marie as being 'calée', these female characters reproduce an attitude conventionally coded as 'masculine' and evaluate each other in terms of intellectual power. The term 'calée' is a particularly interesting lexical choice, insofar as it refers to the quality of being 'instruit, compétent' (an attribute rarely associated with women at the time), but also to the fact of being 'complex'. This second meaning is usually associated with abstract objects, not people, but it nevertheless deepens the resonances of this passage, arguably suggesting the sense of ambiguity and multiplicity that characterizes the notion of modern womanhood. Taking a step further toward the problematization of mainstream

---

[69]Mlle Esther is the female mentor figure in this *Bildungsroman*. This scene can fruitfully be compared with Vautrin's 'leçon' to Rastignac in Balzac's *Le P□ □ □oriot* (1835). Vautrin similarly talks of the 'acharnement du combat', and further indicates that there are two ways to succeed: 'l'éclat du génie' or 'l'adresse de la corruption'. For Vautrin, however, 'le travail' and 'l'honnêteté' are the prerogative of the weak, whereas Mlle Esther's advice to Marie is to cultivate her mind, strengthen her spirit, and work hard. See Honoré de Balzac, *Le P□ □ □oriot* (Paris: Charpentier, 1839 [1835]), pp. 141–42.

[70]The quality generally championed in the Catholic *roman édifiant* is 'fierté', not 'orgueil'. If, according to the Bible, 'Blessed are the meek / for they will inherit the earth' (Matthew 5.5), the juxtaposition of 'orgueil' and 'salutaire' in the title indicates from the outset that this novel presents a strong element of subversiveness. Moreover, it should be noted that, for Marie, the legitimacy of pride is also a matter of class: 'Peut-être l'orgueil est-il blâmable chez les puissants que l'amour devrait incliner vers les humbles. Mais, pour les pauvres, les déshérités comme moi, pour ceux à qui la vie méchante refusa tout, l'orgueil est le cordial souverain qui donne aux plus débiles la force d'accomplir des grandes choses.' Pride is thus represented as the instrument through which Marie can legitimately redress the injustice with which she is confronted at school, in the company of her classmates, and more generally in life. See *Orgueil*, p. 61.

femininity, Marie, in comparing her physical appearance with that of her classmates, dispassionately notes her lack of beauty or femininity and, at an age when most girls focus on securing a good husband, she is entirely indifferent to her schoolmates' first attempts to approach boys (*Orgueil*, 83–85). Questions of class and gender thus appear to be closely interlinked in this novel, as in fiercely asserting her strength and cleverness to counterbalance her social inferiority, Marie refuses to abide by the strict limitations imposed by both categories.

Criticism of the sense of intellectual pride and competition that girls cultivate in the school environment often figures in school manuals and essays of the Belle Epoque, which sometimes blame the new educational system for encouraging (perhaps unintentionally) a behaviour deemed unsuitable for women. More than once, for example, Juranville warns her readers against being envious of their friends or classmates, inviting them instead to emulate those who prove to be more successful and represent a good example for them to follow. In particular, Juranville exhorts young girls to be 'de bonnes camarades dans toute l'acception du mot', by which she means that female students should be 'indulgentes' and 'complaisantes' with one another, 'aimables' for everyone in spite of their personal preferences, and always ready to be of service, all these attributes being compatible with prevailing models of femininity.[71] Indeed, Juranville's repeated recommendations that students avoid improper feelings of jealousy and antagonism ('Les écolières doivent éviter les taquineries, les querelles et les rapports, les délations et la jalousie. La jalousie est un bien vilain défaut')[72] match social expectations for girls to be meek and docile. Competition is here replaced by a gentle camaraderie and by the sort of emulation that allows girls to improve themselves and to exert a positive influence on one another, in a shared effort to attain the self-fashioned ideal of the Third Republican mother and wife.

These recommendations can be read alongside some essays from the same period, which harshly condemn female intellectual rivalry, the pursuit of academic success, and the way in which the development of female subjectivities is influenced by these elements. The *lycéennes* are sometimes accused of being the new *bas bleus*, their pedantry and vanity being regarded as the result of the excessive praise they receive at school for their intellectual achievements.[73] In his critique of the Republican school, one of the contributors of *Les Ennemis de la jeunesse* comments: 'Que n'aurais-je pas à dire sur les mobiles mis en jeu dans presque toutes les écoles et presque tous les lycées? C'est surtout l'appas des

---

[71]Juranville, *Manuel d'éducation morale*, p. 76.
[72]Juranville, *Manuel d'éducation morale*, p. 321.
[73]See, for example, Fanny André, 'Un bas bleu moderne', in *Ennemis de la jeunesse*, pp. 67–75.

récompenses, des distinctions; c'est l'émulation, qui tant et tant de fois dégénère en orgueil et en jalousie.'[74] In evoking the arguments put forward by the opponents of the public school, the aforementioned Mlle L. B. B. writes: 'La jeune fille n'est pas seule sous la direction de maîtresses instruites et expérimentées: elle travaille avec d'autres: il y a forcément comparaison, émulation, rivalité. De là l'esprit de jalousie peut-être, et très certainement dit-on, l'ambition, l'amour du premier rang, la vanité.'[75] In the same collection of essays, Randon describes (and deplores) how students fight against each other in order to gain a degree and access the job market, lured by the false promise of economic independence, social advancement, and intellectual recognition. Referring to the female student, Randon writes:

> [O]n fait appel à l'émulation pour l'exciter au labeur. On l'habitue à considérer l'école comme un champ de bataille et ses camarades comme des ennemies. Ce ne sont pas des compagnes qu'elle doive aimer, mais des concurrentes qu'il lui faut combattre. Remporter sur elles la victoire dans les concours, tel sera son objectif. Elle se persuade que l'existence est une lutte impitoyable qu'il faut poursuivre sans faiblesse, si l'on ne veut pas succomber.[76]

The various references to the lexical sphere of combat and, more generally, to a series of qualities and attitudes predominantly associated with masculinity rather than femininity (e.g. aggressiveness, competitiveness, intellectual ambition) suggest that female homosociality, within the context of the Third Republican school, can contribute to shaping female identities in a way that challenges accepted notions of female essential sweetness and passivity.

As previously discussed, in *Salutaire orgueil* feelings of pride and competition dominate Marie's interactions with her peers, and the author resorts to the same lexicon of conflict and aggression that can be found in essays of this period. However, by contrast with these authors, Prost deploys such lexicon in a non-judgemental way. Interestingly, in a contemporary literary study entitled *La Jeune Fille dans la littérature française* (1910), the critic Jules Bertaut argues: 'C'est à l'instruction obligatoire [...] que la jeune fille doit la personnalité qu'elle s'est acquise', and remarks: 'Face au collège, avec ses professeurs, avec ses condisciples, la voilà [l'adolescente] lancée déjà en pleine *lutte vitale*. On lui

---

[74]Trial, 'Écoles, pensionnats et lycées de jeunes filles', in *Ennemis de la jeunesse*, p. 130.
[75]However, this particular author blames the families, not the school, for this situation. See Mlle L. B. B., 'Les Lycées de jeunes filles', in *Ennemis de la jeunesse*, pp. 138–39.
[76]Randon 'Les Victimes de l'instruction', in *Ennemis de la jeunesse*, pp. 248–49.

reconnaît un caractère, des qualités, des défauts, des tendances, des instincts, on note, on la note, on la classe, elle se classe d'elle-même.'[77] Bertaut further observes:

> [C]e sont des « *lutteuses* » [...] [E]lles ont le beau sang-froid, le coup d'œil professionnel, la vivacité de l'attaque, la promptitude de la riposte, l'entrain aussi et la vitalité profonde. Elles sont égoïstes, parbleu, comme on l'est dans la *lutte*; sèches, ainsi qu'il convient à un adversaire qui se trouve en face d'autres adversaires; sans élans irraisonnés, sans générosité inutile, comme il faut dans un *combat*. Ne leur reprochez ni la mesquinerie de leurs sentiments, ni la férocité de leur cœur. Ce sont des amazones sur le sentier de la *guerre* qui, mieux que leurs frères, ont compris, médité et accepté cette atroce formule de *lutte* pour la vie imposée par les conceptions du jour. Petits animaux féroces, rageurs, dangereux, séduisants, du reste, par leurs *griffes* acérées, que vous pouvez craindre, mais auxquels il vous faut pardonner, car leur égoïsme ne vient pas d'elles-mêmes, mais des conditions sociales dans lesquelles elles se trouvent, leur férocité a une excuse, leur irrespect est un besoin.[78]

Bertaut and Prost employ the same words (e.g. 'lutte', 'combat', 'griffes'); they both draw from the semantic field of combat, attributing unconventional and unfeminine characteristics to the female adolescent, and pointing to the scholastic system and to girls' interactions with their classmates and professors as the causes of their evolution toward new types of femininity. Indeed, Bertaut could have written this passage with Marie Höel in mind.[79]

In promoting rivalry over solidarity, in allowing the students to be driven by their ambitions, in encouraging them to take pride in academic success and cultivate their minds, the school system, as it is portrayed in Prost's novel, condones a kind of female behaviour that does not conform to contemporary ideals of womanhood, ideals that were inscribed in the textbooks and curricula of that time and that the secular school was originally designed to promote.[80] Within this fictional female community, 'masculine' attributes such as 'orgueil', 'ardeur', 'force', 'endurance', 'supériorité', 'domination', are manifested by the heroine by means of her interactions with her peers. This is not to say that Marie lacks femininity entirely, or that her representation would have shocked or upset contemporary readers. On the

[77]Jules Bertaut, *La Jeune Fille dans la littérature française* (Paris: Michaud, 1910), pp. 166, 168. My italics. Note that both Bertaut and Prost employ the term 'lutte'.
[78]Bertaut, *La Jeune Fille*, p. 190. My italics.
[79]Other contemporary reviewers of the novel employ a language similar to that of Prost and Bertaut. For example, Yvonne Sarcey writes: 'Son héroïne [Marie] est une *lutteuse*, une travailleuse qui *conquiert* durement sa place au soleil.' See Yvonne Sarcey, 'Les Lettres de la cousine: *Salutaire orgueil*', *Les Annales Politiques et Littéraires*, 9 June 1907, p. 364. My italics.
[80]For more discussion of the way in which female roles and identities were delineated in the official curriculum of the Third Republican school and in textbooks, see for example Clark, 'The Primary Education of French Girls', and 'The Socialization of Girls'.

contrary, the appeal of Prost's heroine lies in the balance achieved between traditionally masculine and traditionally feminine features, Marie being as rational and resolute as she can be sensitive and passionate. A contemporary commentator aptly expresses this notion of synthesis, when she observes that Marie '[est] douée d'une vive intelligence et d'une âme d'artiste' and that 'ces nerfs, si prompts à s'émouvoir, cette sensibilité, si vive à s'attendrir, ne servent qu'à mieux tremper sa raison'.[81] The fact that these qualities are not mutually exclusive in fictional representations of the *femme moderne*, including in Prost's novel, reflects a more general tendency to blur rigid distinctions between opposite gendered spheres and promote new types of femininity.[82]

The previous chapter on 'Female Mentorship and the Making of the *Femme Moderne* in the Female *Bildungsroman*' highlighted how gender identity could be problematized and reshaped in fiction through the representation of one-to-one, supportive mentorship relationships between female characters.[83] In particular, gender deconstruction is an important feature of Yver's novel *Cervelines*, in which definitions of 'masculinity' and 'femininity' are systematically complicated not only through the portrayal of Jeanne and Marceline's fictional identities (e.g. from the outset these characters are represented as being simultaneously feminine, physically attractive, independent, self-assured, and intellectually superior to men), but also through the depiction of their modes of interaction (e.g. their friendship is 'froide' and 'forte', they smoke cigarettes together). Moreover, the construction of Marceline as a modern woman is presented as the result of the influence exerted by Jeanne on her narrative trajectory (e.g. counselled by Jeanne, Marceline rejects a traditional domestic destiny and pursues her career). Similarly, in *Salutaire orgueil*, Marie's development into a *femme moderne* who can appropriate both male and female prerogatives is partly achieved through the support of her female mentor, Mlle Esther. However, it is important to note that Marie's identity is also constructed by means of the conflictual relations that she entertains with other female characters in the fictional context of the Third Republican school. In addition to this, it should be noted that, as was the case for Aline in *La Cruche cassée*, Hellé, or Jeanne and Marceline, once she accesses adulthood, Marie does not pose a threat to the social order, but rather tries to redefine her place in society outside a traditional marriage.[84] As we shall see in the next chapter on

[81]See Sarcey, '*Salutaire orgueil*', p. 364.
[82]On gender instability and the *femme moderne*, see pp. 35–36 in this thesis.
[83]Gender notions are also complicated in the novels discussed in Chapter One on 'Female Friendship and the Body', insofar as the way in which women's bodily interactions are portrayed in these texts problematizes the dichotomies associated with conventional definitions of womanhood (e.g. sexual vs maternal, active vs passive).
[84]Both Aline and Hellé enter a more progressive form of marriage with sympathetic, enlightened men, whereas Jeanne and Marceline, like Marie, discard the prospect of marriage.

'Female Rivalry and Love Triangles', for all her tendency to defy (literary) conventions and break both class and gender codes, a modern character like Marie is also designed to show that state-educated, free-thinking women can be a great asset for the Republic, insofar as they can contribute to the moral regeneration of the nation.

The originality of *Salutaire orgueil* lies in the fact that, while Marie is extremely lonely and her relations with other students seem non-existent due to her social, material, and physical inferiority, a particular kind of homosocial bond is established between her and her schoolmates, one based on antagonism and on Marie's need to impose her intellectual superiority. If women were often represented in nineteenth-century French novels as sexual rivals competing over men, something that was considered consistent with female nature, schoolgirl fictions of the Belle Epoque portray female intellectual rivals who battle over the recognition and appraisal of their skills and academic worth.[85] In this case, intellectual rivalry is presented as a by-product of class conflict, insofar as Marie's pride and competitiveness are initially motivated by a desire to counteract her social exclusion. The representation of this type of homosocial bond is subversive because it both undermines narratives of social harmony and equality in the Third Republic and pushes the boundaries of acceptable female behaviour. It is in the all-female context of the school that Marie is given free rein to perform femininity in an alternative, unorthodox way. After leaving the secluded world of the *lycée*, the heroine, partly by reason of her adherence to a philosophy of self-control and endurance, generally shows greater restraint in her interactions with both female and male characters, including in situations involving conflict and tension.[86] During her school years, however, within her interactions with both students and teachers, the heroine has learnt to be self-reliant and independent, to value her mind, and even to reduce her initial socio-economic disadvantage by way of her intelligence. These lessons, taught at least in part through social interaction, will be useful to Marie as an adult. Like Jeanne and Marceline, by the end of the novel, Marie has turned into a strong-minded, self-sufficient woman who makes her own choices and finds meaning in her work; after rejecting the prospect of marriage, she travels to Canada to start a new job and contribute to the welfare of others.

The originality of *Salutaire orgueil* can be best appreciated if we compare this novel to Bentzon's *Yette*, which makes some small gesture toward a redefinition of modern femininity but proves unable to embrace it fully. Like *Salutaire orgueil*, this novel is a

---

[85] On female sexual rivalry being treated as consistent with women's nature by writers and philosophers, see Chapter 4 on 'Female Rivalry and Love Triangles', pp. 196–99.

[86] See the episodes in which Marie completely ignores other women's provocations or controls her first, aggressive instincts by reacting in a rather composed and dignified manner. For example, see *Orgueil*, pp. 139–43.

Bildungsroman tracing the development of its (eponymous) heroine from childhood to adulthood. It first appeared in serialized form in *Le Temps* in 1880. Yette is a spoiled, unruly, and tomboyish child, who grows up on her family plantation in Martinique. At the age of nine, her parents, encouraged by the local priest, decide that it is time for Yette to enrol in some serious educational programme and turn into a lady. Therefore, Yette, chaperoned by a faithful servant, is sent to France, where she is entrusted to the care of the Darcey family. Once in Paris, she starts attending the prestigious boarding school directed by Mlle Aubry, where Mlle Polymnie, the Darceys' daughter, has also received her education. Utterly ignorant and rebellious by nature, Yette initially struggles to conform to the house rules and find her place among her peers. However, thanks to the director's efforts, she grows increasingly docile and turns into an exemplary student. Following her parents' loss of fortune and tragic deaths, Yette is rejoined by her younger sister Cora and, instead of accepting the Darceys' help, achieves her economic independence by teaching some classes at the boarding school, while training to become a fully qualified teacher. Although Mlle Aubry plans to make of her her new associate, at the end of the novel Yette decides to accept the marriage proposal received from her former piano teacher, M. Mayer, and renounces all career opportunities in order to become his wife.

Yette's trajectory is designed to show that even the least docile of young girls can be made meek. The opening chapter of the novel is aptly entitled 'Un terrible enfant' and the way in which Yette is portrayed as a child invites comparison with Marie Höel and, of course, with her more illustrious predecessors, Sophie, Fadette, Lamiel or even Jo March and Maggie Tulliver. For example, Yette is introduced to the reader in the following terms: 'Yette entrait comme un ouragan, les cheveux en désordre, sa gaule (blouse) d'indienne déchirée par les branches des arbres auxquels, malgré ses neuf ans révolus, elle aimait encore à grimper' (*Yette*, 3–4). As the local priest observes, at this stage 'ses manières n'ont rien de commun [...] avec celles d'une demoiselle', and during her journey to France, the sailors even comment on the fact that she would make a good seaman's apprentice (*Yette*, 29, 100). Yette's lack of good manners and poor social skills become even more evident when, upon her arrival in Paris, she is introduced to the salon of Mme Darcey and passes for 'une sotte' and 'une petite sauvage' (*Yette*, 111, 113). According to the text, Yette's inability to meet the standards of respectable girlhood can be ascribed to her parents' indulgent attitude and to an inadequate education. The heroine is defined by the priest as 'un diamant brut' that needs polishing (*Yette*, 32), and her fictional trajectory is meant to show that a young girl's shortcomings can be corrected by education and by the right kind of socialization. This process starts with Yette arriving at the school director's office and being abruptly divested both of her identity and her past: first Yette is assigned a number and then she is separated from her black servant, who is accused by Mlle Aubry of exerting a bad influence on the child (*Yette*, 118, 126–27).

Initially, Yette's savagery and rebelliousness make it difficult for her to socialize with the other girls and find acceptance. Since she is illiterate and does not know how to behave in the classroom, her presence provokes the mockery, even the contempt of the other pupils, in particular that of two upper-class girls who rule over the class group, Mlle Raymond and Mlle de Clairfeu. When the teaching assistant, Mlle Agnès, exhorts Yette's classmates to be kinder and asks them to walk her to the refectory, nobody complies but Héloïse, a slow-witted but good-hearted child, who usually serves as the class scapegoat (*Yette*, 136–38). Although Yette immediately finds in Héloïse a trustworthy friend and ally (the two will scheme to send a letter to Yette's mother and Héloïse will be punished for this insubordination, *Yette*, 154–61), she is unable to interact successfully with the rest of her classmates, to the extent that on her first day she is involved in two fights, her fierce attitude somewhat resembling that of Marie Höel (*Yette*, 141–42, 147). However, it should be noted that, thanks to Héloïse's counselling, Yette is quicker than Marie to grasp the school dynamics and promptly learns how to turn a bad situation to her advantage by avoiding direct confrontation. When during recess Yette's doll is stolen by Hélène de Clairfeu, in a scene similar to that in which Marie's Blondine is taken away by her neighbours, Héloïse suggests that Yette trade some jam for the doll instead of fighting or asking for the adults' support. When the other girls are punished for their mean behaviour, Yette goes so far as to ask for the jam to be shared with them, and this gesture earns her everyone's benevolence (*Yette*, 144–47). In this novel, conflict avoidance and the lack of intellectual rivalry are part of a narrative strategy in which the representation of female homosociality reinforces common ideas about female passivity and gentleness.

Moreover, despite the fact that one of the initial fights starts when the girls tease Yette because of her father's profession, the role played by class conflict in this novel is very limited. Not only is Yette, unlike Marie, oblivious to social status, but when Polymnie objects to her befriending the daughter of a grocer (i.e. Héloïse), the remark is lightly dismissed by the school director, who only disapproves of this friendship insofar as Héloïse is a weak student and, therefore, does not provide a good example for Yette to follow (*Yette*, 152–53). The novel thus disguises and minimizes class conflict within the school setting, not least by championing a model of female homosociality in which girls coming from different social backgrounds show kindness and benevolence toward one another, and firmly adopt a kind of female behaviour sanctioned by society. This is certainly true for Yette, who takes an interest in Héloïse and, later on, becomes her tutor at Héloïse's mother's request (*Yette*, 213). Interestingly, Yette's relationship with Héloïse has a lot in common with that between Daniel Stern's Nélida and her best friend at the convent, Claudine. In both cases, the heroines befriend two girls of lower social condition, who are bullied by the rest of the class, and take on a role of protection and guidance similar to that of a charitable *châtelaine*, a role traditionally ascribed to the aristocracy, and later on in the century, to bourgeois respectable women.[87] Yette herself benefits from the kind of righteous pity governing the characters' interactions at school. Indeed, one of the differences with *Salutaire orgueil* is to be found in the fact that, in Yette's case, being an orphan increases the other girls' sympathy and compassion toward her and contributes to her and her sister's integration into the group, whereas Marie firmly refuses to be pitied (*Yette*, 198).[88] Such aestheticizing fictional representations work to support orthodox discourses about female homosociality (and female identities), insofar as these characters' attitudes align them with the generous, caring, and thoughtful behaviour commonly associated with and recommended to girls in manuals and essays of the time, which also posit charity as one of women's duties.[89] Class conflict is not reduced by a sense of intellectual egalitarianism achieved through equal opportunities and common educational experiences, but rather by the characters' engagement with societal expectations for women to act in altruistic and sympathetic ways toward their more unfortunate peers, thus ensuring the stability of a peaceful, unproblematic society, free from contradictions and class warfare. As in the case of *Salutaire orgueil*, questions of gender and class are closely interlinked in this representation of female homosociality: by being 'feminine' and treating each other kindly, the characters avoid controversy in general, and class confrontation in particular, all for the benefit of the Republic.

In a chapter entitled 'Yette sous le joug', an expression that emphasizes ideas of oppression and submission, we learn that in the space of a few months Yette has already turned into a diligent and compliant student. In a letter addressed to her mother, who is still alive at that time, Yette mentions her lovely new classmates, asserting that she cannot remember why she initially disliked them (*Yette*, 177). By the age of fourteen:

---

[87]See Daniel Stern, *Nélida* (Paris: Librairie d'Amyot, 1846).

[88]Yette's parents die in Martinique while Yette is attending the school in Paris. Following their deaths, her little sister Cora joins her in France.

[89]On the behaviour that girls should adopt with one another at school, see for example the aforementioned Juranville, *Manuel d'éducation morale*, p. 76. Juranville, among others, presents charity as one of the requirements of respectable womanhood at pp. 185–86. On the subject of women and charity, see also Maryan and Béal, *Le Fond et la forme*, pp. 164–76.

> Yette s'était fait peu à peu une place à part au milieu de ses compagnes, auxquelles on la citait comme un modèle. Les malheurs qui étaient venus la frapper coup sur coup avaient impressionné toutes ces jeunes imaginations, tandis que le courage avec lequel elle les supportait devait nécessairement inspirer aux plus légères une sorte de respect. Mlles Raymond et de Clairfeu elles-mêmes subissaient cet ascendant, elles qui n'avaient fait aucun cas jusque-là de tout ce qui n'était pas la richesse ou la naissance. (*Yette*, 198)

Unlike Marie, Yette is never represented competing against her classmates or trying to prove her academic worth.[90] She wins the other girls' affection and respect not by way of her intellectual superiority but by becoming a model of female obedience, generosity, and endurance, and by exerting a positive influence over them. This novel dismisses the notion of *orgueil*, which is still presented as a vice, in favour of a (Christian) ethos of dignity and self-abnegation.[91] Yette's subsequent choice to work and study, although allowing her to achieve some independence, is mainly portrayed as an act of devotion and self-sacrifice accomplished for the sake of her little sister, toward whom Yette acts as a surrogate mother (*Yette*, 226). By facing the obstacles put on her path and fulfilling her duty with courage and resignation, Yette ultimately turns from 'un enfant terrible' into 'une héroïne'.[92] The example of perseverance, goodness, and unselfishness offered by this heroine is going to be followed by every other female character in the text, including the idle and frivolous Polymnie, or the egocentric and self-indulgent Cora (*Yette*, 216, 235–37).[93] No room is left for intellectual rivalry or, for that matter, for difference among women, in a context dominated by positive emulation and a respectful camaraderie.

In all these respects, Bentzon's fictional representation of female homosociality in the educational context confirms the ideas found in Belle Epoque conduct books for girls and supports traditional discourses on female relationships and identities. The school effectively moulds Yette into an obliging daughter, sister, and eventually wife, even while providing her with the tools to escape from a conventional female destiny. Although Yette partly defies conservative notions of femininity by claiming the right to work as a man and earn a living,[94]

---

[90]Intellectual competition among students is also absent from Stern's novel, in which the girls' meanness is linked to their frivolity. See Stern, *Nélida* (1846).

[91]Mlle Aubry refers to pride as one of Yette's 'défauts d'enfance'. See *Yette*, p. 225.

[92]The label 'héroïne' is used by Mme Darcey when expressing her new-found admiration for Yette. See *Yette*, p. 215.

[93]Not only does Yette exert her influence on her classmates and on other girls around her own age, like Cora and Polymnie, but even the shallow Mme Darcey is affected by her positive example, and Mlle Aubry, in considering Yette's teaching practice, praises the girl's sweetness and modesty, acknowledging that this affectionate attitude toward the pupils is more effective than her own cold austerity. See *Yette*, pp. 116, 222.

[94]Throughout the text, Yette is defined as 'un garçon manqué', an individual 'taillé pour la lutte', who is going to earn her living 'comme un homme'. See *Yette*, pp. 182, 203, 208.

she is primarily animated by a desire to improve herself by appropriating essentially feminine qualities and by performing traditional female roles, consequently inspiring other women to do the same. The novel's ending brings Yette's possible evolution toward a more progressive type of womanhood to a halt, as the heroine abandons all professional and intellectual aspirations, or any prospect to live her life independently, in order to become M. Mayer's wife. As if to reinforce this message, both Polymnie and Cora readily follow in her footsteps and embrace domesticity by marrying two respectable men, who will now take over from Yette in helping their wives to live up to society's expectations (*Yette*, 279–82).

Even though Yette has the potential to become a modern heroine, not least because she benefits from the increased educational opportunities opening up to girls at the beginning of the Belle Epoque, this character still more closely resembles Monniot's Marguerite than Prost's Marie, or Colette's spirited and provocative Claudine, who both make their appearance in fiction at the dawn of the twentieth century. Overall, Bentzon's novel better fits with orthodox literature rather than with the group of novels considered in this chapter. In particular, the fact that by making good use of her education Yette sets herself on a path to happiness and becomes a successful role model for other girls indicates continuity with the themes and characters of conservative novels intended for girls, such as Naïda Dupuy's *Blanche et Nathalie, ou les effets de l'éducation* (1856).[95] The main purpose of this latter novel is to show the good and bad effects of different types of schooling on women, in order to reassert the preferability of a certain model of education (and by implication of femininity) over the other. The heroine forged into *la femme honnête*, who by the end of the novel is rewarded with marriage, financial security, and a good position in society, tries to save the one who went astray. The latter eventually brings death and misfortune upon herself, but only after having acknowledged the superiority of her charitable friend. Unsurprisingly, Blanche and Nathalie, who by the end of the novel have rekindled their friendship, come from different social backgrounds. This is also the case for the eponymous heroines of *Jeanne et Madeleine* (1902), a republican novel frequently read in the secular classroom and focusing on the friendship between a bourgeois and a working-class girl. Like *Yette*, these texts support Republican ideology by showing the possibility (and desirability) of a stable and coherent society, devoid of class conflict.[96] Reading *Yette* alongside *Salutaire orgueil* thus allows us to trace some of the variations occurring in fictional representations of female communities in early-twentieth-century schoolgirl fiction.

---

[95]See for example Naïda Dupuy, *Blanche et Nathalie, ou les effets de l'éducation* (Paris: P.-C. Lebhuy, 1856).
[96]*Jeanne and Madeleine* (1902) by Alice Dereims is discussed by Clark, 'The Primary Education of French Girls', p. 418.

Rather than showing female characters committed to overcoming their differences and to sustaining each other in a common effort to become exemplary *femmes honnêtes*, novels like *Salutaire orgueil* and, as we shall see below, *Sévriennes*, insist on the heroines' intellectual curiosity and on their ambition to find a better place in society by means of their work, asserting themselves against one another and collectively challenging conservative ideals of female kindness and malleability.

In addition to this, a comparative analysis of Bentzon and Prost's texts permits a consideration of the artistic value of some of the works produced by Belle Epoque female authors. As a novel, *Yette* is characterized by such elements as the readability of its characters, the conformism of its moral judgements, the reinforcement of common ideas about women's identities, relationships, and roles in society, the concealment of conflict and ambiguity, or the presence of a happy ending that restores the status quo. These are all key features of what Daniel Couégnas convincingly identifies as 'paralittérature'.[97] By contrast, gender instability and a focus on difference and contradiction, for example in terms of class tension, lie at the heart of Prost's fictional representation of female homosociality. By dismantling stereotypes and contradicting expectations, *Salutaire orgueil*, like most of the novels analysed in previous chapters, simultaneously undermines clear-cut, hierarchical oppositions between 'popular' and 'high' literature. *Salutaire orgueil*, like those other novels, is therefore marked by a modernism that is expressed primarily at the level of content and that is made available to a large readership in an accessible form.[98]

The novel considered in the next section, *Les Sévriennes* by Gabrielle Réval, portrays a group of female students who, similarly to *Salutaire orgueil*, compete with each other and occasionally feel estranged from one another. However, their relationships play a major role in the text and appear to be more profound and complex than those represented in *Salutaire orgueil*. A close reading of this novel permits access to another facet of female homosociality in Belle Epoque French culture and seems to expand the notion of female friendship, again introducing some values and modes of interaction that do not match the normative model of female bonding prescribed in nineteenth-century conduct manuals, textbooks, and essays.

---

[97]See Daniel Couégnas, *Introduction à la paralittérature* (Paris: Seuil, 1992).
[98]See Holmes' definition of the 'modernisme au féminin', as discussed at pp. 34–35 in this thesis.

Female Competition, Intellectual Friendship, and Camaraderie in *Les Sévriennes*

Published in 1900, *Les Sévriennes* is Gabrielle Réval's first novel. The book is dedicated to her mentor and supporter Jeanne Marni (1854–1910), a contemporary novelist and playwright who often dealt with feminist issues in her texts. One of the first graduates from the *Ecole Normale Supérieure de S□vres*, Réval explains in a preface that this work of fiction is largely based on her memories and describes Sèvres not as a 'couvent' nor as a 'Université féminine', but rather as a 'gynécée liberal' (*Sévriennes*, v, vi).[99] This latter term expresses an ideal that both combines and surpasses the two other models, by introducing the idea of a female community whose purpose and significance lie beyond religion ('couvent') or the simple, somewhat sterile acquisition of knowledge ('Université'). In terms of style and composition, the narrative is fragmented and the focalization shifts throughout the novel. Some episodes are related by an external, omniscient narrator, while others consist in the protagonist's diary entries or letters, other students' letters, a professor's progress report and even a journal article. The story follows a group of girls from the day of their entrance examination at the school of Sèvres and throughout the three years they spend there, until the results of the *agrégation* are made public. The protagonist is Marguerite Triel, a brilliant student who, after the sudden death of her best friend Charlotte and despite ending up first at the *agrégation*, finally rejects the stoic ethos of the school and decides to give up a prospective career in teaching, by choosing to live freely with an artist named Henri (Charlotte's former fiancé, who vowed on her death bed that he would never marry another woman). At the time of its publication, this 'beau roman vécu, féminin et féministe',[100] with its lucid critique of the school's contradictions and shortcomings, and its allusions to suicide, lesbian love, female independent thinking, and free love, was much discussed and provoked some strong, sometimes negative reactions on the part of contemporary reviewers.[101] Before discussing how the topic of female homosociality is treated in this novel, it is important to consider how the school attempts to mould its students and which ideals of womanhood these characters are encouraged to pursue.

According to the director, Mme Jules Ferron, the main purpose of the school is to create 'des êtres libres, formés dans la solitude par une éducation virile' who, by the third year, can demonstrate a strong 'ambition d'agir' and '[une] curiosité morale' (*Sévriennes*,

---

[99]As mentioned earlier, the *écoles normales* were training schools for teachers and were generally attended by girls who needed to work in order to earn a living. These schools often (but not exclusively) recruited from the bourgeoisie and the lower classes, admission depending on an entrance examination.
[100]Séverine, '*Les Sévriennes*', *Le Journal*, 18 June 1900, p. 1.
[101]For example, see Eugène Tavernier, *La Morale et l'esprit laïque* (Paris: P. Lethielleux, 1903), pp. 211–16.

228, 229). Upon her arrival, Marguerite notices that the education offered at Sèvres is designed to infuse the students with a 'force virile'; the girls are not treated as 'des écolières' but rather as 'des êtres responsables et libres', and although every evening they are expected to report to Mme Ferron in her office, they are also free to come and go from the school as they please and to receive other girls in their bedrooms (*Sévriennes*, 29, 38). Among the principles and the stated goals of the school, as listed by one of the teachers, Mlle Vormèse, to first-year students, feature the following: 'Apprendre à penser; Apprendre à agir; [...] [devenir] des femmes d'intelligence et d'énergie'. Moreover, the girls are told: 'Pensez, soyez hardies, allez de l'avant', and are exhorted to become 'des femmes droites, intelligentes et fortes' (*Sévriennes*, 76, 77, 79). Therefore, the students at Sèvres are compelled to subvert, or at least broaden, the definition of femininity by receiving 'une éducation virile' and by enjoying some unprecedented freedoms. As noted by Juliette Rogers, 'Réval offers a model for Belle Epoque women's education that does not insist on sacrifice, duty and submission, [...] but rather on independence, intelligence and creativity.'[102] However, while pointing out the school's potential, Réval also denounces the fact that, as van Slyke contends in her article, Sèvres 'remained a close community, something between a convent and a bourgeois home, where behind high walls virginal mother-surrogates prepared to rear the well-heeled daughters of France'; her characters consequently struggle with the contradictory expectation that they 'be simultaneously virile in thought and womanly in demeanor'.[103] How does this type of education affect the interactions between female characters? What kind of bonds do they establish among themselves in this context?

First of all, the students comment on the extent to which this type of education is transforming them, making them different from other girls. For instance, one of Marguerite's closest friends, the tomboy Berthe Passy, after one year at Sèvres admits to having lost her old friends, thus suggesting the idea that different kinds of education can drive women apart:

> — Tu n'as donc plus d'amies là-bas ?
>
> — Non, depuis que je suis à Sèvres, je n'en ai plus: je suis solitaire au milieu des jeunes filles que je fréquentais; nous n'avons plus rien de commun, ni vie, ni pensée, ni rêves. (*Sévriennes,* 152)

[102]Rogers, 'Feminist Discourse', in '*A Belle Epoque'?*, ed. by Holmes and Tarr, p. 190.
[103]Van Slyke, 'Monsters, New Women and Lady Professors', pp. 349, 350.

Berthe, who believes that 'les femmes [...] ne nous pardonnent pas de nous être déclassées, en gagnant notre vie', further declares: 'Nous sommes en dehors de l'ordre sociale, nous sommes presque un genre neutre, celui des Indépendantes ou des Révoltées' (*Sévriennes,* 153). Shaped into 'un genre neutre' by the education they receive, the heroines of this novel challenge contemporary ideals of femininity and lose their place within the social order; this creates an unbridgeable gap between them and other women. In this respect, Réval's text adopts one of the most recurrent themes of nineteenth-century educational novels: the idea that different types of education set women apart by leading them to adhere to different models of femininity, one sanctioned by society and the other disapproved of, thus determining their futures. In novels such as the aforementioned *Blanche and Nathalie* (1856) by Dupuy, but also Daniel Lesueur's *Névrosée* (1890), the heroine who, as an effect of her education, rejects bourgeois notions of proper womanhood becomes either coquettish or pedantic, and in both cases is doomed to failure and unhappiness.[104] By contrast, if Réval's characters fall short of society's expectations, they become nonetheless capable and admirable women, who can contribute to the progress of the nation. The text does not condemn these women, but rather the society that is still unable to accept them.

Juliette Rogers describes the fictional female community imagined in *Sévriennes* as a reproduction of 'the conventional and patriarchal nuclear family, in which Vormèse takes the role of maternal nurturance and support while Ferron takes the distant and rational role of father figure'.[105] In her discussion of the same novel, however, van Slyke emphasizes instead the discordance within this virtual family, noting the 'fierce competition, dirty tricks and spying that shatter the cozy family model'.[106] A close reading of this text shows that, indeed, some of the heroines refuse to open up to other girls and reject the emotional and physical intimacy characterizing the ideal of female friendship during the Belle Epoque, an ideal that posits a continuity between female friendship and the mother-daughter relationship. For example, on the day of the entrance examination, the students from the Lycée Fénelon, who have known each other for years, greet each other with 'des poignées de mains' instead of kissing or hugging, even though later on they adopt a more affectionate mode of behaviour with their former literature professor (*Sévriennes*, 4, 8). Marguerite, whose best friend Charlotte has not been admitted, initially feels lonely but is not willing to accord her friendship

---

[104] In *Névrosée* (Paris: Alphonse Lemerre, 1890), Lesueur represents two sisters coming from different educational backgrounds and equipped with unequal intellectual skills, who like Blanche and Nathalie grow into antithetical types of women and follow different destinies.

[105] Rogers, *Career Stories*, p. 96. In addition to this, Rogers discusses Marguerite's disappointment in her teachers, her desire for them to be more affectionate and supportive at the emotional level, and the importance, for Marguerite, to emphasize cooperation over competition within the female community at Sèvres. See *Career Stories*, pp. 93–99.

[106] Van Slyke, 'Monsters, New Women and Lady Professors', p. 351.

easily to the other girls and wishes that she had a male friend, who could protect her with his 'affection virile' (*Sévriennes*, 24–25). When Angèle Bléraud, later suspected to be in love with another student, tries to approach Marguerite by showing her tenderness ('elle me poursuit de ses embrassades [...] Elle voulait venir, le soir, me border dans mon lit'), Marguerite rebuffs her without the slightest consideration for her feelings (*Sévriennes*, 31).[107] However, while Marguerite, at least at the beginning, shows no particular desire to foster close and affectionate relationships with her classmates, she clearly expects her teachers, and Mme Ferron in particular, to act in more maternal and sympathetic ways toward the students, and complains when they fail to do so (*Sévriennes*, 27, 29).

Historians have established a link, often confirmed by Belle Epoque novels, between the progressive democratization of female education and the discouragement of female intimacy at school, either between students or between students and teachers, throughout the nineteenth century.[108] Rebecca Rogers, for example, points out that the definition of a rigid set of rules regulating everyday life and the establishment of clear hierarchies within the educational context largely prevented the expression of female intimacy. Instead of encouraging exclusive attachments between pupils or students, the educational system privileged the development of a sense of community within the school based on emulation and competition. This sense of community was promoted, for instance, through the adherence to shared moral principles or the students' affiliation to specific groups (e.g. literary and religious associations), but also by means of uniforms, belts, group challenges, and rankings.[109] Even before the advent of state schooling, between 1830 and 1880:

> Within the boarding-school community the lessons of community involved as well a constant struggle to banish the intimate. Intimacy between students, intimacy between students and teachers, and the intimacy of self-discovery were all vigorously denounced both in rulebooks and in school practices [...] The general evolution within girls' schools during this period was toward greater formality, as institutions abandoned the pretense of being surrogate homes.[110]

---

[107]Like Marguerite, another student, the very stoic, cold, and determined Victoire Nollet, does not seem interested in making friends. In a letter to her mother she drily declares: 'Il faut que j'arrive première à la licence. Mes compagnes ne m'intéressent pas beaucoup: j'ai trop à faire.' See *Sévriennes*, p. 34.

[108]In commenting the character of 'la jeune fille' in early twentieth-century French fiction, Bertaut observes that the educational system prohibits the existence of 'amitiés ferventes'. The female adolescent finds her own personality in her solitude, and by asserting herself against her classmates and friends. See Bertaut, *La Jeune Fille*, pp. 169, 174.

[109]See Rogers, *From the Salon to the Schoolroom*, pp. 186–90.

[110]Rogers, *From the Salon to the Schoolroom*, p. 190.

According to Rogers, the decision to discourage particular bonds between girls was explained by the growing emphasis put by the school on the moral value of community and by the choice to privilege the group over the individual in order to preserve the internal order, to the detriment of a familial model.[111] For Christina de Bellaigue, who in her article compares lay boarding schools in England and France between 1810 and 1867, the greater formality and rigidity of the French institutions, a formality and rigidity that we also find later on in the Third Republican school, can be understood as a legacy of the convent model of schooling. Indeed, in convents a suspicion of female autonomy and a desire to preserve girls' innocence led to the reinforcement of strict regulations that allowed the maintenance of order and discipline; at the same time, the nuns, and the lay schoolmistresses afterwards, tended to cultivate their public personae and arouse the students' respect by presenting themselves as distant figures of authority.[112]

In *Sévriennes*, although Marguerite sometimes yearns for the establishment of warmer and more supportive relationships with other women, both the family model and the traditional model of female friendship described in conduct manuals of the time are compromised by the director's adherence to a stoic model of behaviour, and by the feelings of antagonism and estrangement which come to the surface when the exams approach and competition between the students gets fiercer. For example, the relationship between three of the new first-year students is described in the following way:

> Ce n'est point de l'amitié qui les rapproche, c'est un manège assez curieux de surveillance réciproque; mutuellement, elles cherchent à se voler leurs procédés de travail, afin de l'emporter aux examens. (*Sévriennes*, 184)

Marguerite's friend Berthe Passy, writing to a former student, further observes:

---

[111]Rogers emphasizes that, although boarding schools initially represented alternative families for girls, the female community created within these contexts ultimately diverged from the familial model. Not only was the intimacy of familial relationships precluded, but the figures of the teacher or the headmistress, although often perceived as maternal, were in contradiction with the stereotype of the good mother and wife, the conservative feminine roles toward which girls' education was oriented. These professional women were in fact usually unmarried and economically independent, and they had found a place for themselves outside the domestic sphere. See Rogers, *From the Salon to the Schoolroom*, p. 191. Rogers' work draws in part from that of Vincent-Buffault, who similarly explains that the school system encouraged competition between girls and that moments of interaction, sharing, and solidarity between students were allowed and even promoted mostly by means of collective games or through the custom of the 'petites mères', which implied that the older students took care of the younger ones, thus contributing to instate a mechanism of mutual control between pupils. See Vincent-Buffault, *Exercice de l'amitié,* pp. 154–55. Note, however, that Rogers stresses the difference between her argument and that proposed by Vincent-Buffault, by specifying that: 'She [Vincent-Buffault] emphasizes the medical underpinnings of these prohibitions, whereas for girls, I would argue, the moral underpinnings were more powerful.' Rogers, *From the Salon to the Schoolroom*, p. 190.

[112]See Christina de Bellaigue, 'Behind the School Walls: The School Community in French and English Boarding Schools for Girls, 1810–1867', *Paedagogica Historica*, 40.1/2 (2004), 107–21.

Tu n'as pas idée de cette génération-là ; ces trois gosses, ça n'a pas vingt ans, usent vis-à-vis les unes des autres, d'un faux-semblant qui m'épate. Rivales toutes trois, toutes trois comptent sur la première place à la licence, dans deux ans. Elles s'y préparent en se surveillant étroitement, pour que l'une ne lise pas un livre que l'autre ignore, pour se voler leurs procédés de travail en se récriant d'admiration. Le jour du résultat, si l'une des trois l'emporte, les deux autres, de sa gloire..... feront une hétacombe [sic]!! (*Sévriennes*, 191)

In referring to her own class and in discussing each student's effort to prevail over the others, Marguerite employs the terms 'tactique' and 'lutte', often commenting on her skills and attitudes and on those of her fellow students (*Sévriennes*, 139–40, 208). As we have seen, words that connote competition (e.g. 'lutte'), conventionally coded as masculine in conduct books and essays of this period, are frequently applied to female interactions in Prost's novel, too.[113] Later on, the students who have succeeded at the examination at the Sorbonne are generally admired ('le succès a grandi leurs compagnes'), but the pride of those who have failed, or who have not obtained the result they were hoping for, is wounded. Some of them feel jealousy, or '[une] résignation rageuse', and already plot to rise in the rankings (*Sévriennes*, 227). Finally, near the time of the final examination, Marguerite bitterly remarks: 'en ce moment, c'est fini de la camaraderie, l'égoïsme s'étale et triomphe. L'examen est le Dieu Moloch de tous les bons sentiments' (*Sévriennes*, 290).

In addition to this, some of the students, like Prost's Marie Höel, do not hesitate to use physical violence when they are provoked. For example, Marguerite and Berthe tell their companions the following story:

Savez-vous qu'hier soir, dans le couloir des chambres, cette incorrigible [Berthe] s'est mise à faire de la boxe avec une « troisième année », qui a eu le nez cassé d'un coup de poing!

— C'est vrai, j'ai fait la folle, j'avais de tels grillons dans les jambes, que d'un bout à l'autre du couloir, je me suis ruée sur toutes les épaules que je rencontrais. Mathilde a voulu riposter, et devant sa porte: un, deux, moulinet. (Prudemment les Sèvriennes se mettent hors de portée). Je lui ai envoyé mon poing en pleine figure: ah le beau coup! (*Sévriennes*, 91)

When another student, the deceptive and sly Jeanne Viole, tries to trick Isabelle Mariotte into going to a matrimonial agency, Isabelle slaps her on the face (*Sévriennes*, 123). Most of the time, however, the conflicts do not lead to brutal gestures but remain confined to verbal

[113]See pp. 165, 168, 169 in this thesis.

aggression. These conflicts are caused by a clash of opinions, temperaments, or wills and can result in animated discussions. It is important to note that, according to Belle Epoque codes of proper female behaviour, all the attitudes mentioned above, such as intellectual pride, animosity, and competition, and any kind of friction, either verbal or physical, should be discouraged in girls and are considered unwomanly. In etiquette manuals, for example, women are commonly told not to talk about themselves, not to gossip, not to mock other people, not to strongly express an opinion or to quarrel, and not to be curious or indiscreet.[114] The possibility that girls could have a fight is not even contemplated in these texts. The students in this novel, however, appear to transgress these rules almost on a daily basis within their interactions. The novel thus highlights some of the contradictions inherent to Third Republican ideology. Officially, the school was designed to reinforce conventional ideals of womanhood; female sociability was part of that strategy, insofar as girls were usually expected to perform mainstream femininity in the context of their interactions (inside and outside the school). Conduct manuals and textbooks of this period, for example, generally advise girls to establish deep and sincere relationships with carefully chosen companions and, at the very least, they exhort them to be amiable and gracious with their schoolmates and to suppress any sense of jealousy or rivalry dictated by intellectual pride. At the same time, however, the school system discouraged the expression of intimacy between students and enacted mechanisms of competition, which altered their modes of interaction and led them to display a series of qualities in contradiction with received ideas about girls and their relations. As previously discussed, this conflict is disguised in an orthodox text like Bentzon's, whereas it emerges in Prost's and Réval's novels, which present intellectual rivalry as a form of female homosociality in its own right.

In spite of the considerable role played by conflict and intellectual antagonism in this novel, it should be noted that the fictional school of Sèvres also promotes equality and solidarity between its students and many moments of true camaraderie are depicted in this text. In the preface, Réval underlines the fact that the entrance to Sèvres represents 'une rupture complète avec le passé' and erases social difference:

> Je n'ai point indiqué, ou très peu, ce qu'elles [les élèves] étaient avant d'entrer à Sèvres : l'histoire d'écolières pauvres, mais intelligentes, voulant trouver un gagne-pain dans l'Enseignement, leur est commune à toutes; si elles doivent souffrir de la confusion des milieux, ce n'est qu'une fois professeurs. (*Sévriennes*, VI–VII)

---

[114]Maryan and Béal, *Le Fond et la forme*, pp. 61–67.

This excerpt indicates that the school brings together students belonging to different social backgrounds, all poor in the sense that, at the very least, they do not have a dowry and therefore cannot marry but need to sustain themselves through their work. However, Réval suggests that 'la confusion des milieux' is not problematic for the students at Sèvres, although social difference risks becoming an issue when they leave this secluded oasis to face the outside world in their role as teachers. Upon her arrival, Marguerite confirms that class and age distinctions become meaningless in this context:

> L'esprit de l'Ecole est bon. Il est fait d'une commune estime, d'une entente sympathique entre les trois années. On s'oblige volontiers, les aînées n'affectent pas trop d'être les douairières, elles nous invitent au thé de quatre heures; puis à table, en salle de réunion, au bonsoir, petit à petit les anciennes nous livrent les traditions de Sèvres. Les repas sont amusants ; on se groupe à sa guise, les conversations y gagnent en intérêt: chacune a le droit d'y être sincère, et d'avouer ce qui lui plaît, dans les habitudes de cette vie intime. C'est à l'heure des repas que se prennent les résolutions; de table en table passent les circulaires, les pétitions, les petites notes sur les objets perdus. Au coup de fourchette, bien plus qu'aux conversations, se révèlent soudain les milieux. A ma table, j'ai pour compagnes la fille d'un tisserand et la fille d'un colonel: personne, au cours, ne devinerait une semblable différence de situation; voilà le dîner servi, les tares inconscientes, mais révélatrices, trahissent l'origine. (*Sévriennes*, 39)

A sense of equality reigns among the students, whose social origins are revealed by their manners at table but not by their conversation, an element that points to the school's potential to negate social disparity by promoting intellectual egalitarianism.

Prost, Bentzon, and Réval's novels thus engage with the issue of class in very distinctive ways. Social conflict is certainly a strong theme in *Salutaire orgueil,* where the heroine painfully struggles to improve her status by means of education, and eventually eases social tensions at school by imposing her intellectual superiority on her classmates and by winning their respect. A desire to compensate for her social inferiority and overstep class limitations is at the heart of the narrative trajectory that leads Marie to blur the lines of rigid gender categories and redefine her identity as a *femme moderne*. By contrast, Bentzon underplays the relevance of social division by letting her characters adopt a compassionate, charitable attitude, with the result of strengthening conservative notions about women's innate kindness, generosity, and altruism, as well as supporting Republican ideals of social justice and equality. Social disparities are inconsequential in *Sévriennes*, where the students share a common past of relative poverty, and collectively prepare to face similar destinies (i.e. a career in teaching in the provinces). The novel thus leaves the door open to both intellectual rivalry (the students, provided with similar opportunities, compete to obtain the same jobs and degrees) and, as we shall see, intellectual friendship. What is interesting is that, compared to a conservative text like Bentzon's, *Salutaire orgueil* and *Sévriennes* tend to replace the two contrasting, but equally stereotypical, ideals of female intimate friendship and female sexual rivalry with a form of homosociality based on social conflict and/or intellectual competition, which undermines essentialist assumptions about femininity.

Turning now our attention to female intellectual friendship, it should be noted that Marguerite's observations in the previous excerpt[115] are telling of the general atmosphere of friendliness, esteem, and support characterizing the fictionalized school of Sèvres in spite of the competitiveness of its students. Marguerite describes a close-knit community of girls whose lives are made up of shared traditions and moments of conviviality that heighten their sense of belonging. These girls are free to choose their companions and have open, honest conversations, a practice commonly discouraged in conduct books or in the context of the *salon*. Together, they play active roles and make decisions, for example by signing petitions. Therefore, rivalry, camaraderie, and complicity all add up to compose a picture of female homosociality that is both multidimensional and contradictory, as human relations generally are.

Mlle Vormèse tells her students: 'Faites ici l'apprentissage de la vraie bonté. Aimez-vous les unes les autres. Cherchez un peu votre bonheur dans le bonheur d'autrui' (*Sévriennes*, 79). The Christian overtones of this message suggest continuity rather than rupture with the past, and possibly show that, for all its liberal ethos, the school remains indebted to the dominant model of female education in nineteenth-century France: the convent. What interests us here are the implications of this message for female homosociality. Mlle Vormèse's advice does not go unheard; in *Sévriennes* some of the students prove to be caring and supportive toward each other, and are happy for their friends' achievements. For example, when the older students are going to take their exams, the younger ones get up earlier to cheer them up and prepare their breakfast (*Sévriennes*, 140). When Berthe receives the honour of delivering a class in front of a prestigious scholar, M. Legouff, who then congratulates her, Marguerite feels happy for her friend and praises her for her performance (*Sévriennes*, 131–32). Berthe will prove her loyalty to Marguerite when, at the end of the third year, she prevents Jeanne Viole and Angèle Bléraud from stealing her friend's personal diary with the intention of compromising her reputation and getting rid of

[115]See p. 185 in this thesis.

her (*Sévriennes*, 313). Berthe and Marguerite can also share the physical intimacy that, as our chapter 'Female Friendship and the Body' argued, was common in nineteenth-century female friendship; they hold hands, hug, and kiss (*Sévriennes*, 309, 316, 317). In talking about her class group, Berthe observes: 'Quant à notre promotion, c'est la promotion de famille, on papote, et on potine', her choice of words ('famille', 'papote', 'potine') evoking the comfortable intimacy, the ease of manners and speech that could exist between family members (*Sévriennes*, 191). Therefore, this novel does not entirely reject the modes of female interaction generally praised in conduct books or in more orthodox fiction of the time, but it does present them alongside alternative forms of homosociality, such as intellectual rivalry and intellectual friendship, thus expanding the scope of women's relationships.

Life at Sèvres is marked by episodes involving amusement, discussion, trust, help, and mutual encouragement, some of which call into question received ideas about women's acceptable conduct. For example, when the students come together in the 'grande salle' to dance, the scene is characterized by a 'gaieté folle' (*Sévriennes*, 49). Marguerite describes a situation that has little in common with the great balls held in society as represented in many nineteenth-century French novels, since in this case girls are unselfconscious and physically unrestrained:

> On rit, on chante, on danse, on cause. Les plus graves redeviennent enfants au contact des autres, car c'est l'oubli momentané du travail, des peines, des soucis de l'étude. [...] Et soudain, toutes ces jupes s'emmêlent et se démènent dans un quadrille furieux, où l'on piaffe, où l'on houspille ses voisines, accrochant une main, pinçant un bras, déchirant une robe, dans un vertige de tournoiement barbare. Un bien-être indicible paraît sur tous ces visages en sueur. C'est la détente nerveuse, l'usure brutale d'une fougue vite dépensée, qui renaîtra demain pour s'abattre à nouveau. (*Sévriennes*, 49–50)

The joyous and boisterous fury of a group of girls who dance together, thus finding physical release from the pressures of a demanding academic life, emphasizes ideas of freedom, brutality, and wildness, which are clearly at odds with the strictly coded behaviour that well-bred girls were expected to adopt in society and with one another.

These same characters often share jokes, they mock each other or their teachers, and they have fun. Most of all, they can experience a complete 'communion de pensée' (*Sévriennes*, 73). They occasionally discuss serious topics, like war, and they often debate their ideas and beliefs about their future professions or about women and society. They analyse and criticize their courses and their professors, they have engaging discussions about what kind of teacher they want to become, how they see their futures, what philosophical principles should guide their actions and choices, often disagreeing with each other but usually showing a pronounced ability to build their arguments.[116] At one point, animated by a sense of justice, they come together and decide to protest against the reduction of their allowance of wood logs. They write a letter of complaint to the director and when things get complicated they decide to present a united front, finally winning their little battle (*Sévriennes*, 233–36). The lucidity, sense of purpose, and rationality displayed in these collective scenes, and more generally the intellectual character of these interactions, contradict the common belief that a bond based on reason and virtue can only exist between men. The intellectual female community portrayed in Réval's novel could be compared to the even more idealistic description of Bryn Mawr provided by Renée Vivien in *Une femme m'apparut...* (1904):

> Nous allâmes dans un vaste collège de femmes, où quelques hommes d'études et de travail étaient seuls admis. C'était toute une ville sacrée, une ville d'effort et de méditation. Ces jeunes filles se préparaient à la lutte future, ou élaboraient pour leur contentement, un infini de rêves studieux. La joie de l'esprit, mille fois plus poignante que la joie de la chair, éclairait inexprimablement ces francs visages.[117]

The idea of pursuing 'la joie de l'esprit' and of preparing for 'la lutte future' in the company of other girls and with the support of other women is in fact often reiterated in *Sévriennes*. Both novels construct an ideal female community based on knowledge and shared intellectual interests, which points to new forms of female sociability and how they contribute to the definition of alternative female subjectivities.[118]

Les Sévriennes thus offers a rather nuanced and complex picture of female relationships within the new educational context as depicted in Belle Epoque fiction. My analysis shows that, in the case of this novel, relationships between girls are not hindered by social divisions and are based on both rivalry and solidarity. Even though they do not entirely reject contemporary models of female friendship (e.g. the characters can act in tender, almost maternal ways, and share some physical intimacy), the female students adopt certain modes of interaction normally regarded as unfeminine. Not only do they compete fiercely against each other, driven by a desire to succeed, but the relationships they entertain can have a distinctive intellectual character and are often portrayed as a sort of vivacious

---

[116]For example, see *Sévriennes*, pp. 109–20; 177–86; 212–14.
[117]Renée Vivien, *Une femme m'apparut…* (Paris: A. Lemerre, 1904), p. 72.
[118]Arguably, the female intellectual community depicted in *Sévriennes* is less idealistic than Vivien's, due to the importance attributed to conflict in Réval's text.

camaraderie. By representing female characters who, in their daily interactions at school, can adopt some of the attitudes conventionally praised in women, without being confined to them, Réval's novel implicitly participates in contemporary debates concerning women's identities and their relationships. Free to disagree with one another and to antagonize their classmates, or to establish more intellectual bonds with them, these characters claim their difference and individuality, while also cultivating a series of qualities which are in conflict with prevailing conceptions of femininity.

An additional example of Belle Epoque fictional portrayals of female communities at school is offered by Réval's *Lycéennes.* Published two years after *Sévriennes*, this novel is set in the Parisian Lycée Maintenon and, according to critics, is inspired by Réval's own experience as a student at the Lycée Fénelon.[119] The text invites comparison with the contemporary and hugely popular Claudine series, because of its irreverent and free-spirited heroine, whose rebellion against social conventions is in truth even stronger than Claudine's, given her ultimate decision to become a dancer and not a wife, as in the latter's case. At the beginning of the novel, Françoise, a lively young girl from Lorraine, obtains a scholarship that allows her to move to Paris and attend her final year of studies at the Lycée Maintenon, with the intention of entering the *école normale* and becoming a teacher, like her sister Germaine. As the *lycée* does not offer on-site accommodation, Françoise shares a bedroom with some classmates at the *pension de l'Acropole*, thus enjoying the liberty of a bohemian lifestyle. While increasingly questioning the school's methods and objectives, Françoise falls for her uncle Darbès, an older, married man with whom she entertains a short-lived romance, and who encourages her to pursue her true vocation. Having acquired the ability to reason and make her own choices, at the end of the school year Françoise refuses to take the entrance examination at the *école normale* and announces to her parents her decision to become a dancer. The plot line is mostly sketched out by Françoise's letters to her sister Germaine, or in some cases to her mother, and also by excerpts of her friend Mina's diary.

In *Lycéennes,* Réval further elaborates on some of the issues already treated in *Sévriennes*. For example, the text occasionally criticizes the methods adopted by the school, which pits students (and teachers) against each other and largely prevents the expression of intimacy; the conservatism of the curriculum, which at secondary level is still oriented toward the education of the future mothers and wives of the Republic and does not teach girls any practical skill outside the domestic sphere; and the severity of the conditions imposed on women, even when they obtain their economic independence as teachers.

[119] [Anon.], 'Une animatrice au cœur d'or: Gabrielle Réval', *Les Trésors du si□ le*, July–December 1939, pp. 93–95 (p. 94).

Indeed, like Marguerite, Françoise ultimately rebels against a system that educates women only to turn them into wives or into some sort of lay nuns, in the latter case requiring them to endure a life of solitude, chastity, and sacrifice in order to follow their professional calling. In both novels, although praising some aspects of Third Republican education, Réval insists on the risk of curtailing women's liberties instead of promoting their emancipation through education, and on the need to further women's intellectual, professional, and emotional development at the same time.[120]

From the point of view of homosociality, Françoise, like Marguerite, denounces the sense of antagonism and distrust often characterizing the interactions between students (*Orgueil*, 83–84), and deplores the impossibility of establishing more open, warm, and emotionally supportive relationships with the staff (*Orgueil*, 55–60, 277–78). However, as was the case for the *sévriennes*, the *lycéennes* are also able to share moments of joyful camaraderie and intellectual affinity. In particular, Françoise and Mina, one of her classmates and, in time, her good friend, have long conversations about serious topics; they reason together about the challenges and possibilities of private/religious versus public/secular female education, the condition of women in society, or literature.[121] Françoise sometimes accompanies the devout Mina to church, but the two girls also wander the streets of Paris freely and unsupervised; they visit museums and attend public lectures, thus enjoying a sense of liberty and emancipation unheard of for the students of boarding schools and convents (*Lycéennes*, 221–25). The novel offers various depictions of *escapades entre filles*, for example when, having heard that a famous actor could be hired as their new diction teacher, a group of students decide to go to his house unescorted (*Lycéennes*, 229–30). These characters' freedom, the type of activities they engage in, and the way in which, together, they invest the public space suggest a widening of the possibilities of female homosociality in the Belle Epoque. Réval's novel problematizes the link between female friendship and the private sphere discussed at the beginning of this chapter.[122] Before the advent of the Third Republican school, a sense of confinement and estrangement from the

[120]In the previous chapter, it was noted that Réval's professed opinions on female education, and more generally on women's role in society, are not radical or subversive, insofar as the author, as evidenced in her essays and interviews but also in some of her novels, considers a marriage of equals as the preferable choice for women. For Réval, education is important whether because it allows married women to be better, well-respected companions, or because it provides unmarried women with the possibility of earning a living on their own. See p. 104 in this thesis. Her position and the criticisms she directs at the new school system, it should be noted, are very similar to those of some contemporary feminists, who advocated a revision of the curriculum and insisted on the importance of attributing professional value to the degrees. For more discussion of this, see Offen, *Debating the Woman Question*, pp. 53–72.

[121]Moreover, Françoise's reading of Mina's diary helps to create a real sense of intimacy between them. In this particular respect, their relationship conforms to the model of female friendship described in nineteenth-century essays and conduct manuals.

[122]On the link between female friendship and the private sphere, see p. 144 in this thesis.

outside world were the feelings commonly experienced by French girls in convents and boarding schools.[123] Attendance at the public school, and the array of situations that girls are now allowed to experience in the streets and in other public venues, are game changers in terms of female homosociality, and in novels such as *Sévriennes* and *Lycéennes* they seem to heighten the characters' sense of autonomy.

Lycéennes additionally provides various indications of the formative value, for the female characters, of the shared lives they lead at school and of the relationships they foster within this community. The warning addressed by Françoise to Mina is of particular interest for the illustration of this point:

> Cette culture littéraire est extrêmement séduisante; vous voyez qu'elle exige de nous, moins de docilité que d'indépendance; prenez garde, le souci de n'être point inférieure à vos compagnes de lycées, pourrait vous faire aimer l'esprit d'indépendance et de réflexion qui souffle ici... (*Lycéennes*, 115)

Françoise's words suggest that it is both the type of education provided at school and the constructive sense of rivalry existing between classmates that, despite certain drawbacks, encourage girls to cultivate a spirit of independence and improve their ability to think for themselves. At the end of the novel, she asserts: 'Au contact des autres, j'ai su qui je suis', and tells her mother: 'Il était à prévoir que je ne reviendrais pas à vous telle que vous m'aviez quittée, tout ici devait me détacher de la famille: la Bohème de cette vie de pension, mes amitiés nouvelles, mes études surtout' (*Lycéennes*, 275, 303). It is this combination of experiences, studies, and social interactions that promotes the heroine's self-determination and influences her sense of self.[124]

Both *Sévriennes* and *Lycéennes* highlight some of the contradictions, limits, and opportunities presented by state schooling and call attention to the influence exercised by the new educational system upon female homosociality and, more generally, on female development. At school, the heroines rarely find effective role models or a kindred soul to confide in and rely on; sometimes they wish for their teachers to be more affectionate and caring, or for their peers to be more supportive and open. Rigid hierarchies and fierce competition between students largely prevent the establishment of those intimate bonds usually described in conduct manuals and essays of the time. By contrast, in these novels intellectual rivalry becomes, possibly for the first time, a common form of female

---

[123]On this subject, see Bellaigue, 'Behind the School Walls', p. 115.
[124]Toward the end of *Sévriennes*, Marguerite similarly observes: 'L'École m'a fait femme.' See *Sévriennes*, p. 280.

homosociality, one that is sanctioned by the school and that provides girls with new possibilities. This kind of antagonism, in fact, allows the characters to display qualities commonly discouraged in women because they are in conflict with received notions about presumed female nature. These narratives counteract the reduction of female adolescent characters to the unequivocal standard of the good young girl, and point toward the complexity of modern female identities. Moreover, rivalry is often coupled with alternative forms of female bonding, such as intellectual companionship and the pursuit of new dreams and activities in the public sphere. In this sense, and in response to our initial question about the impact of the creation of new, public spaces of female sociability on women's relationships as described in novels, increased educational opportunities offer the possibility of modifying and extending the content and structure of female homosociality in literature, allowing for a rewriting of gender identities.

Conclusion

In a period characterized by significant evolutions in terms of female education, and by the appearance or reinforcement of female communities and networks of support, schoolgirl fiction served as a forum for discussion of the possibilities of a republican education and the impact of female homosociality on the development of female subjectivities. Products of the school system put in place in the 1880s, the authors considered in this chapter expressed their ideas on these topics not only by means of articles, essays, and public lectures, but also through the novelistic portrayal of women's educational experiences and of the relations entertained by the female characters within the fictionalized world of the secular school. The fact that these novels have often been read simply as fictionalized memoirs or historical accounts of the authors' lives has hindered the appreciation of their literary qualities and a more thorough consideration of what the texts are doing at the ideological and literary level. Indeed, if the school provided French women with new, public spaces of sociability, the novel offered a literary space for the authors to reflect on the meanings and potentials of these female communities, and to engage with some of the issues discussed by the opponents of state schooling in contemporary essays. In particular, anxieties about social mixing and the promotion of values and qualities in contradiction with conservative models of proper female behaviour are tackled in schoolgirl fiction of this period and intertwine with the depiction of female homosociality at school.

In terms of class conflict, while some episodes express a social tension that is at variance with the Republic's self-proclaimed egalitarian ethos, the novels point to a sense of intellectual egalitarianism and present hard work, intelligence, and academic worth as the weapons to fight injustice and promote one's upward mobility. In these texts, much space is given to a striving, competitive femininity, that subverts conventional narratives of collective female docility. Although the heroines, particularly in Réval's novels, sometimes bemoan the impossibility of establishing with other women that kind of heartfelt, supportive, and affectionate homosocial bond often described in nineteenth-century conduct books, unprecedented opportunities to vary their modes of interaction, engage in unorthodox activities, and cultivate new skills open up to them. The school is imagined by the authors as a place where, through a complex play of mirroring and differentiation, the heroine builds her sense of self.[125] Dispassionate competition, lively conversations, and moments of light-hearted camaraderie allow the characters to collectively evolve toward more progressive ideals of femininity. The heroines undermine binary gender oppositions by manifesting a blend of qualities which the authors present as not being inherently feminine or masculine (e.g. energy, ambition, initiative, spirit of competition, rationality), and by bonding over shared intellectual interests and professional aspirations. Even though the school 'was specifically intended to prepare women for cultured domesticity'[126] and '[t]he republican reformers were very eager [...] to make sure that their "new woman" was neither too new nor too independent',[127] in the novels here considered, when the characters leave these sheltered, all-female intellectual communities to enter the world, they prove to be not only cultivated, but also bold and self-assured, to the extent that they reject a predetermined destiny and affirm their own choices, thus confirming the school detractors' worst fears (Marie refuses to marry Luc and pursues her career; Marguerite partly disregards her late friend's wishes and opts for a free union with Henri; Françoise decides to become a dancer against her parents' will).

None of these novels suggest that the new school system can bring women together in a way that completely erases boundaries and encourages them to think of themselves as a united group or develop a feminist collective consciousness. At the historical level, a similar remark has been made by Rebecca Rogers, according to whom:

---

[125]This is particularly true in the case of Réval's novels. By means of her interactions with different kinds of girls and women, including Mina and her cousin Thécla, defined as 'les deux pôles du monde féminin' (*Lycéennes*, 117), Françoise figures out what kind of woman she wants to become. The same applies to Marguerite, who first looks for her identity as a teacher and then, more generally, as a woman, by interacting with the students and teachers of Sèvres.

[126]Offen, 'The Second Sex and the Baccalauréat', p. 257.

[127]Van Slyke, 'Monsters, New Women and Lady Professors', p. 349.

> French women failed to develop a vibrant feminist culture comparable to that which emerged in Great Britain. [...] French schoolgirl culture did not produce rebels, or even many feminists of note. [...] French schoolgirls may have learned to take examinations and to take their studies seriously during this period, but this rarely translated into an awareness of gender inequalities that merited direct challenge in their adult lives.[128]

However, fictional representations of female communities in the Third Republican school variously challenge traditional visions of women's relationships and promote a rethinking of female identities in Belle Epoque French culture. The novels thus testify to the existence of 'un modernisme au féminin',[129] which exists beyond strict oppositions between 'high' and 'popular' literature, and successfully gives form to women's experience of modernity.

---

[128]Rogers, *From the Salon to the Schoolroom*, pp. 194, 195.

[129]See Holmes' definition of the 'modernisme au féminin', as discussed at pp. 34–35 in this thesis.

CHAPTER FOUR

Female Rivalry and Love Triangles

Introduction

In the previous chapter, I discussed the particular kind of antagonism that characterizes relations between female characters interacting in the context of the fictional Republican school. In novels such as *Salutaire orgueil* (1907) and *Sévriennes* (1900), intellectual rivalry constitutes a new facet of female homosociality and not necessarily a negative one, at least insofar as it allows the heroine to broaden her sense of identity and possibilities. In this chapter, I would like to consider a more traditional type of female rivalry, namely sexual rivalry, and explore how Belle Epoque women writers use female-identified erotic triangles in their novels. Unlike intellectual antagonism, women's tendency to compete for the love and attention of men was largely regarded as a natural female disposition, and was treated as such by many nineteenth-century French writers and philosophers. In this introductory section, I will discuss narratives of female sexual rivalry in both didactic literature and fiction from the nineteenth century, and more particularly from the Belle Epoque, subsequently turning my attention to the novel of adultery and to structures of triangular desire therein.

If the term 'homosociality' broadly indicates 'social bonds between persons of the same sex', then rivalry can be considered as one of its many aspects.[1] In this thesis, the decision to undertake an analysis of Belle Epoque novelistic representations of female rivalry is dictated by two considerations. Firstly, there is the need to recognize rivalry as one of the components of human social experience for women as well as for men. Indeed, feminist discourse sometimes celebrates the notion of sisterhood in a way that risks sustaining a conservative, essentialist vision of femininity (i.e. women as inherently selfless, compassionate, and supportive) while reducing or even entirely rejecting differences between women. Tempting as this notion might be, the desire to group all women together unconditionally in an imagined female community devoid of conflict or tension should be resisted, just as reductive representations of female homosociality as conflictual should be resisted, insofar as any such simplification contradicts the reality of women's relationships,

[1]On the definition of 'homosociality', see p. 17 in this thesis.

denying women the possibility of competing or of being at odds with one another.[2] Secondly, the relevance of novelistic representations of female rivalry cannot be ignored given the ubiquity of this topic in Belle Epoque French culture.

In fact, in this period narratives of female rivalry appear in novels as well as in conduct books for girls and essays dealing with women's nature and role in society. As highlighted in the Introduction, historically female friendship has often been regarded as an impossibility by both novelists and philosophers, partly on account of the primacy of love in women's lives, the objectification of women by men leading the former to become sexual rivals rather than friends. Michelet, among others, expresses scepticism about women's ability to foster meaningful and positive relations with one another, alluding to the innate sense of antagonism and distrust that characterizes their interactions:

> Les femmes, qui savent si bien ce que souffre leur sexe, devraient s'aimer, se soutenir. Mais c'est le contraire. Quoi! l'esprit de concurrence, les jalousies, sont donc bien fortes! L'hostilité est instinctive.[3]

In a chapter on female sensibility from *La Psychologie de la femme* (1900), Henri Marion, who writes in defence of female friendship, although in ambivalent terms, evokes a series of famous writers, both from his time and from the past, who invariably claim that female tenderness translates into heterosexual love rather than friendship, and that the latter relationship cannot exist between women because they are 'trop légères, ou trop jalouses, trop naturellement et constamment sur un pied de rivalité'.[4] In *La Vie de l'amitié*, an essay on friendship which in 1913 earned its author the *Prix Montyon* from the *Académie Française*, Louise Barbier-Jussy also observes:

> L'inaptitude de la femme à la profondeur des sentiments (prétextée par le sexe fort comme objection contre l'amitié entre homme et femme) est doublée, selon lui [le sexe fort], dans l'amitié de deux femmes, d'une jalousie qui rendrait impossible le développement de cette affection.[5]

---

[2] For further discussion on the negotiation of sameness and otherness, harmony and conflict in female communities, see for example Michie, *Sorophobia*.

[3] Jules Michelet, *La Femme*, 10th edn (Paris: Calman-Lévy, 1879 [1860]), p. 393.

[4] For example, Marion quotes La Bruyère, Montaigne, La Rochefoucauld, and Paul Bourget. See Marion, *Psychologie de la femme*, pp. 154–57.

[5] Barbier-Jussy, *La Vie de l'amitié*, p. 20.

Barbier-Jussy later goes on to disprove this allegation against women. However, the fact that she feels compelled to answer the accusation points up the fact that the topic of female jealousy was consistently evoked in discussions on female friendship or in speculations about women's nature.

Conduct manuals from the Belle Epoque often confirm these negative views about women and their relationships, but it is worth noting that their treatment of female jealousy is somewhat ambiguous. Female rivalry is in fact both naturalized, in these texts, by being presented as typical of women's nature and, at the same time, condemned as unfeminine. For example, in her *Essais pour l'éducation du sens moral*, the conservative author Louise D'Alq starts her chapter on 'Les Amis' by quoting the popular saying: 'Que Dieu me préserve de mes amis, je m'arrangerai de mes ennemis.'[6] In commenting on the rarity of authentic friendship, for men as well as for women, D'Alq provides several examples of female hypocrisy. To show the catastrophic effects of gossip and envy on a woman's life, she recounts the supposedly true story of two friends, Maria and Jeanne. Jeanne, an honest, beautiful, and innocent girl is deserted by her prospective fiancé because of the slanders uttered by her malicious friend Maria, who resents her beauty and cannot stand the prospect of her marriage.[7] D'Alq concludes by stating that: 'Entre femmes, elle [l'amitié] est synonyme de *trahison*, entre hommes, elle l'est *d'intérêt*.'[8] Other authors of conduct manuals also strive to warn their readers against other women and to reveal the various forms that female jealousy, often disguised as friendship or goodwill, can take. For instance, an anonymous writer claims that: 'Entre femmes, la franchise affectée n'est que le voile de la jalousie, la flatterie est le contre-sens de la pensée.'[9] These examples denounce women's tendency to be envious and duplicitous as perhaps inevitable but at the same time unbecoming. Some authors of conduct manuals point out the incompatibility of traditional female virtues such as self-effacement and benevolence with envy and competition, suggesting that the development of women's intrinsically generous and sympathetic natural dispositions might enable them to overcome jealousy:

[6]Louise D'Alq, *Essais pour l'éducation du sens moral: la science de la vie, la vie intime* (Paris: Bureaux des causeries familières, s.d.), p. 114.
[7]D'Alq, *Éducation du sens moral*, pp. 115–17.
[8]D'Alq, *Éducation du sens moral*, pp. 118–19. Italics in the original.
[9]*Les Usages du monde*, p. 115.

> La nature féminine offre d'ailleurs des ressources précieuses. Le sentiment, qui domine en elle, peut être orienté vers les tendances altruistes. Et le développement des tendances sympathiques et affectueuses peut contribuer à écarter l'envie et la jalousie.[10]

In other cases, however, female cattiness seems to be condoned because it is supportive of the patriarchal order. For example, in highlighting women's hideous propensity to denigrate each other, one author interestingly comments: 'charmantes et délicieuses filles d'Eve, vous seriez trop puissantes, si vous n'aviez pas ce petit défaut-là.'[11]

Not only were female rivalry and jealousy recurrent topics of discussion in etiquette manuals and essays, but during the Belle Epoque these were also well-established literary tropes. Depictions of women competing for men abound in French literature. Nineteenth-century canonical texts such as Stendhal's *La Chartreuse de Parme* (1839), Sand's *Indiana* (1832), or Maupassant's *Une Vie* (1883), to mention just a few examples, all represent female characters as sexual rivals competing for male affection. Moreover, it is interesting to note that novels whose titles either contain the word 'amie' or otherwise imply the presence of two women in the text (e.g. Paul Bourget's *Les Deux Soeurs*, 1904) often turn out to be stories of sexual antagonism and betrayal rather than friendship. Olympe Audouard's *L'Amie intime* (1873), Henry Gréville's *L'Amie* (1878), and Henry Rabusson's *L'Amie* (1886) all fall into this category and portray female friendship as being constantly overshadowed by jealousy; the closer the two friends get, the greater the danger.[12] In these novels, the authenticity of female bonding is threatened by the spectre of heterosexual love looming in the background and readers are tacitly urged to mistrust other women, especially those who try to pass themselves off as their best friends. These representations clearly align themselves with some of the aforementioned ideas expressed in conduct manuals and essays of the same period. For example, in the preface to her novel Audouard addresses her readers with the following words:

> il faut se méfier un peu de certaines *bonnes amies*. [...] C'est incroyable, le génie, la diplomatie, la finesse que les femmes dépensent pour vaincre une rivale, pour la faire

[10]Alphonse Piffault, *La Femme de foyer: éducation ména□ re des jeunes filles* (Paris: Delagrave, 1908), p. 243.
[11]David Emmanuel, *L'Art de plaire: manuel pratique à l'usage des dames et des demoiselles* (Paris: Imprimerie Générale, 1903), p. 121.
[12]Olympe Audouard, *L'Amie intime* (Paris: Dentu, 1873); Henry Gréville, *L'Amie*, 16th edn (Paris: Plon, Nourrit et Cie, 1879). This idea is also expressed by Beauvoir: 'plus deux femmes sont amies, plus leur dualité devient dangereuse. La confidente est invitée à voir à travers les yeux de l'amoureuse, à sentir avec son cœur, avec sa chair: elle est attirée par l'amant, fascinée par l'homme qui séduit son amie.' See Simone de Beauvoir, *Le Deuxi□me Sexe II: l'expérience vécue* (Paris: Gallimard, 1949), p. 365.

tomber de son piédestal, et si elles parviennent à la faire rouler dans la boue, elles ne sont pas satisfaites encore, elles s'acharnent sur le cadavre.[13]

Audouard forcefully deplores this attitude but she also identifies the main cause for women's cruelty toward other women as the fact that they are not given suitable outlets for their energies, instincts, and qualities on an equal footing with men. According to Audouard, the fact that women turn against each other is the result of their confinement to the private sphere and a consequence of the limitation of their agency to the field of romantic, heterosexual love.[14]

Belle Epoque narratives of female rivalry need to be understood in the context of what Nicholas White designates as the 'default narrative' of that culture, namely the narrative of adultery and triangular desire.[15] In *The Family in Crisis in Late Nineteenth-Century French Fiction* (1999), White explores the relationship between the popularity of the topic of adultery in French fiction and the *fin-de-□ □ □*crisis of family values. In particular, White evokes the shifts produced by the *Loi Naquet* on divorce (1884), which 'signalled the fragility of state-sponsored idealism about the indestructibility of the married couple', and by the appearance of the New Woman.[16] While White and other scholars (most notably René Girard and Eve Kosofsky Sedgwick, discussed below) have been mainly concerned with male-authored novels and male-identified love triangles, in this chapter I would like to focus on the novelistic representation by women of female-based love triangles. Belle Epoque female authors often share with their male colleagues a preoccupation with infidelity and desire. The fact that female sexual rivalry should figure recurrently in novels that can generally be labelled as middlebrow, female-centred romances is not surprising, given the frequency with which the erotic triangle pattern is employed in this genre. As we shall see, in Belle Epoque women's novels the female-male-female triangle is used to reflect on the conflicts between female friendship and heterosexual romance and between self-fulfilment and collective good. This device often displaces and eventually defuses anxieties about the blurring of gender roles, the crisis of the traditional family, and the emancipation of women. At the same time,

---

[13]Audouard, *Amie intime*, p. xv. Italics in the original.
[14]See Audouard, 'Préface: Les Petites Pérfidies féminines', in *Amie intime*, pp. v–xxxii.
[15]Nicholas White, *The Family in Crisis in Late Nineteenth-Century French Fiction* (Cambridge: Cambridge University Press, 1999), p. 178. Comparative studies of nineteenth-century British and French fiction highlight the contrast between the British novel of marriage and courtship and the French novels of adultery. Sharon Marcus evokes this contrast in 'Comparative Sapphism', in *The Literary Channel: The Inter-National Invention of the Novel*, ed. by Margaret Cohen (Princeton: Princeton University Press, 2002), pp. 251–85 (p. 251).
[16]See White, 'Introduction', in *The Family in Crisis*, pp. 1–21. See also Holmes, 'Novels of Adultery', in *Currencies*, ed. by Sarah Capitanio et al., pp. 15–30.

paradoxically, the plots of these novels work toward the resolution of female rivalry from within the triangular structure itself.

In literary theory, the notion of triangular desire has been conceptualized in two seminal works: René Girard's *Mensonge romantique et vérité romanesque* (1961) and Eve Kosofsky Sedgwick's *Between Men* (1985), which both deal with erotic triangles in which the two opponents are men.[17] According to both Girard and Sedgwick, the triangle pattern, a device central to male-authored, canonical western fiction, establishes a bond between rivals that is stronger and more significant than the bond that each rival might foster individually with the desired object. While for Girard triangular structures are unaffected by gender, for Sedgwick:

> the radically disrupted continuum, in our society, between sexual and nonsexual male bonds, as against the relatively smooth and palpable continuum of female homosocial desire — might be expected to alter the structure of erotic triangles in ways that depended on gender, and for which neither Freud nor Girard would offer an account.[18]

Sedgwick, however, does not offer any further exploration of the impact of gender on the functioning of love triangles. A few decades later, the specificities of the erotic triangle involving female rivals are considered in more detail by Diana Wallace in *Sisters and Rivals in British Women's Fiction, 1914–39* (2000).[19] Her chapter entitled 'Theorising Female Rivalry' provides a useful overview of previous scholarship on this topic.[20] As explained by Wallace, if Freudian theories tend to normalize female rivalry, works by Nancy Chodorow, Judith Kegan Gardiner, Adrienne Rich, and Elizabeth Abel, on the contrary, contend that women's primary bonds are with women and that women develop their identities in relation

[17]Another useful reference is Rubin Gayle, 'The Traffic in Women: Notes on the "Political Economy" of Sex', in *The Second Wave: A Reader in Feminist Theory*, ed. by Linda Nicholson (New York: Routledge, 1997), pp. 27–62.

[18]Sedgwick, *Between Men*, p. 23. According to Girard, on the contrary, mimetic rivalry 'occurs in an absolutely symmetrical way in both sexes'. René Girard, *Things Hidden Since the Foundation of the World*, trans. by Stephen Bann and Michael Metteer (London: Athlone, 1987 [1978]), p. 337, as quoted by Carole Veldman-Genz, 'The More the Merrier? Transformations of the Love Triangle Across the Romance', in *New Approaches to Popular Romance Fiction: Critical Essays*, ed. by Sarah S. G. Frantz and Erica Murphy Selinger (Jefferson: McFarland, 2012), pp. 108–20 (p. 110).

[19]Diana Wallace, *Sisters and Rivals in British Women's Fiction, 1914–39* (Basingstoke: Palgrave Macmillan, 2000). Terry Castle had been previously concerned with female-identified erotic triangles in lesbian fiction, focusing on bonds of lesbian desire. In her study, Wallace wishes to account for other types of bonds between women. See *Sisters and Rivals*, pp. 59–60.

[20]See Wallace, 'Theorising Female Rivalry', in *Sisters and Rivals*, pp. 46–74. Some of the material discussed below borrows from this chapter.

to one another.[21] The latter claims have been contested, among others, by Luce Irigaray, who in *Ce sexe qui n'en est pas un* (1977) defines women as rival commodities in a male economy. Irigaray argues that in patriarchal societies women's commodification by men prevents them from relating as equal subjects and constructs them as sexual rivals. Their relations are triangular because always mediated through men, the value of each woman measured against that of the other, and their roles (i.e. mother, virgin, and prostitute) defined in relation to men.[22] More recently, Carole Veldman-Genz's discussion of love triangles in popular romance fiction has highlighted the fact that while 'dualistic structures of the male/female/male triangle harbour the potential for female determination and agency', female-based structures split women into antithetical categories ('good/bad, virgin/whore, sane/mad'), thus reasserting female rivalry and erasing female diversity.[23]

If Genz's observations on the popular romance largely support Irigaray's theory, Wallace's use of the model of sibling rivalry and of Bakhtin's dialogic model allows her to provide a more complex understanding of female rivalry. In particular, Wallace's analysis of inter-war British female fiction shows that women also exist in a female economy where they can exchange men in order to establish homosocial bonds among themselves, an idea that challenges Claude Lévi-Strauss' understanding of society as being based on the exchange of women by men.[24] According to Sharon Marcus, the image of women exchanging men is also present in Victorian British novels, in the context of what she calls the 'amity plot'. In the typical amity plot, in fact, female friendship and heterosexual love are interdependent and the female friend acts by 'mediating a suitor's courtship, giving a husband to the friend or the friend to a husband, or helping to remove an obstacle to the friend's marriage'. Marcus further observes that: 'In the plot of female amity, female friendship absorbs, neutralizes, and transmutes female rivalry.'[25] The novels under consideration in this chapter similarly establish a feminine economy based on the exchange of men. However, in these examples, the privileging of a strong homosocial bond over the heterosexual one is not systematic, and stereotypes of female rivalry and friendship are rather subverted by being played off against each other or by collapsing into one another.

---

[21]More recently, the primacy of women's bonds with other women has been reinstated by Bracha L. Ettinger in '*Fascinance* and the Girl-to-m/Other Matrixial Feminine Difference', in *Psychoanalysis and the Image*, ed. by Griselda Pollock (Oxford: Blackwell, 2006), pp. 60–93.
[22]See Irigaray, *Ce sexe qui n'en est pas un*.
[23]Carole Veldman-Genz, 'The More the Merrier?, in *New Approaches*, ed. by Frantz and Murphy Selinger, p. 112.
[24]See Claude Lévi-Strauss, *Les Structures élémentaires de la parenté* (Paris: Mouton, 1967 [1949]).
[25]Marcus, *Between Women*, pp. 82, 97.

As noted by Genz, the love triangle 'is a dynamic structure, capable of producing plural textual effects'.[26] In this chapter, I would like to explore the 'textual effects' produced by the triangle plot in three Belle Epoque female-authored novels: Yvette Prost's *Salutaire orgueil* (1907), Daniel Lesueur's *Nietzschéenne* (1908), and Colette Yver's *Princesses de sciences* (1907).[27] In particular, I will use Hélène Cixous' definition of the gift in a female economy, the notion of female sacrifice, and the nineteenth-century model of normative female friendship as interpretative tools for reading these texts. The term 'Other Woman' will be used with regard to the female character situated outside the traditional, legitimate dyad formed by husband and wife and/or by father and mother.[28] According to Helena Michie, '[p]opular culture uses the transfiguration of female otherness into the mistress to locate it outside the family; the mistress, as the not-wife, becomes the locus of all that is troubling, problematic, unfamiliar about female sexuality and sexual difference.'[29] In the novels considered in this chapter, however, the Other Woman is not the emblem of dangerous femininity, but rather the embodiment of a positive, constructive, moralizing force which contributes to the regeneration of French society by cementing the inviolability of marriage and the family unit.

Salutaire orgueil and the Realization of a Feminine Economy of Generosity

The first novel I would like to consider, *Salutaire orgueil* (1907), has already been discussed in a previous chapter dealing with Belle Epoque literary representations of female homosociality in the educational context.[30] This section will focus on the second part of the novel, in which the first-person narrator and protagonist of the story, Marie Höel, relates in a diary form the events occurring after her departure from the *lycée* at age 22. Before discussing Prost's portrayal of female rivalry and love triangles, it is important to note that *Salutaire orgueil* is a female *Bildungsroman* that partly follows the codes of the romance

[26]Veldman-Genz, 'The More the Merrier?', in *New Approaches*, ed. by Frantz and Murphy Selinger, p. 108.
[27]Daniel Lesueur, *Nietzschéenne* (Paris: Plon, 1924 [1908]); Colette Yver, *Princesses de science* (Miami: HardPress, 2013 [1907]).
[28]Holmes considers the Other Woman as the heroine's foil or negative. For this reason, she defines Lucienne, the wife in *Nietzschéenne*, as the Other Woman, whereas I refer to Jocelyne, the heroine of the novel and Robert's potential mistress, as the Other Woman. See Holmes, 'Daniel Lesueur and the Feminist Romance', in *A 'Belle Epoque'?*, ed. by Holmes and Tarr, p. 207.
[29]Michie, *Sorophobia*, p. 1.
[30]See Chapter Three, pp. 155–77. In particular, for a summary of the novel's plot, see pp. 155–56.

genre but at the same time rejects them, ultimately denying the heroine a happy ending.[31] As highlighted by literary critics, marriage is an essential component of the classic *Bildungsroman* in general, but its significance is even greater when the protagonist is female. According to Odintz, 'female development and maturity seem always bound to a trajectory towards "a sexual fate." [...] Female maturity [...] is inseparable from this journey into heterosexuality, as the only accepted path for women to social integration.'[32] However, in her novel Prost undermines the marriage plot and tries to carve a space for the *femme célibataire* in society.[33] The author thus promotes a diversification of the roles and identities available to modern women outside strictly heterosexual frameworks, while insisting on their compatibility with Third Republican values. Marie is asked to deliver a lecture in the context of the weekly conferences organized by Mme Elder for the association 'Femmes de France'. The title of her contribution is 'Causerie sur la femme de demain', as opposed to the talk previously given by her romantic interest Luc Elder and entitled 'Causerie sur la femme d'aujourd'hui', in which he celebrates the delicate and shallow 'femme-poupée' whose only purpose in life is to please men (*Orgueil*, 153–54). In her passionate speech, Marie condemns women's confinement to domestic and reproductive roles and advocates for the full development of their potential as human beings, her words anticipating those written by Simone de Beauvoir half a century later:

> Je m'élève contre le préjugé séculaire qui ne voit guère dans la femme que le grand instrument de la conservation de l'espèce et la considère comme un moyen, non comme un être libre ayant sa fin en soi. Depuis assez longtemps on déclare qu'il faut faire de la femme une épouse et une mère. Je dis qu'avant tout il faut en faire une personne. (*Orgueil*, 182)

Later in the novel, Luc also converts to a more progressive form of feminism and dedicates to Marie his latest book, *A celles qui sont seules*, in which he promotes the ideal of the single woman whose life is governed by the principles of strength, self-possession, pride, intelligence, and goodness (*Orgueil*, 292–93). If both Marie and Mlle Esther embody this

---

[31]According to Rogers, in the *Bildungsroman* 'the process of evolution is much more important than the (often negative) final outcome'. See Rogers, 'Feminist Discourse', in *A 'Belle Epoque'?*, ed. by Holmes and Tarr, p. 185.

[32]Odintz, 'Creating Female Community', p. 55.

[33]Literary critic Jules Bois observes that Prost's novel 'affirme la faillite de l'amour par le féminisme'. Although he discusses the novel in positive terms, he complains about Prost's rejection of romantic love, and asserts the belief that feminism and love could and should be reconciled. See Jules Bois, 'Revue des livres: Romans féministes', *Les Annales Politiques et Littéraires*, 4 August 1907, pp. 101–103 (p. 103).

ideal at the diegetic level (after reading Luc's book, Marie declares: 'Dans cet ouvrage, j'ai retrouvé toute mon âme', *Orgueil*, 292), *A celles qui sont seules* can be seen as a metafictional device illustrating the overall aim of the novel, which is to create a new narrative trajectory for the single, modern woman, and to contribute to the reshaping of female identities in the Belle Epoque. It is not a coincidence that in 1920 *Salutaire orgueil* is republished as a *roman feuilleton* in the journal *L'Ouest-Éclair* with the title *Celles qui sont seules*. As we can also deduce from a dialogue in which Marie expresses her views on literature and deplores both the romance genre and the artistic creed of *l'art pour l'art*, the ultimate purpose of *Salutaire orgueil* is indeed to address those (female) readers who are alone '[pour leur] rendre l'âpre goût de la lutte et de la vie', giving them a sense of their possibilities outside marriage (*Orgueil*, 174–75).[34] The question that this section will address is: what roles do love triangles and female rivalry play in a text marked by the failure of the romance plot?

One of the most interesting aspects of this novel is the presence of two female-based love triangles which work in very distinctive ways, their opposition allowing us to draw attention to the unconventional use of this pattern made by some Belle Epoque female authors. The first one is the classic love triangle in which two women are pitted against each other to polarize femininity, and the reader, along with the male hero, is compelled to choose between them. Before Marie meets Luc and his mother, her narrow-minded landlady gossips about them and refers to Luc's well-known and scandalous liaison with the married Mme Ladowska, 'miracle de beauté, d'élégance et de perversité' (*Orgueil*, 108). Mme Ladowska is immediately associated with foreignness and is repeatedly referred to by Marie simply as 'la Polonaise', her anonymity also strengthened by the fact that her first name is never revealed. The text completely silences this character, her insubstantial presence only manifested through the 'frou-frou soyeux' of her dress or the perception of her perfume (*Orgueil*, 152). Not even once do we hear Mme Ladowska's voice or have access to her thoughts. When the other characters talk about her, they consistently allude to her striking looks and outfits, defining her as '[une] jolie poupée' but nothing more (*Orgueil*, 145). Represented as a shell, a shadow devoid of any personality or quality, Mme Ladowska is a mere cypher in this story. She is the perfect embodiment of the superficial and uninteresting *femme mondaine* praised by Luc during his talk, this link suggested by the fact that the same word (i.e. 'poupée') is employed to indicate 'la femme d'aujourd'hui' described by him. This 'Sphinx without a secret', a recurrent image in *fin-de-*□ □ □ literature, is represented as

[34]Some contemporary critics actually perceived *Salutaire orgueil* as 'un roman fortifiant', in which 'le travail' is presented both as 'un but' and 'une consolation'. See Sarcey, '*Salutaire orgueil*'.

threatening, and yet, as we shall see, as a figure of the past she is destined to be supplanted by 'la femme de demain'.

Mme Ladowska primarily functions as Marie's rival and foil. On the one hand, she provokes in the heroine predictable feelings of jealousy and anxiety, which are meant to signal her unacknowledged affection for Luc. For instance, when Marie sees Luc and Mme Ladowska together, she confesses: 'une émotion brusque m'a brûlé le visage et a fait trembler mes doigts' (*Orgueil*, 150). When, later on, she perceives their fingers discreetly touching, she feels 'comme un choc dans la poitrine' (*Orgueil*, 155). On the other hand, despite her slim characterization, Mme Ladowska is clearly represented as Marie's antithesis and is called upon to exemplify an evil, dangerous kind of femininity: the *femme fatale*. By contrast with the main heroine, who is rational and self-controlled, yet generous and good-hearted, Mme Ladowska is '[un] bel animal pervers qui ne connaît d'autres lois que les caprices de ses sens' (*Orgueil*, 194). The legitimacy of her womanhood is diminished and compromised by a double association with foreignness ('la Polonaise') and animality. Therefore, in the long run, Mme Ladowska is doomed to be rejected by the male hero, who realizes that she is unworthy of his love and attentions. According to the narrator Marie, Mme Ladowska belongs to that group of contemptible women '[qui] ont cherché à le [Luc] séduire par l'adresse de leur couturière, la savante architecture de leurs cheveux, le charme de leur sourire' but cannot secure his everlasting respect and affection. Marie, for her part, declares that if she was in love with him, 'c'est par une autre voie que [elle] voudrai[t] arriver jusqu'à son cœur' (*Orgueil*, 163–64). Moreover, in noticing Luc's sad expression, she remarks: 'Il me semble que si je l'aimais, moi, il n'aurait pas ce visage-là, en me quittant', thus reinforcing the idea that women like Mme Ladowska only bring sorrow and misfortune, while women like herself can truly love a man and make a difference in his life (*Orgueil*, 189). While this love triangle plays on the classic opposition between *femme fatale* and *femme bienveillante*, the ultimate suppression of the romantic outcome implicitly shows that such polarities are not effective in the modern world.

The erasure of the undeserving, bad woman is one of the most traditional resolutions of the triangular plot.[35] When Luc persists in chasing the fickle Mme Ladowska to Monte Carlo, 'la Fatalité, ou le Destin, ou le Hasard' intervenes: his car breaks a few kilometres down the road and he is forced to turn back. As Marie triumphantly observes, 'le vice [a été] châtié' (*Orgueil*, 202). Some time later, however, Mme Elder complains about the fact that her son is resuming his foolish plan to rejoin Mme Ladowska, and worries that '[elle] finira

---

[35]See Veldman-Genz, 'The More the Merrier?', in *New Approaches*, ed. by Frantz and Murphy Selinger, pp. 111–13.

de le ruiner et de le perdre' (*Orgueil*, 238). Marie unsuccessfully tries to stop him, only to find out, more than a year later, that Luc has spent the whole period since her attempted intervention writing a serious book and thinking about her rather than Mme Ladowska (*Orgueil*, 287–90). Upon his return, Luc declares his undying love for Marie and Mme Ladowska, by then long disappeared from his life, is never mentioned again.

The erotic triangle involving Marie, Luc, and Mme Ladowska conforms to traditional narratives of female rivalry in which women are characterized as polar opposites (i.e. good/evil, virgin/whore, worthy/unworthy) and the hero's decision ultimately reasserts the preferability or even the superiority of a certain kind of femininity over the other. Put in contrast with one another by men and mainly defined through their relations with them, the two female characters never interact and confirm Irigaray's views on the impossibility, for women, of establishing true connections within a masculine economy. By contrast, the second love triangle represented in the text, whose protagonists are Marie, Luc, and Mlle Esther, challenges these conservative views of female sexual rivalry and overturns the power dynamics traditionally generated in triangular plots where two competing women, instead of being desiring subjects, paradoxically turn into desired objects at the hero's mercy. Marie and Mlle Esther's bond is far more complex than the one between Marie and Mme Ladowska and it is also stronger and more meaningful than each woman's relationship with Luc. Not only does this triangular model contradict Irigaray's notion of women as commodities who cannot interact as individuals, but while the man, in Girardian terms, serves as a conduit to reinforce the homosocial relation between the two rivals, this relation already exists outside the triangular structure and its primacy brings about the dismantlement of the triangle itself.

Marie first encounters her teacher Mlle Esther at age 12, in the context of the *lycée* she is attending after her grandmother's death. As a teenage student, she regards her new music and English professor with awe and fear, referring to her as 'une personne qui me glace' and to her lessons as 'un avant-goût du purgatoire' (*Orgueil*, 48, 49). Despite the fact that Mlle Esther is still young and beautiful, she always looks cold and austere, and there is also an air of sadness about her. According to one student, Mlle Esther used to be sweet and full of life, but her demeanour radically changed after a long summer vacation spent in the south of France (*Orgueil*, 49). Later on it will be revealed that during that period Mlle Esther secretly gave birth to Luc's illegitimate daughter. One night, Marie happens to confide her sorrows to Mlle Esther and suddenly realizes that the two of them share the same loneliness and pain ('[Mlle Esther] est, comme moi, seule dans le monde si grand. Personne ne l'aime, elle non plus', *Orgueil*, 57). On this occasion, Mlle Esther, instead of acting maternally and giving Marie the affection she craves, teaches her stoical self-discipline, asserting that 'on ne vit pas pour être heureux, mais pour agir, pour lutter', and urging her to become 'maîtresse de son esprit, de son cœur et de ses nerfs' (*Orgueil*, 57). From then on, Marie sees Mlle Esther as her mentor ('de toute mon âme, je veux la comprendre et je veux la suivre', *Orgueil*, 59), and does her best to impress her and to emulate her. For her part, Mlle Esther takes a real interest in Marie and elects her as her *protégée*, strenuously pressing her to toughen up, to privilege spirit over matter, and to suppress any tendency to sensuality or self-indulgence, while discouraging any expression of affection between them (*Orgueil*, 63–64, 72, 79). Their bond is further reinforced when, during the summer holidays, Mlle Esther offers Marie private piano lessons, thus starting to train her for her future profession (*Orgueil*, 71–73). When, years later, due to her physical condition Marie fails the medical examination to enter the *Ecole Normale*, Mlle Esther first persuades her sister, the director of the *lycée*, to hire her as a school monitor, and then, saddened by the fact that her *protégée* is wasting her talents, advises her to take up a position as a private piano teacher in another town (*Orgueil*, 89–91). By then, their relation has become as much intellectual as emotional, and the two women part with the certainty of being loyal and devoted to one another.

Marie and Mlle Esther's bond ticks all the boxes of a successful (and hierarchical) mentorship relation, enriched by an egalitarian form of friendship. In fact, the school represents for Marie a new shelter and within this context Mlle Esther soon becomes her role model and spiritual mother. Although refusing, in line with her principles, to be overly caring or physically affectionate toward her *protégée*, Mlle Esther nonetheless offers her emotional and moral support, easing her solitude and teaching her to become strong and resilient. She gives her a solid intellectual education not only in her official role as a teacher, but also by sharing with her her passion for literature (*Orgueil*, 81–82). Moreover, she provides her with a professional training and helps her to find her first job, giving her the means to become economically independent and to put her gift for music to good use. Marie is generally considered as Mlle Esther's 'fille adoptive' and Mlle Esther herself calls her 'ma chère enfant', thus suggesting that she sees in her a kind of surrogate daughter (*Orgueil*, 111, 303). In addition to this, Marie becomes Mlle Esther's confidante, the only person in the world whom she could trust with the secret of her illegitimate motherhood (*Orgueil*, 300). While Marie certainly thinks of Mlle Esther as a mother/mentor ('je dois à Mlle Esther le peu que je sais et le peu que je suis') she also refers to her as '[sa] meilleure amie' (*Orgueil*, 111, 304).

After Marie's departure from the *lycée*, however, the relationship between the two women starts to cool off, until Mlle Esther reappears in the story in the unexpected role of Marie's sexual rival. At first, when Marie finds out that in the past Mlle Esther spent some time in the same town where she now lives and was on familiar terms with the Elder family, she cannot understand why her friend never mentioned it or why she appears extremely reticent about visiting or even discussing the matter. Several times she wonders what happened during her friend's time in the town, and Mlle Esther's insistent recommendation to be cautious and to protect her heart puzzles her (*Orgueil*, 106, 119). Only once does she come close to the truth, contemplating the possibility of a past liaison between Mlle Esther and Luc, but she soon dismisses that idea as absurd (*Orgueil*, 195–96). A couple of years after their separation, Marie complains about her solitude and comments on the fact that now Mlle Esther hardly ever writes to her (*Orgueil*, 267). Immediately after Marie and Luc's engagement, however, Mlle Esther gets in touch again, this time to inform Marie that she has contracted typhoid fever and to reveal the secret of her maternity. Her last wish is for Marie to find Luc Elder and to let him know that he has a teenage daughter to take care of (*Orgueil*, 300–303).

Marie's first reaction is one of pure coolness and self-control. After reading the letter, she applies straight away the principles of self-mastery and composure once learnt from Mlle Esther herself, demonstrating the strength of her willpower over her emotions. In the space of a few sentences, Marie, who is considered by Mlle Esther as 'la seule personne au monde qui [ait] pour [elle] une affection réelle', refers to her supposedly sexual rival twice by the word 'amie' ('ma pauvre amie' and 'ma meilleure amie', *Orgueil*, 300, 301, 302). With a clear head, she packs her belongings and takes the first train to visit her. The next few days pass in a sort of painful and confusing blur, but at a certain point Marie strengthens her resolve and, determined to prove her 'grandeur morale', she suppresses her 'amour étroit, égoïste, et lâche' for Luc, and decides to start a new life far away, where she can altruistically put all her energies and love at the service of others. But first, in order for things to happen 'selon la logique et selon la justice', Mlle Esther must survive and be reunited with Luc (*Orgueil,* 309–10). Therefore, Marie risks her own life to nurse Mlle Esther through her illness, and when her friend is finally out of danger, she kisses her forehead, bids a silent farewell, and, still concerned for Mlle Esther's well-being, gets ready to embark for Canada, where she hopes to find 'le grand calmant qui endort les plus cuisantes peines: [...] le travail' (*Orgueil,* 317). Persuaded that her love for Luc would be 'une lâcheté et une cruauté', she assures a now outraged and uncomprehending Mme Elder that her son will soon find 'des tendresses qui vaudront la [sienne]', and leaves with the knowledge that Mme Elder ultimately understands and approves of her decision (*Orgueil,* 320).

The novel ends with Marie's letter to Luc, which he only receives after her departure, in which she begs him to give Mlle Esther the happiness she deserves (*Orgueil,* 323–25). Despite the pain caused by this sacrifice, Marie rejoices in the prospect of cherishing the memory of their love and, most of all, in the fact that her *Bildung* is now complete. Cured from this love and from the temptation to become a wife and a mother, the heroine has fully developed into 'la femme de demain' who is, above all, an independent human being who can support herself financially and psychologically. The degree of agency and independence achieved by the heroine, however, does not pose a threat to society and, on the contrary, is presented as a means to oppose decadence and reinforce the Third Republic's self-fashioned image of a highly moral state. Through her choice of female friendship over romantic union, Marie, a product of secular, state education and the embodiment of *morale laïque*, sets a pattern of modern, non-religious holiness compatible with republican values and profitable to the democratic system. By relinquishing her claim to love to permit the reconstitution of the patriarchal family unit and by putting her talents at the service of others, Marie becomes admirable and provides the reader with a new model of femininity to emulate.

The love triangle involving Marie, Luc, and Mlle Esther is a good example of a Belle Epoque female author's original treatment of the topic of female sexual rivalry. In this case, the triangular structure effectively allows a defusing and reabsorbing of female jealousy and sexual competitiveness, and the female homosocial bond is privileged over the heterosexual one in a way that contradicts the all too common belief, expressed in conduct manuals and essays, that the integrity of women's relationships is usually jeopardized by the primacy of love over friendship in women's lives. While in the first triangle the hero holds decisional power over the two female rivals and the breaking up of the triangle solely depends upon his choice, which enshrines the triumph of traditional femininity, in the second case it is Marie who dismantles the triangular relation by putting her friend's happiness over her own, and the idea of justice over her own feelings and personal interests. While seemingly reinforcing the status quo, this form of female agency is also directed toward the realization of a feminine economy based on generosity. According to Hélène Cixous, the masculine economy, which she calls 'l'Empire du Propre', is characterized by men's fear of loss and separation, and by a desire for appropriation, the act of giving always subordinated to the logic of profit and return.[36] In this masculine order, women are led to turn against each

[36]Cixous, 'Sorties', in *La Jeune Née*, pp. 144–47.

other.[37] On the contrary, Cixous explains, '[s]'il y a un « propre » de la femme, c'est paradoxalement, sa capacité à se dé-proprier sans calcul', which depends on her openness and permeability, and on her ability to include the Other. While Cixous concedes that a gift is never free, the return implied by women's gift is the establishment of relations rather than the securing of profit.[38] In this sense, the novel plays on a tension between traditional (and passive) sacrificial femininity and a form of female empowerment achieved through the act of giving.

In *Salutaire orgueil* Marie's gift certainly reinforces her bond with Mlle Esther and puts female homosociality in a privileged position, thus resolving the tension between female friendship and heterosexual love in favour of the former, but the ending of triangulation also holds additional meanings. In particular, Marie's sacrifice is meant to address and correct what she names 'une faute de jeunesse' (i.e. Luc's pursuing a sexual liaison with Mlle Esther and leaving her alone to face the consequences, *Orgueil*, 324). The decision to give Luc up to Mlle Esther is dictated by a sense of logic — a faculty typically denied to women in that time — justice, and compassion and Marie's action has a feminist resonance. The unfairness of the double standard of sexual morality, the difficult condition of the unmarried mother, and the question of illegitimate paternity were among the main concerns of Belle Epoque feminism. It is only in 1912 that women acquired the right to file paternity suits against the men who seduced and abandoned them.[39] In this case, Luc is compelled to acknowledge his mistakes, to take responsibility for his past behaviour, and to make amends. Marie's 'orgueil' becomes 'salutaire' to him against his own will. Indeed, it is impossible for the hero to resolve the triangulation according to his own desires (i.e. by marrying the woman he truly loves) because Marie and Mlle Esther refuse to be rivals, and also because they resist his attempts at polarizing them. From the hero's perspective, Mlle Esther represents one of those regrettable 'caprices d'une heure' that he once mistook for eternal love (*Orgueil*, 284).[40] Marie, on the other hand, is the woman he truly falls in love with, the one who turns him into a better man and gives a new meaning to his life. However, Mlle Esther is no *femme fatale* and she is a far cry from Mme Ladowska. She is virtuous and loyal, she loves Luc dearly and deserves to be loved in return. Marie herself points this out when she tells Mme

---

[37] 'Contre les femmes ils [les hommes] ont commis le plus grand des crimes: ils les ont amenées, insidieusement, violemment, à haïr les femmes, à être leurs propres ennemies, à mobiliser leur immense puissance contre elles-mêmes, à être les exécutantes de leur virile besogne'. See Cixous, 'Sorties', in *La Jeune Née*, p. 125.

[38] Cixous, 'Sorties', in *La Jeune Née*, pp. 161–62.

[39] Before then, the Article 340 of the Civil Code prohibited paternity suits. See Offen, *Debating the Woman Question*, p. 36.

[40] Mlle Esther employs the same words to describe her liaison with Luc, when explaining what she represented for him: 'j'avais été pour lui un caprice d'une heure.' See *Orgueil*, p. 301.

Elder that Mlle Esther's tenderness will equal her own and that another woman will make her son happy (*Orgueil*, 320). She repeats as much to Luc in her final letter, in which she also exhorts him '[à donner] à cette femme exquise tout le bonheur auquel elle a droit' (*Orgueil*, 324). Marie's generous act is meant to allow Mlle Esther and Luc to reunite and found a (traditional) family for the sake of their child. However, it is important to note that while Marie is denied a romantic happy ending, as a single woman, she is neither ridiculed nor condemned to utter misery. Instead, she claims her rightful place in the world and in the public sphere, determined to live life to its fullest and to realize her potential outside traditional schemas, but in a way that is still reconciliable with the values and expectations of Belle Epoque society. When Marie expresses her resolutions for the future, she vows: 'je penserai, je travaillerai, je me pencherai sur toutes les souffrances, je tendrai la main à ceux qui faiblissent et tombent' (*Orgueil*, 310). Her declaration features an interesting mix of traditionally masculine and feminine prerogatives, associating the masculine sphere of work and thought with the feminine sphere of nurturance and empathy. In breaking the love triangle, Marie thus takes a decisive step toward becoming a *femme moderne*.

Before turning my attention to the other novels, I would like to highlight an interesting parallel between *Salutaire orgueil* and a nineteenth-century British novel which is regarded as one of the major examples of the European (female) *Bildungsroman*: Charlotte Brontë's *Jane Eyre* (1847).[41] The writer and literary critic Henriette Charasson first connected Prost to Brontë in an article from the 1920s in which she noted an affinity between the two novelists in terms of style:

> Yvette Prost est un des rares écrivains de chez nous qui fassent penser aux romanciers anglais, elle a cet humour intime et discret, cette observation profonde attachée aux petites choses, ce don de vie intérieure qui les caractérisent. [...] Et quel sens de la nature, quel respect de l'âme humaine, quelle fierté vivifiante — à défaut de cette foi où l'on voudrait la voir s'épanouir — quelle vivacité de caractère, quelle indépendance et quelle prestesse de répartie aussi, qui font songer parfois à Charlotte Brönte.[42]

Prost's affiliation to Brontë appears even stronger than Charasson's words would suggest, if we take into account the intertextual relation between *Jane Eyre* and *Salutaire orgueil*. In *Salutaire orgueil*, I would argue, Prost revisits Brontë's text and rewrites the love triangle

---

[41]Charlotte Brontë, *Jane Eyre* (London: Penguin, 1994 [1847]). Further references to this novel will be given using the short form *JE* and the page numbers.
[42]Henriette Charasson, 'Des femmes honnêtes vues par des femmes', *Les Modes de la femme de France*, 6 May 1923, p. 24.

between Jane, Rochester, and Bertha Mason in a more feminist direction, by offering a different portrayal of the rejected first wife/mother (Bertha/Mlle Esther). Similarities in plot structure and character types and a series of thematic and verbal echoes provide evidence of the lineage between these two works of fiction.

Both novels are coming-of-age stories presented from the heroine's perspective, the first-person narrative inviting the reader's identification with a strong female protagonist. Jane's description as 'poor, obscure, plain, and little' (*JE*, 251) perfectly fits Marie, and both heroines are represented as proud, solitary, quiet, and stubborn. As children, they show a feisty, rebellious disposition, and once they become adults, they question women's traditional roles in society, denouncing female confinement to the private sphere.[43] Two orphaned girls without wealth, beauty, or connections, they both spend most of their lives at a boarding school until they move to another town where they take up a position as teachers. Their lives then intermingle with those of the inhabitants of a rich and prestigious house (Thornfield/Villa Blanche). These inhabitants are an elderly, somewhat maternal woman (Mrs Fairfax/Mme Elder), a young child who becomes the protagonist's pupil (Adèle/Yvonne), and a dark, mysterious hero, several years her senior, who is frequently absent from home and who publicly pursues a vain and cold-hearted society beauty (Blanche Ingram/Mme Ladowska). Like Rochester, Luc, a worldly and restless man, is disenchanted, moody, and emotionally tormented, although usually appearing charming and lively in society. Each hero is struck by the heroine's talent (for music in Marie's instance and for drawing in Jane's). He admires her frankness, kindness, and wittiness as well as her calm and dignified demeanour. However, being generally disillusioned with women, he initially doubts his own feelings and motives ('j'ai eu peur de me tromper [...] Je ne savais pas à quelle profondeur j'étais pénétré de vous; je m'en voulais de ce que j'appelais un nouveau caprice', *Orgueil*, 288; and 'I was for a while troubled with a haunting fear that if I handled the flower freely its bloom would fade [...] I did not then know that it was no transitory blossom', *JE*, 311). Indeed, for some time the hero of each novel treats the young heroine with overt coldness and indifference, adopting a contradictory attitude that confounds her while generating romantic tension. Eventually, the hero falls deeply in love with the sensitive and innocent girl that he comes to perceive as his means of salvation ('Cet amour, si nouveau et si pur, survenu un peu tard

[43]As a child, Jane tells her friend Helen Burns: 'When we are struck at without reason, we should strike back again very hard.' See *JE*, p. 60. As discussed in a previous chapter, Marie reacts fiercely any time she suffers an abuse from her schoolmates. See pp. 156–57 and 164 in this thesis. Marie's aforementioned passionate speech about 'la femme de demain' echoes Jane's belief that: 'It is thoughtless to condemn them [women], or laugh at them, if they seek to do more or learn more than custom has pronounced necessary for their sex', even though Marie's condemnation is more specifically directed toward the institution of marriage and toward love as the unique outlet for female energy. See *JE*, p. 111, and *Orgueil*, pp. 181–84.

dans ma vie, m'a refait un cœur neuf', *Orgueil*, 291; and 'I believe I have found the instrument for my cure', *JE*, 218).[44] When confronted with the possibility of a marriage that would defy social conventions or her own sense of justice (Rochester is still legally married to his first wife, Bertha, while Luc has a duty toward Mlle Esther, the mother of his child) the heroine holds to her principles and renounces love. In fact, Charasson's remark about Prost's unmarried heroines applies to both Marie and Jane: 'elles aimeraient à aimer mais elles ne jugent pas que l'amour vaille de descendre au-dessous de soi-même, et, quand il le faut, elles n'hésitent pas à mutiler leur cœur.'[45]

However, the two texts also differ in significant ways. As discussed above, Prost's novel ends with the heroine's attempt to rectify the past by giving up the man she loves for the sake of Mlle Esther. In her final letter to Luc, Marie writes:

> le sacrifice est déchirant; m'arracher de vous, mon ami, c'est tuer en moi pour jamais toute joie et toute espérance; c'est m'enfoncer de nouveau dans la nuit morne et dans le froid d'où votre amour m'avait tirée... (*Orgueil*, 324–25)

Marie's choice is utterly painful, but her sacrifice is unconditional; in spite of her sorrow, this heroine has no regrets or hesitation and looks forward to setting herself on a new path. Her rejection of a form of love that she considers too narrow and egoistical, is paralleled by an intention to dedicate her life to others, as well as to labour, by embracing a life that could be compared to that of a missionary (*Orgueil*, 309–10). This is not the case for Jane, who can never resign herself to a life devoid of love. Indeed, when asked by St John Rivers to go to India with him as his wife, Jane, although willing to become a missionary, cannot abide by his idea that she is 'formed for labour, not for love' and cannot consent to a loveless union (*JE*, 398). She insists on accompanying him as his sister instead, but St John objects: 'Do you think God will be satisfied with half an oblation? Will He accept a mutilated sacrifice?' (*JE*, 401). Unlike Marie, then, Jane cannot sacrifice love altogether and refuses to see work (or the prospect of an intellectual relationship with St John) as a viable or sufficient means to self-actualization. In this case, the heroine's journey toward maturity ends with marriage.[46]

---

[44]Marie also expresses the wish to save Luc's soul: 'Je me sentirais animée d'un zèle édifiant pour sauver l'âme de M. Elder.' See *Orgueil*, p. 212.

[45]Charasson, 'Des femmes honnêtes', p. 24. With regard to Jane Eyre, Maria Lamonaca talks of an 'emotional self-mutilation [that] is infinitely preferable to spiritual ruin'. See Maria Lamonaca, 'Jane's Crown of Thorns: Feminism and Christianity in "Jane Eyre"', in *Studies in the Novel*, 34 (2002), 245–263 (p. 255).

[46]Although marriage is the traditional outcome of the (female) *Bildungsroman* set in patriarchal societies, in this case critics have observed: 'While the reader may question whether Brontë's Jane has achieved fully realised independence, her marriage to Rochester does place her in an increased position of power; she can return to him because, finally, she controls her own decision. Her return is no longer mandated by money,

Turning now our attention to the third element of the love triangle, i.e. the heroine's sexual rival, it should be noted that Bertha Mason, at the plot level the principal moral/legal impediment to Jane and Rochester's union, conveniently commits suicide during the fire that destroys Thornfield after Jane's departure. In other words, the fulfilment of Jane's romantic aspirations comes at the expense of the emotionally abandoned first wife, whose erasure from the text is necessary to the heroine's happiness. This plot element, along with Brontë's unsympathetic and dehumanizing portrayal of Bertha Mason, cast a shadow over the novel's feminism. For example, Cora Kaplan observes that 'Bertha must be killed off [...] so that a moral, Protestant femininity, licensed sexuality, and a qualified, socialized feminism may survive. Yet the text cannot close off or recuperate that moment of radical association between political rebellion and gender rebellion'.[47] According to Elaine Showalter, 'Jane, unlike the contemporary feminist critics who have interpreted the novel, never sees her kinship with the confined and monstrous double, and [...] Brontë has no sympathy for her mad creature. Before Jane Eyre can reach her happy ending, the madwoman must be purged from the plot.'[48] In particular, Brontë associates Bertha Mason with foreignness, madness, and animality. For instance, in the space of the same page, this character is referred to by Jane herself as a 'beast', a 'strange wild animal', a 'clothed hyena', a 'maniac', and a 'lunatic' (*JE*, 291). In Rochester's eyes, Bertha is a 'monster' and her very company is 'degrading' (*JE*, 304, 306). The unhappy marriage into which he, as an inexperienced young man, has been deceived by his family for reasons of money and prestige, is all in all too great a punishment for the 'blindness of youth' and positions him, at least to some extent, as a victim (*JE*, 303). Prost, on the other hand, creates a love triangle in which not only the rejected female figure, Mlle Esther, is represented as fully human and worthy of love and respect, but Luc is unequivocally accountable for his 'faute de jeunesse' (i.e. the deception of Mlle Esther). His ignorance of the consequences (i.e. the birth of a daughter) represents his only extenuating circumstance (*Orgueil*, 324).

Prost, I would argue, rewrites the outcast woman, Mlle Esther, in an original way by lending her the features of both Bertha Mason and Ms Temple (i.e. Jane's teacher at Lowood

---

status or Rochester, but by her own desire and from her own choice.' See Sarah E. Maier, 'Portraits of the Girl-Child: Female Bildungsroman in Victorian Fiction', *Literature Compass*, 4.1 (2007), 317–35 (p. 332).

[47]Cora Kaplan, 'Pandora's Box: Subjectivity, Class and Sexuality in Socialist Feminism', in *Making a Difference: Feminist Literary Criticism*, ed. Gayle Greene and Coppélia Kahn (London: Methuen, 1985), pp. 169–75 (pp. 172–73).

[48]Elaine Showalter, *The Female Malady: Women, Madness and English Culture, 1830*–1980 (London: Virago, 1987), pp. 68–69. As usefully summarized by Laurence Lerner in a now outdated but still relevant article, (feminist) criticism about Bertha Mason interprets this character as a representation of Jane's repressed sexual desire, of her anger at patriarchy, or as the colonial 'Other'. See Laurence Lerner, 'Bertha and the Critics', *Nineteenth-Century Literature*, 44, (1989), 273–300.

and, according to one critic, 'the ideal of female independence compatible with eventual marriage'), thus creating greater ambiguity around the identities of her female characters instead of polarizing them.[49] Mlle Esther can be compared to Ms Temple insofar as Jane, like Marie, considers her teacher as a 'mother, governess, and, latterly, companion' (*JE*, 86). Moreover, Jane declares:

> I had imbibed from her [Ms Temple] something of her nature and much of her habits: more harmonious thoughts; what seemed better regulated feelings had become the inmates of my mind. I had given in allegiance to duty and order; I was quiet; I believed I was content; to the eyes of others, usually even to my own, I appeared a disciplined and subdued character. (*JE*, 86)

Even though Mlle Esther and Ms Temple act in distinctive ways (e.g. unlike Ms Temple, Mlle Esther never adopts a warm or tender demeanour to interact with her pupils) the effect of their influence on the heroine's development is similar, in that they teach her to become more stoic, controlled, and self-reliant. In addition to this, both Ms Temple and Mlle Esther generously put their lives at risk to nurse their students during a typhoid epidemic (*JE*, 78; *Orgueil*, 300). As for Bertha Mason, her association with Mlle Esther might look less obvious. However, Bertha and Mlle Esther, both dark-haired and sexually attractive (at first glance, Bertha looked 'tall, dark, majestic', *JE*, 302; Mlle Esther is described as being 'belle, comme les statues de marbre', *Orgueil*, 48), for some time excite the hero's passion (Rochester declares: 'I was dazzled, stimulated; my senses were excited; and being ignorant, raw, and inexperienced, I thought I loved her', *JE*, 302; Luc, referring to his past mistresses, among whom figures Mlle Esther, asserts: 'Tant de fois déjà j'avais pris mes caprices d'une heure pour un amour éternel!', *Orgueil*, 284). Even more importantly, toward the end of the novel Mlle Esther shows the signs of madness. In her delirium, she incessantly calls for her daughter, she mistakes Marie for Luc, and looks utterly hysterical (*Orgueil*, 311–14). For example, Marie notices 'ses yeux révulsés dans un visage méconnaissable' (*Orgueil*, 313). However, Mlle Esther is not demonized by the narrator or the other characters, and the causes of her troubled state are to be found in a medical condition (i.e. typhoid), not in her origins or in her supposedly vicious nature.

Unlike Bertha Mason, Mlle Esther is given a voice and a subjectivity. Only for the briefest moment does Marie contemplate the possibility of her friend's death being the key to the fulfilment of her own romantic dreams, and she rejects this thought abruptly, without

---

[49]Lerner offers this definition of Ms Temple in 'Bertha and the Critics', p. 295.

even fully formulating it (*Orgueil*, 310). As Marie puts it to Mme Elder: 'votre fils et moi pourrions être heureux d'un amour qui serait, à la fois, une lâcheté et une cruauté?' (*Orgueil*, 319–20). Marie assists Mlle Esther through her illness, saving her life at her own risk. Moreover, she actively puts an end to her friend's moral and emotional 'martyre' by reuniting her with Luc (*Orgueil*, 324). Luc, like Rochester, was not mistaken in believing that the heroine would save his soul. However, Marie does so by renouncing him and not by claiming him for herself or by becoming his wife. The hero's atonement requires in fact the sacrifice of true love and a complete allegiance to the good woman whose trust he once betrayed as well as to their child.

Certain contemporary critics judged *Salutaire orgueil* unfavourably and expressed a negative view of the novel's ending. In particular, in a 1907 review appearing in the *Mercure de France*, Rachilde observes:

> Il faut se méfier des femmes trop parfaites. Cette fille rancie dans l'étude, dont la joie suprême était d'apprendre et de comprendre, demeure pourtant une sotte. Elle n'a pas compris que le suprême orgueil est de savoir prendre. Refuser ce que le pacte de la vie vous concède est avouer ne point s'en trouver digne. Si ma meilleure amie a un enfant clandestin de l'homme que j'aime et qui m'épouse, elle ne saurait m'en vouloir d'adopter son enfant à sa place. Quand il n'y a que le nom de la mère qui change, de quoi se plaindrait le père, mon Dieu? Maintenant le salutaire orgueil fera quatre malheureux au lieu d'un et, dans un roman, plus on est malheureux, plus c'est beau.[50]

Rachilde's ironic rejection of the sacrificial paradigm ('dans un roman, plus on est malheureux, plus c'est beau') and her criticism of the novel probably have more to do with art than morals, considering that in her own fictional works this author aims at producing aesthetic emotions by breaking moral rules. A novel like this one, written from an edifying perspective, could only be received with sarcasm and contempt by someone like Rachilde. What interests us here is that she considers Marie's gesture as self-denying, to say the least, and that she adopts a rather phallocentric take on the subject, as she remonstrates that a man would have nothing to complain about if another woman was to take care of his child. As for the fact that, were she a true friend, Mlle Esther should be happy for Marie to adopt her daughter, this character is never confronted with such a possibility, given that she is unaware of Marie's engagement to Luc. Therefore, what Rachilde fails to see is that in

[50]Rachilde, '*Salutaire orgueil*, par Yvette Prost', *Mercure de France*, 1 September 1907, p. 12. A few years later, referring to *Salutaire orgueil*, Jane Misme denounces Prost's portrayal of the conflict between heart and brain as 'anti-feminist'. See Jane Misme, 'Cœur ou Cerveau'.

offering a more complex and sympathetic representation of the physically confined (Mlle Esther is in fact confined to the walls of the *lycée*, if not to an attic) and emotionally rejected woman, and in making the heroine acknowledge and respect her friend's claims to love and happiness, Prost recalibrates the love triangle in a way that allows the establishment of a feminine economy of generosity which upsets the patriarchal order, even while protecting some of its core values (i.e. the centrality of the family). Many parallels suggest that *Jane Eyre* is a source for *Salutaire orgueil*, but, from a feminist standpoint, Prost's rewriting of the main love triangle situates her text on more progressive grounds, at least in its portrayal of female homosociality.

The next section will examine a female-based love triangle which defuses female sexual rivalry not as much by privileging the homosocial bond between rivals, as by stressing the indispensability of sacrifice for the preservation and betterment of society.

Nietzschéenne and Sacrifice as the Foundation of Society

First published in 1907 as a *feuilleton* in *L'Illustration*, *Nietzschéenne* is one of Daniel Lesueur's most socially engaged and intellectual works.[51] In the preface to its 1919 edition, the author, who claims to have read all of Nietzsche's works, expresses her satisfaction at realizing that some readers have found in it a source of comfort, the book's purpose being to familiarize the French readership with Nietzsche's doctrine of energy and self-mastery, and to strengthen women's courage, willpower, and spirit of sacrifice (*Nietzschéenne*, 7–10).[52] The novel recounts the encounter between Robert Clérieux, a businessman in the French car industry, and Jocelyne Monestier, an unmarried heiress in her late twenties and the founder of a philanthropic society, *La Cité Fraternelle*, which provides accommodation for working-class families. Robert is immediately intrigued by Jocelyne, even though he is already happily married to the irreproachable but weak-minded Lucienne. Soon enough, the mysterious and reserved Jocelyne, who wishes to secure Robert's trust, shares with him the truth about her past. When she was still a careless and romantic young girl, Jocelyne entertained a compromising correspondence with her father's protégé, the ruthless and

[51] Holmes defines this novel as a 'roman à idées'. See Holmes, 'Novels of Adultery', in *Currencies*, ed. by Capitanio et al., p. 18.

[52] This claim can fruitfully be read alongside Marie's words in *Salutaire orgueil*: 'Je voudrais [...] que ma pensée fût capable d'affermir une volonté chancelante, de consoler un cœur découragé, de lui rendre l'âpre goût de la lutte et de la vie. Je voudrais que ma pensée, fût un cordial bienfaisant, non un dissolvant des énergies déjà défaillantes.' See *Orgueil*, pp. 175–76.

ambitious Eugène Sorbelin. Some years later, Sorbelin used those letters to blackmail her and to break off her engagement with the man to whom she impetuously offered her virginity. This event destroyed her family and her reputation, but Jocelyne found in herself the resources to face the situation. She became an enthusiast of Nietzschean philosophy and started to lead a simple life, apart from high society and dedicated to the welfare of those in need. Jocelyne's aim in opening up to Robert is to warn him against Sorbelin, who has now become Robert's right-hand man at the factory. Robert consequently confronts Sorbelin, finds out about his schemes to take over his business, and promptly fires him. From that moment on, with Jocelyne's guidance, this young entrepreneur, until then a somewhat ineffectual and insecure boss, turns into a more capable and self-assured man. The two quickly fall in love but their relationship, although platonic and primarily based on mutual respect and esteem, is broken off by the jealous Lucienne, who is unaware of Jocelyne's efforts to resist Robert's advances and to suppress her growing feelings for him. During a strike promoted by the resentful Sorbelin, Robert's safety is seriously threatened. At that point, Lucienne unexpectedly turns to her rival, asking for her help. At the end of the novel, in the midst of the chaos generated by the strike, Jocelyne sacrifices her life by taking a bullet that was meant for Robert.

Unlike *Salutaire orgueil*, a novel of courtship in which the main love triangle is composed by two 'women on the market' (i.e. Marie and Mlle Esther) who both need to secure a husband, *Nietzschéenne* is a novel of adultery focusing on the rivalry between wife and mistress. More precisely, this novel provides an example of what White calls the 'plot of subtraction' or 'adultery *manqué*', a tale in which adultery is not consummated and whose nineteenth-century model is Flaubert's *L'Éducation sentimentale* (1869).[53] However, while, as noted by White, in nineteenth-century bourgeois cynical plots of subtraction, 'restraint looks like a mixture of boredom and indecisiveness', *Nietzschéenne*, I would argue, maintains the idealism of a previous model identified by White: Madame de La Fayette's *La Princesse de Clèves* (1678).[54] In fact, as in the case of Mme de Clèves, Jocelyne's self-restraint is primarily the result of a noble moral choice, and the heroine's conduct is intended to be worthy of admiration and emulation on the part of readers. The representation of Jocelyne as a positive model of femininity needs to be understood in relation with the anxieties about degeneration and the fears regarding women's changing roles in society which characterize the context of *fin-de-siècle* France. As highlighted by Venita Datta, women authors' creation of female role models like Jocelyne reflects a Belle Epoque

[53]White, *The Family in Crisis*, pp. 12–13.
[54]White, *The Family in Crisis*, p. 13.

obsession with the redefinition of the hero and a widespread interest in Nietzsche's thought, which in certain cases provided the means to reshape ideal womanhood and to promote female heroism.[55] According to Datta, at the time of the novel's publication Jocelyne's chastity and her feminine attributes (e.g. gentleness and charm) rendered her an acceptable or even commendable model for French women, whereas her most subversive traits, for example the fact that she is Robert's moral and intellectual superior, passed unnoticed. Indeed, Datta's analysis of Belle Epoque reviews of the novel shows that this heroine was largely perceived by critics as the ideal French woman. Strong and energetic, yet feminine; intellectual and self-possessed, yet loving and self-sacrificing, Jocelyne embodied the vision of woman as a 'civilizing agent', unthreatening to men and able to support the moral regeneration of the nation.[56]

Jocelyne's worth is put on display within the dynamics of the love triangle, through a comparison with her foil, Lucienne. The difference between these two female figures is primarily defined through the description of the relationship they each entertain with the male hero and, most of all, through his gaze. At the beginning of the novel, Robert is perfectly content with his marriage and even worries about the possibility of unnecessarily provoking his wife's jealousy by visiting Jocelyne (*Nietzschéenne*, 49, 85). However, the more he gets to know Jocelyne, the more he realizes that Lucienne is not his equal and tires of her. Although possessing all the characteristics traditionally deemed desirable in a wife (e.g. loyalty, faithfulness, submissiveness), Lucienne, a woman 'sans épreuves ni expériences, une cervelle d'oiseau, un corps de poupée frêle', cannot provide the support Robert requires in his role of entrepreneur (*Nietzschéenne*, 164). In fact, having recently inherited his father's factory, Robert has to face unforeseen problems and responsibilities, and in this new situation he finds himself unable to rely on his 'femme-enfant', later coming to the conclusion that what he feels for Lucienne is tenderness, not love (*Nietzschéenne*, 125, 149). Surprisingly enough, while Robert is still physically and sexually attracted to his wife — his passion for her governs his reason and awakens his instinct (*Nietzschéenne*, 167) — the relationship he fosters with the Other Woman is mainly intellectual and leads him to privilege the mind over the senses. This is clearly indicated at their first encounter, when the narrator

---

55Venita Datta, 'Superwomen or Slaves? Women Writers, Male Critics, and the Reception of Nietzsche in Belle-Epoque France', *Historical Reflections/Réflexions Historiques*, 33.3 (2017), 421–47.

56Datta, 'Superwomen or Slaves?', pp. 438–40, 446. Recently, Laurent Robert has commented on the figure of Jocelyne and on the novel's outcome. His argument, by contrast with Datta's, implies that Jocelyne is a failed model, insofar as she is unable to live up to her moral standards and cannot be either a free woman or an effective promoter of collective welfare. My own reading of *Nietzschéenne* is more in line with Datta's. See Laurent Robert, 'La Tentation du roman à thèse chez Daniel Lesueur', in *La Littérature en Bas-Bleus III : Romanci□ □ en France de 1870 à 1914*, ed. by Andrea Del Lungo and Brigitte Louichon (Paris: Garnier, 2017), pp. 145–55 (p. 154).

observes that, looking at each other, '[Robert et Jocelyne] sentirent un lien, un secret. Rien de sensuel. Ils oubliaient, par miracle, ce qui veille toujours entre un homme et une femme: l'amour'; the expression 'par miracle' underlines the exceptionality of the situation (*Nietzschéenne*, 37). In defining Jocelyne's appeal, Robert talks of '[u]ne sorte de soif psychique' and even declares: 'Jocelyne, ce que vous m'inspirez est tellement supérieur au désir! C'est une soif de votre présence, de votre pensée, de votre âme' (*Nietzschéenne*, 125, 154). The words 'pensée' and 'âme' firmly situate their relationship in a platonic, mental sphere. Unlike Lucienne, who has never set foot in the factory, Jocelyne actively helps Robert in the management of his business. Her essential contribution is readily acknowledged by Robert himself, who asserts: 'Vous avez donné une âme à mon usine' (*Nietzschéenne*, 194). Although Jocelyne is considered competent and skilled in a way deemed unusual for women — Robert initially marvels at the fact that 'un cerveau de femme' is behind the organization of her charity (*Nietzschéenne*, 28) — her role in supporting Robert's activity is purely feminine, insofar as she gives 'a soul' to the factory. Indeed, Jocelyne's influence exerts a humanizing effect upon this mechanical, masculine world, in a way that reminds us of Denise's nurturing, maternal power in Zola's *Au bonheur des dames* (1883).[57] This mix of traditional and less conventional feminine values allows Lesueur to create a *femme moderne* who oversteps certain boundaries while still embodying a perfectly acceptable model of femininity.[58]

Half way through the novel, Jocelyne already appears as a more suitable companion for Robert, who fantasizes about replacing Lucienne with her (*Nietzschéenne*, 126). Compared to marriage, the hero's involvement with the Other Woman constitutes here an updated, more progressive and fulfilling form of heterosexual relationship, one in which women are the equals (or even the superiors) of men, this equality being represented not only as unthreatening but as beneficial to men.[59] The positive effect exerted by Jocelyne's presence on Robert's life and on his very sense of self is aptly described through the use of free indirect speech:

[57]'Elle [Denise] se voyait arriver en jupe pauvre, effarée, perdue au milieu des engrenages de la terrible machine; longtemps, elle avait eu la sensation de n'être rien, à peine un grain de mil sous les meules qui broyaient un monde; et aujourd'hui, elle était l'âme même de ce monde, elle seule importait, elle pouvait d'un mot précipiter ou ralentir le colosse, abattu à ses petits pieds.' Émile Zola, *Au bonheur des dames* (Paris: Fasquelle, 1906 [1883]) p. 402. For more on this subject, see Hennessy, 'Maternité stérile'.
[58]As already noted by Datta, while Jocelyne displays strength and other unconventional qualities characteristic of the New Woman, her energy is directed toward the support of men, and for this reason Jocelyne was not considered threatening by the novel's contemporary critics. See Datta, 'Superwomen or Slaves?', p. 438.
[59]In referring to Lucienne as 'l'idéal féminin de l'époque dans toute sa passivité', Holmes observes that the novel shows the unsuitability of such an ideal for the achievement of a happy heterosexual relationship. See Holmes, 'Modernisme et genre', p. 56. For further discussion of Belle Epoque female authors' representation of heterosexual relationships, see *Ecrire les hommes,* ed. by Grenaudier-Klijn et al.

> Qu'était-il, voici quelques mois à peine, lorsqu'il l'avait rencontrée? Un enfant timide, tenu en lisières, trahi sans le savoir, prêt d'être réduit à néant. Et aujourd'hui?... Un homme. Un homme agissant par lui-même, dirigeant les autres. Un homme qui avait pris conscience de sa force, de son jugement, de sa clairvoyance. Un homme qui commandait, qui réussissait. Un maître. Un victorieux. (*Nietzschéenne*, 194)

Robert's transformation into the Nietzschean *Übermensch* is only made possible by the intervention of a Superwoman, in a way that illustrates the important role women can play in the renewal of French decadent society. Although the heroine may be seen simply as embodying the traditional (and passive) role of muse who inspires the male poet/hero to found a new order (in this case, a welfare-state factory), it is worth asking whether any irony is intended here, given Jocelyne's intellectual and moral superiority. What is certain is that some contemporary critics of the novel reacted strongly against Lesueur's not-so-veiled insistence on the male characters' passivity and ineptitude.[60]

The characterization of Jocelyne and Lucienne challenges the way in which wife and mistress are traditionally portrayed in triangular narratives of adultery. In particular, the maternal/sexual, virgin/whore dichotomy usually found in literature, for example in canonical texts such as *La Cousine Bette* where the difference between Adeline Hulot and Valérie Marneffe could not be more clear-cut, is blurred in this novel, insofar as Lucienne represents a combination of the maternal-sexual woman, whereas Jocelyne is mostly portrayed as a *femme moderne* and an intellectual being rather than as a *femme fatale*, although she first appears in the novel as an indecipherable Medusa (*Nietzschéenne*, 39). Lesueur's rewriting of the Other Woman is in line with the nuanced and complex representation of female characters that she also offers in other novels.[61] In *Nietzschéenne*, the subversion of rigid gender norms is matched by an awareness of the constructedness of women's traditional roles within the love triangle. The word 'rôle' is employed by Jocelyne herself when she refuses to become Robert's mistress: 'Je ne pourrais pas vous partager avec une autre. Je ne veux pas vous arracher à cette autre. Je ne veux pas d'un tel rôle' (*Nietzschéenne*, 200). Moreover, while throughout the novel the reader is invited to side with Jocelyne rather than with the weak, possessive, and childish Lucienne, at one point the omniscient narrator tones

---

[60] M. Cabs comments: 'Si Jocelyne existait en chair et en os, elle suffirait seule à justifier toutes les prétentions du féminisme le plus échevelé. L'homme n'aurait plus qu'à déposer son sceptre en ses mains pour lui servir d'esclave…'. The critic further adds that the novel gives 'une idée assez piètre des qualités du mâle, réduit au rôle d'enregistreur passif de la volonté supérieure de son héroïne'. See M. Cabs, 'Le Livre du jour: *Nietzschéenne*, par Daniel Lesueur', *Gil Blas*, 22 July 1908.

[61] See the discussion of *Justice de femme* and *L□ □res closes* in Chapter One. On this point, see also Holmes, 'Daniel Lesueur and the Feminist Romance', in A 'Belle Époque'?, ed. by Holmes and Tarr.

down this assessment. When Robert falls in love with another, arguably better woman, Lucienne, an exemplary wife by Belle Epoque standards, becomes helpless, embittered, and generally disagreeable, suddenly turning into 'CELLE A QUI L'AMOUR DONNAIT TORT' (*Nietzschéenne*, 212. Capital letters in the original). Having lost the position of beloved and respected wife, Lucienne finds herself unjustly trapped in a new role which does not suit her (i.e. that of the betrayed wife). The text underlines how all these different identities (e.g. mistress, beloved or betrayed wife) are imposed on women by men. 'Comment réussir dans un rôle [celui de bonne épouse] quand, aux yeux de l'unique spectateur [le mari], le rôle disparaît?', asks the narrator referring to a woman's crisis of identity following her husband's changing perception of and feelings for her (*Nietzschéenne*, 211). Not only does the narrator assert that Lucienne 'valait peut-être mieux que son sort' (*Nietzschéenne*, 211), but in the same passage the reader's sympathies are further aroused by the use of the form 'vous', which constitutes a direct appeal for him/her to join in the narrator's speculations and identify with this character.[62] The narrative voice thus treats Lucienne with indulgence despite her shortcomings, leading the reader to sympathize, at least to a certain extent, with the heroine's self-styled rival.

In terms of the relation between the two rivals, most of the time Lucienne's attitude toward Jocelyne follows a traditional pattern. A victim of circumstances, Lucienne acts as a scorned wife driven by jealousy and anger. She confirms the malicious rumours concerning Jocelyne and shows a profound contempt for her rival, calling her 'drôlesse' and 'fille misérable' (*Nietzschéenne*, 163). She also proves to be particularly vengeful and cynical when, following the financial ruin and consequent suicide of the investor Nauder, Jocelyne's legal tutor, she revels in the possibility of her rival having lost all her fortune (*Nietzschéenne*, 213). When Lucienne finally puts her pride aside, asking for Jocelyne's help to rescue Robert, her first words to her are: 'Nous nous haïssons… C'est entendu' (*Nietzschéenne*, 239). Unlike Marie and Mlle Esther, these characters are not bound by affection or mutual admiration. However, in turning to Jocelyne in a time of need, Lucienne recognizes her superiority and, even more importantly, she attests to women's ability to overcome their differences and act selflessly for the sake of men. As observed by the narrator, '[l]a première [Lucienne] eût juré la veille que rien au monde ne la conduirait vers la seconde [Jocelyne]', and yet there she is, sacrificing her *amour propre* for Robert. Ultimately, this self-denying act, as anticipated by the narrator ('[Lucienne était] capable (elle devait en fournir la preuve)

[62] 'C'est l'aventure de beaucoup de femmes négligées ou délaissées. […] Celui pour qui vous combinez tant d'effets subtils ne vous voit pas. Il ne vous voit plus, ni telle que vous êtes, ni telle que vous voulez paraître. Craignez que, d'autre part, il ne vous voie trop. Vous n'êtes plus pour lui une femme, vous n'êtes plus que *sa* femme. Vous êtes l'obstacle.' See *Nietzschéenne*, p. 211. Italics in the original.

d'un accidentel geste de beauté', *Nietzschéenne*, 211), redeems her character.[63] As for Jocelyne, her behaviour largely contradicts that of the cynical temptress who considers the wife as a rival to defeat. In fact, she actively resists both Robert's attempt to substitute one woman with another and his efforts at imposing fixed roles on them. From the outset, Jocelyne is determined not to cause Lucienne any pain and constantly reminds Robert of his duties as a husband and father. When Lucienne intercepts and misinterprets a note that Jocelyne sent to Robert, the heroine firmly tells him: 'je suis résolue à faire tout — vous m'entendez bien: tout — même des démarches humiliantes pour rendre à votre femme un peu de ce bonheur que j'ai brisé si involontairement', and subsequently advises him on how to fix things with his wife (*Nietzschéenne*, 152).[64] Jocelyne's refusal to become Robert's mistress is dictated by a sincere concern for Lucienne and a willingness to defend the sanctity of marriage, but also by a need to preserve her self-esteem and master her instincts.[65] Even though at one point her resolve falters and in a moment of weakness Jocelyne is suddenly ready to follow her heart against her better judgement (*Nietzschéenne*, 234–36), the final encounter with Lucienne sets things straight: 'Elle ne braverait pas cette femme. Elle respecterait le droit de l'épouse' (*Nietzschéenne*, 239–40). Jocelyne pushes this decision to the extreme, sacrificing her life along with her happiness. Her respect for Lucienne, and more generally for the institution of marriage, does not prevent her from falling in love with Robert or occasionally being jealous of his wife, but she stands by her principles nonetheless.

The love triangle portrayed in *Nietzschéenne* defuses female rivalry by depicting two women who, at the end of the novel, come together and unite their efforts for the benefit of a man. Even more interestingly, this device is used to reflect on the conflict between personal fulfilment and collective good, presenting women's sacrifice as the cornerstone of French society. This idea is consistent with Lesueur's other works, a similar message being conveyed, for example, in *Justice de femme*.[66] As noted by Margaret Cohen in her discussion of what she calls 'sentimental (social) novels' of the first half of the nineteenth century, adultery is one of the most common scenarios in which novels 'bring individual

---

[63]In his review of the novel, Jean Lionnet observes: 'On plaint Mme Clérieux, quoique sotte, et on l'admire presque lorsqu'elle va chercher Mlle Monestier pour sauver Robert.' See Jean Lionnet, 'Les Livres: *Nietzschéenne*, par Daniel Lesueur', *La Revue hebdomadaire*, 29 August 1908, pp. 673–77 (p. 673).
[64] Later on, Robert is indeed grateful to Jocelyne for preventing him from cheating on his wife. See *Nietzschéenne*, p. 164.
[65]As Jocelyne explains to Robert, after having struggled for years to gain a sense of self and rise above social prejudice, she cannot compromise her hard-won independence for a man, nor is she willing to experience the humiliation that an adulterous liaison would entail. See *Nietzschéenne*, p. 200.
[66]See Holmes, 'Novels of Adultery', in *Currencies*, ed. by Capitanio et al., p. 26. See also Holmes' discussion of the conflict between duty and desire in 'Daniel Lesueur and the Feminist Romance', in *A 'Belle Epoque'?*, ed. by Holmes and Tarr.

freedom into conflict with collective welfare'.[67] Belle époque female-authored novels such as *Nietzschéenne, Salutaire orgueil*, and even *Princesses de science* still explore adultery in the context of the theme of freedom and represent what Cohen names the conflict between the 'heart' and the 'code', but they do so through the depiction of female-based love triangles and through the adoption of a particular philosophical stance.[68] In this instance, the character who experiences a tension between the heart and the code is not the wife within a male-based love triangle, who is usually torn between two valid but mutually exclusive alternatives (sentimental novel) or oppressed by the code (sentimental social novel), but the Other Woman. Jocelyne, like Marie, breaks off the triangular structure and privileges the consolidation of the bourgeois family over her own aspiration to love, thus voluntarily putting the code above the heart. 'Voluntarily' represents here a key word. By contrast with the sentimental social novel, in which the code always reasserts itself against the heart and turns the heroine into a victim, in both *Nietzschéenne* and *Salutaire orgueil* the act of renunciation is primarily represented as an heroic, Nietzschean demonstration of power over the self, rather than a passive form of abidance by social rules explicitly meant to reinforce the status quo.[69] Unlike that of Marie in *Salutaire orgueil*, however, Jocelyne's sacrifice does not open up a different path for the single, independent woman, as the novel ends with her tragic death.

Some contemporary, conservative critics stressed this aspect of the novel and praised Lesueur's heroine for her ability to meet social expectations about women by sacrificing herself, a gesture interpreted as anti-Nietzschean.[70] More recently, Marie Kawthar Daouda has identified Jocelyne as one of the figures of the 'anti-Salomé', in her

[67]Cohen, *Sentimental Education*, p. 38.

[68]See Cohen, 'The Heart and the Code; George Sand and the Sentimental Social Novel', in *Sentimental Education*, pp. 119–62.

[69]Both novels show a preoccupation with acting in compliance with moral and philosophical principles rather than social conventions, even while the result of the heroines' actions is indeed the consolidation of the traditional family, whose solidity is a matter of national importance in Third Republican France. Marie, who has read Nietzsche as a student and who later in her life quotes him in a speech, follows the ideal of 'la Grandeur' over 'le Bonheur', and her sacrifice is dictated by the conviction that 'au dessus de l'amour le plus ardent et le plus pur, il y a la justice et il y a la pitié'. See *Orgueil,* pp. 79, 183, 207, 320.

[70]For example, see Gaston Deschamps' review of the novel 'La Vie Littéraire: *Nietzschéenne*, par Daniel Lesueur', *Le Temps*, 7 June 1908, in which Jocelyne's death is discussed in the following terms: 'Oubliant Nietzsche à ce moment suprême, la « nietzschéenne » fait simplement le geste instinctif que la vocation du génie féminin dicte à toutes les vraies amies de l'homme, même lorsqu'elles ne sont pas des amantes. Elle s'offre en sacrifice.' Moreover, Lionnet observes: 'Et la mort de Mlle Monestier? Ce sacrifice absurde (je parle en nietzschéen) à un être qui lui est inférieur, puisqu'elle le dirige, ce mouvement bête de femme amoureuse, comment l'aurait qualifié Nietzsche? Je lis dans la Volonté de puissance chère à Mlle Monestier: « On cède à un sentiment généreux, mettant sa vie en danger sous l'impulsion d'un moment; mais ceci est de peu de valeur et ne représente pas même un acte caractéristique... » Un Nietzsche découvrirait chez Mlle Monestier, malgré l'hyperesthésie de l'orgueil, assez de christianisme inconscient pour l'excommunier.' See Lionnet, '*Nietzschéenne*', p. 675.

definition 'celle qui se sacrifie pour faire advenir une ère nouvelle'.[71] In her study, Daouda points out the links between *Nietzschéenne* and the genre of the fairy tale, a genre which Lesueur appropriates to highlight women's role within 'la crise épique de la fin du XIXe siècle'.[72] An embodiment of the 'féminité féerique [...] vaincue et asservie à une grande œuvre fondatrice', according to Daouda Jocelyne undergoes a Christianized death in which the idea of self-sacrifice replaces Nietzschean hubris.[73] Nuancing Daouda's argument, and while recognizing the influence of the fairy tale and the *roman édifiant* on Lesueur's novel, I would like to call attention to the ways in which *Nietzschéenne* also breaks off from tradition and challenges conservative representations of women.

Both Nietzsche and the American philosopher Ralph Waldo Emerson are referred to in Lesueur's novel and constitute part of the background against which her representation of female identities and homosociality, but also her representation of suicide, should be interpreted. In an article published in *Le Matin*, Lesueur quotes the same excerpts from Nietzsche that Jocelyne reads out loud to Robert, and elaborates on the principles enacted by the heroine: 'obéir fièrement' and 'tenir bon'.[74] In discussing her novel, Lesueur carefully distances herself from radical feminism. Although writing 'le roman de l'énergie féminine', she insists that energy is not to be confused with 'révolte' or 'indiscipline', claiming that 'la femme est la créature qui a la meilleure grâce à manifester son énergie dans la soumission' and wishing 'que son énergie cesse de se disperser et se tende pour soutenir celle de l'homme'. According to Lesueur, a woman submits to 'la loi de son sexe' in that she needs to be graceful, good, and respectful of social conventions. However, this otherwise conservative discourse is nuanced by the following statement: 'Commencer par se soumettre à l'ordre établi est le meilleur argument qu'on puisse se donner pour en réclamer la réforme au nom de l'intérêt général.' Lesueur cautiously expresses a dissatisfaction with the status quo, which needs reforming.[75] However, in her view changes are to be promoted from within the system itself rather than by fighting it from the outside. This idea is reflected in Jocelyne's attitude, which Lesueur describes as being 'plus fière que la révolte, plus féconde en magnifiques résultats individuels et sociaux', and it seems consistent with her

[71]Daouda, 'L'Anti-Salomé', p. 15.

[72]'Le héros rencontre la fée, celle-ci, d'abord inquiétante, gagne sa confiance en s'humiliant devant lui, il reçoit d'elle une mission et la force pour l'accomplir, puis elle disparaît, engloutie, dès que la quête est accomplie, en se sacrifiant pour lui.' Daouda, 'L'Anti-Salomé', p. 238.

[73]Daouda, 'L'Anti-Salomé', pp. 238. As already mentioned, Jocelyne was praised by conservative critics because they considered both this character and its creator as anti-Nietzschean. On this subject, see also Datta, 'Superwomen or Slaves?', p. 446.

[74]Daniel Lesueur, 'Nous avons une maladie de la volonté. Qui la guérira?', *Le Matin*, 4 June 1908. The same excerpts are quoted in *Nietzschéenne*, pp. 101–03.

[75]Note that Lesueur's preoccupation with common welfare implies a dismissal of Nietzsche's anti-social conception of history and his ideal of a world made solely by and for the *Übermensch*.

characterization.[76] As previously discussed, Jocelyne combines traditional feminine virtues with some of the features of the New Woman. Strong, smart, and self-reliant (as opposed to delicate, naïve, and subservient), she is held up as the ideal French woman to the detriment of a more conventional character like Lucienne, her brand of femininity subtly undermining bourgeois, conservative models of womanhood.

By the same token, if on the one hand her death can be understood as a Christianized act reflective of traditional femininity and a sign of submissive abnegation, on the other hand this choice is, for Lesueur at least, an expression of self-assertion, a manifestation of women's strength and freedom. In her article on female suicide, Margaret Higonnet interestingly remarks that in literature '[w]hile some "heroic" suicides become encoded as masculine and exemplary (such as self-sacrifice in war, or a republican challenge to tyranny), others which appear to constitute a surrender rather than a choice become encoded as feminine'.[77] In other words, suicide tends to be read differently according to gender. The assumption that Jocelyne's sacrifice for the man she loves is a purely self-negating act and a proof of failure is in line with these views.[78] However, as Higonnet argues, death in fictional narrative can produce multiple meanings and can be open to different interpretations.[79] Could Jocelyne's suicide represent more than the fulfilment of a traditional female destiny? The consideration of Nietzsche's position on suicide allows us to interpret the novel's ending in an alternative way. Indeed, Nietzsche thinks of voluntary death as a rational choice and 'a supreme affirmation of freedom and will', the adequate coronation of a meaningful existence for those who have achieved their goal.[80] By the end of the novel, Robert's education is completed and Jocelyne, the one who provides him with the means to become a good entrepreneur and a better man, has accomplished her mission. In commenting upon her own death, a death in which she plays an active role, Jocelyne whispers to Robert: 'Cela vaut mieux ainsi, mon amour' (*Nietzschéenne*, 249). This sentence does not suggest passive surrender, but rather confirms the consistency between Jocelyne's behaviour and Nietzschean philosophy. Her task being completed, death represents the ultimate outlet for Jocelyne's energy, the domain where she can exert her agency and free

---

[76]Lesueur, 'Nous avons une maladie'.

[77]Margaret Higonnet, 'Frames of Female Suicide', *Studies in the Novel*, 32 (2000), 229–42 (p. 232).

[78]For example, the critic Jules Bois considers Jocelyne's death as a defeat and claims that the *dénouement* contradicts the novel's thesis: 'Mais comme il est malheureux que la trame du roman ne confirme pas jusqu'au bout la thèse! A quoi sert de « tenir bon », si c'est pour être irrémédiablement vaincu? En somme, voilà un livre pessimiste par le dénouement, mais excitateur d'énergie et de moralité par le conseil et par le souffle.' Jules Bois, '*Nietzschéenne*, par Mme Daniel Lesueur', *Les Annales Politiques et Littéraires*, July–December 1908, pp. 5–7 (p. 6).

[79]'[D]eath does not give final determination to meaning; it does not close the sentence as a signifying totality. Instead, it generates multiple textual readings.' Higonnet, 'Female Suicide', p. 230.

[80]See Paolo Stellino, 'Nietzsche on Suicide', *Nietzsche-Studien*, 42 (2013), 151–77 (pp. 154–62).

will one final time, asserting her authority over the novel's conclusion. Her suicide adopts the paradigm of the founding (male) hero whose sacrifice marks both the fulfilment of a fate and the beginning of a new era, and in this sense it transcends gender frontiers.

Moreover, if we look at her trajectory as a character, not only does Jocelyne actively translate Nietzsche's precepts into actions, but she also appears to live by Emerson's notion of the gift, in that she offers Robert and Lucienne the only valuable gift one can give, namely 'a portion of herself'. According to Emerson, while the act of giving may be painful for the giver, it also puts him/her in a position of superiority, challenging the receiver's independence.[81] In this sense, Jocelyne does not appear as a self-effacing victim or a Christian martyr, but rather as a heroine who chooses her own destiny and affirms her subjectivity. Her sacrifice can be read as a self-determining act, as the final step she takes in a non-Christian path toward the accomplishment of a sublime, heroic mission. Jocelyne's death certainly differs from that of Gisèle and Sabine, the Other Women of Lesueur's *Justice de femme* and *Haine d'amour*, respectively, who commit suicide out of despair, unable to cope with the irreducibility of their desires to social dictates. Indeed, in this respect Jocelyne more closely resembles Marie of *Salutaire orgueil*, Marceline and Jeanne of *Cervelines*, Renée of Colette's *La Vagabonde* (1910), or even sister Sainte-Sophie, the protagonist of Anna de Noaille's *Le Visage emerveillé* (1904), who all choose an alternative to romantic love, whether this is their career, convent life, or, as it is the case for Jocelyne, death. Should the fact that death usually tends to be perceived by critics as a more conventional plot outcome lead us to dismiss the ways in which Jocelyne is also an untraditional character, whose extreme sacrifice might be more consistent with Nietzschean philosophy, as its author intends it, rather than with the requirements of normative femininity or with a narrative of female capitulation?[82] 'Demi-vierge et martyre', 'Méduse', 'Amazone incoercible' or 'femme nouvelle qui trouble et qui intrigue – en apparence toute intelligence et toute logique, au fond tout cœur et toute bonté', Jocelyne and her death are invested with an ambiguity

[81]'The only gift is a portion of thyself. Thou must bleed for me'. However, '[s]ome violence, I think, is done, some degradation borne, when I rejoice or grieve at a gift. I am sorry when my independence is invaded'. See Ralph Waldo Emerson, 'Gifts', in *The Logic of the Gift: Towards an Ethic of Generosity,* ed. by Alan D. Schrift (New York; London: Routledge, 1997), pp. 25–27 (p. 26). Emerson is also quoted in *Nietzschéenne*, p. 87: 'The man who stands by himself, the universe stands by him also.'

[82]Not only does Jocelyne (and her actions) represent for Lesueur an embodiment of Nietzschean philosophy, but when asked during an interview how she responded to the accusation of her novel's ending betraying a certain pessimism, she answers: 'Mais est-ce bien être sceptique, pessimiste, que de peindre une femme versant son sang pour défendre une créature qu'elle aime?'. These words suggest that female suicide, in *Nietzschéenne*, is invested with a positive connotation. See Charles Doury, '*Nietzschéenne*', *L'Intransigeant*, 21 August 1908, p. 3.

which ultimately reflects Lesueur's position vis-à-vis feminism and her engagement with women's issues, but also her tendency to leave her fiction open to interpretation.[83]

Where do men stand within this seemingly feminine economy of self-sacrifice? In both *Nietzschéenne* and *Salutaire orgueil* the undoing of the love triangle depends on female initiative and is enacted through a logic of renunciation and generosity. As (disempowered) objects of exchange between women, the male characters are not exempted from contributing to national regeneration and, instead of indulging their egotistical dispositions, they are invited to join in the sacrifice by privileging justice and collective good over their personal aspirations. As already noted, Marie's 'gift' in *Salutaire orgueil* has a corrective power, insofar as it allows the rectification of Luc's wrongdoing and promotes the formation of the rightful family, regardless of the hero's feelings and desires. In *Nietzschéenne*, Jocelyne, as Robert's moral superior, acts as a 'civilizing agent' fighting against the supposed degeneration of French society not only by overcoming her passion and sacrificing her life, but also by requiring a similar sacrifice from Robert. While the female characters choose which course of action to follow, freely deciding to adhere to a logic of energy and self-discipline and to put the code above the heart, or another woman's happiness over their own, this is not the case for the male characters, who usually appear to experience the whole situation as an imposition. In Lesueur's novel, this idea is suggested twice. Firstly, when Jocelyne asserts that she would do anything in order to restore Lucienne's happiness, and Robert desperately exclaims: 'Et mon bonheur, à moi? Et notre bonheur, à nous?' (*Nietzschéenne*, 152), the heroine opposes Robert's selfish claim to individual happiness with the following words:

> Comment voulez-vous m'intéresser à une possibilité de bonheur si peu vraisemblable, qui, sans doute, ne se réalisera jamais, quand vous me montrez chez une autre une souffrance véritable, immédiate, atroce… — dont nous sommes la cause, que nous pouvons soulager. Allons, Clérieux, soyez vous-même, soyez plus que vous-même. (*Nietzschéenne,* 153)

Not only does Jocelyne display a greater capacity for compassion than Robert, she also proves to be wiser and more rational than him, contrasting the illusory promise of future bliss with the cogency of factual reality. In encouraging Robert to adopt her own behaviour, Jocelyne is asking him to surpass himself and to contribute to the reinvigoration of society's

[83] The words 'demi-vierge et martyre' and 'Méduse' are employed in *Nietzschéenne*, pp. 27, 39. The expressions 'Amazone' and 'femme nouvelle' appear in Fernand Vandérem, 'Réception de Mme Daniel Lesueur', *Femina*, 15 Janvier 1910, p. 43.

moral health. Robert subsequently decides to follow Jocelyne's advice; he reassures his wife about his fidelity, and in a letter to Jocelyne he writes: 'Vous ne voulez pas qu'elle [Lucienne] souffre. C'est donc moi qui souffrirai' (*Nietzschéenne*, 160). In this way, Robert describes himself as a victim of the situation, and unlike Jocelyne's, his sacrifice looks more like a self-denying act imposed by someone else and accomplished unwillingly rather than an act of heroism. This represents a complete reversal of gender stereotypes, insofar as sacrifice is free and heroic for the heroine, whereas it is forced and self-effacing for the hero. The suppression of male adulterous desire brought about by the dismantlement of the love triangle is both a way to preserve traditional values (e.g. the institution of marriage on which the bourgeois, nuclear family is founded) and to promote a more equal society, one in which the unfairness of the double standard of sexual morality can be addressed and corrected by women.[84] Sacrifice, either female or male, freely chosen or imposed, is represented, in *Nietzschéenne*, as necessary to the welfare of society.

Princesses de science and the Fine Line between Rivalry and Friendship

If both *Salutaire orgueil* and *Nietzschéenne* problematize received notions about female sexual rivalry and propose new versions of the Other Woman, suggesting, respectively, that female friendship can overrule romantic love, or that a form of complicity can exist between wife and mistress, if only for the sake of man or more generally for that of society, our third and final example blurs the lines between ruthless female sexual competition and the nineteenth-century prescriptive model of female friendship, subverting these two stereotypes about female sociability by combining them.

Published in 1907, Yver's controversial novel about professional women in the medical field, *Princesses de science*, stirred up heated debates in the press and was awarded the *Prix Vie Heureuse* in the same year.[85] The plot revolves around the 'brainy woman' Thérèse Herlinge, a smart, driven, and very promising medical intern who falls in

[84]As noted by Holmes, in Belle Epoque France 'l'adultère féminin était un acte criminel, punissable par l'État, alors que le mari disposait du droit « naturel » des hommes à la polygamie, pourvu qu'il observe un peu de discrétion'. Bill Overton calls attention to the centrality of the question of gender in representations of adultery in nineteenth-century fiction, and remarks that 'male sexual transgression plays only a minor role in the Western novelistic tradition'. See Holmes, 'Écrire les hommes', in *Écrire les hommes*, ed. by Grenaudier-Klijn et al., p. 100, and Bill Overton, *The Novel of Female Adultery: Love and Gender in Continental European Fiction, 1830–1900* (Basingstoke: Macmillan, 1996), p. 1.

[85]For a discussion of the debates generated by the novel's publication, see Mesch, *Having It All*, pp. 123–24, 139–41.

love with a fellow doctor, the attractive Fernand Guéméné, and only agrees to marry him when he promises not to interfere with her career. However, Fernand fails to keep his word and their marriage soon turns into a battle field in which Thérèse's desire to pursue her ambitions is set against Fernand's unrelenting wish for her to give up her job and become a traditional wife and mother. Even though at first Thérèse seems able to balance her private and professional life, a series of events proves the impossibility, for this heroine, of having it all, to borrow Mesch's expression. More specifically, after an unplanned pregnancy and the premature death of their son, left in the care of a negligent wet nurse following Thérèse's refusal to breastfeed, the couple grows increasingly apart, both spouses immersing themselves in their work, but with different results. While Thérèse is making a name for herself in the medical field, Fernand sets himself the unrealistic goal of finding a cure for cancer. Resenting his uncaring and far too successful wife, he slowly falls for the thoughtful, naïve, and forbearing Mme Jourdeaux, the widow of a patient whose life he failed to save, and nurtures the idea of leaving Thérèse in order to start a new family with her. Thérèse, on the brink of losing her husband for good, finally decides to renounce her medical career, but it is too late; Fernand has already moved on and does not appreciate her sacrifice. Determined to save their marriage, Thérèse pleads with Mme Jourdeaux to give up Fernand, a request to which her scrupulous and principled rival agrees. The novel ends with a devastated Fernand who, like a patient, turns to his now devoted and submissive wife in order to mend his broken heart.

Princesses de science has much in common with the novels previously discussed in this chapter. The love triangle represented in this text is in fact disrupted by women, who act behind the hero's back and regardless of his desires, and presents a reversal of the usual direction of 'dramatic irony' in novels that feature adultery. White considers this figure in his discussion of literary male-based love triangles, and explains how the superior knowledge of the 'extra-domestic situation' acquired by the 'fallen wife' creates an 'imbalance which undermines the patriarchal family structure'.[86] In this case, however, the tables are turned, in the sense that in this female-based love triangle it is both the betrayed wife and the mistress who acquire a superior knowledge of the situation at the expenses of the cheating husband, their actions and decisions determining the outcome of the novel.[87] While female knowledge and power are once again aimed at the reinforcement of the status quo and not

[86]White, *The Family in Crisis*, p. 16.

[87]In *Salutaire orgueil*, it is Marie alone who dismantles the love triangle without Mlle Esther ever realizing it, while in *Nietzschéenne* it is Jocelyne who resists the temptation of becoming Robert's mistress. Lucienne, however, is aware of the situation and even appeals to Jocelyne to save Robert's life. In this third case, it is the wife, Thérèse, who persuades the Other Woman to break off the triangle. In each example, it is the heroine, and not the hero, who has full knowledge of the situation and decides how to proceed to resolve the triangle.

at its subversion, this unbalancing of gender hierarchies still threatens strict gender divides by putting women in a superior position.

The notions of female sacrifice and generosity, which are central to both *Salutaire orgueil* and *Nietzschéenne*, also play an important role in this novel. Indeed, *Princesses de science* focuses on Thérèse's *apprentissage du sacrifice*, drawing a narrative path that leads the heroine to espouse the values of normative femininity. At the beginning of the novel, when Fernand first proposes, he outlines a very conservative ideal of marriage, one entirely based on female abnegation and on women's confinement to the private sphere ('je réclame de vous le don absolu', '[que] la femme s'abandonne tout entière à sa fonction souveraine, qui est de vivre pour son mari, pour ses enfants', *Princesses*, 12, 19). Thérèse firmly refuses Fernand's repeated offers of love until he (temporarily) renounces all demands for her obedience and asks her to be his wife without conditions ('Je ne vous demande plus rien', *Princesses*, 81). After their first-born's tragic death, Thérèse briefly contemplates the idea of surrendering herself to her husband's will and giving up her career, but eventually confesses: 'L'acte que tu m'as demandé aurait requis de l'héroïsme, Fernand. Je te jure que je me suis essayée au renoncement: je n'en suis pas capable' (*Princesses*, 275). These words would suggest that Thérèse, like Marie and Jocelyne, or like the narrative voice, associates female sacrifice with heroism, but in truth at this stage Thérèse still considers women's self-effacement and lack of aspirations outside the domestic sphere contemptible and cannot comply with her husband's request. A brief visit to a former fellow student, Dina, who earlier in the novel happily renounces her career in order to become a devoted wife and mother, confirms the impossibility, for Thérèse, of resigning herself to a traditional female destiny ('cette sorte de bonheur indigna Thérèse [...] La belle abnégation qui mettait toute cette charmante Dina, si spirituelle et instruite, au service d'un homme, la révoltait', *Princesses*, 274). Later on, during a quarrel with Fernand, Thérèse makes a list of all the compromises she had to accept in order to protect their marriage, enumerating the various ways in which her family life and Fernand himself have hindered her career (*Princesses*, 295). However, she quickly regrets her outburst and the text goes on to prove that Thérèse is mistaken in her conviction that a partial sacrifice could secure the stability of her marriage. In fact, Fernand soon finds in Mme Jourdeaux the selfless and dutiful companion who more closely resembles his ideal wife. In a surprising turn of events, Thérèse suddenly repents all her past choices, renounces her ambitions, and turns into a docile, subservient wife, although fearing that it might be too late to make amends. In fact, not only must a woman's sacrifice be absolute but, for it to be heroic, it also needs to be timely ('j'imite ces aéronautes qui, près d'être engloutis, jettent à la mer leur trésor [...] [P]ersonne ne songerait à admirer leur sacrifice', *Princesses*, 373). As a matter of fact, Fernand does not love Thérèse any more and her decision to stop practising medicine both saddens and infuriates him ('Fernand la contemplait, le cœur serré, plein de pitié et aussi de rancune pour ce sacrifice trop tard accompli qui ne servait plus à rien, sinon à lui donner un rôle méprisable', *Princesses*, 391).

As, according to the logic of female-authored Belle Epoque novels, the husband cannot be trusted to choose duty over desire, it is up to the Other Woman to defend the inviolability of marriage and restore the wife's rights. After a long period of hesitation, the virtuous Mme Jourdeaux, who sees Thérèse as a heartless and undeserving wife ('[Mme Jourdeaux] voyait en elle une créature détestable, maussade, méchante', *Princesses*, 345), briefly surrenders to her feelings for Fernand and kisses him. Not only does the latter declare his undying love for her but, like Robert, he tries to convince his prospective mistress of the rightfulness of their common claim to passion and freedom (*Princesses*, 397–98). Thérèse unexpectedly interrupts this meeting and during a subsequent tête-à-tête with Mme Jourdeaux she appeals to her rival's goodness and sense of honour in order to get her husband back. If, for Thérèse, it is a question of choosing her marriage over her career, Mme Jourdeaux, as the Other Woman, is called upon to put the institution of marriage and another woman's legitimate claims above her own aspirations to happiness. Like Marie and Jocelyne, Mme Jourdeaux readily acknowledges 'la souveraineté de l'épouse' (or 'de la mère' in Marie's case) and sacrifices love, thereby reminding the husband/father of his duties and engagements (*Princesses*, 404, 405). Therefore, she proves to be, morally, Fernand's 'aînée, la plus forte' (*Princesses*, 394). Recently, Hope Christiansen has rightly observed: 'One might even say that it is Mme Jourdeaux, who selflessly gives up the man she loves, who makes the real sacrifice in the end, not Thérèse.'[88] As for Fernand, as in the case of both Luc and Robert, he is also compelled to deny his desires and to privilege the code over the heart. In this instance, however, the text tries to resolve the dichotomy between heart and code not by appealing to some superior, philosophical ideal of strength and self-possession, but by conflating the idea of happiness with marriage, duty, and collective good. Thérèse and Mme Jourdeaux both agree that, despite his heart's wishes, Fernand 'vivra misérable tant qu'il errera loin de la paix, de l'ordre, de la famille', and this explains why Thérèse, in fighting for her own happiness, claims that 'pourtant le bonheur n'est pas seulement pour moi au foyer' (*Princesses*, 404). Mme Jourdeaux similarly explains to Fernand:

[88]Christiansen, 'Grappling with Feminism', p. 958.

> [Notre] grand amour [est] un bonheur sans base, établi en dehors de tout ordre, de toute loi [...] Vous avez votre femme et j'ai mon fils. Voilà pour chacun de nous les assises de l'existence véritable, de la vie morale, du bonheur. (*Princesses*, 405–406)

According to this novel, happiness, for women as well as for men, can only be found within the family. Any expectation of pleasure and contentment outside its boundaries is illusory. This argument clearly resonates with Jocelyne's condemnation, in *Nietzchéenne*, of what she calls 'une possibilité de bonheur si peu vraisemblable' (i.e. love outside marriage), but also with Marie's refusal, in *Salutaire orgueil*, to build a precarious happiness over the ruins of another woman's misfortune.[89] *Princesses de science* thus confirms and even strengthens the idea that collective good can only be achieved at the price of a sacrifice accomplished by both men and women. Each novel suggests that it is women who, as moral agents, actively promote the regeneration of society by forcing the often reluctant men to participate in this logic of sacrifice along with them. Self-indulgence is never the answer, least of all in Yver's novel, where individual happiness and social duty are equated.

The relationship between Thérèse and Mme Jourdeaux is represented in a way that neutralizes female rivalry and turns it into a different kind of homosocial bond, one that in the end appears to be more consistent with normative female friendship than with rivalry. Mme Jourdeaux plays a double role in this novel. On the one hand, as the Other Woman, she provokes Thérèse's jealousy and makes her realize that she is losing her husband. As noted by Juliette Rogers, jealousy and fear are the 'new' and 'surprising' emotions that Thérèse only experiences at the very end of the novel and that determine its *dénouement*, leading to her sacrifice.[90] On the other hand, Mme Jourdeaux and her rivalry with Thérèse do not represent a real threat to the stability of the married couple, insofar as the Other Woman becomes Thérèse's main ally in saving her marriage. Even more importantly, Mme Jourdeaux ultimately serves as a role model for Thérèse. Yver's love triangle thus obeys the laws of 'mimetic desire': here the rival functions as a catalyst and a mediator of the heroine's desire; she embodies both an obstacle to overcome and a model to imitate.[91] Indeed, throughout the novel, Thérèse is unable to find positive models of behaviour in the women around her. These female characters can be read as Thérèse's doubles, women who face the same moral dilemma and who offer different, but equally inappropriate and disappointing responses to it. One of them is the aforementioned Dina, whose choice to give up her career for her husband Thérèse disapproves of. Thérèse similarly questions Dr. Lancelevée's life

---

[89]See pp. 128 and 208–209 in this thesis.
[90]Rogers, *Career Stories*, p. 141.
[91]Girard's notion of mimetic desire has already been discussed in this thesis, pp. 61 and 128–29.

choices. This very successful and well-respected doctor could never let marriage jeopardize her career, so she engages in a free union with a colleague, a solution that Thérèse finds unacceptable (*Princesses*, 292). The overworked Dr. Adeline, utterly unhappy and incapable of balancing family life and career but forced to work for financial reasons, constitutes yet another negative example for Thérèse.[92]

If the heroine initially refuses to become like her self-effacing mother, by the end of the novel she decides to conform to similar standards of normative femininity, following the example provided by Mme Jourdeaux, and also by the 'tantine', the deceased wife of Fernand's uncle. Fernand clearly endorses these two figures of femininity.[93] During one of their discussions, he resolutely tells Thérèse: 'Il n'y a pas d'épouse nouvelle', this short sentence summarizing the main point of Yver's novel (*Princesses*, 256). The expression 'épouse nouvelle' is to be understood in parallel with and in opposition to *femme nouvelle*. As the novel suggests, New Women can and do exist, but only because they cannot marry and have no choice but to provide for themselves. However, once a woman is blessed with marriage, she should abandon her career and turn into what Fernand calls 'l'amante éternelle' (*Princesses*, 256). In other words, the *femme nouvelle* cannot exist within marriage as '[une] épouse nouvelle'. Thérèse comes to this very conclusion toward the end of the novel (*Princesses*, 384–85), and Yver confirms this view in a journal article that appeared after the novel's publication.[94] In the same speech about the ideal wife, Fernand explicitly refers to the 'tantine' and more subtly to Mme Jourdeaux. In particular, he associates womanhood with motherhood and compares heterosexual relations to the mother/child bond: 'Les hommes [...] ont besoin de leur femme, comme l'enfant de leur mère' (*Princesses*, 256). This image is repeated later on in the text, when Fernand tells Mme Jourdeaux: 'Je voudrais [...] me faire un petit enfant comme André [Mme Jourdeaux's son], et me mettre sous votre garde', and subsequently begs her: 'Soyez cette mère jeune et

---

[92]Rogers also comments on the fact that Thérèse is unable to find positive role models in the other women doctors represented in the text. See Rogers, *Career Stories*, p. 140.

[93]For the purpose of this chapter on love triangles, I am going to focus primarily on Mme Jourdeaux, although it should be noted that the text also creates a parallel between Thérèse and the 'tantine', presenting the latter figure as a positive model of femininity for the heroine to emulate.

[94]See Yver, 'Le Choix d'une carrière'. In a letter written in 1928, Yver states: '*Les Cervelines*, *Princesses de science*, *Les Dames du Palais* sont successivement trois volumes antiféministes dans le sens qu'ils subordonnent le développement de la personnalité de la femme à son rôle d'épouse, de mère et de gardienne de foyer.' Yver's conservative views on women and marriage have been criticized, among others, by Jules Bois, who observes: 'Dans *Princesses de science*, Mme Colette Yver avait pris nettement parti contre les savantes, pour les « servantes de l'ignorance ». Seules, ces dernières, de l'avis de cette femme intellectuelle pourtant, pouvaient être aimées et faire des épouses et des mères.' See Comité d'histoire de la sécurité sociale, '*Princesses de science* (1907) de Colette Yver', in *Bulletin d'histoire de la sécurité sociale*, 2000/07, pp. 187–203 (p. 187), and Jules Bois, 'Revue des livres: *Les Dames du Palais*, par Mme Colette Yver", *Les Annales Politiques et Littéraires*, 20 March 1910, pp. 277–80 (p. 277).

adorable qui guérit tous les chagrins' (*Princesses*, 393, 397).[95] Indeed, Mme Jourdeaux is much like a Republican Virgin Mary, her association with a pure, saintly kind of womanhood strengthened by the fact that she is compared to the 'Marthe évangélique' and described as having '[des] airs de madone' (*Princesses*, 312, 344). Mme Jourdeaux confirms Fernand's view of heterosexual relationships when she compares him to a sort of adopted child: 'je vous ai adopté dans mon cœur. [...] Parfois je me figure avoir deux fils: l'un petit, l'autre très grand [...] ils me sont également chers' (*Princesses*, 394). In another passage, Fernand lists 'les vertus qu'il aurait aimé en sa compagne, et qui étaient précisément toutes celles de la douce femme [Mme Jourdeaux]', leaving no doubt about the type of woman he desires (*Princesses*, 319). The only way for Thérèse to have a happy marriage then is to emulate the 'tantine' and Mme Jourdeaux, who both meet Fernand's expectations about women. According to Christiansen, the idea that Yver could offer the insipid Mme Jourdeaux as a model for her readers is inconsistent with the fact that this author created 'the brainiest female characters that the French novel had ever seen' and with the low consideration in which she held this particular female figure.[96] Whether Mme Jourdeaux was considered by its creator as a positive example of femininity or not, what interests us here is that her narrative function is to allow the 'anti-heroine' Thérèse to turn into a conventional female character who sacrifices herself by choosing love and family over her own ambitions.[97]

When Mme Jourdeaux is first introduced in the text, at a dinner where she meets Thérèse, the narrator immediately highlights the similarities between the two women: 'Elles étaient également belles, de même âge, de même taille' (*Princesses*, 164). However, despite their physical resemblance, these two characters could not be more different, their contrast being repeatedly highlighted throughout the novel by both the narrator and Fernand. For example, during this party, Mme Jourdeaux, the single-minded wife whose entire life revolves around the care of her family, does not exist as an individual entity, but rather as an appendage of her husband, whose health is her main concern and whose state of being determines her own ('Madame Jourdeaux semblait absorbée par un sentiment unique: la pitié pour son mari', *Princesses*, 168). Moreover, talking with Fernand, Mme Jourdeaux candidly asserts that 'elle aurait été médecin, elle, pour soigner son pauvre mari', the

[95]Earlier in the text, Fernand also tells Mme Jourdeaux: 'Vous m'avez choyé depuis quelque temps avec des raffinements qui m'ont rappelé mon *enfance*, ma maison, les *douceurs maternelles*, mes lointaines vacances.' See *Princesses*, p. 281. My italics.

[96]Christiansen comes to this conclusion through the reading of Yver's 1920 treatise *Dans le jardin du féminisme*, where the author of *Princesses de science* observes that: '[Mme Jourdeaux] forme avec Thérèse le plus pathétique et le plus troublant contraste.' See Colette Yver, *Dans le jardin du féminisme* (Paris: Calmann-Lévy, 1920), p. 211, as quoted by Christiansen, 'Grappling with Feminism', pp. 955–56. Christiansen also comments on the fact that Mme Jourdeaux is Thérèse's double.

[97]Oberhuber defines Thérèse as an 'anti-héroïne' in 'Cervelines ou Princesses de science?', p. 61.

possibility of becoming a doctor subordinated to the fact of being of service to her husband (*Princesses*, 177). By contrast, Thérèse, who spends the night trying to impress her colleagues, is described as 'rayonnante de fierté, satisfaite, épanouie', while completely mindless of her husband (*Princesses*, 181). Later on, when Fernand tells his wife about his research, she complains about not having been told earlier, and he justifies his reticence by explaining: 'Tu ne peux pas être une petite compagne naïve, s'extasiant devant les moindres idées de son mari...Tu as d'ailleurs ta vie en dehors de moi' (*Princesses*, 231). Fernand is right, given the fact that Thérèse laughs away or at least treats with manifest scepticism his foolish and fruitless attempts at finding a cure for cancer (*Princesses*, 230, 310). On the other hand, despite the fact that Fernand patently fails in saving M. Jourdeaux's life, he finds in his widow that 'compagne naïve' who can comfort his ego and who can put him at the centre of her universe. In fact, Mme Jourdeaux, 'cette simple femme dépourvue de toute science, qui ne comprenait même rien à ses travaux', enthusiastically encourages him to continue his research (*Princesses*, 262, 315). At one point, she even goes as far as to suggest that she serve as his human guinea pig, just to prove the unconditional faith she has in him (*Princesses*, 321). This unequivocal aptitude for self-sacrifice is exactly what his competent, rational, and self-absorbed wife lacks and will need to learn. Therefore, even when Fernand mistakes Mme Jourdeaux for his wife ('Fernand la prenait parfois de loin pour sa femme', as if the two women 'avaient été intimement parentes, presque sœurs', *Princesses*, 285), he is painfully aware of the fact the they have nothing in common. Thérèse, regretting her inability to be 'l'épouse qu'il [Fernand] avait rêvée', because '[a]vant d'être sa femme, j'étais la doctoresse', acknowledges the fact that he has found elsewhere (i.e. in Mme Jourdeaux) 'l'amie dévouée que je n'ai pas été' (*Princesses*, 372). This is when she renounces her career as a doctor and becomes a woman like Mme Jourdeaux, the one who almost replaced her. Interestingly enough, when Thérèse and Mme Jourdeaux part after their confrontation, the text reinforces the theme of the double by precising that '[e]lles s'embrassèrent comme deux soeurs' (*Princesses*, 404). Not only do the two heroines look alike, but now their dissonant identities seem to have reconciled and merged, Thérèse finally conforming to the traditional model of femininity represented by Mme Jourdeaux. As if to confirm this evolution, while evoking their physical resemblance once again, the narrator this time observes: 'Leur commune élévation de cœur, sinon de cerveau, les faisait *égales*, dignes l'une de l'autre' (*Princesses*, 400. My italics). Such a statement underlines a female-centred society in which women, through their homosocial bonds, appropriate and reinvent the ideals of virtue, nobility, and equality traditionally inscribed in models of male friendship. Thérèse might well be a *femme nouvelle* and Mme Jourdeaux's intellectual superior, a condition that usually creates an unbridgeable gap between female characters,[98] but in marriage there is no room for the 'épouse nouvelle'. Her only option is to revert to the *épouse traditionnelle*, as represented by Mme Jourdeaux herself, and this choice brings her closer than ever to her enemy.

One of the reasons why it is possible, for Mme Jourdeaux, to act as Thérèse's role model is that the relationship she establishes with Fernand, although adulterous, actually provides an example of what a bourgeois marriage looks like. On this subject, it is useful to refer to White who, quoting works by Michael Wood and Alain Corbin, observes that adultery 'is a parody of the marriage it undoes [...] [T]he quest of the adulterous spouse is often a search for another [...] "home". This is then a quest for refamiliarization'.[99] This is particularly true in the case of Yver's novel, in which Fernand, constantly disappointed in Thérèse and dissatisfied with their marriage, finds a surrogate wife in Mme Jourdeaux, who puts all her energies into creating a domestic paradise for him. Indeed, Mme Jourdeaux acts as the ideal nineteenth-century wife, patiently waiting for Fernand while embroidering at the window, and spoiling him with succulent meals. Not only does Fernand start to imagine 'sa vie écoulée auprès d'une épouse pareille à madame Jourdeaux', but her house actually turns into 'un foyer illusoire' for him, and we learn that Fernand, surrounded by Mme Jourdeaux and André, 'se complaisait à ce simulacre d'une famille auquel il se leurrait par instants' (*Princesses*, 318, 348).[100]

In consolidating Thérèse's marriage, both by giving up Fernand and by providing the model of womanhood, and the model of marriage, that Thérèse ought to reproduce, Mme Jourdeaux acts more as a friend than as a rival. As highlighted in the Introduction, emulation was one of the elements most frequently evoked in nineteenth-century discussions of female friendship. Conduct books and essays of this period suggest that women, as friends, should encourage each other (and learn from each other how) to adhere to conservative gender norms and perform their duties as mothers and wives, while always giving priority to marriage over friendship.[101]

The relation between friendship and marriage was indeed a crucial one in nineteenth-century France, since family was the 'primary theatre of private life' and any other social formation needed to be defined in relation to it.[102] On this topic, Vincent-Buffault has pointed out a striking difference between Latin and Anglo-Saxon cultures:

---

[98]This topic has been discussed at p. 180 in this thesis.
[99]White, *The Family in Crisis*, p. 15.
[100]Moreover, Mme Jourdeaux's son, André, is constantly compared to Fernand's lost child.
[101]For a discussion of these models of female friendship, see pp. 19–23 and 119–20 in this thesis.
[102]*A History of Private Life,* ed. by Perrot, p. 97.

> Au moment du passage à l'état de femme mariée, l'abandon des amitiés intenses est préconisé. Le phénomène est plus net en pays latins. En contrées catholiques, les amitiés de jeunes filles constituent une éducation sentimentale de l'intimité qui prépare les femmes à leur destination privée dont le mariage est l'étape essentielle. Dans les pays anglo-saxons, une tradition d'amitié spirituelle et de liberté des consciences ménage davantage les continuités et les choix individuels.[103]

As argued by scholars, nineteenth-century America was in fact characterized by the existence of a female world that, although exclusive, was widely accepted and existed alongside traditional family structures, while in Victorian England female friendship, marriage, and family life were complementary.[104] By contrast, the status of female friendship in nineteenth-century France appears more ambiguous and controversial and, in one way or another, friendship always tends to be subordinated to or reinserted within the familial sphere. Henri Marion, quoted at the beginning of this chapter, asserts:

> Il est certain qu'elle [l'amitié féminine] n'est pas très fréquente, que les belles amitiés de jeunes filles, si expansives et si profondes à la fois, ne durent pas ordinairement avec le même caractère, après que le mariage ou de l'une ou de toutes les deux les a séparées en leur apportant de nouvelles affections.[105]

Indeed, a woman's first allegiance is usually to her husband rather than to her female friends, or at least this is the sense of the recommendation that Michelet addresses to women in *La Femme*: 'Madame, ne partagez pas votre cœur [entre votre mari et votre amie].'[106] This is partly due to anxieties about the fact that female friends can act as bad counsellors, their influence possibly constituting a threat to marriage. In order to prove that love requires exclusivity and that friendship could undermine it, Michelet employs a metaphor in which marriage is symbolized by a beautiful, strong orange tree, progressively killed by the apparently harmless presence of a bunch of strawberries at its feet. The small, pretty, unsuspected strawberries clearly represent female friends.[107] Similarly, the author of *La Voix de l'amitié* (1879), an essay in which the idea of friendship intermingles with religion and Christian values, strongly warns women against making themselves vulnerable to unsuitable

---

[103]Vincent-Buffault, *Exercice de l'amitié*, p. 245.
[104]See Smith-Rosenberg, 'The Female World', and Marcus, *Between Women*.
[105]Marion, *Psychologie de la femme*, p. 156.
[106]Michelet, *La Femme*, p. 336. Michelet also insists that the husband should serve as the primary and possibly only confidant of his wife. See Michelet, *La Femme*, p. 347.
[107]Michelet, *La Femme*, pp. 336–38.

friends and exposing their hearts to dangerous influences, in particular when they wish to confide a problem concerning their unfaithful husband:

> Mais malheur, malheur à elle, si elle choisit un cœur sans pitié, sans religion, sans convictions profondément chrétiennes! Au lieu d'étancher la plaie de cette âme meurtrie, au lieu de la consoler, de la fortifier, ce cœur frivole et mondain, où n'habite pas la crainte de Dieu, lui conseillera peut-être les plus tristes compensations aux infidélités d'un époux.[108]

At the same time, however, this and other authors express the conviction that a good friend could, by contrast, act as a model of proper behaviour and promote the durability of marriage.[109]

Normative female friendship as described (and prescribed) in conduct manuals and essays of this period can be understood as a form of 'horizontal homosociality', which not only exists in harmony with the social order but even reinforces it.[110] Charlotte of *L□vres closes* (1898), Suzanne of *Névrosée* (1890), and Mme de Lorris in Octave Feuillet's novel *Un mariage dans le monde* (1882), for example, are all represented as the wiser female friends who defend the sanctity of marriage and encourage the unhappy wife to become more obedient and to remain faithful to her husband.[111] In *Princesses de science* it is Mme Jourdeaux who takes up the role of friend and confidante, and contributes to turn the proud and strong-minded heroine into a docile and selfless wife. Indeed, during their final encounter, Thérèse confides in Mme Jourdeaux as if she were '[son] amie la plus fidèle', and after some initial reticence, Mme Jourdeaux welcomes her as 'une amie' (*Princesses*, 402, 403).[112] At the same time, it should be noted, Thérèse reminds Mme Jourdeaux of the inviolability of marriage, of the rights of the legitimate wife, and of the need, for the Other Woman, to sacrifice love and personal happiness for the greater good (*Princesses*, 402–04). The relationship between Thérèse and Mme Jourdeaux thus contradicts negative views about women's interactions in general and about female rivalry in particular. As highlighted at the beginning of this chapter, writers of conduct books and novelists were often at pains

---

108 J. L. M. N, *La Voix de l'amitié*, p. 114.
109 See pp. 19–23 and 119–20 in this thesis.
110 On the definition of 'horizontal homosociality', see p. 99 in this thesis.
111 Octave Feuillet, *Un mariage dans le monde*, 18th edn (Paris: Calmann-Lévy, 1882).
112 As already noted, the two women part as sisters. According to Vicinus, in the nineteenth century sisterhood was the most egalitarian relationship women could experience within the family circle and the sororal metaphor was often employed to indicate an equal friendship between women. On the continuity between friendship and kinship in nineteenth-century France, Vincent-Buffault observes: 'entre l'intensité des relations familiales et celle des amitiés, il n'existe pas vraiment de rupture. L'ami(e) devient le frère ou la sœur que l'on se choisit.' See Vicinus, *Intimate Friends*, p. xxvi, and Vincent-Buffault, *Exercice de l'amitié*, p. 161.

to prove the inauthentic or even insidious nature of intimate female friendship, discussing how close friends could in fact reveal themselves to be a woman's worst enemies and a serious threat to the solidity of her marriage.[113] In a complete reversal of the situation, Yver portrays two female rivals who ultimately behave like friends, in the most conventional sense of the term, or at the very least like allies, and who ensure the preservation of society's moral health by participating in a logic of sacrifice that implies the exchange of men. If in the 'amity plot' of the Victorian novel of marriage the female friend promotes the heroine's union with her suitor,[114] in Belle Epoque novels dealing with the topic of adultery (or love outside marriage), the female rival promotes the wife/mother's re-union with the husband/father. Thus, two seemingly opposing forms of female homosociality (i.e. friendship and rivalry) play important roles in both kinds of novel, and the effects they produce are surprisingly similar.

Conclusion

Structures of triangular desire, a common device in Belle Epoque fiction, are appropriated and used by some female authors of this period in a way that challenges conventional literary representations of female rivalry as well as common assumptions about female jealousy, as expressed in conduct manuals and essays of that time. However, this is not to say that the texts always take a further step toward the reshaping of women's images in literature or that they create a fictional world in which the status quo is systematically undermined. The way in which female characters refuse to be polarized and chosen by the male hero, taking upon themselves the task of breaking off the erotic triangle, usually behind his back and to his chagrin, can arguably be read as an expression of female agency. Moreover, sexual competitiveness is neutralized through the privileging of a strong and sincere homosocial bond, as in the case of *Salutaire orgueil*, or through a disposition, on the part of the Other Woman, to respect the rights of the wife/mother and to acknowledge the inviolability of the State-sanctioned couple, as in the cases of *Nietzschéenne* and *Princesses de science*. As a consequence, the line between female rivalry and normative friendship tends to be blurred. Such paradoxes (e.g. the Other Woman as the guarantor of the family and the wife's best ally) are created by exploiting and highlighting inconsistencies in stereotyped representations of women and their relationships, and this allows the texts to carry out a

[113]See pp. 196–99 in this thesis.
[114]On the 'amity plot' as discussed by Marcus in *Between Women*, see p. 201 in this thesis.

subtle form of subversion, one that is not explicitly disruptive. Sometimes, the undermining of the traditional romance plot, a recurring element in Belle Epoque women's fiction, opens up a new path for the heroine, a path that is more attuned to the requirements of modern womanhood. This is the case for Marie, in *Salutaire orgueil*, who renounces love and goes on to build a different life for herself, pursuing a professional career abroad instead of getting married and having children. Even when the plot outcome is death, as in *Nietzschéenne*, it is worth asking whether the heroine's sacrifice could be read as an act of heroism more indicative of her adherence to a (Nietzschean) doctrine of energy, courage, and self-mastery rather than to normative femininity.

None of the Other Women represented in these novels could be identified with the figure of the *femme fatale* or the evil mistress, a signifier of dangerous and unrestrained female sexuality, an emblem of destructive passion that must be erased from the text. The redefinition of the Other Woman nuances and complicates the dichotomous categories to which women are usually reduced to in novels. In particular, both Marie and Jocelyne are intelligent, resourceful, and strong-willed heroines, who to some extent defy social conventions and reject conventional femininity, but who are clearly intended to be worthy of admiration and emulation by even the most conventional readers of the time for their integrity and high sense of morality. If the saintly Mme Jourdeaux could in no way be mistaken for an enterprising *femme moderne*, it is precisely her purity and her attachment to bourgeois values that set her apart from the *femme fatale* or the dangerous mistress. Through the use of internal focalization and first-person narration, or by the intervention of a sympathetic and non-judgemental omniscient narrative voice, the text usually invites the reader to side with the Other Woman, whose behaviour provides an example to follow: the single woman Marie represents 'la femme de demain' and her story is meant to comfort and guide the reader; Jocelyne is an embodiment of female energy, that primary force upon which the regeneration of French society depends, and was generally perceived by contemporary critics as the ideal French woman; Mme Jourdeaux's status as a possible role model for readers is more controversial, as argued by Christiansen, but the fact that the heroine Thérèse finally espouses the values promoted by this character leads us to believe that she constitutes an example of positive femininity. As in the case of the novels analysed in the preceding chapters, the fictional representation of female homosociality, in this instance female rivalry, is once again embedded in definitions of modern womanhood and in negotiations around the meanings of femininity.

Offering readers such fictional role models is not an anodyne gesture on the part of the authors, and it can be better understood if we take into account the context in which these novels were produced. The female writers considered in this thesis, for the most part born around 1870, belong to that generation of citizens brought up with the idea of fighting decadence and opposing the decline of French society after the fall of Napoleon III. Their first memories were probably linked to the emergence of a secular, republican state which wanted to claim its own legitimacy as a highly moral system in opposition to the corrupt Empire, but also to the Church.[115] As we have seen in the previous chapter, female education was one of the main battlefields in which the war between State and Church was fought at the time. Having such freely educated female characters (Marie attends the public *lycée*, Jocelyne is an avid reader of Nietzsche, and Thérèse is a trained doctor) lend their support to the bourgeois, patriarchal system of the Third Republic boils down to asserting that women do not need to receive a religious education in order to remain the pillars of the nuclear family, whether they belong to it or not. Although, as argued in the chapter 'Female Communities in Schoolgirl Fiction' and particularly with regard to *Salutaire orgueil*, the Third Republican school is often portrayed as a context in which the female characters transgress both social and gender boundaries and collectively redefine their identities as *femmes modernes*, the novels here considered show that none of these learned, free-minded heroines represent a real menace to the social order. On the contrary, in the context of Belle Epoque anxieties about degeneration, the (intellectual) Other Woman reinforces the family unit and contributes to securing the stability of marriage, the unexpected complicity between female rivals being portrayed as unthreatening and even partly supportive of the status quo, while also disregarding contemporary gender stereotypes about female jealousy, disloyalty, and pettiness. Through the exchange of men, the female rivals of a love triangle realize an economy of generosity and sacrifice in which everyone, including the recalcitrant hero who unabashedly professes his right to happiness, is considered responsible for society's welfare and needs to prioritize collective good over individual happiness. The texts thus support one of the main principles underpinning Third Republican ideology, a principle shared by many feminists of the time: the primacy of the family over the individual. Indeed, as noted by Karen Offen, '[i]f there was one thing these progressive-minded men and women agreed on, it was that the family, not the individual, remained the basic socio-political unit.'[116]

Although these representations of female rivalry promote the consolidation of patriarchal institutions like marriage and, in *Princesses de science*, reinforce conventional female identities, the establishment of a feminine economy also allows the novels to voice

[115]The French law on the Separation of the Churches and State was passed in 1905, only a couple of years before the publication of these novels.
[116]Offen, *Debating the Woman Question*, p. 18.

feminist concerns and to question gender inequality. For example, Marie's giving up of Luc to Mlle Esther raises questions about illegitimate paternity and about the status of the unmarried mother, her gesture being invested with a corrective power, in addition to being noble. More generally, the injustice of the moral double standard is addressed through the suggestion that female sacrifice must be paired with male sacrifice. In *L'Éternelle Sacrifiée*, a famous lecture delivered several times between 1905 and 1906, the feminist activist Nelly Roussel interestingly points out the difference between men and women's education and sense of morality in Belle Epoque France:

> I find the difference between the two moralities and the two educations in everything: we are always reminded of duties, while you, Gentlemen, are insufficiently reminded of them. We are taught only sacrifice, the abdication of all pride, of all our natural rights, and of our most legitimate desires, while a man is told only about his freedom, his power, his greatness, and his virility.[117]

The heroines of the novels considered in this chapter are certainly well-versed in the art of self-sacrifice, but they also constantly remind the men of their duties and responsibilities, and prevent them from exerting their 'natural right' to experience passion outside marriage and from treating their wives as a nuisance that stands between them and their happiness. If self-sacrifice is posited as an ideal for women, an ideal supportive of masculinist, patriarchal conceptualizations of womanhood, this sacrifice is made both for the sake of another woman and in the name of the collective good and, for the same reasons, it is also recommended to and eventually imposed on men. As historians remind us, the application of a single standard of morality for both sexes set by women was among the stated objectives of first-wave feminism; it was understood as a way to subvert the French sexual culture, break male codes of behaviour, and encourage political change.[118]

The neutralization of female rivalry and the reinforcement of female homosocial bonds, the rewriting of the Other Woman and the heightening of female agency, the creation of a feminine economy of generosity and sacrifice based on the exchange of men are among the most interesting elements characterizing Belle Epoque female authors' unconventional use of the erotic triangle. Moreover, if we stand by Bill Overton's remark that '[n]o classic novel, let alone any fictional tradition, is based on male adultery', the writers' concern with

---

[117]See 'Nelly Roussel, *She Who Is Always Sacrificed*', in *Feminism of the Belle Epoque*, ed. by Waelti-Walters and Hause, pp. 17–41 (p. 32).
[118]For more discussion on this, see for example Offen, *Debating the Woman Question*, p. 422, who quotes Andrea Mansker, *Sex, Honor and Citizenship in Early Third Republic France* (2011).

this topic, as expressed through their novelistic representations of female-based love triangles, also marks the originality of their works within the literary panorama of the Belle Epoque.[119]

[119]Overton, *The Novel of Female Adultery*, p. vi.

Conclusion

The Troublesome Noisiness of the 'Troubling Silence between the Lines'

My interest in Belle Epoque fictional representations of female homosociality has been triggered by an observation about the limited narrative space dedicated to female friendship in the nineteenth-century French literary canon and the small number of studies devoted to this topic in nineteenth-century French scholarship. These elements, along with women's frequent marginalization from the cultural history of friendship, their exclusion from androcentric definitions of this bond, and their seeming absence from ongoing discussions on the value of this relationship, constitute what I initially referred to as 'the troubling silence between the lines'. A desire to address and explore this 'silence' has led to a close examination of some female-authored, middlebrow novels published between 1880 and 1914, in an attempt to re-establish women's writing of the Belle Epoque within the narratives of the literary and cultural history of friendship in the long nineteenth century. A difficulty in mapping out the contours of female friendship and defining its content and structure once and for all, and a realization of the convoluted, multilayered nature of the notion of 'homosociality' itself have widened the scope of this study to include the related themes of female physical intimacy, mentorship, solidarity, community, camaraderie, and intellectual or sexual rivalry; these are, it has seemed to me, the most pertinent narrative configurations concerning female bonding that recur throughout many female-authored novels of this period. However, as the thesis progressed, it became evident that the interest of these novels does not lie in the way in which they portray female homosociality as a stand-alone subject, as much as in the way in which the imagined models and ideals of female bonding proposed in these texts engage with contemporary debates about women's nature and roles, and contribute precious insights to our understanding of gender identities in nineteenth-century French culture. This thesis has consequently explored Belle Epoque novelistic representations of female homosociality as a way to discuss notions of modern femininity and devise a 'modernisme au féminin' which problematizes the dichotomy between 'high' and 'popular' literature.

In a complex and contradictory time — during which the Third Republic was consolidating its power, the feminist movement was gaining momentum, and French society was torn between its underlying conservatism, fears of degeneration, and enthusiasm vis-à-vis progress and modernization — fictional representations of female friendship, mentorship, solidarity, intellectual or sexual rivalry participate in the definition of modern female subjectivities and, more largely, in the social history of ideas. In the novels analysed, interactions between two or more female characters are constantly characterized by a tension between traditional and modern womanhood, which mirrors and complicates contemporary concerns about the female body, love, marriage, career, education, degeneration, and the family. The practice of comparing these representations with the prescriptive models of female interaction found in nineteenth-century conduct books, didactic manuals, and essays, or with the more conventional ideals inscribed in orthodox literature of the time, allowed us to highlight how the authors variously embrace, reject, or problematize received notions of essential femininity and use fiction as a means to discuss what it means to be a woman in the modern world. If, in the dominant discourse, female friendship is variously presented as playing second fiddle to love, as fleeting and inauthentic, as a disguise for rivalry, as something to be policed or, at most, as a social mechanism aptly reinforcing traditional gender norms, in the novels under analysis the relationships that the heroines foster with other female characters are central both to the development of their fictional identities as *femmes modernes* and to the establishment of their somewhat unusual narrative trajectories.

These depictions of female homosociality, created by female authors for the enjoyment of a predominantly female, cross-class readership, give form to an intra- and extra-diegetic feminine economy in which women can sometimes elude the restrictive gender definitions imposed on them by men or constructed in relation to men, and can claim instead the possibility of defining themselves in relation to or against one another, in a way that often challenges the dichotomization of women (sexual vs maternal) and deconstructs sexual difference (male vs female, active vs passive, reason vs emotion). The creation of the *femme moderne* as 'un soi-en-relation', to borrow Diana Holmes' expression,[1] and, what is more, as 'un soi-en-relation' with other female characters, is one of the hallmarks of a female modernism whose originality is often expressed in terms of content, rather than in the systematic employment of radically experimentalist narrative forms. The subversively liberating power ascribed to certain female relationships, the ambiguities created around gender identity, the undermining of predominant expectations about women's identities and behaviours, coupled with the positive representation of how women, in the expanded roles they encourage each other to take on, can nonetheless contribute to the welfare of society,

[1]See Introduction, p. 34.

constitute part of the interest and appeal of these works of fiction for past and contemporary readers alike.

The *femme moderne* who comes into being, on paper, through intricate plays of female mirroring, support, and conflict, is a complex figure who stands with one foot in the past and one foot in the future. Indeed, many of the heroines portrayed in our novels correspond to Rachel Mesch's definition of the modern woman as one who embraces the new opportunities opening up to her during the Belle Epoque without rejecting traditional femininity *in toto*.[2] Thus, more often than not, in their portrayal of female homosociality, the novels carry out a sort of quiet subversion, or a subversion that does not necessarily upset the status quo at every turn (and that sometimes even reinforces it), but that creates new, alternative spaces for the female characters within said order. By exposing the constructedness and deficiency of mainstream femininity, by challenging common assumptions about presumed female nature and conduct, and by showing the permeability of the binary gender system, these texts widen the spectrum of women's possibilities as active agents in the modern world and give shape to more progressive types of femininity in fiction.

My analysis of the discursive treatment of female homosociality in nineteenth-century France has been narrowly focused upon didactic literature and middlebrow, female-authored novels of the Belle Epoque. This necessarily entails some questions about the generalizability of the findings and points toward future paths of enquiry. Within the context of the chosen time frame, evidently not all female authors, not even the few considered in this thesis, were unanimously disruptive in their portrayal of women's relationships and gendered identities. Some texts take rather moderate, conservative stances on these subjects, and certain representations of female bonding align themselves with the models of female sociability (and femininity) that can be found in much didactic or orthodox literature of the time. With regard to the same time period, occasional parallels have been drawn with male-authored novels; however, further investigating male representations of female friendship and asking whether it would be possible to differentiate literary discourses on female homosociality along gender lines could provide us with a more comprehensive picture of this topic's treatment in Belle Epoque French fiction.

Efforts have been made to identify variations and specificities in women's novelistic representation of female homosociality during the Belle Epoque, especially with regard to earlier nineteenth-century French literature and in consideration of the particular social,

---

[2]See Introduction, p. 25.

political, and cultural climate in which these works were produced. However, the number of studies looking at this theme in previous or subsequent fiction is far too limited to allow us to make systematic comparisons and trace clear patterns, repetitions, or evolutions within the French literary tradition. Conducting comparative analysis not only within the same literary culture at different times, but also with other literatures could help us to shed more light on this topic.[3] A comparative analysis of representations of male, female, and cross-sex modes of social interaction could also further our understanding of gendered identities in literature.

Clearly, more needs to be done in order to understand the value and practice of friendship in nineteenth-century French women's lives. Looking at the topic of female homosociality through the prism of fiction only allows us to draw some conclusions about the discursive treatment of women's relationships in Belle Epoque France, but other types of investigation could be possible. For example, there is still much to be gained from the analysis of the authors' correspondence and life-writing material, an endeavour that we were unable to undertake at this stage due to the limitations imposed by a PhD in terms of time and resources, but that could constitute the object of future research projects.

My stated purpose at the beginning of this thesis was to include women's writing of the Belle Epoque within the narratives of the literary and cultural history of friendship in the long nineteenth century and investigate the inscription of female subjectivities in French women's fiction through the analysis of their representations of female homosociality. Such representations are one of the devices through which female authors engage with the tension between tradition and modernity/modernism, both at the sociological and literary level, and negotiate the meanings and possibilities of womanhood. If we pay these literary works the attention they deserve, we realize that 'the troubling silence between the lines', referred to in the Introduction, is largely the result of the exclusion of many Belle Epoque female authors from the French literary canon. The troublesome noisiness of women's voices is still there to be heard.

---

[3]Admittedly, in this thesis, occasional parallels have been drawn with American and British Victorian culture. In particular, the Introduction offered some discussion of the notion of 'female romantic friendship', and in Chapter Four on 'Female Rivalry and Love Triangles' I mentioned the notion of 'amity plot' and referred to the difference in the status of female friendship after marriage in Latin (French) and Anglo-Saxons nineteenth-century cultures. See pp. 11–19, 201, and 237–38 in this thesis.

www.ingramcontent.com/pod-product-compliance
Lightning Source LLC
LaVergne TN
LVHW010054170826
845678LV00012B/2137
* 9 7 8 4 4 7 5 8 5 5 1 8 1 *